OXFORD ENGLISH MONOGRAPHS

Self as Narrative

Subjectivity and Community
in Contemporary Fiction

KIM L. WORTHINGTON

CLARENDON PRESS · OXFORD
1996

FOR MY PARENTS
Robert and Denice Worthington

Acknowledgements

The substance of this book was initially submitted as a doctoral dissertation at Oxford University in 1992. I am extremely grateful to a number of awarding bodies whose generosity, in the form of grants and scholarships, made it possible for me to begin, and complete, the dissertation: the British Universities' Overseas Research Student Award Scheme, which granted me an ORS Award from 1989 to 1992; the Oxford University Overseas Research Student Scholarship Fund; St Hilda's College, Oxford, which provided me with a scholarship from the Raymond–Sisam Bequest Fund between 1989 and 1992; and the British Federation of University Women which awarded me their annual Fellowship between 1991 and 1992. I would also like to thank the Governing Body at Christ Church, Oxford, for electing me to a teaching lectureship from 1990 to 1993. In addition to the financial support this provided, Christ Church proved a stimulating and supportive environment in which I was able to proceed with my work.

Without question my most significant debt in this project is to my research supervisor at Oxford University, Christopher Butler. His wisdom and generosity sustained me through my years as a research student and beyond. He has my deepest admiration and affection. Special thanks, too, are due to Robert Neale and E. Warwick Slinn at Massey University, New Zealand, for the gift of their teaching and encouragement; and to Sally Mapstone at St Hilda's College, Oxford, for support and advice along the way.

Throughout this book I stress the constitutive importance of intersubjectivity and community. Accordingly, I express my deepest love and gratitude to my family and to my husband, Paul James White—the two significant communities, both given and chosen, that have shaped and accepted my changing self-narratives.

Material from *Lady Oracle*, by Margaret Atwood is reprinted with the permission of Simon & Schuster (© Margaret Atwood, 1976), Andre Deutsch Ltd (Virago Press Ltd, 1982; © Margaret Atwood, 1976), and the Canadian Publishers, McClelland & Stewart, Toronto. Material from *The Book of Evidence*, by John Banville is reprinted with the permission of Reed Books (Martin

Secker & Warburg Limited, 1989; © John Banville, 1989). Material from *Foe*, by J. M. Coetzee is reprinted with the permission of Murray Pollinger (Martin Secker & Warburg/Penguin Books, 1987; © J. M. Coetzee, 1987). Every effort has been made to obtain all necessary permissions. Any omissions will be rectified in future editions.

Contents

Introduction

By lifting the ego out of its immediate entanglement in the
world and by thematizing the subject of thought itself,
Descartes established the apodictic certainty of self as a
result of the clarity and the distinctness with which it perceives itself. Through self-reflection—the ego, the subject—
is put on its own feet, set free from all unmediated relation
to being. In giving priority to the human being's determination as a thinking being, self-reflection marks the human
being's rise to the rank of a subject. It makes the human
being a subjectivity that has its center in itself, a self-
consciousness certain of itself.

Gasché, *The Tain of the Mirror*

The self [in recent thought] . . . suffers disgrace abounding.
It has become an essentially contested category continually
revised, devised, supervised, or denied. The denial seems
most pervasive regarding an ontological, originary, coherent
self. After putting everything in doubt, consciousness ends,
reflexively, by turning that doubt upon itself.

Hassan, *Selves at Risk*

The Inward Turn

Modernity, broadly understood as the past several hundred years
in Western history, may be defined by the rise to prominence of
the self, or at least as the phase in which the concept of the
self became fixed in Western culture.[1] The late sixteenth-century
Galilean-Newtonian world-view forced a revision of the old Aristotelian conception of a universe within which human beings,
securely placed in a vast, hierarchical Chain of Being, fulfilled a
predetermined role and looked outwards to the ordered cosmos
for intimations of meaning and value. This new way of conceiving

---

[1] One of the most comprehensive of recent accounts of the rise of the self in
modernity is that provided by Charles Taylor in *Sources of the Self: The Making of
the Modern Identity* (Cambridge, Mass.: Harvard University Press, 1989).

the universe brought about a significant reconception of the previously held relationship between human beings and their physical environment. The inner realms of human consciousness and the external world were now thought to be radically separated; meaning was no longer deemed given, to be found in the world around or beyond individuals. Increasingly, human beings turned inward in the search for certainty. In the centuries that followed, the idea of the distinct, autonomous nature of the self became entrenched in Western thought. In the upheavals of the Reformation, individuals were ostensibly freed from clerical control, and the Enlightenment encouraged free-thinking, reasoning subjects to challenge prescribed dogma and turn inward in the search for grounding authority. Rationality was triumphantly acclaimed, and the capacity of human beings to contain and control the world about them seemed certain. Descartes' famous *cogito ergo sum* valorizes precisely such a withdrawal into the interior realm of one's own mind as the means of affirming the one secure certainty of being: self-consciousness. In the Romantic period, the celebration of self-expression and the inner sanctity of the autonomous mind achieved a status of almost religious significance. And in our own century, fascination with the self seems to have ousted religion as the central focus of the moral and ethical concerns of individuals.[2]

These historic events could be read as episodes in a story of progressive human emancipation, a story charting the liberation of humankind from subservience to extra-personal authorities, a story celebrating the ascendancy of human reason, freedom, and dignity. On such an account, human beings in modernity achieved the liberation, if not the invention, of the self; they usurped the authority of external, transcendent grounds of meaning and value, and internalized authority in the prioritization of their immanent and self-reflexive knowledge. Indeed, as many commentators have noted, Western culture over the past few hundred years may be characterized by the mistrust it displays in the inherited 'metanarratives' or overarching mythologies that once structured human interactive communities: traditional theology, empirical philosophy, scientific rationality, social protocol, literary and

[2] See Louis A. Sass, 'The Self and its Vicissitudes in the Psychoanalytic Avant-Garde', in George Levine (ed.), *Constructions of the Self* (New Brunswick, NJ: Rutgers University Press, 1992), 17–58.

conversational conventions. Post-Enlightenment thought might be understood, as Rodolphe Gasché avers in the first epigraph above, as a metaphysics of subjectivity grounded in the self-reflexive capacity of autonomous human subjects.

On such a world-view, there is no certainty beyond the conceptual processes of the individual psyche; deference to external authorities is supplanted by a cult of individuality in which truth, meaning, and value, if they are to be found at all, become radically subjective. The much vaunted late nineteenth-century 'death of God' proclaims the birth of a new deity, the autonomous Self, immanent ground of certainty. Orthodox theology gives way to a cult of 'liberated' subjectivity which is, unavoidably, characterized by the contradictory impulses of hope and fear. Anthony Cascardi, in *The Subject of Modernity*, points to the ambiguous consequences of this modern 'secularization', which he understands as the tendency to 'speak in terms of inner-worldly progress and self-improvement rather than the possibility of [extra-personal] perfection'.[3] Modern secular subjects are liberated from a belief in the determining authority of God, and assert their own subjective and transformative power as a means of containing the potential meaninglessness of an unauthorized world, a world in which God is dead. This secular focus, as Cascardi observes, 'yields a world that is in principle open to transformation from within, but also raises fears that the world may be governed by no authoritative point of view'.[4] For some, the celebrants of modern subjective liberation, the adoption of an antinomian, iconoclastic stance offers a release from mandates of conformity imposed by extra-personal meta-narratives of value. This is viewed as emancipatory and as a cause for celebration, for it is seen as heralding an era of (tolerant) unfettered individuality and a diverse plurality in which previously excluded or marginalized alternatives gain credibility.

But the response to this broad cultural desacralization has been deeply ambivalent; the celebration of autonomy is seemingly inseparable from the fear of uncertainty and the spectre of meaninglessness. For if it is true that the breakdown and loss of shared systems of belief in transcendental meta-narratives has facilitated the rise to supremacy of the individual, then it is also true that this

---

[3] Anthony Cascardi, *The Subject of Modernity* (Cambridge: Cambridge University Press, 1992), 126.
[4] Ibid.

new individualistic focus brings with it the attendant dangers of alienation, solipsism, and isolation. Too readily the intuition of 'release' from systematization and order slides into a nostalgic lamentation for lost certainty and a fear of relativistic anarchy. The loss of belief in the transcendent gods of metaphysical certainty (and loss it is, not simply lack, a loss that is tainted with the residue of a more substantial past) may entail not the ecstatic liberation of creative pluralism, but the terror of alienation, atomistic monism, and groundless relativism. For some, life lived without recourse to the undisputed authority of extra-personal grounds of value is unbearable. So Israel Scheffer on such an imagined state of affairs:

Independent and public controls are no more, communication has failed, the common universe of things is a delusion, reality is itself made . . . rather than discovered. . . . In place of a community of rational men following objective procedures in the pursuit of truth we have a set of isolated monads, within each of which belief forms without systematic constraints.[5]

For Scheffer, abandoning the systematic constraints of objective reasoning and the public controls of community leads fast down the slippery slide towards the irremediable, antagonistic alienation of isolated monads. In the late nineteenth and early twentieth centuries the euphoric Romantic celebration of inwardness gave way to an anguished intuition of solipsistic alienation. This concern, in a variety of ways, is central theme of many of the great writers of the period of high modernism: Eliot, Woolf, Joyce, Beckett. It was feared that human beings, locked into the cells of their own intellections, might have no access to the minds of others. It would seem that in terms of a philosophy that valorizes self-reflexive subjective immanence, knowing or understanding others, beyond the mere perception of their external characteristics, is impossible. Without external structures of communicative and ethical authority, the division between self and others becomes an impassable gulf.

From our late twentieth-century perspective, fortified by new

---

[5] Israel Scheffer, *Science and Subjectivity* (Indianapolis: Bobbs-Merrill, 1967), 19. Scheffer writes in response to Thomas Kuhn's subjective challenge to orthodox methods of scientific inquiry in *The Structure of Scientific Revolutions* (Chicago: University of Chicago Press, 1961).

ideas about discursive functioning, Scheffer's pessimistic invocation of anarchic relativism and solipsistic isolation seems easily countered by positing the shared communicative medium of language. In *Modernity and Self-Identity*, for example, Anthony Giddens responds to the proposition that a 'transcendental philosophy of the ego terminates in irremediable solipsism' as follows:

The difficulty is avoided in the position of the later Wittgenstein, as well as in the more sophisticated versions of existentialist phenomenology. Self-consciousness has no primacy over the awareness of others, since language—which is intrinsically public—is the means of access to both. Intersubjectivity does not derive from subjectivity, but the other way around.[6]

Subjectivity, in short, is understood to derive from intersubjectivity. That is, our conceptions of selfhood are deemed to be constituted by, not merely reflected in, the terms of language, which is social and public. In thinking myself, therefore, I speak (or write) myself in the terms of a language which is prior to, and has primacy over, my self-conception. I speak myself, to myself and to others, in the language of others. The self-immanent, self-reflexive subjective centre of modernity is dethroned, and a new determining force gains eminence: language and the discursive processes which structure social interaction.

The Prioritization of Language

Far from assuaging modern fears, this conception of linguistically constituted subjectivity opens the door to a raft of new and unsettling questions. The ramifications of a prioritization of language as prior to and the condition for self-consciousness have been widely felt through a variety of disciplines, not least those of literary, social, and political theory. Hans-Georg Gadamer, building on Dilthey's stress on interpretative method and incorporating Heidegger's existential analytic, offers the hermeneutic posture of (linguistic) interpretative procedures as universal and all-encompassing. Language loses its pragmatic representational function, and becomes the very medium for the interpretative

---

[6] Anthony Giddens, *Modernity and Self-identity: Self and Society in the Late Modern Age* (Cambridge: Polity Press, 1991), 51.

conceptualization of one's self and one's relation to the object-world: 'there cannot be a position that is not drawn into the reflective movement of consciousness coming to itself.'[7] Emphatically, and enigmatically, Gadamer writes: '[b]eing that can be understood is language.'[8] Interpretation is understood as the fundamental activity by which human beings realize their world (as text) and their being-in-the-world as (self-) interpretative subjects:

The hermeneutic consciousness does not compete with that self-transparency that Hegal took to constitute absolute consciousness and the highest mode of being. . . . In the last analysis all understanding is self-understanding, but not in the sense of a preliminary self-possession or of one finally and definitely achieved. For the self-understanding only realizes itself in the character of a free self-realization. The self that we are does not possess itself: one could say that it 'happens'.[9]

Or, as the hermeneutic philosopher Paul Ricoeur puts it, '[t]here is no direct apprehension of the self by the self, no internal apperception or appropriation of the self's desire to exist through the short-cut of consciousness, but only by taking the long road of the interpretation of signs.'[10]

Jacques Derrida's poststructuralist account of human subjectivity similarly prioritizes linguistic operation as the medium of self-conception. Selfhood, on his account, takes on the contours of *écriture*, the operations of endlessly mediated and deferred (conceptual) 'writing'. The meaning of the human subject is reduced to an 'effect' of *différance* (a neologism that conflates the ideas of deferral and difference) and the impossible attempt to bridge the gap between signifier and signified.[11] The self as discursive construct is deemed equally prey to the dispersals and mediations of

[7] Hans-Georg Gadamer, *Truth and Method* (New York: Seabury Press, 1975), 308.

[8] Ibid. 432.

[9] Gadamer, *Philosophical Hermeneutics*, trans. and ed. David E. Linge (Berkeley: University of California Press, 1976), 55.

[10] Paul Ricoeur, *The Conflict of Interpretations* (Evanston, Ill.: Northwestern University Press, 1974), 170.

[11] The most extensive account of *différance* is provided by Derrida in *Positions*, trans. A. Bass (Chicago: University of Chicago Press, 1982). For an explication of Derrida's variable definitions of *différance*, see Rodolphe Gasché, *The Tain of the Mirror: Derrida and the Philosophy of Reflection* (London and Cambridge, Mass.: Harvard University Press, 1986), 194–205.

Derrida's famously theorized 'movement of *différance*' which renders the notion of presence a discredited metaphysical illusion, pointing as it does to the forever incomplete, deferred nature of the significatory process: 'Presence is a determination and an effect within a system which is no longer that of presence but that of difference.'[12] When applied to the human subject and her thought processes, the notion of *différance* invokes a radical decentring and displacement. If self-reflexive conceptual processes are beset by the hermeneutic uncertainty and open-endedness which characterize all interpretative endeavour, then knowing oneself with certainty is an impossibility: 'you are indefinitely referred to a concatenation without basis, without end, and the indefinitely articulated retreat of the forbidden beginning as well as of hermeneutic archaeology, eschatology or teleology'.[13] Self is never separable from, or directly available to, linguistic appraisal: 'the movement of difference is not something which occurs to a transcendental subject. It is what produces it.'[14]

In the terms of Lacanian psychoanalysis, relations between language and consciousness are equally problematic. For Jacques Lacan a sense of selfhood which precedes linguistic formulation is inconceivable; self-certainty is an illusory, misrecognized construct; the human subject is always split asunder in the attempt to know or 'speak' itself. For Lacan human beings must not be conceived as the masters of language, able to convey pre-existing meanings through language. Rather, '[t]he subject is born insofar as the signifier emerges in the field of the Other.'[15] The illusion of subjective agency is an effect of language, an effect which paradoxically entails the loss of the subject in its objectification in a pre-existing system of signification. Self-scrutiny reveals not the presence of the autonomous self but its absence in the (mis)recognition of oneself as a unified object: 'the I is precipitated in a primordial form, before it is objectified in the dialectic of identification with the other, and before language restores to it, in

---

[12] Jacques Derrida, *Speech and Phenomena: And Other Essays on Husserl's Theory of Signs*, trans. David B. Allison (Evanston, Ill.: Northwestern University Press, 1973), 147.

[13] Derrida, *Dissemination*, trans. B. Johnson (London: Athlone Press, 1981), 333–4.

[14] Derrida, *Speech and Phenomena*, 82.

[15] Jacques Lacan, *The Four Fundamental Concepts of Psycho-analysis* (London: Hogarth Press, 1977), 199.

the universal, its function as subject.'[16] Thus, for Lacan, 'I identify myself in language, but only by losing myself in it like an object.'[17] The linguistic turn evident in such philosophical reflections ushers in a host of problems with which we have yet to deal adequately. Centrally, linguistic scepticism has called into question the possibility of the self-certain subjective immanence necessary to validate the claims of post-Cartesian modern philosophy. In the rhetoric of postmodernity, *all* absolutes, including the ostensibly free-thinking subject of modernity, are deemed to be the product of the kind of deluded metaphysical thinking which seeks to ground the contingencies of experience in an authoritative, substantial presence. The ontological security of the modern subject is ravaged in postmodernity by epistemological and linguistic uncertainties turned inward, against itself and its own processes of introspection. In much contemporary thought the self is no longer understood as a pre-linguistic given, but as a linguistic construct. In the words of Anthony Kerby, it is no more than 'the *implied subject* of self-referring utterances', construed as 'a result of discursive praxis rather than either a substantial entity having ontological priority over praxis or a self with epistemological priority, an originator of meaning'.[18]

One of the most disturbing notions which such theorizing forces us to confront is the idea that personal authenticity and subjective agency are impossible, given their constitution in the terms of social discourse. There can be no private language, no private morality. Even the most private, intimate contours of selfhood are written and read in the extra-personal terms of social language: human beings are 'subjected' by the language in which they conceive themselves. In other words, human beings are made into subjects by language, and are subjected to the ideological values, the systems of representations, repressions, hierarchies, and stereotypes with which social language is imbued. Pursuing this line of thought, Roland Barthes writes in *The Pleasure of the Text*, '[t]he language I speak *within myself* is not of my time: it is prey, by nature, to ideological suspicion.'[19]

[16] Lacan, *Écrits: A Selection*, trans. Alan Sheridan (New York: Norton, 1977), 2.
[17] Ibid. 86.
[18] Anthony Paul Kerby, *Narrative and the Self* (Bloomington and Indianapolis: Indiana University Press, 1991), 4.
[19] Roland Barthes, *The Pleasure of the Text*, trans. Richard Miller (London: Jonathan Cape, 1976), 40–1.

The stance is familiar to students in any number of (post)-modern disciplines, as are its major theoretical acolytes: Derrida, Lacan, Barthes, Foucault, to name a few. Although their interests and concerns are often divergent and even oppositional, each theorist practices some form of subjective dissolution or deconstruction with recourse to the discursive operations of self-reflexive consciousness. In short, in the light of postmodern scepticism, the linguistic-constructivist turn may be thought to herald the ascent of a new era in the history of thought, that of the 'death of man'. The phrase is that of Michel Foucault in *The Order of Things*. In this work he boldly proclaims the dissolution of the *episteme* of subjective ascendancy and of the post-Kantian anthropocentric tendency of philosophical thought. Here Foucault offers human subjects as the 'being[s] of language' not in possession of pre-linguistic essentiality, and propounds the view that human interrelations and conceptions are fundamentally linguistic and symbolic in character:

From within language experienced and traversed as language, in the play of its possibilities extended to their furthest point, what emerges is that man has 'come to an end,' and that, by reaching the summit of all possible speech, he arrives not at the very heart of himself but at the brink of that which limits him . . . where the promise of the origin interminably recedes.[20]

Between Structure and Agency: Plural Communities of Resistance

The idea that selves are constituted as subjects in intersubjective discursive processes, is one that I endorse. It is to oversimplify, however, to reduce selfhood to the processes of infinitely deferred, ideologically complicit language, as the pervasive contemporary metaphor of textual self-consciousness encourages us to do. The consequences for subjectivity evoked by this rhetorical, reductive trope are untenable. Among others, my central concerns are ethical: the deterministic ethos of constructivist conceptions of 'textual' subjectivity evacuates agency; it is, moreover, politically enervating. How can we even begin to theorize the possibility of (social and personal) change, except as the consequence of the

[20] Michel Foucault, *The Order of Things: An Archaeology of the Human Sciences* (1966; New York: Vintage Books, 1973), 382–3.

most arbitrary, contingent circumstances, when the self, as social subject, is always only the product of predetermined and determining social norms encoded in language?[21] It is one of my central claims in this book that we do not have to accept either the bleak determinism of theories which subscribe to constructivist notions of subjectivity, with the attendant dangers of ideological subjection and moral and political ennui, or the vague (not to say dangerous) utopianism which wishfully imagines we can simply step outside the webs of social interaction and interpersonal discourse to attain 'undetermined' selfhood which is still meaningful.

The tension between individual autonomy and communal constructivism animates all the chapters which follow. The framework for my discussion will be outlined in the first chapter, which moves from a consideration of the stand-off between Lyotard's avowed explosion of meta-narrational structures and Habermas's advocacy of consensual intersubjective communication to a consideration of the debate in political philosophy between advocates of rights-based liberalism and those of communitarianism. It is my contention that in the overlap between the liberal version of the self and the communitarian stress on intersubjectivity we may find a more viable model of subjectivity—that is, of subjectivity as constituted in the complex interactions of multiple communal determinants and interpersonal affiliations. Subjectivity, as I conceive it, involves far more than fixed, passive positioning within the symbolic order; the webs of social structuration offer a wide range of potentially transgressive communicative sites ('communities') from which to speak or write. I suggest, in other words, that positing an interlinked network of plural interpretative sites or communities, within which human beings are simultaneously situated and between which they move, might point to a way of overcoming the narrowly conceived dualisms paraded in contemporary thought between, for example, structure and agency, relativism and totalitarianism.

My second chapter focuses on the capacity possessed by human agents for deviant play within the rule-bound arenas of meaningful intersubjective discourse, and on the possibility of internal criticism by self-reflexive social agents. Rules, I argue, are necessary to

---

[21] This is the question asked by George Levine in his introduction to the collection of essays *Constructions of the Self* (ed. George Levine); debate on this issue stimulates many of the essayists who contribute to the collection.

make deviance from the rules both meaningful and intentional. Unless we are to abandon ourselves to a concept of change which is merely evolutionary, we need to acknowledge the possession by human subjects of the capacity for revolutionary rule-breaking—and potentially rule-making—play. The rules that order intersubjective interaction are never undisputed natural laws, and should more rightly be conceived as revisable protocols—protocols that are procedural rather than prescriptive. Human subjects are able to actively change, and hence in some measure create, the protocols which structure the communities and communicative procedures within which they are constituted. This results in an understanding of deviance as intentional and potentially creative, rather than simply destructive, an idea that will animate the chapters that follow. The key here lies in recognizing the creativity of language use and the possibility it offers for 'rule-bound' deviance.

In articulating a more pragmatic account of intersubjective communicative procedures, I do not wish to dismiss the very real fears of subjection which may inhere in the notion of selfhood constituted in intersubjectivity. One of the most important features of contemporary critical theory is that it has made us aware of the way in which minorities and other marginalized groups may be subjected, even subjugated, by the discourses of prevailing social practices and institutions. Feminist (and cultural theorists) have done much to articulate the practical consequences of the determination by dominant (patriarchal) discourse of marginalized subjects. Too often, however, this has led to the postulation of the entrapment of the subject in (patriarchal) discourse and a consequent advocacy of ex-communicative escape to a wilderness outside (patriarchal) community.

In contradistinction, for some feminists (like Rita Felski, Nancy Fraser, and Marilyn Friedman) and cultural critics (like bell hooks, Giyatri Chakravorty Spivak, and Homi Bhabbha), subjectivity is to be understood and celebrated as constituted in the positive terms of chosen, potentially transgressive, plural communities. Such accounts seek to dismiss the myth of passive entrapment, resisting the binary of inside/outside and the unpalatable alternatives (meaningless escape or insider complicity) it offers to human subjects. Social transformation is understood as possible *within* the protocols of plural intersubjective communities; social subjects may choose to situate themselves in a variety of interconnected communities of resistance. This in turn promotes a notion of the development and modulation, through inter-animation and cross-communal borrowings, of alternative sites for self-definition. Such an understanding holds it possible for communal and communicative alternatives to exist, and, moreover, requires that subjects possess the capacity to assess, choose between, and even create these meaningful alternatives. In other words, it theorizes a subject who is always constituted by the communities in which she has being, yet who has the (qualified) ability to modulate and move between the communities that will determine her.

Self as Narrative

I am unwilling to accept the consequences for notions of morality and agency which are often thought to follow from a poststructuralist account of indefinitely deferred or always-already subjectivity—that is, of subjectivity understood as 'text', either as endlessly inconclusive hermeneutic endeavour or as pinioned in linguistic structures that pre-exist (yet facilitate) its construction. The lived experience of our lives as human beings forces us to reconsider the conclusions toward which such theorizing points. If I do not possess some kind of personal identity through time, a sense of myself which, if not fixed, is at least coherent, how can my actions have any guarantee of consistency? If I am only the always-already product of discourse, how can I speak with originality or act with intention? If I am always (an)other to myself, how can I make judgments and choices, or hold beliefs? Indeed, what happens to notions of culpability and responsibility if we scrutinize the human subject as a poststructuralist text, as a discursive construct made up, not merely reflected, in words? What possibility is there of autonomy or individuality if human beings are understood to be forever subjected or violated by the linguistic medium in which they know themselves or are known by others? How can socially constructed subjects ever be the agents of social change?

Rather than understanding subjectivity as the passive product of extra-personal discursive operations or as an endlessly deferred textual process that remains opaque to interpretation, in this book

I suggest that the construction of a subject's sense of selfhood should be understood as a creative narrative process achieved within a plurality of intersubjective communicative protocols. In the act of conceptualizing one's selfhood, one writes a narrative of personal continuity through time. That is, in thinking myself, I remember myself: I draw together my multiple members—past and other subject positions—into a coherent narrative of selfhood which is more or less readable by myself and others. Understanding personhood in this way, I argue, leaves open the possibility of revision of one's conceptions of self, and also acknowledges the potential for misreading and misinterpretation of the narratives of self and others. At the same time it recognizes that a narrative of self provides the human subject with a sense of self-continuity and coherence that enables the projection of desire and intention towards an imagined future. In short, it allows the subject to function as a purposive, morally responsible agent.

This is in no way to suggest that selfhood is a fiction, if fiction is understood as something that is untrue, fallacious, opposed to fact, but rather to suggest that selfhood is an active interpretative process. My use of the term 'narration' is more than simply descriptive; it is intended to denote the constitutive process by which human beings order their conceptions of self and of the world around them. Increasingly, theorists in a number of disciplines are promoting the idea of narration as a model for human conceptualization.[22] Anthony Kerby is representative: 'narratives

[22] The value of narrativity as a means of ordering and understanding reality is debated by essayists in W. J. T. Mitchell (ed.)*On Narrative* (Chicago and London: University of Chicago Press, 1981). Readers are also directed to Kerby, *Narrative and the Self*, and Mark Freeman *Rewriting the Self: History, Memory, Narrative* (London and New York: Routledge, 1993). Both Kerby and Freeman are greatly indebted to the work of Paul Ricoeur, particularly *Hermeneutics and the Human Sciences* (Cambridge: Cambridge University Press, 1981), and the three volumes of *Time and Narrative* (Chicago: University of Chicago Press, 1984-8), in which Ricoeur promotes the idea of the text as a model for human action. Other recent works which explore the narrative nature of human conceptualization include the edition edited by George C. Rosenwald and Richard L. Ochberg, *Storied Lives: The Cultural Politics of Self-Understanding* (New Haven and London: Yale University Press, 1992); the collection of essays edited by John Shotter and Kenneth Gergen, *Texts of Identity* (London: Sage, 1989); the collection of essays edited by Theodore R. Sarbin, *Narrative Psychology: The Storied Nature of Human Conduct* (New York: Praeger, 1986); and Arthur Danto, *Narration and Knowledge* (New York: Columbia University Press, 1985). Lois O. Mink defends narrative as a primary form of human comprehension in 'Narrative Form as Cognitive Instrument', in Robert H. Canary and Henry Kozicki (eds.), *The Wiring of History* (Madison: University of Wisconsin Press, 1978), 129-49.

are a primary embodiment of our understanding of the world, of experience, and ultimately of ourselves. Narrative emplotment appears to yield a form of understanding of human experience, both individual and collective, that is not directly amenable to other forms of exposition or analysis.'[23] Theodore Sarbin offers 'the narrative as an organizing principle for human action', and suggests that 'human beings think, perceive, imagine and make choices according to narrative structures'.[24] In the introduction to a collection of essays which consider narrative as a means of understanding the interpretative and investigative procedures followed across a wide range of disciplines, Christopher Nash writes of the contemporary 'obsession' with the notion 'that our sensations and understandings are inextricable from the system of signs through which we articulate them to ourselves'.[25]

One of the characteristics of narration is temporal and spatial emplotment: narratives are concerned not with isolated moments or particular acts, but with *sequences* of acts and events.[26] They are orderings and interconnections of phenomenological perceptions, or the memories of these perceptions, in time and space. In the process of narration, discrete moments and acts are contextualized: they are enmeshed in a history.[27] Historical narrative contextualization is crucial to human understanding. It is because we can understand or conceptualize the connection and interrelation between remembered, experienced, and anticipated actions and events, and because we can situate them in space and time, that the plethora of stimuli and experiences that constitute our lived world (and our selves) come to have a meaning. The history

---

[23] Kerby, *Narrative and the Self*, 3.

[24] Theodore R. Sarbin, 'The Narrative as a Root Metaphor for Psychology', in Sarbin (ed.), *Narrative Psychology*, 3–21; 9, 8.

[25] Nash (ed. and intro.), *Narrative in Culture: The Uses of Storytelling in the Sciences, Philosophy and Literature* (London and New York: Routledge, 1990), p. xi.

[26] For a discussion of the minimum conditions of narrative, see Nelson Goodman, 'Twisted Tales; or, Story, Study, and Symphony', in Mitchell (ed.), *On Narrative*, 99–116. On plotting, see Peter Brooks, *Reading for the Plot: Design and Intention in Narrative* (1984; Cambridge, Mass. and London: Harvard University Press, 1992); on plot and sequence in narrative, see Frank Kermode, 'Secrets and Narrative Sequences', and Paul Ricoeur, 'Narrative Time', in *On Narrative*, 79–97 and 165–86 respectively.

[27] See Hayden White, 'The Value of Narrativity in the Representation of Reality', *Critical Inquiry*, 7 (1980), 5–28, and *Metahistory* (Baltimore: Johns Hopkins University Press, 1973).

one tells of one's self, through the process of one's own memory and facilitated by the memories of others, is a narrative in which moments of the past achieve some kind of interconnection, even coherence. Granted, this meaning constituting narrative does not guarantee permanent fixity or access to *the* meaning or truth of the self, but it provides a more or less stable conceptual framework from which to begin to understand the present and anticipate the future. Moreover, historical narratives need not—indeed cannot— have direct correspondence with the past as it *really was*, but rather mediate and modulate the events of the past from a present interpretative moment.[28] In remembering the past, events and actions are set within a framing, contextualizing present narrative, a narrative which is in no way comprehensive, but full of gaps and omissions and weighted by partisan understandings and desires.[29] Despite the fallibility of memory and the partiality of our subject- ive interpretations, the narratives we tell about our world and ourselves anticipate coherence and closure or, at the very least, followability.[30] They are more or less 'readable', which is not to suggest that their meanings are transparently and unproblem- atically available to an objective viewer. Patently, many (self) narratives are open-ended, and their meanings and purposes un- clear. But narrative itself, as a mode of conceptualization, anticip- ates an end (which may be revised), and aspires to order (which may be provisional). Narrative conceptualization enables the cre- ation of a revisable, provisional, but more or less readable self, and facilitates the experience of self-continuity through time. Much of this book comprises an exploration of the human capacity for self-revision, or more precisely the capacity to reconceptualize the self though the revision of narratives of selfhood. In this inheres a degree of personal autonomy.

That said, my focus is not simply individualistic. In my discus- sion of the human capacity for revisable self-narration I do not wish to lose sight of social analysis. I argue for a conception of the human subject as agent of both personal and social change. As I have already noted, the dimensions of the personal and the social

[28] See Hayden White, *Tropics of Discourse* (Baltimore: Johns Hopkins University Press, 1978), and Robert Young, *White Mythologies: Writing History and the West* (London: Routledge and Kegan Paul, 1990).
[29] See Stephen Crites, 'Storytime: Recollecting the Past and Projecting the Future', in Sarbin (ed.), *Narrative Psychology*.
[30] See Kerby, *Narrative and the Self*, 32–64.

are fundamentally entwined, for the medium and materials in which individuals narrate their versions of self are ineluctably intersubjective. All narratives are told (and interpreted) in social language, within the bounds of communal and communicative conventions that render them intelligible; and in this respect narration might be understood as conservative, as an act that merely sustains and perpetuates the already existing discursive and cultural norms of the communities in which the narrating individual exists. The intersubjective nature of discursive procedure and the vicious circle of hermeneutic endeavour would seem to disavow the possibility of original authorship or authentic narratives of self, and to severely constrain the production of alternative modes of social formation. Questions about the nature and possibility of authorial originality and narrative authenticity have fuelled much debate in those modes of contemporary literary criticism which have followed the constructivist, hermeneutic turn, and have encouraged a tendency to self-reflection in many contemporary fictions. There is much insight to be gained from the concerns with textual authenticity and issues of narratology that animate many contemporary literary critical debates, particularly as they impact on questions of subjectivity, and it is to a consideration of these that I turn in my fourth and fifth chapters.

Literary Critical Perspectives

If human (self-) conceptual processes are narrative in kind, then contemporary literary critical perspectives on narration and discursive process might offer fruitful paths for exploration in a discussion of subjectivity. Given the linguistic turn in Western thought, it is not surprising to find that many contemporary writers—philosophers (Ricoeur, MacIntyre, Taylor), psychologists (Sarbin, Gergen, Schafer), sociologists (Bertaux, Giddens), and geographers (Massey, Soja)[31]—have utilized literary theory and the analysis of literature in their writings about the nature and status of the human subject and her social placement. These writers do

[31] Contemporary geography is increasingly informed by the insights of literary theory. See Michael Keith and Steve Pile (eds.), *Place and the Politics of Identity* (London and New York: Routledge, 1993), many of the contributors to which utilize fictions and literary theory to further their arguments. See esp. chapters by Michael Keith and Steve Pile, George Revill and Doreen Massey.

not seek to elide fiction and narrative conceptualization, texts and selves, or fictions and perceived reality; but, despite their very different theoretical assumptions and ends, all hold in common an understanding of the linguistic nature of conceptualization and concur in their use of metaphors of textuality and narration to facilitate the understanding of personhood.

The consideration of any narrative artefact, the manner of its production, and the interpretation of its meanings might open windows on the kinds of questions raised here. I have chosen to focus my attention on contemporary fiction. Generated and consumed in the late twentieth century in a climate of linguistic scepticism, many contemporary fictions (although by no means all) evidence a specific concern with the problematics of textual production, interpretation and narration. This is particularly the case with those fictions that self-reflexively scrutinize their own processes of production (meta-fictions) and those fictions which ostentatiously bend and break the rules of traditional narration (anti-narratives). In meta-fictions and anti-narratives (and the categories are by no means exclusive), the activity of narrating is foregrounded at both the formal and the substantive level. These fictions invite the reader to share in the kinds of epistemological and ontological uncertainties engendered by the self-conscious inspection of narrativization as a mode for understanding: the fiction of Martin Amis, Margaret Atwood, John Barth, Donald Barthelme, Italo Calvino, Angela Carter, J. M. Coetzee, John Fowles, Sara Maitland, Thomas Pynchon, Salman Rushdie, and Kurt Vonnegut is representative.

In Chapter 4 I turn to a close analysis of recent critical discussions of meta-fictional strategies, and consider a variety of meta-fictional or anti-narrative texts. In part, my critique focuses on the manipulative, perhaps self-deceptive nature of the rhetoric in which the contemporary theoretical appeal for textual/personal liberation, through acts of radical dispersion and dissemination, is often couched. The moral and political intimidation which frequently inhere in the rhetorical ploys of such criticism is particularly disturbing, and bears closer scrutiny. In the course of my discussion I consider a number of contemporary meta-fictions/anti-narratives in order to defend my claim that many contemporary fictions in fact explore and exemplify the creative, constitutive capacity of subversive linguistic play, and encourage the same playfulness in their interpreting reader, despite a theoretical climate in which 'textual' processes are frequently dismissed as passively reinscriptive. Many contemporary theorists, I contend, have mistakenly appropriated iconoclastic contemporary fiction, claiming for it an aesthetics of negativity in line with sceptical and constructivist philosophical assumptions. I conclude that such theorizing may be misguided, even dangerous, particularly in those forms which advocate the wholesale rejection of communal and communicative conventions as the condition for authenticity in the creation of fictions and the narratives of self.

My fifth chapter, the final chapter in Part I, returns to and elaborates the notion of narrativized selfhood as a metaphor which attempts to retain the value and the possibility of human subjects as accountable, reflexive agents who exist and have some power to transform themselves *within* the contexts of particular social settings or discursive structures (communities). Rather than look at the experimental strategies of self-reflexive fictions as reflecting an intuition of the endless regress of hermeneutic endeavour and the impossibility of narrative authenticity, I suggest that we might consider such fictions to be engaged in an exploration of the possibility of narrative creativity within communicative protocols and a simultaneous enquiry into the transformative possibilities of creative self-narration.

In the second part of the book I take a close look at three contemporary novels: John Banville's *The Book of Evidence*, J. M. Coetzee's *Foe*, and Margaret Atwood's *Lady Oracle*. My purpose is threefold. First, I hope to draw out some of the ethical and political consequences of the claims I make in the first part of the book in an analysis of the narrative content of these novels. In particular, my readings stress the inescapable embeddedness of persons in intersubjective communities, an aspect of being that both facilitates and constrains the capacity for purposive agency in individual subjects. In Chapter 6 I submit that excommunication, the wholesale separation of self from others/language, is an untenable theoretical goal. Severance of self from community has pathological consequences: intersubjective engagement is a condition of healthy personhood. *The Book of Evidence* invites us to consider the ethical consequences of a theoretical advocacy of a posture of wholesale subjective construction or excommunicative dissolution, beneath the cover of which an intentional agent (such as Freddie, the novel's protagonist) may perform the most heinous of intentional acts (in this case, murder). Focusing on the figure of Friday in Coetzee's *Foe* in Chapter 7, I suggest that entrance into preexisting systems of signification does not merely constrain but is a condition of personal autonomy, for only in language can one speak (for) oneself and begin to contest the will-to-power of interpreting others. Only as speaking subjects do we have any chance of challenging the prescriptive interpretations others would impose on us. I conclude, in Chapter 8, with a look at the celebration of creative self-narration offered in Atwood's *Lady Oracle*. Joan, the novel's heroine, an author of conventional Gothic romances, writes a subversive version of herself into the errant script of her latest novel. This act of creativity suggests to her the power of (re)writing her own life narrative and the necessity of engaging with, rather than escaping from, the communities that define her.

Second, I aim to substantiate my assertion that many contemporary fictional texts reveal the possibility of linguistic creativity on the part of writers and readers, rather than simply exposing the limitations and restrictions of discursive determinism. Despite ostensibly lamenting the paucity of language as medium for creative expression and the restrictive nature of fictional conventions, in practice, each of the novels I consider displays a remarkable resistance to always-already strands of predetermined constructivism; each self-consciously revels in the ludic strategies available to creative players in the game of language. Overtly, and at times intrusively aware of their own processes of fictionalization, these meta-fictional novels affirm that the author is anything but dead and that contemporary literature is far from exhausted.

Finally, I argue that these fictions explore (and invite the involved reader to explore) the subjective capacity for the expression of personal autonomy in the creative construction of narratives of selfhood within the rule-bound arenas of meaningful communicative procedure. Each of the books I consider is, in part or in sum, a fictional autobiography, a novel in which a first-person narrator selectively tells his or her life story. Moreover, the meta-fictional nature of the texts encourages us to scrutinize not only the processes of fictionalization and interpretation pursued by writer and reader, but also the protagonist-as-author's activity of self-narration in the act of autobiographical writing. In other words, these meta-fictional autobiographies offer a triple focus with regard to the activity of narration: first on the part of the self-conscious authors, second on the part of the self-conscious narrators, and third, on the part of the interpreting reader.

Recently we have witnessed an upsurge of critical interest in the genre of autobiography.[32] More than simply fuelling the contemporary fascination with the self, autobiography is of particular critical interest because it provides a model for the manner in which we (re)write the self in acts of retrospective self-conceptualization. In particular, it highlights the gap between the self who remembers and authorizes the narrative of the past (I), and the self who is remembered, written as a protagonist in that narrative (me). This gap has been lamented, by writers such as Benveniste, Lacan, and Derrida, as the divisive condition of inauthentic being: the reflecting subject and the reflected object of introspection can never cohere into a transcending self. Autobiographical writing works towards creating a synthesis, or continuity, between the self who tells and the self (selves) told in the narrative of one's life; and examining its processes might reveal the way in which a similar continuity is achieved in the act of retrospective self-conceptualization. Most significantly, autobiographical writing offers for scrutiny the creativity of (self-) remembrance, and suggests the constitutive importance of the present interpreting self to the historical self re-membered. As Stephen Crites writes, 'the remembered past is situated in relation to the present in which it is re-collected. The child is not the father of the man. The man, in this respect, is the father of the child.'[33] And further, in elaborating on the activity of recollection:

[32] See e.g. Kathleen Ashley, Leigh Gilmore, and Gerald Peters, *Autobiography and Postmodernism* (Amherst, Mass.: University of Massachusetts Press, 1994); Robin Henley, *Turning Life into Fiction* (Cincinnati: Story Press, 1994); Leigh Gilmore, *Autobiographics: A Feminist Theory of Women's Self-Representation* (Ithaca, NY: Cornell University Press, 1993); John Sturrock, *The Language of Autobiography: Studies in the First Person Singular* (Cambridge and New York: Cambridge University Press, 1993); Phillipe Lejeune, *On Autobiography* (Minneapolis: University of Minnesota Press, 1989); Shari Benstock (ed.), *The Private Self: Theory and Practice of Women's Autobiographical Writings* (Chapel Hill, NC: University of North Carolina Press, 1988); Robert Elbaz, *The Changing Nature of the Self: A Critical Study of the Autobiographical Discourse* (London: Croom Helm, 1988); Paul John Eakin, *Fictions in Autobiography* (Princeton: Princeton University Press, 1985); and the collection of essays in James Olney (ed.), *Autobiography: Essays Theoretical and Critical* (Princeton: Princeton University Press, 1980).

[33] Crites, 'Storytime', 158.

What I own as my self is always present as the character in the story from whose perspective its episodes are recalled, claimed as its own self by this 'I' who recalls. By telling the story from the perspective of this self, as in a first person narrative, usually told in the past tense, I distance this self from the intersubjective matrix of experience in order to claim it as my own, as that personal past with which I claim identity. Still there is always some hiatus between the 'I' who recollects and the self who appears as a character in a succession of episodes, a hiatus that I artfully bridge by owning this self, claiming it as my own.[34]

To a certain degree, when remembering, we make, rather than simply retrieve, our past. Certainly, this act of making is subject to constraints: not least those imposed by the circumstances within which the interpreting and socially embedded 'I' narrates and the intersubjectivity of the linguistic medium of remembrance and narration. None the less, it is the idea of *making* the self, through self-conscious narrative acts of remembering, that I wish to emphasize and explore. Each of the narrating protagonists in the novels I consider wilfully performs the rewriting of self in the process of writing his or her life-story, in ways that impact on the present and offer new configurations for the future. The limitations and potentialities of their enterprises may provide new ways of conceiving our situated subjectivity and the transformative power that inheres in constructive self-narration.

[34] Ibid. 159. For Crites this bridging is achieved linguistically as the differentiation between the grammar of past and present.

Part I

THEORIES OF SUBJECTIVITY

1

Self as Text: The Political Agenda

> It is in and through language that man constitutes himself as
> a subject, because language alone establishes the concept of
> 'ego' in reality, in *its* reality which is that of being.
>
> Benveniste, *Problems in General Linguistics*

Human beings are to be understood as texts: this metaphoric claim
has frequently been made by contemporary critical theorists for
whom the acts of writing and interpretation which constitute
textual meaning are thought to be paradigmatic of the conceptual
processes through which we come to know ourselves and our
world: in thinking myself, I write (and read) a text of self. So
conceived, the self-reflective act of introspection is one of hermeneutic endeavour, not of factual discovery, and self-knowledge is
subject to precisely the same limitations of doubt and uncertainty
which characterize all interpretations. In our century, linguistic
scepticism has become intimately bound up with concerns about
selfhood, personal agency, and individual autonomy, for it is
claimed that only through language and acts of (linguistic) interpretation do we arrive at a conception of who we are. Increasingly,
in a variety of disciplines, theorists have recognized language as
the epistemological (and some would say ontological) foundation
of subjectivity. Only through the medium of language, it is argued,
can we come to know what it means to be human, or, even more
devastatingly, do we know that we are. Ever more frequently,
(meaningful) being is situated in the linguistic processes of intellection.

It is a post-Wittgensteinian philosophical commonplace that the
medium for our introspective reflections, the languages (or alternative significatory structures) in which we read and write our texts
of self, are never personal and private. In this respect there is a
dimension of selfhood which is irreducibly social. It seems only a
small step from this understanding to the poststructuralist claim
that existence as a writing/speaking subject inescapably involves

reproduction of the logic of the prevailing symbolic order, a blind reinscription of its ideological norms and values. Once the constitution of human subjectivity is understood in textual terms, as written in a system of social language that is the prior condition for one's (self-)conceptions, linguistic practices and aesthetic endeavour no longer seem able to offer an escape from external systems of authority into the realm of creative authenticity.

On a poststructuralist account, one's selfhood can no longer be conceived of as an independent, autonomous essence, but as the product of significatory processes which pre-exist it. As Derrida comments, famously, in *Speech and Phenomenon*, 'the movement of [significatory] difference is not something which occurs to a transcendental subject. It is what produces it.'[1] Lacanian psychoanalytic theory has been used extensively to bolster this position. Selfhood, on such a view, is always realized in terms whose social and temporal character construct it as an unoriginal representation, and this discursive subjectification amounts to writtenness by extra-personal systems of signification. One's sense of oneself can only ever be a retrospective re-cognition, a belated realization of something which is always already written in the structures of symbolic language, never a spontaneous apprehension of an original self. Many critics find this despairing sense of personal and textual 'inauthenticity' to characterize contemporary fiction. In an existence deemed to be perpetually reconstructed in language, where perceived 'reality', however personal, is always the retrospective product of interpretative *différance*, and where even our most private inner thoughts are already written in systematized social language, aesthetic endeavour offers no retreat from the enslavement wrought by all conceptualization. The authority and autonomy of the human subject are no less open to challenge than all the other gods discredited by the linguistic turn of sceptical postmodernity; the individual mind enjoys no ontological priority as an unmediated reality confirmed by a priori self-reflection. Inauthenticity as the fear of inherited systems of authority becomes inauthenticity as the fear of one's own creative mind:

Writing, the very act of taking personal vision and formulating it in terms of a pre-established, innately social system of signs and symbols,

[1] Jacques Derrida, *Speech and Phenomena: And Other Essays on Husserl's Theory of Signs*, trans. David B. Allison (Evanston, Ill.: Northwestern University Press, 1973), 82.

can come to be the most intimate form of self-betrayal, the most insidious form of inauthenticity.[2]

It would seem that the metaphors of textualized identity wielded by poststructuralists urge the pessimistic conclusion that there is no escape from the mediations of social systematization into the subjective certainty of personal creativity (except perhaps in the negative 'escape' of radical, non-representational fragmentation). The activity of writing is itself devalued as paradigmatic of the treachery of all conscious activity—a reinscription of prescriptive social patterns and values. There can be no expression of individuality through creativity, no private (meaningful) language. All conceptual texts are defiled by the traitorous taint of otherness.

Much impetus for such theorizing arises from the abstraction of language as a static, atemporal system or code from the web of historically specific communicative practice. This bracketing of the socio-historic communicative context reveals a negative loyalty to structuralist principles: at root, poststructuralists such as Lacan and Derrida rely on a Saussurean devaluation of *parole* in order to focus on the repressive procedural operations of *langue*. This structuralist foundation is severely damaging to any emancipatory politics, as Nancy Fraser claims:

Because it abstracts from *parole*, the structuralist model brackets questions of practice, agency, and the speaking subject. Thus it cannot shed light on social identity and group formation. Moreover, because this approach brackets the diachronic, it will not tell us anything abut shifts in identities and affiliations over time. Similarly, because it abstracts from the social context of communication, the model brackets issues of power and inequality. Thus, it cannot illuminate the processes by which cultural hegemony is secured and contested. Finally, because the model theorizes the fund of available linguistic meanings as a single symbolic system, it lends itself to a monolithic view of signification that denies tensions and contradictions among social meanings. In short, by reducing discourse to a 'symbolic system,' the structuralist model evacuates social agency, social conflict, and social practice.[3]

    [2] Frank D. McConnell, *Four Post War American Novelists: Bellow, Mailer, Barth and Pynchon* (Chicago: University of Chicago Press, 1977), p. xxii.
    [3] Nancy Fraser, 'The Uses and Abuses of French Discourse Theories for Feminist Politics', *Boundary 2*, 17/2 (1990), 87. A similar claim underlies Paul Smith's critique of contemporary theories of subjectivity in *Discerning the Subject* (Minneapolis: University of Minnesota Press, 1988): such theories construct 'a purely theoretical "subject," removed almost entirely from the political and ethical realities in which human agents actually live' (p. xxix).

According to Lacanian theory, subjects are constituted as subjects only by entry into a pre-existing symbolic order (understood variously as a totalizing significatory system or a universal set of cultural traditions). But with Fraser I would argue that submissive subjection to the prevailing symbolic order is a dangerous myth of determinism that wholly precludes the possibility of linguistic innovation, political intervention, and social change. It is a gross simplification to reduce the heterogeneity of social practices and discourses to a single monolithic structure of the power, the symbolic order. Doing so wilfully evades the fact that at any given moment social subjects are able to take up positions, or are situated, in a variety of signifying communities (if signifying communities are understood, as here intended, not as coherent entities locatable in space and time, but as discursive sites that reveal certain common allegiances). Poststructuralism's negative structuralism ignores the contingency of communicative practice and social protocols; it amounts to fallacious scaremongering in its inattention to the very real presence in and between signifying communities of contestation, contradiction ambiguity, perspectival differences, and interpretative alterity.

Familiar poststructuralist procedure sets up the straw target of humanist individualism, in order to promote a conception of the human subject as discursive position, or text, where 'sublimity' or escape from conservative reinscription inheres only in radical identity-fragmentation. In such theorizing, metaphoric tenor and vehicle are frequently elided: human subject is/as (poststructuralist) text. Under such conditions, the political claims of literary theory are particularly relevant to concerns with human subjectivity. Frequently in contemporary theory, textual and personal autonomy are promoted as the refusal to conform to prevailing conventions of value and practice, and as the shattering and dispersal of received, normalized modes of expression—in other words, as the refusal to comply with expectations of narrative followability. Literary theory rooted in deterministic poststructuralism finds itself in a precarious double bind. Human subjects, as poststructuralist texts, are condemned either to numb resignation and conformity with institutionally complicit codes of practice or to the empty gesture of non-significatory fragmentation as anti-structural escape. There is a significant problem with such thinking, for it renders nonsensical (quite literally) any possibility of progressive political intervention. Poststructuralist rebellion against narrative constraints must be, and must remain, meaningless and ineffectual unless deeply at odds with its own determinist premiss. A theory of linguistic constructivism, in which authoritative agency is dismissed as delusion, offers no possibility for revolutionary practice, be it in the texts of fiction or those of the self. Such a theory makes no allowance for the possibility of deliberately conceived aesthetic novelty and innovation; and it disavows the possibility of willed rebellion and revision on the part of social subjects condemned forever to reinscribe the symbolic order in all their meaningful signifying practices. Ostensibly, for poststructuralist theorists, the only true escape from reinscription lies in radical unreadability, the wholesale rejection of the orderings and connections of narrative—hence the valorization, frequently seen in contemporary theory, of 'anti-narrative' fictions. But this is disingenuous, for such fictions frequently only posture at unreadability. As long as a text, despite all its flaunting of the rules, remains understandable—because its flaunting of the rules is understood—then it is clearly no longer free from the constraints of followability, and it is not wholly given over to non-narrativizable, formless excess. Quite simply, as David Carroll avers, 'in pure . . . formlessness, there is no place for art and no place for discourse either. Art and discourse can approach this limit, but are necessarily destroyed when they plunge into the abyss beyond it.'[4] Many unconventional contemporary experimental fictions, understood as experimental fictions, do not take this abysmal plunge, although they gesture towards it. The indeterminacy, open-endedness, and multivalency evident in some contemporary literature do not equate with wholesale anti-narrational escape from narrative conventions so long as these characteristics are recuperable as strategies in a narrative of emancipation.

In much contemporary literary criticism we witness the politicization of contemporary fictional writing, in which experimentation across the board is theorized as a ubiquitous (and laudable) exemplification of poststructuralist claims with respect to the desirability of anti-narration. These fictions are appropriated to serve dubious critical ends; they are critically defined not in

---

[4] David Carroll, *Paraesthetics: Foucault, Lyotard, Derrida* (New York and London: Methuen, 1987), 43.

relation to their instrumentality with respect to content, but to the disruptive forms they utilize: texts which display plurality, diffuseness, multiplicity of meaning, and the fracturing of narrative order are extolled as radical and subversive. Certainly, writers as diverse as Walter Abish, Alasdair Gray, Angela Carter, Raymond Federman, Donald Barthelme, John Barth, Margaret Atwood, Thomas Pynchon, Toni Morrison, and Russell Hoban revel in a huge array of anti-realist tactics in their experimentation with the form and content of their fictions. All seek, in divergent ways, to unsettle and defamiliarize the reading experience, to disavow the prescriptions of received narrative conventions, and to challenge complacent readers to conceive of their relation to the world in new and different ways. But fictional novelty has long progressed according to procedures of rebellion and experimentation; tension between traditional and revolutionary literary forms is clearly not unique to the twentieth century. The anxiety of influence, to borrow from Harold Bloom, may be seen as a fundamental impetus towards innovation throughout the history of Western literature.[5] New generations of writers continuously challenge, revise, rewrite, and even overturn their textual antecedents. This does not mean that they reject outright the tenets of narrativization. Radical aesthetic practice is clearly not the exclusive preserve of (post)modern writers. Moreover, claims with respect to the liberating efficacy of contemporary anti-realist novels rely too heavily on the mythical bogeyman of novelistic realism (which certainly wasn't the despotic ruler of all creative enterprise prior to the twentieth century). What is exceptional in our age, perhaps, is not formal experimentation but the political urgency with which the critical debate about experimental contemporary aesthetics is informed. This is not surprising, given the extent to which much contemporary philosophical thought centres on the operations of language and discursive practice, finding these to be at the root of our acts of self- and world comprehension. For this reason the way in which literary texts operate has been given new, unprecedented attention in recent thought.

If postmodern art/writing, as Jean-François Lyotard famously avers in his appendix to *The Postmodern Condition*, is that which would categorically refuse to conform to 'pre-established rules',

[5] Harold Bloom, *The Anxiety of Influence* (New York and Oxford: Oxford University Press, 1973).

then this is not an aesthetic practised by contemporary fiction.[6] As I will argue, contemporary fictions are better understood as engaged in transformative practice within the procedural bounds of inherited communicative and literary 'rules'. Certainly, many contemporary fictions destabilize the conventions of (realistic) representation, challenge naïve assumptions of teleological closure and linguistic transparency, and proceed by breaking some of the established conventions of more traditional modes of narrativization. Arguably a number may conform to the characteristics of Lyotard's hypothetical postmodern aesthetic 'events' in so far as they strive to '[put] forward the unpresentable in presentation itself', deny the reader (or viewer) 'the solace of good forms', and impart a 'sense of the unpresentable' (if only by negation). But in no way does this iconoclastic practice amount to a condition in which writers 'are working without rules',[7] or rejecting narrative procedure, as Lyotard characterizes postmodern aesthetic endeavour.

Far from disavowing rules and wholly scuttling consensual communicative practices, contemporary fictions are busily making new ones, and celebrating their capacity to do so (despite continual institutional appropriation) in self-reflexive narratives that flaunt this capacity for creative deviance. Writers of contemporary experimental texts do not work without rules, but rather work within the constraints of old rules in order to invent and experiment with new ones. In what follows I will argue that contemporary experimental fictions do not simply lament rule-bound writtenness and linguistic determinism, but explore the possibilities for individualistic expression within the discursive structures that ensure their meanings and identities as fictional texts. In doing so, they provide an analogy for the qualified creative

[6] Jean-François Lyotard, 'Answering the Question: What is Postmodernism', trans. Régis Durand, in *The Postmodern Condition: A Report on Knowledge*, trans. Geoff Bennington and Brian Massumi (1979; Manchester: Manchester University Press, 1984), 81. Further references to *The Postmodern Condition* will be cited parenthetically in the text.

[7] Lyotard declares that if rules are realized in postmodernist aesthetic practice, then this realization is retrospective—'the rules of what *will have been done* . . . always come too late for their author' (ibid.). In this manner he tries to evade what may appear to be major inconsistency in his theorizing, for throughout *The Postmodern Condition* Lyotard insists on the importance of rules, without which there can be no art. By claiming that postmodern art is retrospectively recognized as rule-bound, Lyotard seeks to avoid the issue of conscious anticipation of, or complicity with, predetermined rules on the part of the artist/writer.

autonomy available to the human 'textual' subject. *Pace* Lacanian and Derridean negative structuralism, the pragmatic conception of subjectivity I develop holds that human social agents live under a plurality of historically specific social conditions, existing as the complex manifestations of multiple communal determinants and interpersonal affiliations. Pragmatic subjectivity involves more than fixed, passive positioning within the symbolic order and the blind reinscription of repressive practices; the webs of social structuration offer a wide range of communicative sites from which to speak and write. It goes without saying that not all of these discursive positions and perspectives are equal in value, but this is precisely the point: conflict and contestation are part of the picture when significatory acts are understood as performative and potentially oppositional. In this light the politics of post-structuralist textuality, particularly as applied to notions of subjectivity, needs closer scrutiny. In the section that follows I will consider some of the ramifications of the politicization of linguistic analysis, specifically as they pertain to the notion of the human textual subject, in a brief consideration of the oppositional work of Lyotard and Habermas. I will follow this with a discussion of the debate between the advocates of rights-based liberalism and communitarianism, a debate which, while very different from that between Habermas and Lyotard (if we can call debate that which is not characterized by open discussion), similarly confronts the issues of relativism and universalism, liberty and restraint, in its probings of the ontological status of the human subject.

Relativism or Totalitarianism: The Debate between Lyotard and Habermas

> There is no unity of language but islets of language, each governed by a different order that is untranslatable into that of the others.
> Lyotard, cited in Rorty, *Objectivity, Relativism and Truth*, 215.

Lyotard's analysis of postmodernity in *The Postmodern Condition* is representative of contemporary concerns in the emphasis it places on the importance of linguistic practices and in the linking of these to political ends. Lyotard's work may be read as an expression of relativistic optimism in a cultural climate sceptical of metaphysical certainties. He characterizes postmodernity in terms of its 'incredulity towards received metanarratives' (p. xxiv), that is, towards unifying and legitimating historical and anticipatory accounts of personal, social, and communal progress. For Lyotard, in the late twentieth century the post-Cartesian conception of history as a story of liberation is no longer credible; the Enlightenment prioritization of rationality as the means of ordering and controlling both society and nature has clearly failed to procure its promise of greater world stability and individual freedom. In the space of this new, incredulous, sceptical post-modernity, Lyotard finds not a nostalgic lamentation for lost narratives of stability (41) but an increasing openness to, and celebration of, plurality and multiplicity in an outright rejection of received narratives. Lyotard characterizes postmodernity in terms of an increasing resistance to a consensus or shared belief, and posits instead the flourishing of a proliferation of localized, relative 'language-games' or partisan conceptions of meaning, value, and social practice. Assimilating narrative and totalizing desire, he promotes a vision in which the decentring of legitimating meta-narratives results in diverse and innovative productivity, a fertile field of multiplicity and pluralism which will (he claims) remain resistant to the totalizing impulses of narrative ordering. Lyotard's formulation of full-scale cultural and linguistic deregulation is exemplary of the manner in which some contemporary theorists view the notion of subjective, and cultural, 'deregulation'—as a means of escape from servitude to outmoded, restrictive conventions imposed on individuals from without, as the means to attain a utopian 'sublimity' which is uncircumscribed by meta-narrational order.

Lyotard's indulgent vision is open to criticism on many fronts. Where, it is asked, do we draw the line between meaningful vocal multiplicity and mere babble? How do we define the point at which a free market of individualistic pluralism disintegrates into anarchism? What regulatory meta-narrative permits and enables this deregulation to take place? What value underlies the call for devaluation? In short, what *orders* the postmodern aesthetic of sublimity, the valorization of non-narrativizable extremes: open-endedness, non-representation, permanently revolutionary anti-narratives? Steven Connor is one critic who consistently challenges Lyotard's hypothetical postmodernity. In *Postmodernist Culture*, he decries Lyotard's work as

> one of the most powerful instances of the will to the sublime in contemporary thought and [it] joins with the work of Deleuze and Foucault in suggesting the possibility of deliverance from the epochal delusions of metaphysical thinking into the 'nomadic', unregulated freedom of pure difference. . . . Lyotard paints a picture of the dissolution of science into a frenzy of relativism in which the only aim is to bound gleefully out of the confinement of musty old paradigms and to trample operational procedures underfoot in the quest for exotic forms of illogic.[8]

If one is wholly subjected within determining social paradigms (and this is the presupposition upon which the critical imperative to escape them is founded), how *does* one 'bound gleefully' out of their confines? This question finds repeated expression in contemporary theory: if one is constituted in pre-given paradigms of meaning and value, how is one able to articulate and act on original challenges to such paradigms? How does one even come to contemplate rebellion against restrictive social structures if one is the repressed subject of their operations? We might ask with Stanley Fish, '[h]ow, if the tyranny of ideologically imposed "facts" is so complete, if the lines of communication and thought are so wholly in bondage . . . how, if distortion is everywhere and everywhere controlling (the first thesis, after all, of critical thought), does one ever *begin* to get a purchase on that which is *not* distorted?[9] If one is able to make the leap urged by Lyotard, when surely his initial premiss of containment and repression needs revision.

Furthermore, and just as importantly, we must ask *why* it matters that we follow Lyotard's urgent imperative to fracture the narrativizable and thus escape meta-narrative control: what (meta-narrative of) value lingers in decentred postmodernity that we should accord worth to the eradication of meta-narratives? For if the revolutionary abolition of paradigms of received value is to

---

[8] Steven Connor, *Postmodernist Culture: An Introduction to Theories of the Contemporary* (Oxford: Basil Blackwell, 1989), 34–5. See also his *Theory and Cultural Value* (Oxford: Basil Blackwell, 1992), 110–19.

[9] Stanley Fish, *Doing What Comes Naturally: Change, Rhetoric, and the Practice of Theory in Literary and Legal Studies* (Oxford: Clarendon Press, 1989), 450.

have any meaning, let alone the (emancipatory) *value* Lyotard accords to this activity of deregulation, it is only in so far as it is conceived within the terms of an ethical stance which accords great value to individuality, individual rights, and liberty as necessity. Lyotard's postmodernity is conditional on the existence of intersubjectively understood (if not universally valued) cultural paradigms and linguistic parameters, which regulate, and indeed make possible, the value (and the comprehension) of the deregulation he urges. In this respect it is itself a legitimating meta-narrative, one which deems a postmodern multiplicity of language-games to be a *better* mode of being than the tyranny of received meta-narratives.[10] In other words, Lyotard's notion of productive plurality presupposes a shared framework of understood ethical values without which liberated subjects cannot even begin to mean. Timothy H. Engström suggests that a pragmatic response to Lyotard's theoretical sublime might be 'that we sense sublimity only by relative comparison to what is culturally paradigmatic (or normal), that we work or play in the spaces between paradigms and their margins as these become figured'.[11] Rejecting the veracity and possibility of absolute meta-narrational certainty does not preclude partial, provisional comparisons and assessments: intersubjectively understood norms need not be abstract and unchallengeable (or, for that matter, inherently repressive). Indeed, these understood norms may be local and provisional; they may even facilitate the expressive autonomy of the individual. Just because a totalizing and objective comparative standpoint is impossible, 'there is no reason to presume there are *no* good and obviously relative ways to assess local or regional achievements of progress or emancipation'.[12]

Several strands of thought need to be unwound here. First, I am suggesting that Lyotard's hypothetical postmodernity is underwritten by fundamentally humanistic values such as those of individualism, personal autonomy, and liberty. In this Lyotard is by no means alone. In fact, it may be argued that essentially humanistic values such as personal liberty, independence, privacy,

[10] See Alphonso Lingis, 'Some Questions about Lyotard's Postmodern Legitimation Narrative', *Philosophy and Social Criticism*, 20/1–2 (1994), 1–12.

[11] Timothy H. Engström, 'The Postmodern Sublime?: Philosophical Rehabilitations and Pragmatic Evasions', *Boundary 2*, 20/2 (1993), 194.

[12] Ibid. 200.

and democracy underscore many poststructuralist accounts of subjectivity; certainly these values are frequently evoked in order to legitimate the deviant experimentation of many postmodern texts. Meili Steele suggests as much in her critical assessment of the critiques of reason offered by Lyotard, Foucault, and Derrida: '[these critiques] make strong ethical appeals to liberty at the same time that they refuse to theorize how, why, or through whom this transformation is to take place or what it might look like.'[13] Appeals to these values are not always overt, but they are none the less prioritized by evoking the horror and terror of contrary concepts such as determinism, repression, and institutional control, as if negative exemplification of opposing conditions might be enough to secure the unexamined primacy of the values they espouse.

Second, I am claiming that in order for a proliferation of individual or local language-games to be understood as meaningful alternatives to universal meta-narratives, there needs to be some regulating medium for communication which cuts across local and personal specifics, and which allows the understood communication of pluralistic perspectives. It is a gross error to conflate the linguistic codes and conventions which enable intersubjective and intelligible communication with the ideological values which discursive processes may reinscribe. Again, in this regard, Lyotard is a representative case, rather than an isolated voice in the rhetoric of postmodernity. Too often in contemporary theory we find the reductive, invalid collapse of language or discourse, conceived as monolithic structures of domination, into concrete, contextual instances of speech and writing. This abstract bracketing of *parole* from *langue* reveals a structuralist bias which leaves no space for questions of agency and practice on the part of a speaking subject. The obvious fact that many alternative, often contestational discursive communities and ideological subcultures can and do exist among users of the same language reveals just how mistaken it is to elide the procedural operations of language with the discourses (ideological, ethical, or political) it makes possible. I will argue throughout this book that speaking subjects have a capacity, limited certainly by situation and circumstance, for critical reflection on the (signifying) communities in which they are structured

---

[13] Meili Steele, 'The Ontological Turn and its Ethical Consequences: Habermas and the Poststructuralists', *Praxis International*, 11/4 (1992), 428–46, 434.

and for the modulation of, and choice between, a variety of determining structures or communities.

Third, as Peter Dews has noted, Lyotard obfuscates the social consequences of his programme for postmodernity through the use of metaphors which efface the disturbing consequences of his vision. He utilizes, in Dews's words, the 'anodyne connotations' of the term 'language-game' in a manner which suggests that the consequences of the unregulated proliferation of plural perspectives would involve no more than a kind of 'verbal jousting'. Doing so effaces or minimizes the potentially crippling relativism which must lurk beneath Lyotard's espousal of cultural deregulation:

Had [Lyotard] employed an alternative term such as 'social practices' and had he considered that this category would have included pumping pollutants into the environment, closing down industries in depressed areas, and driving under the influence of alcohol, he would have found it less plausible to portray conflict merely as a kind of verbal jousting ('agonistics') internal to each language game.[14]

The failure to specify adequately the tenor of a metaphorical vehicle or the rhetorical manipulation of metaphorical associations is of course one of the most prevalent features of contemporary theoretical discourse, as Patrick Colm Hogan, amongst others, has pointed out.[15]

Finally, in the passages cited above, Lyotard uses the metaphor of 'gaming' to suggest the activity of the artist/writer 'working without rules' (81), in opposition to conformist rule-governed behaviour or the determinations of some shadowy rule-giver. But in doing so, he goes against his own post-Wittgensteinian intuition that game play is a rule-bound practice *within* which there is scope for transgression. The actions of the social rebel who rejects the norms of 'proper' practice are no less constrained by the terms of social rules than those of the most strictly conforming subject, albeit that the actions of the former are conceived in negative relation to those rules. There is no possibility of meaningful gaming, be it aberrant or conformist, without intersubjective rules that order play. In much of *The Postmodern Condition* Lyotard

---

[14] Peter Dews, Editor's Introduction to *Jürgen Habermas: Autonomy and Solidarity: Interviews* (London: Verso, 1986), 24.

[15] See Patrick Colm Hogan, *The Politics of Interpretation* (New York and Oxford: Oxford University Press, 1990), 28–95, for an excellent account of rhetorical manipulation by poststructuralist theorists.

acknowledges as much: 'if there are no rules, there is no game' (10)—and certainly no possibility of transformation of the game. Rules are necessary for (language-) games to progress meaningfully, a notion that sits uncomfortably with his assertions towards the end of *The Postmodern Condition* to the effect that postmodernist art will proceed 'without rules'. Moreover, Lyotard asserts that 'even the least privileged among us, is never entirely powerless . . . [and possesses] mobility in relation to these language game effects' (15). In comments such as these, in which he recognizes the space for movement within the rule-bound games, Lyotard seems to be suggesting something less radical than many commentators would assume. Far from advocating the wholesale abandonment of rules, he appears merely to challenge unquestioning belief in their fixity, and with this encourages a concomitant recognition and development of our capacity for mobility within rule-bound language-games. Given this tacit acknowledgement of agency, Lyotard's postmodern agonistics are perhaps less radical than they are sometimes interpreted to be.

Counter to Lyotard's claims, I will suggest that meaningful subjectivity or linguistic value may in fact be conditional on the existence of shared communicative frameworks *and* the intersubjective acknowledgement of certain (provisional) values (for example, those pertaining to the importance of individuality and personal freedom). This does not necessarily entail the ahistorical or transcendental constitution of these frameworks; nor does it endorse the notion that interpersonally understood values are necessarily repressive, monolithic, and totalizing or that they encroach on the preserve of personal autonomy. It is simply not enough to assert that a human subject, constituted in communal language, is simply 'a function determined by language and not an origin "outside" the textual-linguistic systems surrounding it'.[16] The experience of moral dilemmas and divided loyalties and the complexity of human relationships and interactions suggest the paucity of a theory which would reduce human subjects to the determined functions of controlling language and the ideological values it purportedly reinscribes. Ideological or linguistic deter-

---

[16] David Carroll, *The Subject in Question: The Languages of Theory and the Strategies of Fiction* (Chicago and London: University of Chicago Press, 1982), 15. Carroll is concerned in this book to probe the limitations of the conception of situated subjectivity which he outlines in the passage cited.

mination (if this *is* in fact the premiss from which Lyotard works) is not the only alternative to a discredited account of subjective immanence or a pessimistic vision of solipsistic atomism and individualistic relativism. A degree of social embeddedness may well be compatible with a degree of personal autonomy. An element of 'freeplay' may inhere in our rule-bound gaming. Too often, however, theorists manipulate the reductive reasoning which slides from one undesirable pole of the spectrum of theorized subjectivity to the other, from essentialism to unconstrained *différance*, from the devil of linguistic or ideological subjection to the deep blue sea of textual and personal atomism. The reiteration of this seemingly intractable double bind is everywhere apparent in modern philosophy and contemporary theory.

The Postmodern Condition is commonly understood as a polemical critique of Jürgen Habermas's concept of a 'legitimation crisis' and his vision of communicative rationality. Habermas's ambitious project in *The Theory of Communicative Action* attempts to reconcile systematization (seemingly autonomous social processes, including language) with individuality (the 'life-world' of historical human subjects).[17] He seeks to provide a normative foundation for critical and social theory which is neither transcendental (for this must imply absolutism) nor immanent (for this must evoke the spectre of relativism). Habermas shares with Lyotard, as with many other contemporary thinkers, the assumption that language and linguistic operations are the most fundamental area of political-ethical enquiry. However, he utilizes this vision towards a far more redemptive end than do Lyotard, Foucault, Derrida, Lacan, and others who have followed the 'linguistic turn' in philosophical thought, who are far more pessimistic.[18] In the current theoretical climate, in which problems of consciousness have to a large extent been replaced by problems of language, it is not surprising that Habermas's optimistic project has been dismissed as 'immoderate' or 'outrageous'.[19] For it is in linguistic

[17] Habermas, *The Theory of Communicative Action*, Vol. 1: *Reason and the Rationalization of Society* (Boston: Beacon Books, 1984).

[18] Of course, there are crucial distinctions to be made between the philosophies of these various thinkers, and in subsuming them under the rubric of 'poststructuralism', it is not my intention to obfuscate their difference. Habermas's lectures on the 'philosophical discourse of modernity' attempt to engage with the consequences and ramifications of poststructuralist thought (*Philosophical Discourse of Modernity*, trans. Frederick Lawrence (1985; Cambridge, Mass.: MIT Press, 1987).

[19] Connor, *Theory and Cultural Value*, 104.

processes themselves, in the operations of intersubjective communication, that Habermas seeks to salvage human rationality and the values of personal freedom, truthfulness, democracy, and equality.

Central to Habermas's account in *The Theory of Communicative Action* is the now (in)famous notion of the 'ideal speech situation' —a consensual, rational intersubjective act of communication which he finds at the heart of even the most biased, manipulative, and ill-motivated speech. Habermas suggests that in ideal discourse the willingness to reach agreement or consensus—normative rationality—prevails over the limitations of action and individual prejudice or self-interest. Discussion in such a situation is ordered only by the 'unforced force of the better argument',[20] and achieves 'an agreement that terminates in the intersubjective mutuality of reciprocal understanding, shared knowledge, mutual trust, and accord with one another'.[21] For Habermas, then, intersubjective communication is immanently rational; there is a fundamental, internal connection between communicative action and communicative rationality. Even disagreement presupposes shared rational norms between antagonistic speakers. Communicative rationality, argues Habermas in *The Theory of Communicative Action*,

carries with it connotations based ultimately on the central experience of the unconstrained, unifying, consensus-bringing force of argumentative speech, in which participants overcome their merely subjective views and, owing to the mutuality of rationality motivated conviction, assure themselves of both the unity of the objective world and the intersubjectivity of their lifeworld.[22]

From this conception Habermas moves on to make his fundamental claim: that discursive practices are themselves the locus for a reclamation of ethics for a postmodernity disenchanted with

[20] Cited in Rick Roderick, *Habermas and the Foundations of Critical Theory* (Basingstoke: Macmillan, 1986), 82. Roderick provides a useful account and critique of the development of Habermas's thought up to an including *The Theory of Communicative Action*. Pertinently, Roderick asks, 'Why is genuine understanding/agreement based only on the force of the better argument? Couldn't it also be based on love, compassion, solidarity or sympathy?' (160).

[21] Habermas, 'What is Universal Pragmatics?', in *Communication and the Evolution of Society*, trans. Thomas McCarthy (1976; London: Heinemann, 1979), 3. McCarthy provides a full account of Habermas's work in *The Critical Theory of Jürgen Habermas* (Cambridge: Polity Press, 1984).

[22] Habermas, *Theory of Communicative Action*, 1. 10.

notions of ethical universals.[23] The immanent rationality of communicative practices, as he conceives them, enables communicators to make claims with respect to rights and truths without
coercion and prescription or the exclusion of a variety of modes of
being. Claims of universal validity are to be tested discursively in
rational discourse; they are those maxims to which all rational
communicators can agree. Throughout, he insists on the rational
adjudication of these claims. From the conditions of the ideal
speech situation we may, he argues, extrapolate the values of
mutuality, democracy, and autonomy, finding here a counter to
the relativistic bent of much contemporary philosophy.[24] In order
to make this assertion, Habermas develops the idea of an intersubjective 'life-world' or shared 'background' of everyday social
assumptions, receptivities, and relations which provides the basis
for the rational defence of claims to truth, rightness, and authenticity. Within the horizons of the life-world communicating subjects
are able to achieve mutual understanding: 'the life-world . . .
stands behind the back of each participant in communication and
. . . provides resources for the resolution of problems of understanding.'[25] The continuity of tradition and horizon of unity that
comprises the life-world is 'pre-reflexive', intuitively known by
participants and not subject to critical appraisal:

the moment this background knowledge enters communicative expression, where it becomes explicit knowledge and thereby subject to
criticism, it loses precisely those characteristics which life-world structures always have for those who belong to them: certainly, background
character, impossibility of being gone behind. . . . [O]ne can label as a
life-world only those resources that are not thematized, not criticized.[26]

In all communication aimed at reaching understanding, Habermas suggests, the following validity claims are immanent (if not
explicit): the comprehensibility of the utterance, the truth of the

---

[23] See Habermas, *Moral Consciousness and Communicative Action*, trans.
C. Lenhardt and S. Nicholson (Cambridge, Mass.: MIT Press, 1990).
[24] In an interview with Axel Honneth, Habermas disparages contemporary conditions in which 'forms of relativism have the upper hand under the sign of a dubious
revival of Nietzsche (or of irrationalism in general)': 'The Dialectics of Rationalization', in Dews (ed.), *Jürgen Habermas*, 103.   [25] Ibid. 109.
[26] Ibid. Compare Habermas's claim that a life-world is something 'which can be
accounted for more or less only narratively and intuitively, in everyday language—
not theoretically': quoted in 'Life-forms, Morality and the Task of the Philosopher',
in Dews (ed.), *Jürgen Habermas*, 211.

utterance, the rightness or appropriateness of what is spoken, and the sincerity of the speaker. Rick Roderick elaborates this idea thus:

Communication depends upon the presupposition that each participant can justify the validity claims he raises. Although this presupposition may prove false, Habermas holds that it is unavoidable. For him, the goal of communication is coming to an understanding in regard to each of the types of validity claim that culminates in 'reciprocal understanding, shared knowledge, mutual trust, and accord with one another'.[27]

Importantly, Habermas stresses that these validity claims pertain in only the most ideal—perhaps impossible—speech act, but are none the less implicit in all communicative encounters. The *expectation* of comprehensibility, truth, rightness, and sincerity is what makes communicative understanding possible, and the expectation of the realization of these attributes structures all acts of communication. These expectations may not always be fulfilled —in fact, it is more likely that they will not be, given the distorting and manipulative nature of many of our communicative acts. But it is the *belief* in their efficacy which enables communication to occur. Belief need not concur with actuality for a belief system to provide a sense of orientation and meaning to the believer.

Habermas's notion of the ideal speech act has been subject to severe and incredulous criticism. So Terry Eagleton: 'To claim to detect a *promesse de bonheur* in an exchange of obscene insults would seem either ridiculously gullible or faintly perverse. . . . Do not such proposals move at such a rarefied level of abstraction as to be effectively worthless? Can a political ideal really be projected from the invariable, universal "deep structures" of human conversation?'[28] Similarly, Barbara Herrnstein Smith acerbically observes of Habermas's vision of rational consensus:

Habermas has secured a category that is quite sublime . . . but also quite empty: for having thus disqualified and bracketed out what is, in effect, the entire motivational structure of verbal transactions, he is left with an altogether bootstrap operation of magical reciprocality, in which the only thing that generates, sustains, and controls the actions of speakers

---

[27] Roderick, *Habermas and the Foundations of Critical Theory*, 89.
[28] Terry Eagleton, *The Ideology of the Aesthetic* (Oxford: Basil Blackwell, 1990), 404.

speakers and listeners is the gratuitous mutuality of their presuppositions.[29]

One of the most common objections to Habermas's account is that it implies the coercive unity of plurality and the reduction of the multiplicity of language-games to the universal logic of linguistic rationality; in Lyotard's phrase, it 'does violence to the heterogeneity of language games'.[30] But such objections, as Peter Dews has cogently formulated in his introduction to *Jürgen Habermas*, rest on several mistaken assumptions.[31] The first of these is Lyotard's erroneous confusion of language-games and validity claims. He fails to recognize Habermas's differentiation between three distinct value spheres in the life-world (cognitive, moral, and aesthetic) and a 'pluralization of diverging universes of discourse' (Habermas's phrase). Validity claims, as Habermas conceives them, are able to '*cut across* this multiplicity' of language-games. Differences in opinion with respect to cognitive, moral, and aesthetic questions may well exist, but 'we cannot claim that these conflicts are *in principle* unamenable to discussion, and to possible resolution' (23). In short, Lyotard fails to distinguish between the regulation of discourse procedures and the variable content of discourse. Secondly, if Lyotard is to avoid the slide from productive plurality to antagonistic relativism, his valorization of language-game plurality must rest on a higher-order recognition of intersubjective validity claims, for how else can he secure the priority he accords to such plurality? Arguably, Habermas's theory of consensual rationality does not theorize the homogenization of

---

[29] Barbara Herrnstein Smith, *Contingencies of Value: Alternative Perspectives for Critical Theory* (Cambridge, Mass., and London: Harvard University Press, 1988), 110. Cited in Connor, *Theory and Cultural Value*, 105.

[30] Lyotard, *Postmodern Condition*, 66. Cf. David Held's objection that the notion of communicative rationality grounded in the universal traditions of the life-world fails to account for localized cultural traditions, ideology, false consciousness, repressive force, or specific material conditions, all of which are, as Held comments, 'important determinants of the possibility of discourse and, more generally, of a rational, free and just society: in *Introduction to Critical Theory* (Berkeley: University of California Press, 1980), 396. See also Seyla Benhabib, *Critique, Norm and Utopia: Study of the Foundations of Critical Theory* (New York: Columbia University Press, 1986), ch. 8, for an expression of similar concerns.

[31] See Dews, Editor's Introduction to *Jürgen Habermas*. Further references to this essay will be cited in the text. Dews remains one of the staunchest defenders of Habermas's theory against the claims of poststructuralism; see *The Logics of Disintegration: Post-structuralist Thought and the Claims of Critical Theory* (London and New York: Verso, 1987).

language-games or the supremacy of one game over the others, but rather the very conditions that enable the possibility of plurality (24). Furthermore, we may in fact conceive of the universalization of discursive principles as part of the same process that ensures and enables the diversification of individual life-styles: 'It is possible for a proliferation of sub-cultures to take place precisely because the need for agreement on basic rules of social interaction is satisfied at ever higher levels of abstraction' (24).[32]

For many, the Habermasian account of rational consensus smacks of (Kantian) transcendentalism. Does the foundational rationality proposed by Habermas only amount to a replacement for a Kantian conceptual-transcendental argument, as Terry Eagleton suggests?[33] If so, how does this relate to the Marxian impulse contained in the socio-empirical stress on historicity and social embeddedness? In what relation, moreover, does Habermas's version of Kant stand to Lyotard's version of the same? Does Habermas's theory, urging rationality, consensus, and intersubjective good will, represent only a secular resurrection of theological imperatives? What prevents 'rationality' from becoming (or being) repressive? What scope is there in such theorizing for individuals who object to or reject the universal deep structures of Habermas's pragmatics? If the foundations for discourse (and socio-political values) are already encoded in the communicative acts we perform, how can dissent or debate ever be discursively articulated; how can we ever step outside and criticize or challenge something so deeply embedded in the very terms of our criticism? How do we scrutinize the rational foundation of Habermas's theory without a circular appeal to that very foundation? What allowance is there in Habermas's notion of communicative consensus for input from those, like children or animals, who are not able to partake in adult human discourse, or from those, like immigrants to a new

[32] For a comparable argument, see Axel Honneth, 'An Aversion Against the Universal: A Commentary on Lyotard's *Postmodern Condition*', *Theory, Culture and Society*, 2/3 (1985), 247–57.

[33] Eagleton, *Ideology of the Aesthetic*, 405. See Thomas McCarthy, 'Kantian Constructivism and Reconstructivism: Rawls and Habermas in Dialogue', *Ethics*, 105 (Oct. 1994), 44–63. McCarthy writes of Habermas's view that 'it is geared like Kant's ethics to what everyone could rationally will to be binding on everyone alike; but it shifts the frame of reference from Kant's solitary, reflecting, moral consciousness to the community of moral subjects in dialogue; and it replaces his categorical imperative with a procedure of practical argumentation aimed at reaching reasoned agreement among those subject to the norms in question' (46).

community, whose grasp of linguistic and discursive procedures is limited?[34]

These criticisms are only partly met by the frequently cited rejoinder that Habermas's 'ideal speech situation' is precisely this, an *ideal*. Steven Connor has formulated this line of defence as follows:

> the force of Habermas's account lies precisely in its evocation of a utopian orientation within the structure of discourse; although this may indeed imply the desire to close the gap between actuality and ideal, it does not stake everything on the accomplishment or the possibility of accomplishing that convergence. Just as the improbable prospect of universal peace and goodwill on earth does not and should not prevent one trying to minimalise actual conflicts in the here and now, so one might think, in a similar way, that the ideal speech situation may be described and recommended as a motivating and operational orientation within discourse without needing to be or necessarily to become actual.[35]

Richard Kilminster has argued that the ideal speech situation is a 'regulative principle' in the Kantian sense, that is, a utopian ideal that cannot be concretely realized without losing its critical function: 'the critical theorist can only work towards achieving an ideal situation that is inherently unachievable.'[36] Indeed, in reply to critique, Habermas himself has stressed the 'counterfactual' nature of the ideal speech situation.[37] His more recent work seems to deny the transcendental status of claims for the rational foundation of discursive procedure, and rejects claims to their immanence as well. But where does this leave us? In this weaker, if more amenable, form of Habermas's theory, as Rick Roderick has suggested, the value of Habermas's account seems to be no more than a rather tenuous empirical concept: '[e]ntirely abandoning the attempt to provide a foundation for this normative dimension

---

[34] This point is made by Steven Connor in *Theory and Cultural Value*, 109, and echoes a similar objection made by Lyotard in *Postmodern Condition*, 19.

[35] Connor, *Theory and Cultural Value*, 105. Connor is quick to reject this line of defence, suggesting that 'Habermas seems to want to establish the visible *actuality* of the orientation towards ideal consensus in the structures of discourse, as well as the potential for or desirability of such consensus' (106).

[36] Richard Kilminster, 'Structuration Theory as World View', in *Giddens' Theory of Structuration: A Critical Appreciation*, ed. Christopher G. A. Bryant and David Jary (London and New York: Routledge, 1991), 93–4.

[37] Roderick, in *Habermas and the Foundations of Critical Theory*, 81–7, provides an account of the counterfactual nature of Habermas's claims and a defence of them as such against sceptical critics.

would leave Habermas with no way to avoid the ethical scepticism of [a relativistic account]. And this would seem to reduce Habermas's project to a mere academic sociology without practical and political implications.'[38] Indeed, without transcendental (or immanent) status, on what authority does Habermas's communicative rationality derive its imperative force? Why should anyone submit to the rationality Habermas proposes? How is 'free' intercourse to proceed without immanent or transcendent guide-lines to contain their potential relativism or repression? And even if (a big if) we were to agree that there was some fundamentally rational foundation for discursive practice, and that the formal and procedural characteristics of consensual speech were unproblematically available for our scrutiny and critique, how then would we derive actual, material ethical norms (like democracy, respect for individuality, the priority and value of truthfulness) from this formal account? Habermas's theory seems unable to clarify how individuals are to be brought into line with the communicative ethics he announces.

Lyotard's objections to Habermas's theory are well known. Towards the end of *The Postmodern Condition* he argues that Habermas's appeal turns on two mistaken assumptions:

The first is that it is possible for all speakers to come to agreement on which rules or metaprescriptions are universally valid for language games, when it is clear that language games are heteromorphous, subject to heterogeneous sets of pragmatic rules.

The second assumption is that of global consensus. But . . . consensus is only a particular state of discussion, not its end. Its end, on the contrary, is paralogy.[39]

Once we recognize 'the heterogeneity of the rules and the search for dissent', Lyotard believes that we can no longer endorse Habermas's notion that collective human emancipation is to be attained in a consensual regulation of (communicative) game rules. For Lyotard, Habermas's theory of communicative consensus offers dangerous justification for a state of rhetorical will-to-power in which those unable to speak, or not as adept at speaking, are without voice in a community of spoken 'accord'. He goes further,

---

[38] Roderick, *Habermas and the Foundations of Critical Theory*, 163–4. Roderick writes in response to McCarthy's claims that Habermas has 'detranscendentalised' his project (McCarthy, *Critical Theory*, 6–7).
[39] Lyotard, *Postmodern Condition*, 66.

suggesting that the homogenization of rules in ostensible consensus can only be achieved by the repression of those whose rebellious moves threaten to destabilize the hierarchical power structures implicit in prevailing games: 'Such behaviour is terrorist. . . . By terror I mean the efficiency gained by eliminating, or threatening to eliminate, a player from the language game one shares with him. He is silenced or consents, not because he has been refuted, but because his ability to participate has been threatened' (63–4). Fascism lurks beneath the surface of proclaimed consensuality. For Lyotard, individual freedom must lie in the irreducible heterogeneity of language-games, the fragmentation and plurality of discordant, incommensurable genres of discourse. But, as I have suggested, he fails to indicate how this multiplicity is to be controlled and remain productive without disintegrating into crippling, self-defeating relativism unless by an implicit reliance on fundamentally normative notions such as those of individual liberty, intersubjective tolerance, and the respect for difference. This implicit self-contradiction appears to paralyse his postmodern ethics, as Steven Connor notes in his discussion of the Lyotard–Habermas impasse in *Theory and Cultural Value*. Perhaps the implicit control in Lyotard's hypothesized postmodernity is precisely the Habermasian discursive rationality he so vehemently rejects.

Driven on the one hand by a positively Habermasian commitment to universal norms which would guarantee preservation of discursive diversity and freedom (though, as we have seen, this commitment rarely comes to discursive consciousness), Lyotard's bitter antagonism to what he sees as the dominative form of ethical universalism espoused by Habermas's philosophy is an antagonism against himself.[40]

Indeed, we might ask with Connor whether Lyotard's passionate refutation of universals is simply 'a different form of universalism' (118), so that the very form of his argument in fact reflects the imperative obligation toward rational consensus that underpins Habermas's theory. Moreover, does this latter in fact attempt to secure precisely the conditions necessary to sustain Lyotard's vision of productive heterogeneity? Or does Habermas's theory seek to promote, as Lyotard claims, the dominant, repressive force

---

[40] Connor, *Theory and Cultural Value*, 117. Further references in this book will be cited parenthetically in the text.

of one particular language-game (his) over all others under the claims of false universality? If this is the case, then perhaps Lyotard's refutation of Habermas's claims is in fact premissed on an acceptance of them in so far as he is using 'the Habermasian orientation towards universalism to criticize Habermas's false universalism' (ibid.). Rather than simply refuting Habermas's notion of the ideal speech situation, Lyotard appears to use it as the normative foundation of his very critique of that notion.

Autonomy or Community: The Debate between Liberals and Communitarians

> [T]he liberal psychology of human nature is founded on a radical premise no less startling for its familiarity: man is alone. We are born into a world of strangers, live our lives as wary aliens, and die in fearful isolation.
>
> Barber, *Strong Democracy*

Although seemingly intractable, the Lyotard–Habermas deadlock is instructive. Need we accept either extreme in the debate? Need a concept of individual liberty wholly preclude shared beliefs, intersubjective norms, or shared narratives of value? Otherwise put, is subjective liberty contingent on the abandonment of all intersubjectively understood rule-bound procedures? If not, at what point *do* beliefs merely reinscribe, norms become repressive, and narratives totalize? Does acknowledging the possibility of intersubjective understanding (and willed dissent) entail the subordination of all to the repressive rules of (transcendent or immanent) communicative practice or rationality? On the contrary, I will argue that the intersubjectively understood procedures of communicative practice which enable us to communicate and interact must be held distinct from the variant beliefs and meanings which may be negotiated within them, beliefs and meanings which may delineate the contours of numerous subcultures and partisan communities. Understanding certainly does not equate with belief. Intersubjective beliefs need not be transcendent, immanent, or universal, but can be (and frequently are) local, specific, provisional, and open to revision. Their values can, and frequently do, change across time and according to context.

One of my primary concerns in this book will be to explore the extent to which human beings possess the capacity for self-reflexive monitoring, and a consequent ability to adapt and revise those norms and beliefs that order their social interaction and individual action, *within* the procedural structures of language. Lyotard's notion of plural language-games might be constructively developed as the productive social arena of (inter)action for reflexive and choosing social agents—providing we abandon his insistence on the incommensurability of 'islets of language' and temper the dangers of irremediable relativism this implies by an understanding that persons can simultaneously belong to numerous language-games or communities of discourse, and that the interrelation of speaking community members provides a web of internal interconnections between them.[41] From Habermas's account we might develop the idea of communal and communicative consensus as a positive ideal, provided we counter potentially repressive totalization with an understanding that consensus in language-use communities is never universal but always local and revisable. Together, rather than in opposition, Habermas's idea of communal consensus and Lyotard's of agonistic gaming may point towards an alternative conception of subjective constitution, a conception which acknowledges the social determination and contextual situatedness of subjects while also allowing for the possibility of partial individual self-determination.

This claim will need substantiation. One way of approaching the problem is to look at an important debate which has taken place in political theory over the last two decades between the advocates of communitarianism and those of rights-based liberalism.[42] Communitarianism arose largely as a challenge to the claims

[41] The term 'language-game' remains vague in *The Postmodern Condition*, subsuming a variety of discursive practices and rhetorical uses of language. In his more recent work (like *The Differend*, trans. Georges Van Den Abbeele (1983; Mineapolis: University of Minnesota Press, 1984) Lyotard has begun to differentiate between various dimensions of language use and practice such as 'phase regimes' and 'genres of discourse'.

[42] I make a distinction here between the utilitarian liberal position, derived from the philosophy of J. S. Mill, and rights-based liberalism, which rejects many of the claims of utilitarianism and propounds a strong thesis of individualism in the Kantian tradition. The latter enjoys precedence in contemporary liberal thought, largely due to the influential publication of John Rawls, *A Theory of Justice* (Oxford: Oxford University Press, 1971). Further references to this book will be cited parenthetically in the text.

of liberal individualism, a theoretical position developed around the central thesis of justice as fairness advocated by John Rawls in *A Theory of Justice* (1971). Yet the two groups hold much in common, not least their concern with the nature and status of selfhood and the relations between subjects and community. It is my belief that when one attempts a pragmatic adoption of either liberal or communitarian policies, or when one tries to bring the theoretical stance of either into line with the complexity of lived human relations, one view invariably collapses into the other. Pragmatism, in other words, rejects the theoretical positions of both hardline communitarianism and hardline liberal individualism in favour of a middle position which draws from the extremist reserves of both. This claim finds support in the most recent developments in the debate between liberals and communitarians. Political theorists in both camps have not been immune to the critiques offered by their adversaries, and a pragmatic revision of liberal and communitarian positions has been notable in recent years. Evidence of a more temperate adaptation of an earlier version of liberalism may be found, for example, in the recent work of John Rawls or in that of Joseph Raz and Nancy Rosenblum. Each of these accounts maintains the fundamental liberal stress on the priority of personal autonomy, but may be seen to incorporate many aspects of the communitarian critique. Likewise, the recent work of communitarians such as Charles Taylor, Michael Sandel, and Alasdair MacIntyre may be read with a view to the tacit or latent liberal assumptions (such as the value of choice between communities) which inhere in them.

Broadly, we can say of liberalism that it stresses the priority of individual liberty and autonomy over intersubjective relations and responsibilities; and of communitarianism that it is the reverse, a theoretical stance which gives priority to communal contexts over personal autonomy. But this is too simple. Such pedestrian definitions are clearly inadequate, and may (and often do) result in caricatures of each position which are easily, and unfairly, attacked by adversaries. The difficulty in defining each of these theoretical stances is compounded by the fact that the word 'liberalism' has a rich associative and connotative history, one which in everyday use is imbued with a range of values and concerns not always compatible with the rather narrower stance of political theorists who are defined as liberals (nor is the liberal position to be confused with the libertarian one).[43] 'Communitarianism' similarly resists easy definition. It implies a univocal stance and a coherent theoretical position, whereas in fact it is applied to a range of very different theorists, despite the fact that these theorists often advocate varying and even contradictory positions. Those defined as communitarians—Michael Sandel, Alasdair MacIntyre, and Charles Taylor, for example—have little sense of belonging to a distinct theoretical group, and sometimes have little in common beyond their critique of liberalism.

In *A Theory of Justice* Rawls outlines a liberal society founded on the notion of justice as fairness. In order to do so, he uses a thought-experiment which invokes a pre-societal condition, which he calls the 'the original position'. In this imagined state of affairs, individuals who are veiled in ignorance (about their material circumstances, social status, learned skills, given attributes, *and* about the values or goods they hold supreme) are imagined to enter into a contract which organizes their society in the manner most likely to foster value pluralism. The complete circumstantial ignorance of individual contractors is necessary in this scenario in order to protect against the weighting of the contract in any way that would favour one person, particular situation, or set of values over another. If, 'veiled in ignorance', I do not know what personal attributes and features I have, or the material circumstances with which I am endowed, or the values and goods I hold, then I will not contract to anything but the fairest social structure, one which offers equal opportunity and freedom to all. The society structured on the contractual notion of justice as fairness envisioned by Rawls does not favour one value over another, and holds no particular conception of the good life: the rights of the autonomous individual always supersede the social goods which she may or may not contract to uphold. The state has no authority to censure or promote one way of life over any other, except in cases where one's free actions cause another person harm, threaten to violate the autonomy of another, vitiate the freedom of choice of another, or jeopardize the egalitarian foundation of the state. In the words of Rawls in *A Theory of Justice*, 'the self is prior to the ends which are affirmed by it; even a dominant end must be chosen from among numerous possibilities' (560). In short, the

---

[43] See Robert Nozick, *Anarchy, State, Utopia* (Oxford: Basil Blackwell, 1984), for an account of the libertarian position and a critique of the liberal one.

state envisioned by Rawls is non-perfectionist and neutral (except in the sense that it accords utmost priority to the values of individual liberty and personal choice). For Rawls, state neutrality is essential if there is to be the greatest possible range of valuable life-styles and moral options within which individuals can exercise unquestioned, uncoerced personal choice. In other words, a distinction is made between individual rights and social goods, with priority being given to the former: the concept of right is prior to that of the good.

The ideal of state neutrality is notoriously problematic, for while it promises complete individual autonomy, it offers no suggestion as to how a neutral state is to allow the productive expression of personal choice, what Rawls terms 'free social union with others' (534), without disintegration into a mêlée of individual will-to-power (unless it relies on the intrinsic good will of its citizens). In A Theory of Justice, Rawls insists that in no way is 'the coercive apparatus of the state' necessary to ensure the productivity of interpersonal deliberation (329). State endorsement of any particular conception of the good, he contends, will inevitably result in the prioritization of majority (or dominant) social interest over the intrinsic rights of individuals; it will sacrifice the sanctity of individual rights to a coercive vision of communal good. State neutrality or anti-perfectionism is fundamental to his conception. The liberal departure from utilitarianism is clearly stated by Rawls: 'Each person possesses an inviolability founded on justice that even the welfare of society as a whole cannot override . . . . the rights secured by justice are not subject to political bargaining or to the calculus of social interests' (3–4). Anti-perfectionism has its roots in what Rawls sees as the fundamental, inescapable pluralism of humanity. It seeks to give equal credence to all possible permutations of human desire, need, and belief. People must be allowed to live their lives without interference from others or the state, except in those cases where their actions infringe on the liberty of others.

But the liberal account is problematic on many counts. It is open, for instance, to charges of irremediable solipsism and isolation on the part of its citizens. MacIntyre, in espousing his version of Aristotelian community over a Nietzschean rejection of the authority of moral tradition, suggests that the modern liberal person 'is a citizen of nowhere, an exile wherever he lives.[44] In a similar vein, Samuel Beer writes that '[f]reedom and equality can be cold. People can be free and equal—and strangers.'[45] MacIntyre finds the liberal account to be inherently emotivist in as much as individual choices are the arbitrary expression of personal preference. Moral judgements under liberalism, he argues, can be no more than the expression of personal feelings and predilections, and moral debate nothing more than the attempt to persuade others to adopt one's own position using any means available to achieve this end. Indeed, it seems that moral objectivity, the notion that some modes of being are clearly more valuable than others, is incompatible with a liberal vision of anti-perfectionism. The grounds on which one is to make choices between one mode of being and another seem precarious, if not non-existent. Charges of anarchic relativism are commonly levelled at liberalism; fragmentation and even downright antagonism between individuals seem to follow the valorization of wholesale individual liberty. Without some form of state regulation and control, it is claimed, how is an anti-perfectionist society, neutral among ends, to function effectively without deteriorating into the anarchy of a multiplicity of incompatible versions of the good life, personal preference, or individual desire? It is easy to see how the non-interventionist liberal notion of state neutrality could be open to charges of subjective relativism, emotivism, and asocial individualism, unless some account is given of the way in which persons are capable of interacting and communing productively, are meaningfully able to share language, knowledge, and experience, and to understand and respect the choices of others. Liberal rights-based neutrality is thought by some to presuppose (or impose?) the shared, understood value of personal liberty and consonant values which comprise a legitimating framework that prevents degeneration into the atomistic relativism of unregulated individual desire and expression. Merely proclaiming the amorality of such values or the neutrality of such a framework is deemed insufficient to guarantee their amoral or neutral status. Still others

---

[44] Alasdair MacIntyre, *After Virtue* (London: Duckworth, 1981), 147. In ch. 9 MacIntyre poses the stark question, repeated in his final chapter, 'Nietzsche or Aristotle?' (238).

[45] Cited in Nancy Rosenblum, *Another Liberalism: Liberalism and the Reconstruction of Liberal Thought* (Cambridge, Mass., and London: Harvard University Press, 1987), 177.

posit the existence of 'latent community' or 'underlying consensus' in the purportedly neutral structures of a liberal economy.[46]

The communitarian counter to the purported emptiness, ennui, and monadic atomism of liberal neutrality appears to be equally problematic. In situating not only self-fulfilment but the individual's very sense of self in community, communitarianism appears to lay itself open to the charge of coercive social control levelled at it by its liberal detractors. Communitarians such as Sullivan, Sandel, MacIntyre, and Charles Taylor stress that selves are 'embedded' or situated in existing social practices in ways that are deeply constitutive of their conceptions of selfhood. But for liberals, communal embeddedness must ultimately connote an enforced complicity with, and reinscription of, existing communal norms: communal embeddedness is in fact 'self-immolation'.[47] How can it ever be possible for an individual to evaluate, challenge, and even reject the ideological values implicit in her community if she is wholly immersed in it? How desirable is a conception of the person who is without the ability to opt out of contextual and communal goods in favour of more intrinsic personal rights? Equally problematic is the inability of communitarians to adequately theorize the position of minorities and marginalized individuals.

Certainly, it seems that hardline communitarianism does prioritize the pursuit of communal goods over the personal liberty and private ends of individuals, a prioritization which runs counter to the ethic of subjective freedom which has such high currency in contemporary thought. That said, I can see no solution in the liberal affirmation of the possibility of retreat from potentially coercive community into the essentiality of an unencumbered self and the solipsistic isolation and anarchic relativism this seems to entail. As the above discussion of Lyotard's postmodernity suggests, subjective multiplicity without structures which allow for meaningful interpersonal understanding and exchange is incomprehensible. The purely unprincipled profusion of incommensurable partisan narratives results not in a progressive plurality of voices, but rather in the drowning of all voices in a babble of

---

[46] See e.g. Michael Walzer, *Spheres of Justice* (New York: Basic Books, 1983). Nancy Rosenblum provides a critical account of the notion of latent community in *Another Liberalism*, 169–74.

[47] Rosenblum, *Another Liberalism*, 153.

relativistic non-communication. Some form of organization or systematization, one which promotes the value of cultural plurality and individual freedom, seems necessary to safeguard individual interests and regulate interpersonal exchange. But at what point do we distinguish between democratic protectionism and autocratic perfectionism, between free-market regulation and wholesale market control? At what point do purportedly neutral organizing procedures become repressive and restrictive? Liberal individualists insist that such a distinction is impossible to make. Communitarianism, they contend, inevitably endorses a model of state control in which maintenance of the *status quo* severely limits, by marginalization or exclusion, the capacity of an individual to determine herself. As Will Kymlicka avers, 'the problem of the exclusion of historically marginalised groups is endemic to the communitarian project'.[48]

Communitarian objections to the liberal invocation of a neutral state regulated by justice as fairness, and liberal replies to these objections, have been well documented.[49] Consistent with my concerns in this book, I will focus on one set of objections in particular, those concerned with the nature and status of the person. Arguably, at the heart of the liberal–communitarian debate are two antithetical conceptions of the self. Central to the critique of liberalism articulated by communitarians such as Sandel, MacIntyre, and Taylor is the claim that the liberal position presupposes an invalid, incoherent ontological conception of the self, namely that the self is antecedently individuated, understood as a meaningful agent that exists prior to and independent of the communities, interactions, and relationships into which she chooses to enter. This in turn promotes a disturbing vision of monadic isolation as the existential condition of human beings. In

[48] Will Kymlicka, *Contemporary Political Philosophy: An Introduction* (Oxford: Clarendon Press, 1990), 227. See Kymlicka's defence of liberalism as a means of evading the exclusivist tendencies of communitarianism in *Liberalism, Community and Culture* (Oxford: Clarendon Press, 1989).

[49] See e.g. Stephen Mulhall and Adam Swift, *Liberals and Communitarians* (Oxford and Cambridge, Mass.: Blackwell, 1992); and Shlomo Avineri and Avner de-Shalit (eds.), *Communitarianism and Individualism* (Oxford: Oxford University Press, 1992), for a collection of essays about the debate. For an account of the liberal position see Dworkin's essay, 'Liberalism', in *A Matter of Principle* (Cambridge, Mass.: Harvard University Press, 1985), 181–204. For the communitarian reply to liberalism, see Walzer, 'The Communitarian Critique of Liberalism', *Political Theory*, 18/1 (1990), 6–23.

contradistinction, for communitarians, personhood is inconceivable without reference to interpersonal interactions and communal participation, the social and linguistic matrices in which our selfhood is constituted. According to the representative communitarian claims made by Michael Sandel in *Liberalism and the Limits of Justice*, the liberal vision, in stressing the priority of the self over its social ends, presupposes an incoherent metaphysical self which is unencumbered by its goals and attachments and which possesses the (ironic) ability to stand back, choose, assess, and revise them. Sandel characterizes the Rawlsian liberal self thus:

> The priority of self over its ends means that I am not merely the passive receptacle of the accumulated aims, attributes, and purposes thrown up by experience, not simply a product of the vagaries of circumstance, but always, irreducibly, an active, willing agent, distinguishable from my surroundings and capable of choice.[50]

Sandel dismisses this account as nonsensical, for if selves are constituted in community (the first premiss of communitarianism) and do not exist as meaningful persons prior to it, then talk of a pre-communal self who orders and contracts into communal unions is logically impossible. Selves are already always *in* community, and cannot simply choose or contract to enter the social context in which they have meaningful being.

Communitarians thus insist that it is inconceivable to think of persons as the individual and essential possessors of intrinsic rights, as selves independent of and prior to their social placement or historical conditioning. Personhood is always embedded in the social (and significantly, linguistic) context in which one has meaningful being; selves are constituted in and by a society and that society's history.[51] Here is William M. Sullivan:

> [S]elf-fulfilment and even the working out of personal identity and a sense of orientation in the world depends upon a communal enterprise. This shared process is the civic life, and its root is involvement with others: other generations, other sorts of persons whose differences are significant because they contribute to the whole upon which our par-

---

[50] Michael Sandel, *Liberalism and the Limits of Justice* (Cambridge: Cambridge University Press, 1982), 19.

[51] The dual allegiance of communitarianism to Aristotle and Hegel is clear. For an account of the communitarian debt to Hegel, see Charles Taylor, *Hegel and Modern Society* (Cambridge: Cambridge University Press, 1979). MacIntyre, in *After Virtue*, attempts a revisionary reformulation of Aristotelian ethics for the twentieth century.

ticular sense of self depends. Thus mutual interdependency is the foundational notion of citizenship. . . . Outside a linguistic community of shared practices, there would be biological *homo sapiens* as a logical abstraction, but there could not be human beings.[52]

As Sandel formulates it in *Liberalism and its Critics*, 'I am . . . embedded in a history which locates me among others, and implicates my good in the good of the communities whose stories I share.'[53] The hardline communitarian view, such as that offered by Sandel, rejects what it perceives to be the mistaken metaphysical platform upon which liberals base their substantive moral conception of personal essentialism. 'What goes on in the original position', claims Sandel, in discussing the theory of Rawls, 'is not a contract after all, but the coming to self-awareness of an intersubjective being.'[54] Persons, argues Sandel, are constituted in community, and in no way exist prior to and aloof from communal contextual situatedness. In *Liberalism and its Critics* many of Sandel's arguments for communitarianism turn on the critique and rejection of the putative liberal conception of the self. The liberal position, as Sandel interprets it in this book, is one in which we are the 'bearers of selves wholly detached from our aims and attachments'; the liberal self is 'a choosing self, independent of the desires and ends it may have at any moment' (5).

Certainly for Rawls, as for other liberals, the capacity for autonomous choice is fundamental to the notion of personhood, but this stress on autonomy does not appear to necessitate a commitment to the metaphysical essentiality of selfhood. As I see it, in making this claim, Sandel attempts to strengthen the communitarian position only by misrepresenting the (Rawlsian) liberal one.[55] He presents an unjust caricature of Rawls's theory with regard to persons, in order to promote his opposing communitarian conception. The value of his communitarianism is secured almost exclusively by means of devaluing the conception of personhood which he claims underlies liberalism. But what if

[52] William M. Sullivan, *Reconstructing Public Policy* (Berkeley, Calif.: University of California Press, 1982), 158, 173.
[53] Michael Sandel, *Liberalism and its Critics* (1984; Oxford: Basil Blackwell, 1987), 9.
[54] Sandel, *Liberalism and the Limits of Justice*, 132.
[55] This is precisely the point made by Amy Gutman in her essay 'Communitarian Critics of Liberalism' (1985), repr. in Avineri and de-Shalit (eds.), *Communitarianism and Individualism*, 120–36.

this conception of personhood is not essential to the liberal account, as Nancy Rosenblum, among others, has argued?[56] Rosenblum suggests that communitarians such as Sandel and Taylor are deeply mistaken in understanding the liberal notion of the abstract self to be anything other than a conceptual tool for political thought:

Abstract individualism is meant to serve a particular kind of sociability. It does not claim that men and women are essentially or only consumers or legal persons. Abstract individualism does not deny eroticism, camaraderie, ideological affinity, and so on; liberalism asks men and women to ignore all the other things they are in order to treat one another fairly in certain contexts and for certain purposes. This does not mean that men and women are always and in every context strangers, or if they are strangers, they are aliens.[57]

Rawls's more recent work attempts to deny that this conception of the person lies at the heart of his liberalism. In articles such as 'Justice as Fairness: Political not Metaphysical' and 'The Domain of the Political and Overlapping Consensus' and in his most recent book *Political Liberalism*,[58] he responds to the communitarian attack on the supposed liberal conception of an essential metaphysical self by refuting that the liberal position entails such a conception. He is at pains to dismiss and disown any metaphysical charges with regard to the ontological status of human beings. His theory, he avers, makes no ontological claims for essential personhood. Nor does it claim to be a comprehensive moral or philosophical doctrine. Rather, the theory is to be understood strictly as political, one which offers a conception of people as citizens. He writes:

we adopt a conception of the person framed as part of, and restricted to, an explicitly political conception of justice . . . persons can accept this conception of themselves as citizens and use it when discussing questions of political justice without being committed in other parts of their life to comprehensive moral ideals often associated with liberalism, for example, the ideals of autonomy and individuality.[59]

---

[56] Rosenblum, *Another Liberalism*, 160–5.   [57] Ibid. 161–2.

[58] John Rawls, 'Justice as Fairness: Political not Metaphysical', *Philosophy and Public Affairs*, 14/3 (1985), 223–51; idem, 'The Domain of the Political and Overlapping Consensus', *New York University Law Review*, 64/2 (1989), 233–55; idem, *Political Liberalism* (New York: Columbia University Press, 1993).

[59] Rawls, 'Justice as Fairness', 224–5.

In other words, Rawls appears to be suggesting that the way in which people understand themselves in political matters, as citizens, may be wholly different from the way in which they understand themselves in their private, non-political lives. It is only in the realm of the political that the principle of autonomy holds supreme importance; in private it may be subordinate to alternative comprehensive conceptions of the good, ones which do not accord supreme authority to the value of individual autonomy. The concept of the person given in the original position outlined in *A Theory of Justice*, suggests Rawls, must be understood to adhere only in the political domain, even if this conception differs from, or even runs counter to, any personal comprehensive moral or philosophical belief or value system. In making the claim that persons possess the ability to stand back and revise only those goods which are political, and that this capacity for detachment does not extend to the realms of private comprehensive moral doctrines, Rawls is able to answer the communitarian challenge which finds an unacceptable metaphysical essentialism at the heart of the liberal account: 'Note that what is impracticable is not *all* values of community . . . but only a *political community* and its values.'[60]

The communitarian response to Rawls's political liberalism may be readily anticipated. To begin with, if it is true that selves are wholly constituted in community and are thus utterly implicated in the social matrix, as communitarians aver, then it makes no sense at all to talk of a split between the personal and the political realms or to propose that the personal and the political might be ordered by different, perhaps even incompatible, doctrines of value. Moreover, communitarians might justly question the *origin* of the value of political justice as fairness. On what authority, if not a private, substantive liberal doctrine, does Rawls make his claims for the concept of the person as citizen? Furthermore, communitarians might question the desirability of Rawls's political liberalism, which implies a disturbing, and perhaps disabling, split between whatever distinct conceptions of the good people *qua* private selves may hold in their personal lives and those that they are required to hold in their lives as people *qua* citizens. As Mulhall and Swift comment of Rawls's political liberalism:

When it comes to thinking about politics and what justice demands, we are to suspend or bracket our beliefs—beliefs that perhaps give our life

[60] Ibid. 241.

its meaning and make up our very identities as individuals—in favour of a particular understanding of citizenship and society. And it is important to recognise that, for Rawls, it is always the political conception that wins: it is not just that there is a hint of schizophrenia here, there is the further claim that in cases of conflict it is always the political conception that must have priority. The demands of justice, the requirements of the political, must come first, before the claims of those comprehensive doctrines with which they must simultaneously and schizophrenically be held.[61]

Clearly, although Rawls's more recent work leaves open many areas for communitarian attack (not least the problematic prioritization of political conceptions over individual beliefs and his blithe positing of the distinction between the personal and the political), it represents an engagement with, and an attempt to address, some of the objections raised by his communitarian critics, particularly the mistaken claim that an abstract metaphysical conception of the person lies at the heart of his theory.

There is another way in which communitarians misrepresent the liberal position as a way of strengthening the appeal of their own, namely in suggesting that liberalism ignores or disavows communal attachment, group loyalties, and relationships. It is necessary for communitarians to make such claims in order to further the emotive argument that liberalism entails isolation, alienation, and atomism on the part of its citizens, who are without a sense of belonging or placement. Communitarians, in other words, might be thought to 'exploit longings for wholeness' by stressing the sense of belonging, unity, and purposiveness that can be afforded by group solidarity, while playing down the secondariness of personal liberty to group purpose or the sublimation of individuality to group ends which this might entail.[62] But few liberals deny that selves can and do form expressive groups and communities, the communities of friendship being one notable example. Their objections are not to the notion of communal groups as such, but rather to the putative communitarian claim that community attachments are always simply discovered, not chosen, and that community attachments are all-encompassing, offering no possibility of adaptation or change on the part of their mem-

[61] Mulhall and Swift, *Liberals and Communitarians*, 178. See also McCarthy's critique of Rawls's claims in 'Kantian Constructivism and Reconstructivism', 58–63.
[62] Rosenblum, *Another Liberalism*, 152.

bers. Ronald Dworkin, for one, has stressed the importance of community in the liberal conception of personhood, in essays such as 'Liberal Community';[63] and in *Another Liberalism* Rosenblum makes similar moves to suggest the openness of liberalism to a variety of community attributes.[64] Joseph Raz, in *The Morality of Freedom*, has given what is perhaps the strongest liberal argument for the importance of community in the formation of the person, to the extent that one could even talk of his 'communitarianism' were it not for his fundamental liberal stress on the importance of personal autonomy and the capacity of individuals to make choices between various communal group attachments.[65] In an important move against traditional liberal thought, Raz disavows the connection between state perfectionism and the liberal ethic which demands autonomous choice between a variety of viable alternatives. Need plurality of options be conditional on state neutrality, as Rawls claims in *A Theory of Justice*? Not at all, Raz argues. According to Raz, the state *can* be perfectionist, endorsing certain moral values and life-styles over others, without reneging on the liberal requirement that persons be able to make uncoerced choices between a range of valuable alternatives. Raz declares that 'the autonomy principle is a perfectionist principle. Autonomous life is valuable only if it is spent in the pursuit of acceptable and valuable projects and relationships. The autonomy principle permits and even requires governments to create morally valuable opportunities, and to eliminate repugnant ones.'[66] In the complex account of liberal perfectionism which Raz provides in *The Morality of Freedom*, he acknowledges the dependence of individuals on the social matrices within which they are embedded, giving the lie to communitarian claims that liberals overlook this aspect of personhood.

While acknowledging that persons are situated in a social matrix, liberals such as Dworkin, Rosenblum, and Raz insist that persons are able to judge, question, and challenge the goods of the

[63] Ronald Dworkin, 'Liberal Community' (1989), repr. in Avineri and de-Shalit (eds.), *Communitarianism and Individualism*, 205–24.

[64] See Rosenblum, *Another Liberalism*, ch. 7, 'Repairing the Communitarian Failings of Liberal Thought', 152–86.

[65] Joseph Raz, *The Morality of Freedom* (Oxford: Clarendon Press, 1986). Mulhall and Swift provide an instructive account of Raz's 'communitarianism' in *Liberals and Communitarians*, 249–88. I am indebted to Mulhall and Swift in the discussion of Raz which follows.

[66] Raz, *Morality of Freedom*, 417.

various communities in which they are currently situated and the ends to which these communities currently aspire. These liberals argue that individuals are capable of objectively transcending the limitations of their formative environments, and are able to re-examine their (present) goals and relationships, replacing them by others deemed more suitable. This is hardly to suggest that individuals exist 'wholly detached from [their] aims and attachments' —the position which Sandel mistakenly attributes to liberals in the passage cited above—but rather that, at any given time, particular encumbrances, particular situations of embeddedness, are open to question and revision. This view is not compatible with liberal individualism as portrayed by MacIntyre in *After Virtue*, where contemporary liberal society is considered to be 'nothing but a collection of strangers, each pursuing his or her own interests under minimal constraints' (233). Very few liberals in fact endorse a position in which the freedom of the person is pursued exclusively at the expense of social projects and commitments, recognizing the unpalatable consequences of such radical individualism: asocial relativism, life experienced as the battle of antagonistic and contingent individual wills, solipsistic alienation, and the reduction of moral judgements to the arbitrary expressions of individual preference. The more recent liberal stance, which acknowledges the importance of contextual placement and communal ties, is entirely different from the implied position of wholesale detachment from social roles and ends which is too often laid at the liberal doorstep.[67]

If we concede these qualifications of the contemporary liberal stance with respect to the importance of communal ties for a conception of the person, the liberal position begins to appear less starkly antithetical to communitarian claims. Recent versions of the liberal–communitarian debate certainly require us to abandon crude dualisms between placement and exile, purpose and drift, communal embeddedness and autonomous choice. It might be

[67] William Corlett, in *Community without Unity: A Politics of Derridean Extravagance* (Durham, NC, and London: Duke University Press, 1989), dismissively writes that the 'enterprise of making community safe for liberalism has flourished in the last decade' (24). He considers the work of liberals such as Gutmann, Gaus, and Hiske in this respect, but reserves his strongest criticism for Rosenblum. Corlett rejects both the liberal conception of community ('remunity') and the communitarian one ('communion'), and finds the attempt by theorists (such as Rosenblum) to balance communion and remunity to be mistaken (32).

thought that recent liberal concessions are still inadequate in the eyes of communitarians, for whom membership in a community is deeply and fundamentally constitutive of an individual's sense of self, not merely a variable, adaptable *aspect* of liberal individuality. But is this truly the position defended by the various contemporary theorists labelled 'communitarians'? A closer examination of recent communitarian arguments suggests not. Contemporary communitarian tracts reveal the inclusion of what may appear to be qualified gestures toward the human capacity for personal autonomy and individual choice, even if this capacity is rather more limited in scope than the wholesale personal liberty which is the foundation of the liberal tradition. Sandel, for example, is often charged with promoting a typically communitarian vision in which a self discovers, never elects, the constituting frameworks in which she has meaningful being. In *Liberalism and the Limits of Justice*, for example, he insists that the relationships and contexts in which persons are situated are 'not [ones] . . . they choose (as in a voluntary association) but an attachment they discover, not merely an attribute but a constituent of their identity' (150). At the same time, Sandel would disavow the determinism towards which such a position invariably points, by positing an ill-defined notion of 'self-determination'. He claims, for example, that 'the subject is empowered to participate in the constitution of its identity' (152), a claim for (partial) self-constitution which would seem to run counter to the notion that one merely discovers the constitutive social attachments with which one is encumbered. Prevarication, or at the very least uncertainty, seems implicit in the many qualifiers which punctuate his arguments. In representative claims in *Liberalism and its Critics* he suggests that subjects are 'defined *to some extent* by the community of which they are part' (150; my emphasis), and that allegiances are held 'in virtue of those *more or less* enduring attachments and commitments which taken together *partly* define the person I am' (172; my emphasis).[68] He writes of our capacity for qualified self-interpretation: 'As a self-interpreting being, I am able to reflect on my history and in this sense distance myself from it, but the distance is always precarious and provisional' (172).[69]

---

[68] Such qualifications are not uncommon in the work of Sandel. In 'Morality and the Liberal Ideal', *New Republic*, 7 May, 1984, p. 17, he writes that we are 'partly defined by the communities we inhabit'.

[69] See Charles Taylor's distinction between human agents as 'simple weighers' and

Self-interpreting being? This seems a far cry from the claim of wholesale social determination of persons that liberals would attribute to communitarianism. If interpretation of the narrative of self is bound to some extent by what is given to be interpreted (past happenings, character traits, genetic coding, circumstances, discovered community attachments, and so on), it is also true that there is space for creativity in the reading of these discovered attributes and qualities. Human subjects, as (self-)interpretative agents, never merely discover, but also invent connections and relations between the events that are given on the pages of memory and personal history. Furthermore, self-interpretation requires a certain capacity for ironic detachment on the part of the reflective self-interpreter, an ability to distance oneself from one's past self (selves). While this conceptual 'split' may be (and is) lamented by some as evidence of the human inability to achieve personal identity (for the coherence of self is forever deferred in the ongoing processes of self-interpretation), it also provides the space necessary for self-evaluation and critical reflection.

If in the above citation Sandel concedes some element of personal autonomy in the notion of self-interpretation, equally important is the move he makes from the locus of determinism as 'community' to that of 'more or less enduring attachments and beliefs'. This qualification is crucial. In no small part, the seeming intractability of the traditional liberal–communitarian debate might be seen to rest on the failure of communitarians to adequately define what the nebulous term 'community' connotes.[70] Without adequate definition, 'community' too readily assumes the all-encompassing contours of society or political state (usually marked by the parameters of a bounded geographical location). It is such concepts of community that liberals find so deeply repulsive, for they seem to quash any possibility of personal autonomy or the expression of individual desire. But perhaps communitarian aims can be served by appealing to a less prescriptive notion of community, in which communal attachments

'strong evaluators' in 'What is Human Agency?' in Theodore Mischel (ed.), *The Self: Psychological and Philosophical Issues* (London: Basil Blackwell, 1977), 103–38.

[70] Corlett attempts to unravel some of the connotations of 'community' in *Community without Unity*, stressing the distinction between *reciprocity* and the geographic use of *community*. Sandel, in *Liberalism and the Limits of Justice*, contrasts instrumental and sentimental community with constitutive community.

are understood as plural ('attachments and beliefs') and provisional ('more or less enduring'). Personhood might be conceived of as constituted in a variety of smaller collectivities and unions based on associations that are sometimes unchosen and circumstantial (family, nation of birth or tribe, school), and sometimes voluntary or consensual (circles of friends, unions of colleagues, adopted citizenship). In *Another Liberalism* Rosenblum writes that the task facing communitarians is to 'show whether their aim can be met by voluntary and perhaps temporary associations formed for limited purposes and capable of attaching only some of our loyalties, or whether it is necessary to be violently gripped by feelings of attachment' (157). While maintaining the vision of communal embeddedness (although communal constitution is now spread widely over a variety of community bases), the idea of plural constitutive communities—which attach only *some* of our loyalties—might combat liberal fears about repressive totalitarianism and minority exclusion in the traditional communitarian account:

Communitarianism based on voluntary associations blunts both threats. There is a potentially infinite number and kind of groups, and because they are incorporated within the liberal frameworks of separate spheres, membership remains partial. Both characteristics insure that from the point of view of personal liberty, communitarianism is benign. (159)

Plural Communities and the Politics of Place

Recasting the notion of community in terms of plural associations beings other problems. One of these is definition. Abandoning the definition of community as clearly visible social structure(s) or geographical location(s), and widening it to include a multitude of variable associative and collaborative unions, both local and global, real and imagined, opens a hornet's nest of interpretative possibilities. Pluralist theorists cite widely different examples of community, including familial and tribal affiliations, work-places, a multitude of institutions and corporations, religious groups, ideological and political allegiances, and so on. This leads to a second problem. Clearly not all community memberships are consensual or voluntary. Many communities are not chosen at all, birth or mere circumstance being the sole condition of membership; membership in some communities is enforced or coercively maintained. Invariably some collectivities are instrumental and exploitative, serving the interests of dominant members at the expense of others. Patently not all communities cater to the psychological desires or even the physical needs of their members (abusive families and exploitative work situations might be cited as examples). Feminist theorists are particularly concerned that community should not be defined in terms of traditional, conventional structures, such as the family, which are frequently (traditionally) coercive or exploitative. Voluntary associations are no less problematic than involuntary ones, and may be formed for reasons such as altruism, patriotism, or paternalism. Some voluntary collaborations are strategic, founded on mutual distrust rather than mutual respect. Others may require the repudiation of certain needs and desires in order to secure the gain of others.

Against these objections we must stress the notion of pluralism. Only plurality safeguards against totalitarianism (although the price of this freedom may well be conflict on intra- and interpersonal levels). People belong to many different communities. Voluntary, supportive, and mutually beneficial communities may be formed and consensually joined within or alongside even the most repressive conditions of other, less voluntary, attachments. (Besides, not all involuntary attachments are of necessity repressive; some provide supportive structures and conventions that promote positive and productive personal ends.) One might, for example, belong to a repressive family unit, but find support in a positive community of friendship; one might be the exploited member of a self-serving work-place, yet find one's emotional needs met by voluntary association in a community of religious belief, a community of admiring readers of the works of Milton, or a community of avid cricket supporters. It is inconceivable to imagine persons who do not belong to a variety of communities, even under the most repressive conditions, and thus whose sense of self is not determined by more than one set of prescriptions, values, and beliefs. Supportive voluntary associations may be formed within or alongside even the most horrifically repressive communities: friendships within concentration camps, the maintenance of shared religious and moral beliefs under extreme situations of oppression. This is not to deny that inequalities will prevail. Certain communities (or members of them) may be more powerful, or possess the ability to exert more coercive pressure than others. Shifting, revisable relations of equality are the inevitable condition of plurality; conflict and contestation are a necessary condition of theorizing the human ability to evaluate conditions and make (some) choices between competing communities. As George Revill notes, support for the notion of community does not entail

that a shared sense of purpose, consent to action, means a consensual commitment to a common intersubjectively transparent set of social assumptions. Recent work by social anthropologists has addressed the tension between conformity and individuality within even so-called 'traditional' communities. The importance of community's symbolic rallying points are recognized precisely because they are polyvalent, providing an all-embracing concept which can contain the multiplicity of individual objectives and expectations.[71]

My use of the term 'community' is not intended to play to what might be deemed twentieth-century nostalgia for group purpose and collective guidance.[72] The word, as I intend it, is far more inclusive. In no way do I use the term to denote a fixed set of rules or system of beliefs, but rather to denote a set of shared, mutable communicative protocols that facilitate intersubjective understanding while accommodating plurality and supporting internal criticism (the possibility of which I will argue for in my next chapter): it denotes a *symbolic rallying point* rather than a concrete, transparent set of social assumptions or a fixed geographical location. Community should not be understood as signifying a particular bound arena or a political constituency, but rather as a *spatial metaphor* referring to a shared discursive 'space' that may be concrete or imaginary. The interrelation of the local and the global (facilitated in modern society by the emergence and expansion of a variety of communication technologies and increased opportunities for travel and mobility) is an important facet of our

[71] George Revill, 'Reading Rosehill: Community, Identity and Inner City Derby', in Michael Keith and Steve Pile (eds.), *Place and the Politics of Identity* (London and New York: Routledge, 1993), 117–40. See also Anthony Paul Cohen, *The Symbolic Construction of Community* (London: Tavistock, 1985).

[72] See Revill, 'Reading Rosehill', 128, where it is suggested that the term 'community' is too often exploited this way by politics of the Right that in fact threaten basic liberties in an appeal to the desirability of community: the 'communities' of religious fundamentalism or, in Britain, policies such as 'Care in the community' and the 'Community charge'.

contemporary existence. Social subjects are constituted not only in local communities, but in global ones as well. Contemporary human beings are situated in a vast, complex web of interconnections, able to 'commune' with distant and radically different others by telephone, fax, and internet. The mass media further extend the possibilities of (imaginary) identification between individual subjects; they encourage cross-fertilization between individuals and communities, and facilitate adaptations in any given community in response to the external influences of other communities.

Some contemporary geographers—among them Doreen Massey, Edward Soja, and David Harvey—have recently turned their attention to the exploration of space, real and imaginary, as a constitutive dimension of cultural politics and personal identity. They note that in attempting to articulate relations of oppression and dominance in a variety of social dimensions (such as class, gender, sexual orientation, and race), theorists from a broad spectrum of disciplines have increasingly relied on a range of spatial metaphors: embeddedness, displacement, mapping, positionality, situatedness, centre-margin, and, of course, community. Until recently, this spatial terminology has remained largely unexplored, despite its proliferation in critical discourse.[73] Spatial terminology has been assumed to be self-evident, and is frequently used to provide the metaphorical 'ground' for a multiplicity of contemporary cultural debates.[74] In postmodern discourses keen to challenge all manner of essentialisms, the assumed essentiality of space—dismissed as either opaque or transparent—is all the more surprising.[75] These contemporary geographers urge re-examination of the implicit assumptions that operate within the spatial terminology so frequently employed in contemporary cultural theory. They seek to address what they perceive as the theoretical prioritization of history and temporality over geography and spatiality: space has traditionally been regarded as fixed, static, and undialectical, while time/history is conceptualized as the medium of movement and

---

[73] See the collection of essays edited by Michael Keith and Steve Pile, *Place and the Politics of Identity*.

[74] See Neil Smith and Cindi Katz, 'Grounding Metaphor: Towards a Spatialized Politics', in Keith and Pile (eds.), *Place and the Politics of Identity*, 67–83.

[75] See Henry Lefebvre, *The Production of Space* (1974; Oxford: Basil Blackwell, 1991).

permutation.[76] Spatiality and temporality, they argue, are existential and experiential dimensions that cannot be separated, permutable dimensions within which cultural and personal identity is constituted. Alongside this critique of historicism has grown a considerable body of recent theory which explores what might be termed the 'politics of place', where place is understood as produced and reproduced in the processes of social formation: politics, time, and space are far from antinomic, being intrinsically interrelated. The explorations of spatial metaphors such as 'community' point towards a crucial reconceptualization of the politics of plural 'spaces' within which human beings exist.[77]

Gayatri Chakravorty Spivak, and other advocates of polyvocal pluralism reject a static model of binary opposition in the formulation of cultural dynamics in favour of the persistent recognition of heterogeneity.[78] We need to stop thinking of the proliferation of heterogeneous 'communities' in contemporary culture as a relativistic 'horror of multiplicity' (the phrase is Fredric Jameson's[79]) but rather as offering a vast, fertile web of *interconnected* sites of

[76] See Doreen Massey, 'Politics and Space/Time', in Keith and Pile (eds.), *Place and the Politics of Identity*, 141–61; Edward Soja, *Postmodern Geographies: The Reassertion of Space in Critical Social Theory* (London: Verso, 1989); and Dick Hebdige's introduction to the special issue 'Subjects in Space', *New Formations*, 11 (1990), pp. vi–vii.

[77] See David Harvey, *The Condition of Postmodernity* (Oxford: Basil Blackwell, 1989).

[78] See Gayatri Chakravorty Spivak, 'Can the Subaltern Speak?', in Cary Nelson and Lawrence Grossberg (eds.), *Marxism and the Interpretation of Culture* (Basingstoke: Macmillan, 1988), 271–313. The Jan. 1995 imprint of *PMLA* 110/1, an issue devoted to the topic of 'Colonialism and the Postcolonial Condition', offers a number of essays that explore the heterogeneity of cultural practice. As Linda Hutcheon suggests in her introductory essay 'Colonialism and the Postcolonial Condition: Complexities Abounding', these essays 'do not deconstruct an existing subjectivity or posit an essentialist, universal, unitary subject; instead they investigate the "multiplication" of identities' (11). Rosemary Jolly, in discussing post-apartheid South Africa, dismisses 'a static model based on binary oppositions' in favour of a theory that 'constantly recogniz[es] dissident practices in the context of change' (in 'Rehearsals of Liberation: Contemporary Postcolonial Discourse and the New South Africa', *PMLA* 110/1 (1995): 23).

[79] Fredric Jameson, *Postmodernism, or, the Cultural Logic of Late Capitalism* (London: Verso, 1991), 363. Sharings and borrowing between communities (religious, social, cultural, linguistic) is clearly not a feature only of contemporary Western culture, although the difference between our own age and earlier/other ones in this respect is certainly one of degree, due to the increased mobility of individuals and the proliferation of mass media and communication technologies in the late twentieth-century.

borrowing and adaptation. Communities—spaces of intersubject-ively shared (communicative) protocols—are not intended here as radically isolated and independent, set apart with clearly defined boundaries and all-or-nothing membership conditions. They are interdependent and interconnected in so far as their constituent members *simultaneously* share commitments to numerous other communities. Meanings, purposes, and values are frequently trans-communal, shared not only by members within specific groups but across and between them as well. Relationships exist between communities as well as within them, the result of the plurality of simultaneous attachments of their individual community members. Community attachments are variously voluntary, non-consensual, and need- or interest-governed; they may change radically accord-ing to context and circumstance. Precisely because individuals are situated as members in a plurality of formative groups and com-munities, the boundaries between them are often blurred, and considerable overlap may exist between them. Communities share interests, meanings, and values, as do their members. This is not to deny that certain communities are radically different from others, or are structured around incommensurate aims and values, or share no members in common. But no community is an island, hermetically sealed and self-contained: a web of trans-communal interconnections exist, constituted in the plural situation of indi-viduals in a variety of communities. I am not suggesting that the simultaneous placement of individuals in a variety of communities will lessen, let alone eliminate, conflict and antagonism between communities. Choices and decisions have to be made by individuals when evaluating competing communal demands and values. But these choices and evaluations are not made in a vacuum; they are the complex product of an individual's cumulative knowledge and experience, knowledge and experience gained through multiple formative communal attachments and placements in the course of her lifetime. We must conceive of plural communities as a complex web of interdependencies and interconnections, in which relationships never simply settle into petrified patterns of difference and dominance, but remain open to movement and change precisely because of the multiple, simultaneous commitments of their members. To add to this vision of complexity and further develop the notion of subjective liberty, I will argue in later chapters that persons possess not only the ability to evaluate and move between a variety of determining communities, but also the capacity to adapt and change the contours of the communities in which they are situated. Trans-communal cross-fertilization and borrowing are, in part, what enables the extension and modification of the 'boundaries' of the discursive 'spaces' in which subjects can and do meaningfully commune and communicate.

One further aspect of a notion of plural community attachment needs to be mentioned before moving on: it allows us to account for the possibility of change and development in persons, which must otherwise be inconceivable. If one is simply born into *a* constitutive community (or even *a* fixed structure of communities), conceived as singular and monolithic, how could we account for changes in beliefs and knowledge through a person's lifetime? If the structures that determine us are always fixed and prior to our self-conceptions, how can changes in personality and belief be understood except as psychotic, as the loss of meaningful selfhood? The fact that human beings can and do learn and change, and adapt or even abandon previously held values and commitments, accords with their induction, through the course of their lives, into an ever increasing variety of determining communities, and with their capacity to evaluate and make choices between the competing demands of these communities. Pluralism, as I conceive it, need not be stymied by the conception of a fixed hierarchy in which certain (more repressive) communities putatively sanction a variety of increasingly marginal and minimal communities beneath them. It must be conceived as a fluid, flexible web of trans-communal interrelations. Positing *a* dominant determining community, within which exist a number of increasingly subordinate sub-communities in fixed relations, would disavow the anguished choices we frequently face when we have to choose between conflicting allegiances and loyalties.

Between Dualisms: Pragmatic Plurality

My purpose in pairing two very different debates in this chapter—that between Lyotard and Habermas and that between liberals and communitarians—is not to suggest direct parallels or hidden convergences between them. Nor is it, quite clearly, my intention to provide a comprehensive review of either. My aims are more modest. I hope to suggest that the dualistic deadlock which characterizes both debates might be fruitfully tempered by the adoption of a more pragmatic perspective, one that affords some points of mediation between unpalatable extremes. In evaluating the debate between Lyotard and Habermas, need we choose between totalitarian communicative rationality or the relativistic frenzy of incommensurate language-games? It seems to be the case that Lyotard's arguments against Habermas can be sustained only by a tacit assumption of a normative foundation that makes possible his claims in the first place. On the other hand, need it be the case that accepting, with Habermas, the possibility of shared intersubjective understanding wholly precludes differences of opinion between subjects or renders invalid the adoption by subjects of variant, even opposing, discursive language-use positions within the structures afforded by communicative procedure? My discussion of contemporary moves in the debate between liberals and communitarians suggests not.

At their more politically pragmatic moments, both contemporary liberalism and recent communitarianism seem to qualify the extremism of their more traditional positions by a partial (or veiled) acknowledgement of the validity of the other's claims: contemporary liberals seem willing to affirm the importance of intersubjective attachments and communalities, and in much recent communitarian writing there is a tacit acknowledgement of the possibility of (partial) self-interpretative autonomy and the capacity of subjects to evaluate and sometimes choose between competing communal frameworks of belief and value. This is not to suggest a collapse of one position into the other; clearly differences remain. But they are differences of degree rather than insurmountable antagonisms: the work of theorists like Rosenblum, Raz, and Walzer reveals an increasing openness to the claims of their opponents. Rather than opting for one of two diametrically opposed theories of personhood, we might be able to find useful insights at the points of overlap between the two. In these spaces of convergence—between the extremes of personal essentialism and coercive communal authoritarianism—we may begin to theorize a more pragmatic notion of subjective agency: of personhood constituted in the variable, shifting matrices of a productive multiplicity of chosen and given communities, allegiances, loyalties, and commitments.

2

Rules and Protocols, Beliefs and Understandings

> The subject is no longer defined only in its essence as the place and the placing of its representations; it is also, as a subject and in its structure as *subjectum*, itself apprehended as *a representative*. Man, determined first and above all as a subject, as being-subject, finds himself interpreted throughout according to the structure of representation.
>
> Derrida, 'Sending: On Representation'

What scope is there for creative representation, if the human subject is simply the structural determinant, the 'subjectum', of 'the structure of representation', as Derrida seems to aver in the above citation? When considering the value and validity of the poststructuralist challenge to subjective essentiality we need to return to questions raised in my previous chapter: if my knowledge of myself and my world is wholly constituted within the boundaries of delimiting representative structures, how do I ever gain the (external) critical perspective which allows me to recognize, let alone challenge, them? How does the possibility of contestation ever arise if all thought is wholly constituted by social structures which reinscribe conventional norms and practices? Indeed, how do we begin to question the terms of our social and linguistic embeddedness when the terms, the questions, and the answers too are all performed in the circumscribed arena of social discourse? One needs to be sufficiently independent, and possess a degree of autonomous objectivity, a capacity for critical self-reflection, in order to become aware of one's structural incarceration and to contemplate (let alone act on) alternative modes of being. Quite simply, a hardline poststructuralist conception of subjectivity fails to provide an adequate account of the human capacity for contestation, and certainly fails to account for the possibility of its own anti-authoritarian posture. In consequence, it has, in the words of Meili Steele, 'kept poststructuralism tied to an ethics of difference and a politics of negative freedom—that is, freedom as opportunity rather than freedom as capacity'.[1]

A softer version of poststructuralism, and one which is more amenable to the political claims which underwrite its emancipatory project, would understand determinism not as absolute but partial. Derrida seems to suggest as much in his use of qualifiers in the first sentence of the citation, writing that the 'subject is no longer defined *only* in its essence as the place and the placing of its representations' (my emphasis) but *also* 'as a subject . . . apprehended as *a representative*'. I am willing to accept this softer version of the poststructuralist conception of subjectivity, one in which human subjects are understood not *only* as essential agents, but *also* as the partial products of extra-personal structures of representation (the plural form here is crucial). Such a conception is a necessary check on the naïve predication of subjective essentialism. But in his second sentence Derrida seems to point towards a far more all-encompassing determinism: 'Man' is determined *'first and above all* . . . as being-subject [and] *finds* himself interpreted *throughout* according to *the* structure of representation' (my emphasis). Subjectivity, in this formulation, is merely discovered, the product of an all-pervasive structure that seems to offer no scope for reflective agency. The slide from soft to hard determinism in these two sentences is devious and misleading. It is to such manipulative rhetorical play that we must take objection.

There are obvious parallels between certain poststructuralist accounts of the human subject as an inauthentic discursive process and the communitarian account of subjective constitution which claims, as William M. Sullivan does in the extract cited in my previous chapter, that 'outside a linguistic community of shared practices . . . there could not be human beings'.[2] Both reject the notion of an objective, originating self who is able to stand outside social processes. Both find the language of the society in which a subject is embedded to be constitutive, to a significant degree, of that subject's very sense of selfhood. It might be thought that my objections to the (hardline) poststructuralist account of subjectivity

[1] Meili Steele, 'How Philosophy of Language Informs Ethics and Politics: Richard Rorty and Contemporary Theory', *Boundary 2*, 20/2 (1993), 169. See also Charles Taylor, 'What's Wrong with Negative Freedom', in *Philosophical Papers*, vol. 2 (New York: Cambridge University Press, 1985), 211–29.

[2] William M. Sullivan, *Reconstructing Public Philosophy* (Berkeley: University of California Press, 1982), 158, 173.

favours a liberal conception of an essential subject who exists prior to the communities to which she elects or contracts to belong. But it is in no way my aim or intention to endorse the tenets of hardline liberalism. For, as I have suggested, the liberal version of subjectivity fails to account for how it is that the autonomous self it promotes may productively commune with others without recourse to certain intersubjective conventions and protocols (not least linguistic ones) which may impinge on the sovereignty of individuality. Just as the impasse between hardline liberal and communitarian conceptions of the human subject may find some resolution in a pragmatic vision of communal plurality, so too it may be possible to reach and understanding of the linguistic positioning of the person which does not result in either the pessimistic claim that persons are wholly 'written' in extra-personal social terms and which finds human freedom to lie in the wholesale rejection of *all* systematization or the opposing liberal-humanist claim that we live as essential, autonomous selves with the undisputed capacity for individual expression and creative articulation.

Given the extent to which human conceptual processes are understood in linguistic terms in contemporary thought and the consequent politicization of textuality discussed in the previous chapter, it will prove useful to take a closer look at two prevailing contemporary literary theories that hold distinct and antagonistic understandings of the interpretative (reading) process, theories which I will call, following Robert Scholes in *Protocols of Reading*, deconstruction and fundamentalism.[3] These opposing stances in the discipline of literary criticism shadow the wider theoretical dualisms discussed in my previous chapter: that between communal, communicative determinism and liberal essentialism, that is, between those who believe human beings to be 'subjected' by their social embeddedness and those who believe subjective autonomy to be the fundamental condition of personhood.

The stand-off in literary criticism results in part from the inherent absolutism of both the deconstructionist and the fundamentalist accounts of textuality, a surprising claim, perhaps, given the proclaimed anti-foundationalism of the former. Critical fundamentalism may be defined as the belief that texts are transparent

[3] Robert Scholes, *Protocols of Reading* (New Haven and London: Yale University Press, 1989).

vehicles which represent truths about the world and unproblematically convey an author's intentions to readers. Deconstructionism, by contrast, holds that the meaning of a text, far from
being unproblematically fixed by its author and clearly available
to a reader, inheres in the interpretation of that text by a historically situated reader, indefinitely suspending the number of possible
interpretations of that text. A deconstructive account stresses the
fact that reading takes time, and temporality precludes objectivity
(hence the key importance of deferral in Derrida's notion of
différance). Texts are not simply transparent, atemporal vehicles
which carry pre-given meanings from a determining author to a
passive reader, but are the product of a reader's imposition of
meaning, at a particular historical junction, on the signs which
compose the text. Signs, moreover, do not unproblematically
represent meanings; language is the very medium in which meanings are differentially constituted. Deconstruction reveals, moreover, that certain terms are privileged in the construction of signs,
and thus that signing and interpretation are never neutral. The
deconstructive position is abundantly familiar, as are the limitations it ascribes to more traditional modes of reading and
interpretation. Deconstructive textuality may be viewed as emancipatory in so far as it gives interpretative licence to readers who
may themselves *determine* the meaning of a text and the signs that
comprise it: if there are no true, objective meanings, then there are
no false ones either, and all textual interpretations are equally
valid. But this is deeply problematic for a number of reasons. A
stress on subjective interpretative validity can result in the disturbing intuition that if everything means anything, then it is
pointless to talk about meanings at all. In the place of traditional
notions that legitimate singular textual meaning (such as intentionality), there flourishes instead a profusion of partisan narratives,
of subjective interpretations. If objective certainty is an impossibility, then arbitrary subjectivity appears to rule the day: the
spectre of relativistic incommensurability rises once again. Indeed,
it is precisely the fear of an unchecked proliferation of interpretations that is used by fundamentalists to fuel the anti-deconstruc-
tion fire. We can see clear parallels between the kind of textual
deregulation urged by advocates of deconstruction and Lyotard's
hypothesized state of emancipated postmodernity in which the
authority of meta-narratives is to be abolished once and for all.

We can also see how the fear of anarchic individualism called upon to discredit Lyotard's call for meta-narrative abolition might be used to discredit a deconstructionist theory of textuality.

Yet it is precisely the capacity for subjective (interpretative) autonomy that poststructuralist theorists seek to challenge when situating social language prior to, and as the necessary condition for, the constitution of the human subject (and thus her texts and interpretations). This being so, to attack deconstructive textuality on the grounds of its endorsement of arbitrary subjectivism could be deeply mistaken—unless, of course, deconstructive theorizing carries a deep, inherent contradiction, positing at once a bleak, inescapable ideological determinism *and* the intrinsic capacity for rebellious deviance by individuals from determining structures. This it appears to do, at least in its softer versions: much deconstructive rhetoric is a curious amalgam of deterministic lamentation and emancipatory jubilation. Contrary to overt, antinormative claims, there appears to be a shared substantive premiss that underlies all poststructuralist accounts: the value (and goal) of antinomian subjective autonomy is a key feature in—one might even say the tacit normative foundation of—the deconstructive appeal. A politics of individual liberation presupposes the *value* of subjective individuality. To speak of freedom or oppression must predicate the existence of individuals who are capable of being freed or oppressed. This is certainly the case if the theory is to have anything more than utopian appeal. The worth of deconstructive practice is measured, time and time again, by the yardstick of its promise to 'release' subjects and texts from determining authority, be it metaphysical illusionism, phallocentric subjection, or ideological determinism. Frequently the consequences or nature of this release remain unexplored, but are gestured towards in a kind of irresponsible rhetoric that relies heavily on metaphorical equations of release with madness, amorality, unbounded wilderness, silence, and so on. It is my claim that the appeal of deconstructive theory in no small measure lies in this inherent contradiction between the predication of an encompassing determinism and the possibility of individual release from determining authority, a contradiction which is obfuscated in the emotive use of manipulative rhetorical language. This contradiction between a deterministic ethos and a textual ethic which promotes, above all, the value of freedom is one that contemporary writers manipulate and exploit in a number of significant ways, as I will suggest in Chapter 4.

The critical fundamentalist stance—the belief that textual meaning is an authorial given, that the interpretative process is always one of careful excavation and never of creation—does not provide an adequate alternative to deconstructionist claims. Fundamentalism presupposes that textual meaning is an ideal object which is equally accessible to all readers (if they read *properly*). It relies heavily on notions of metaphysical essentialism and linguistic transparency, suppressing the problems of temporality and historicity which have become such urgent considerations in recent philosophy and literary criticism. It assumes that the meanings of words are fixed and transparent; it denies the existence of a gap, temporal and conceptual, between authorial intention and reader comprehension. And in doing so, it runs counter to the recognition of contextuality and historicity and the discreditation of objectivity which is our century's philosophical heritage.

Avoiding the naïve predications of the fundamentalist account of textuality and interpretation as transparent activities of reflection and archaeological discovery does not require that we wholly abandon the task of interpretation and the possibility of meaningful communication. Just because there is no definitive, unquestionably right way of interpreting a text (spoken or written) does not mean that *all* interpretations are equally valid or, for that matter, that some might simply be wrong. Avowedly temporal deferral and contextual displacement of original intention are conditions of all our acts of reading, ones which always distort the 'purity' of our interpretations. But does it matter that we are unable to access ideal meanings or absolute truths? Robert Scholes is one critic who consistently suggests not. In *Protocols of Reading* he writes:

> If everything in our world is impure, insofar as we know anything about it, this means that purity is not a concept that we can use, except in a relative way, more or less pure, more or less impure. Similarly, if none of us ever experiences the pure presence of anything, then we can stop talking about pure presence as if it mattered. (69)

If absolute certainty or full presence is not available to us, then why bring it into the equation of meaning-interpretation as a measure of (impossible) perfection to which we must hopelessly aspire? Scholes continues, '[i]f we have no Truth with a capital T, we must stop using the notion of such Truth—in whatever guise—to measure what we then take to be our failure to achieve it. But we must not give up distinguishing between truth and lies within whatever frameworks we can construct to make such determinations' (154). The abandonment of a singular foundation of truth as *the* normative ground for interpretation need not entail the wholesale refutation of meaningful intersubjective communication or the possibility of interpretative discernment or provisional belief. Meaning is not infinitely deferred; it comes to rest (if momentarily) in concrete instances of communication and interpretation. *These* are what need analysis, not some abstract system of language operation and the totalizing violence it ostensibly sustains. Certainly these moments are not points of access to invariable, fixed truths, they are open to revision and revaluation, a process that may continue indefinitely. But we need to distinguish truth from meaning, and to resist the fallacious reasoning which suggests that because we can never, with certainty, gain access to the former, we must also relinquish any possibility of the achieving the latter. As I have suggested in the previous chapter, meanings can be communicated and beliefs shared within the various interconnected frameworks provided by many partisan, local communities. Interpersonal communication and textual interpretation are achieved within multiple, shifting communal frameworks of (referential and moral) value, frameworks which need not be conceived of as transcendent or universal.

Of central importance to Scholes's discussion in *Protocols of Reading* is his claim, evident in the previous citation, that not only are human subjects able to communicate meaningfully within intersubjective frameworks of value but also, crucially, they possess some capacity to construct and adapt the procedural protocols that structure their interpretative communities: 'we must not give up distinguishing between truth and lies within whatever frameworks we can construct to make such determinations' (154). We may recognize that 'structure[s] of representation' (Derrida's term, cited above) are necessary to ensure the possibility of intersubjective communication, meaningful representation, and a sense of selfhood, but these need not be conceived of as singular or absolute. How much better, with Scholes, to understand the shared frameworks within which we read and interpret as local and revisable 'protocols', rather than ahistorical, fixed structures.

In Chapter 1 I suggested that positing an interlinked network of plural interpretative sites or communities, within which human subjects are simultaneously situated and between which they move, might be a way of overcoming the narrowly conceived dualisms so often paraded in contemporary thought between, for example, structure and agency, relativism and totalitarianism. Persons are situated as subjects in a variety of (sometimes conflictual) communal frameworks which provide a range of interpretative possibilities and different signifying practices that may be adopted by the subject at any given moment. Consequently, one's conception of self is never fixed simply in one permanent structure of representation, but in a plurality of shifting affiliations.

Thus, no-one is simply a woman; one is rather, for example, a white, Jewish, middle-class woman, a philosopher, a lesbian, a socialist, and a mother. Moreover, since everyone acts in a plurality of social contexts, one's womanhood figures centrally in the set of descriptions under which one acts; in other words, it is peripheral or latent. Finally, it is not the case that people's social identities are constructed once and for all and definitively fixed. Rather, they alter over time, shifting with shifts in agents' practices and affiliations. . . . In short, social identities are discursively constructed in historically specific social contexts; they are complex and plural; and they shift over time.[4]

One way of blunting the barb of totalizing determinism with respect to the placement of the subject within community structures is to maintain the notion of a plural web of interactive, reciprocally influential discursive communities between which the subject has some freedom to choose and move. The matrix of interpretative communities is not monolithic and a priori, but a plurality of constantly changing activities, beliefs, and events that are open to constant re-evaluation and reinterpretation in the light of specific historic conditions. This communal, communicative matrix should not be conceived in opposition to individuality, but rather as the medium for individual constitution: individuals draw on the fund of interpretative possibilities available to them in a variety of communal contexts in constructing their own assessments and interpretations of self and others. Although many communal structures are inherited, they are open to reinter-

---

[4] Nancy Fraser, 'The Uses and Abuses of French Discourse Theories for Feminist Politics', *Boundary 2*, 17/2 (1990), 84.

pretation by new generations, enabling individuals, in Lawrence E. Cahoone's words, to 'reconstruct their inheritance':

The inheritance provides a context of cultural activities, events, artifacts, and meanings which serve as an interpretive reservoir on which each individual draws both in order to create his or her own interpretative patterns and in order to communicate and share meanings with others . . . . The communal-communicative-cultural matrix of relations is not the antithesis of individuality, it is the field of becoming for the individual, the pluralistic context in which individuality is located and on which it feeds and draws meanings and raw-material for its own meaning-construction and interpretation.[5]

When the protocols that enable communication are understood as prescriptive rather than procedural, the concepts of understanding and belief may coalesce. Retaining the distinction between these two notions—understanding and belief—is vitally important. Communicative protocols engender understanding but do not, perforce, prescribe belief. Understanding something does not mean accepting or believing it; in fact, understanding is a prior condition for the possibility of willed transgression or disbelief. If there are many different communities of understanding, there are many more sub-communities of belief. It is, in part, the shared understandings between individuals, like their common language, which enable them to accommodate (and challenge) variant belief and value distinctions.

The English language community, for example, includes a wide variety of different (un)believing discursive communities—Christian, Jewish, Muslim, Hindu, agnostic, atheist, and so on. Members of one discursive community, English-speaking Christians,

[5] Lawrence E. Cahoone, *The Dilemma of Modernity: Philosophy, Culture, and Anti-Culture* (Albany, NY: State University of New York Press, 1988). Cahoone is here developing a notion of non-subjectivist culture, but his articulation is useful for the definition of community I wish to articulate. Cf. Neil ten Kortenaar, in 'Beyond Authenticity and Creolization: Reading Achebe Writing Culture', *PMLA* 110/1 (1995), 30–42): 'People fashion their identity by identifying with cultural symbols and by narrating a place in the world. Of course, a community's narratives are shaped according to conventions, and narrative conventions change from age to age, and differ from clime to clime. Narratives and symbols are social institutions that outlast the lives of individuals, and cultural agents must construct their lives within these inherited parameters. But individuals to not merely replicate their inheritance. Culture . . . is not a prescriptive grammar but rather a reservoir of often contradictory potential practices that social actors can make use of when communal identity is being renegotiated, as it always is' (31).

for example, are themselves not reducible to one interpretative community, but may include people who hold a wide range of incompatible political beliefs and loyalties: left-wing English-speaking Christians may or may not be heterosexuals, feminists, beer-drinkers, animal rights activists, or Arsenal football supporters. The number of partisan subdivisions and permutations of belief and allegiance possible within a given language community is endless. What prevents the atomism of this community into a multitude of antagonistic, solipsistic (un)believers is not the forced control of some transcending authority which renders all difference the same, but the many shared alliances, allegiances, and interconnections that exist between individuals who coexist in numerous communities of belief. An English Jewish feminist (subject A) shares some beliefs with a French Christian feminist (subject B), who likewise shares some beliefs with a South African Christian Fascist (subject C). It would clearly be ridiculous to suggest that A, B, and C are reducible to 'subjects' of the same community, and that therefore their interpretations or beliefs would collapse into singular agreement. But it would be equally facile to deny that in certain contexts they have common allegiances and are members of the same discursive community. The points of intersection between the various intersubjective divisions and subdivisions of understanding believers form a vast, complex network which cannot be reduced to a structure of determination in which one set of ideological values or beliefs enjoys supremacy. At any given moment, religious belief may have supremacy over nationality for subject A, the reverse may apply for subject B, whereas both religion and nationality may be subordinate to political concerns for subject C—but these individual prioritizations can, and frequently do, change from one moment or situation to the next. In the words of Daniel Schwartz,

we each belong to multiple interpretive communities; and as we read, we draw upon our participation and experience in several interpretive communities. Not only do those interpretive communities change as well as modify and subvert one another, but our relationship to them varies from text to text. . . . How we read the texts—and the world—depends on an ever-changing hierarchy of interpretive strategies.[6]

[6] Daniel Schwartz, *The Case for a Humanistic Poetics* (Basingstoke and London: Macmillan, 1990), 28–9. See also Schwartz's essay, 'The Ethics of Reading: The Case for Pluralistic and Transactional Reading', *Novel*, 21/2–3 (Winter/Spring 1988), 197–218.

We cannot glibly relegate all interpretative communities and strategies to the same plane, positing a single set of beliefs, a single interpretative community or fixed hierarchy of communities, which controls all our acts of reading and interpretation. Moral dilemmas, like debates about the meaning of a text, arise precisely because of conflicting loyalties, within each subject (and between subjects), to the various communities and sub-communities to which that subject *simultaneously* belongs. Choices must be made, often at great cost, between one set of allegiances and another, choices which may well be influenced by the circumstances of time and place—contexts which can and will change, often requiring revision and sometimes evoking regret. Our 'agonies of choice', as Scholes calls them in *Textual Power*,[7] are inseparably linked with and expressive of our capacity for interpretative freedom:

Different, even conflicting, assumptions may preside over any reading of a single text by a single person. It is in fact these very differences within the reader, who is never a unified member of a single unified group—it is these very differences that create the space in which the reader exercises a certain measure of interpretive freedom.[8]

Our value- or meaning-determining beliefs, like our many community loyalties, are not fixed but continually changing, perpetually being re-evaluated in the light of the counter-demands, challenges, and reshuffling of priorities brought about by circumstantial change and temporal contingency.

To say this is not to deny that the codes which operate to bind communities of understanding and the conventions of authorization which enable meaningful narrative exchange can and do impose limits and constraints on action or interpretation. Of course they do; but it is never simply a case of one code or forced allegiance to one code. There are many different, sometimes conflicting, beliefs and interpretations which can be (and are continually) renegotiated and re-evaluated within a communicative system that engenders intersubjective understanding. The interpenetration of, and fluidity of movement between, the multiplicity of interconnected codes of authority and planes of

---

[7] Robert Scholes, *Textual Power: Literary Theory and the Teaching of English* (New Haven and London: Yale University Press, 1985), 163.
[8] Ibid. 154.

belief which coexist within the interpretative network of discursive communities to which individual persons belong is far greater than the monoptic vision of a single, controlling extra-personal discursive structure credits. Such a position too easily lends force to the injunction to abandon (the) community in a celebration of unqualified individuality—a credo of self-exile or excommunication. The postmodernist alternative to the hypothesized totalitarian repression of individuality in community—the fragmentation of identity in the endless regression of difference, the subversion and deconstruction of meta-narratives into a plurality of incommensurate individual language games—is equally untenable. The sense of loss which fundamentally characterizes this theoretical position is in no way abated by the ecstatic 'bliss' of dissolution, the insufficiency of meaninglessness.

The multiplicity of diverse perspectives we hold as members situated within an array of often antagonistic communities (some given, some chosen) never amounts to the limited vision of a single rule-bound perspective. Recognizing that we are situated as meaningful agents in relation to a variety of determining discursive communities need not divest us, as individuals, of our responsibility and purpose by condemning us to the role of produced 'subject' within these communities. Likewise, theorizing subjectivity as discursive product need not condemn individuals to the always-already writtenness of belief. Rather, it can offer us an enhanced understanding of how communication between individuals takes place despite (or because of) the diversity of individual belief. An exploration of selfhood in the metaphorical terms of textuality need not result in pessimistic assumptions of determined inauthenticity, but rather can affirm our status as the productive co-authors of our texts of social and personal value, texts which are, and must be, subject to a variety of (sometimes radically different) interpretations. As individuals, we are responsible for the self-reflexive monitoring of the communal conventions that structure our discursive communities and which generate textual (and personal) meaning. Furthermore, our placement in communities is rarely permanently fixed and unrevisable: we are able to move between, and contract allegiance to, many different interpretative and discursive communities; in many cases we even have the capacity to defect from one (moral, linguistic, religious, geographic) discursive community to another. We have, in short, the qualified potential to choose and move between the communities which will determine us. Herein lies both our human freedom and our pain.

Communities of Choice: The Model of Friendship

In an essay entitled 'Feminism and Modern Friendship', the feminist concerns of political theorist Marilyn Friedman enable her to achieve a synthesis of the ideas of subjective constitution and personal autonomy.[9] Friedman's essay adds valuable insights with respect to the communal situation of subjects in so far as she seeks to promote the idea that human subjects are, to an extent, able to move between a number of different determining communities. Friedman's position may be seen as one which straddles the divide between liberals and communitarians (see Chapter 1). This is not surprising if one considers that some strands of revolutionary feminism have for many years championed the cause of the (female) individual and her right to autonomy (a liberal tenet), which acknowledging the formative role of community in the individual's conception of personal identity (a communitarian tenet). For such thinkers, autonomy is not a matter of absconding from all communities, but of belonging to the right ones. The notion of a traditional (patriarchal) community modelled on the nuclear family is anathema to many feminists, to be avoided at all costs; the enforced subordination of women in many traditional domestic communities has had dire consequences for female autonomy. This understanding has sometimes resulted in a despairing belief that women can only ever be free in the 'wilderness', in an excommunicated realm apart from traditional communal structures and the machinations of patriarchal language. A variety of poststructuralist conceptions with respect to the efficacy of anti-narrational and anti-structural dissemination have fuelled this assumption, giving rise to impossible demands for an exclusive female language, or an *écriture feminine*. However, not all feminists subscribe to this utopian ideal founded on the ethics (and

---

[9] Marilyn Friedman, 'Feminism and Modern Friendship: Dislocating the Community' (1989), repr. in Shlomo Avineri and Avner de-Shalit (eds.), *Communitarianism and Individualism* (Oxford: Oxford University Press, 1992), 101–19. Further references to this essay will be cited parenthetically in the text.

aesthetics) of negative freedom. Some, like Friedman, hold out, and actively promote, the reformative power of female subjects *within* community and the movement of female subjects between a plurality of communal contexts. Indeed, it is precisely the reconstitutive power of (positive) communities and communicative protocols that some feminists would utilize toward the end of liberation.[10]

While endorsing an understanding of selfhood as communally constituted, Friedman rejects the patriarchal model of 'familial' community which she finds central to the traditional communitarian account and which 'seems to hark back to the repressive . . . world of family, neighbourhood, school, and church, which so intimately enclosed women in oppressive gender politics' (107). Communities such as these are ones we simply discover; we are placed in them by the accidents of birth or some other non-voluntary circumstance. They are, Friedman argues, 'characterised by practices of exclusion and suppression of non-group members, especially outsiders defined by ethnicity and sexual orientation' (106). In order to counter the prescriptive force of a traditional communitarian theory which suggests that we only 'discover' the communities in which we are situated, she proposes a model of community based on the 'communities of choice' which characterize the circle of friends we choose to join or establish, or the cities or countries to which we, as adults, may choose to move. A subject does not simply discover the intersubjective relationships which characterize her friendships, Friedman contends, but chooses to enter into them, to make and fulfil certain expectations and demands within them, and to leave them if she so desires. These 'more voluntary communities', remarks Friedman, 'foster not so much the constitution of their subjects but their reconstitution' (117). The communities of friendship play an important role in defining one's sense of selfhood, and to this extent may be thought of as definitional or constitutive (a communitarian notion). However, entrance into these communities is frequently the result of choice, not coercion.

There are problems here. Friendships *may* of course be coercive rather than supportive, destructive rather than reconstructive, an

---

[10] Numerous contemporary feminists take this line: Rita Felski, Nancy Fraser, Diana Fuss, Linda Nicholson, Sally Robinson, Patricia Waugh, and Patricia Yaeger spring immediately to mind.

idea explored by Margaret Atwood in her sensitive portrayal of childhood friendship in *Cat's Eye* (1989). Distinguishing a 'true' from an 'artificial' friend requires an objectivity perhaps attainable only by (temporal and spatial) distance—the ironic distance granted, for example, to the reader of Atwood's text or the adult perspective of her retrospective narrator. Moreover, the bond of affection between friends can be impulsive, frequently beyond elucidation by appeals to norms of rationality: in many cases we like people whose values we do not respect or dislike those whose behaviour is none the less deemed 'right' or 'good'. Nancy Rosenblum warns against the romanticism of friendship promulgated by theorists who offer the expressive attachments of 'direct relations' as a model for normative social interaction. The moralistic and erotic case of the language of direct relations ('faithfulness', 'intimacy', 'sharing', 'love') glosses over negative aspects of friendship like fickleness, self-interest, and unreliability. This is further exacerbated by the mistaken reliance of many political theorists on an Aristotelian notion of friendship as a model for community agreement and unity, such as that offered in the *Politics*: 'for Aristotle both citizenship and friendship resting on shared virtue are available only to men of wealth and leisure who enjoy specific physical and psychological capacities for ethical life; the exclusion of women and slaves from both justice and friendship indicates how central election and exclusion are.'[11]

Certainly, the sense of belonging and familiarity afforded to subjects by friendship communities may be bought at the cost of marginalization, exclusion, and separation of others. Those who are different, unfamiliar, and alien are traditionally excluded from these sorts of communities, which are frequently based on shared characteristics such as religious belief, sexual preference, and race. We might rightly question the desirability of such communities as a model for social interaction on political levels, stressing instead, with liberal theorists, the value of a society based on justice as fairness and the purportedly neutral framework of equality which it provides for all its citizens. But to raise these objections is to miss Friedman's point. She is surely not advocating the affective bonds between members of friendship communities as *the* model

[11] Nancy Rosenblum, *Another Liberalism: Liberalism and the Reconstruction of Liberal Thought* (Cambridge, Mass., and London: Harvard University Press, 1987), 181.

for *all* interpersonal social relations. She is suggesting that friendship attachments can be expressive of personal choice, and that the movement of subjects between a variety of affective associations reveals a degree of subjective autonomy.

Many of the communities of friendship are willingly chosen. *Why* they are chosen, whether to further self-interested aims or mercenary ends or to provide positive mutual support, is another issue entirely. So too is the question of the exclusionist nature of affective ties. What is vital is that they are *chosen*, not simply discovered by virtue of the accident of circumstance. If we see Friedman's conception of chosen friendship-community definition as a model for the way in which human subjects (not simply women) are at once defined by their embeddedness in certain intersubjective structures, yet also possess a degree of choice with regard to the communities in which they choose to be situated, then we may find here a model which accords to human subjects a limited, but not insubstantial liberty, one which is more commensurate with the experiential reality of being human than either the hardline communitarian or the hardline liberal account of selfhood. Community, as I define it, includes this element of choice.

But we need to go further. I have claimed that not only are we able to exercise a degree of choice with regard to the formative communities we opt to enter, leave, and move between, but also that we are able to actively change, and in some measure create, the protocols which structure these communities. The key here, as I have hinted, lies in the creativity of language *use*. Communities are to be understood as collectivities of shared language use: communal members share discursive protocols which enable them to communicate meaningfully. Abstract theorizing about the totalitarian procedures of language understood as monolithic and universal offers no help here. An ahistorical semantics focused on the abstract structures of *langue* needs to be replaced by a context-specific consideration of language use in and between individual communities of discourse. In particular, we need to consider the ways in which discursive communities and their members are able to adapt and revise the protocols of reading and interpretation, the 'rules' for language use which order their communicative interactions. Maintaining the notion of plural communities and multiple attachments is important. Meaningful communication or interpretation does not simply entail following prescriptive, pre-given rules. When interpreting texts (whether fictional texts or the texts of selfhood), individuals draw on their plural participation in a changing hierarchy of discursive communities, each of which offers alternative (albeit sometimes conflictual) protocols and strategies for interpretation and language use. Strategies learned or developed in one community may be used creatively to modify or subvert those that prevail in other communities. The ever changing communicative matrix makes available to subjects inter-pretative resources from a variety of discursive communities which may cross-fertilize, challenge, and subvert the rules of others.

Language-games and Rule-bound Free Play

> We need protocols of reading for the same reason that we need other codes and customs—because we desire a frame-work in which to negotiate our differences.
>
> Scholes, *Protocols of Reading*

Clearly, no community of discourse is 'neutral' in the sense that it simply functions as an apolitical arena within which the free play of individual (ex)change can occur. Communities are bound by shared conventions which order the meaningful interactions of their members. Too readily, however, these legitimizing conven-tions and protocols may be naturalized as abstract and indisputable laws or rules. Compliance with them, in acts of understood com-munication or comprehensible behaviour, or in the presentation of a consistent, readable personal identity, is thought to be enforced conformity, the mere reinscription of the mandates of coercive or hegemonic control. So conceived, intersubjective protocols sustain certain correct procedures which do not permit transgression except at the cost of reprobation, exclusion, or even punishment (endorsements of conventional behaviour through praise, tax-breaks, promotion, and so on may also function as more covert means of procedural control). It might be argued that, regardless of the manner of their constitution, whether adopted by 'free' choice or ostensibly instituted on the basis of majority or even consensual agreement, once in place, the rules that facilitate meaningful communication inevitably limit and constrain the agency of the speaking subject or the meaning of a text.

Such a conclusion is founded on a misguided equation of (negotiable) conventions and (prescriptive) rules. Within the necessarily restrictive terms of communal conventions, we possess a great deal more freedom than deterministic philosophies are willing to concede. This freedom is not absolute, of course, but qualified by the requirements of interactive consistency and referentiality. This qualified freedom remains distinct from the radically individualistic freedom of excommunication, by which I mean a wholesale severance of self (or one's self-expressions) from the norms of some discursive community, an impossible condition of alienation that is sometimes naïvely predicated as the necessary condition for existential freedom. *Anomie*, understood by Emile Durkheim as a lamentable consequence of the late nineteenth-century deterioration of traditional social relationships, has become in the twentieth century the desirable goal of radical individualism:

What Durkheim did not foresee was a time when the same condition of *anomie* would be assigned to the status of an achievement by and a reward for a self, which had, by separating itself from the social relationships of traditions, succeeded, so it believed, in emancipating itself. This self-defined success becomes in different versions the freedom from bad faith of the Sartrian individual who rejects determinate social roles, the homelessness of Deleuze's nomadic thinker, and the presupposition of Derrida's choice between remaining 'within,' although a stranger to, the already constructed social and intellectual edifice, but only in order to deconstruct it from within, or brutally placing oneself outside in a condition of rupture and discontinuity.[12]

The injunction to alienated excommunication is an unfortunate feature of much iconoclastic literary theory. Contemporary authors are urged to employ, or are interpreted as employing, radical tactics of excommunication in their deviance from conventional norms of narrative procedure. It is claimed, moreover, that deviant contemporary novels provide models for wider social subversions. Textual fragmentation, discontinuity, and dissemination are read as acts of political emancipation, and the martyrdom of anti-narrational self-erasure is celebrated as heroic. Texts, it is argued, should reach 'beyond' or 'beneath' or 'outside' the communicative boundaries of the articulable and narrativizable, into the unknown, the unknowable. Poststructural liberation is theor-

[12] Alasdair MacIntyre, *Whose Justice? Which Rationality?* (London: Duckworth, 1988), 369.

ized as inexpressible, formless, unarticulable, 'the undefined work of freedom' in Michel Foucault's phrase.[13] Without a fundamentally conceptual framework which theorizes the (re)cognition of radically disruptive and experimental art in ways which allow for the development of critical knowledge (albeit negative), the political value of radically anti-narrative texts is hard to imagine. If they are wholly excommunicated, if they abstain from conforming to some manner of communicative convention, their radical gestures will be without (understood) value. In order for such art to *mean*, to have *value*, it must be conceptually apprehended and interpreted within the intersubjective values of a community of discourse, even if in a negative or challenging relation to that community. The cost of a wholesale rejection of communicative conformity in disruptive art must surely be meaninglessness: texts must be utterly unreadable, radically discontinuous, for only in this way can they escape the containment of readerly apprehension. But this is not the case in numerous contemporary fictions which, while rejecting established narrative conventions, do not abandon meaning. Their iconoclasm is recognizable as a narrative of rebellion, in which the author/text (and perhaps the reader) features as antinomian hero. It seems inescapable that if acts of excommunicative martyrdom are to be understood *as such*, they must be recognizable *as* strategies within the tactical repertoire of a political movement, or at least inscribed within the value system of a particular theoretical stance. Putative self-destructive rupture or discontinuity becomes a means of proclaiming autonomy. Moreover, as Tobin Siebers asks, 'What happens to this moral triumph [of textual or critical self-sacrifice] . . . when martyrdom assumes the form of a theory, when it acquires the magnitude of a movement, when martyrdom becomes systematic?'[14]

[13] Michel Foucault, *The Foucault Reader*, ed. Paul Rainbow (New York: Pantheon, 1984), 46; cited in Steele, 'How Philosophy of Language Informs Ethics and Politics', 169. Steele calls into question the logical validity of 'the utopian desires in poststructuralist texts [that] seek forms that are so discontinuous with the present that they cannot be formulated'.

[14] Tobin Siebers, *The Ethics of Criticism* (Ithaca, NY: Cornell University Press, 1988), 99. Siebers provides an interesting critique of the limitations of such a stance of self-marginalized exile in his analysis of contemporary criticism. He suggests that critics like Edward Said, Paul de Man, and Jacques Derrida maintain 'the persona of the exile', and aspire to a Lukácsian ideal of 'transcendental homelessness' (11). These critical thinkers try 'to capture an aura of innocence and moral

How valid is the theoretical injunction to what I have been calling excommunicative freedom—the radical break from all communal norms and conventions? Does contemporary fiction truly concur with the abolition of readable narratives in order to avoid the insidious self-betrayal of ideological reinscription? Is the innovation and experimentation we find in contemporary fiction only a defeated and defeatist attempt to deny the closure of intellectual apprehension? It is my contention that anti-realist contemporary fictions, far from endorsing a despairing ethic of self-mutilation (of mute silence or disseminated dismemberment), in fact works towards an entirely different end. They offer models of (partial) self-determination through narrative creativity in which the human 'textual' condition is viewed as constructive and potentially redemptive. They reveal the way in which alternative communities of discourse may be structured through the invention of new (but intersubjectively understood) conventions, and how existing communities may be modified through self-reflexive monitoring of their own procedures and protocols. My consideration of a number of radically experimental novels in Chapter 4 is intended to explore the limits of our qualified (because convention-bound) personal freedom and the capacity we possess for its expression, without retreating to a theoretical position which situates personal (and textual) authenticity only in a tactical stance of self-annihilation.

Instead of insisting that social situatedness always precedes our self-conceptions and that for this reason voluntarism is simply an illusion, we should begin, rather, with the fact that contestation, challenge, and the need to make choices can and do occur within the bounds of social discourse and everyday human interaction. Moral dilemmas, personal and public, are a feature of daily life; disputes and disagreements frequently arise between speakers of the same language or inhabitants of the same community;

disinterestedness by cultivating personal marginality . . . [and] to represent the critical consciousness as exiled and marginal' (12). He contends that this rhetoric of homelessness and exile is 'proof that the critic is not implicated in either repression or normality, but . . . also represents the critic as exclusive and different when compared to other mortals' (12). Siebers warns, however, against 'the dangers of turning marginality and suffering into a commodity or privileged claim to critical insight'; the 'power of marginality', he asserts, 'is purchased at an enormous expense by modern critics', because it threatens 'to achieve a distance from the real issues of living and choosing in the world' (12–13).

misinterpretations and reinterpretations are commonplace; and ambiguity is a fundamental feature of both written and spoken language. Debate, discrepancy, conflict, and confusion, on both inter-and intra-personal levels, seem central to our experience of what it is to be human. Social criticism and protest, that which 'takes place when we determine that social institutions and arrangements contradict our social norms and ideas', is a fact of modern society which constructivist theories are hard put to explain.[15] Likewise, internal criticism and self-evaluation—-the capacity for an individual to discern conflict among her beliefs, experience doubt about her values, or reassess her convictions—is a familiar aspect of existence that is rendered inexplicable by determinist theories of always-already subjectivity. A pluralist theory goes some way towards explaining how such circumstances and experiences of conflict, criticism, and protest might arise. An understanding of the capacity of individuals to subvert and modify the rules or conventions of the communities within which they are constituted takes us even further.

In *Textual Power* Robert Scholes draws a useful analogy between the conventions that order linguistic processes and game-play, and the law of gravity:

If you play chess you can only do certain things with the pieces—or you will no longer be playing chess. But those constraints in themselves never tell you what move to make. Language does not speak, any more than the law of gravity falls. Furthermore, language is changed by speech, though gravity is not changed by any act of falling or flying. (153)

Despite (and because of) the existence of game rules, individual chess-players exercise a high degree of autonomy when choosing the moves they will make, albeit that these choices are limited by the functional possibilities of the piece they are moving, its position on the board, the moves of their opponents, their own intellectual resources, their experience of playing the game, and so on. Game rules facilitate individual choice—without them, the movements of pieces on the chess-board would be arbitrary. The difference between the intersubjectively understood conventions that order interaction in (language or communication) games and

[15] Mark S. Cladis, 'Wittgenstein, Rawls and Conservatism', *Philosophy and Social Criticism*, 20/1–2 (1994), 18.

the law of gravity is that the former are open to revision and change, while the latter is not. Put another way, the former are mutable, potentially negotiable conventions, whereas the latter is a non-negotiable physical law. The distinction is vital in terms of theories which explore the linguistic constitution of the texts of selfhood and all too readily urge resignation to their rule-bound determinism.

Situated within the bounds of a variety of rule-bound communities, human subjects have the capacity for creative play. A number of contemporary literary critics have developed a theory of playful creative transgression in the writing and reading of literary texts, and from this the possibility of free-playing creativity by human textual subjects. Patricia Yaeger, in *Honey-Mad Women*, is exemplary in this respect. In her first chapter she approvingly quotes from Teresa de Lauretis's *Alice Doesn't*:

As a form of political critique or critical politics, feminism has not only 'invented' new strategies, new semiotic contents, and new signs, but more importantly it has effected a habit-change in readers, spectators, speakers, etc. And with that habit change it has produced a new social subject, women. The practice of self-consciousness, in short, has a constitutiveness as well as a constituency.[16]

However, Yaeger dismisses the high-minded seriousness of de Lauretis's work and her 'negative reading of women's linguistic powers' (20). 'Why', she asks, 'is it fashionable to dramatise "male" language as the chief source of our danger rather than as an opportunity for dialogue and revision?' (22)—a question which is not intended to deny that 'male' language can be dangerous, but rather to point towards a revisionary conception of language: language as a rule-bound structure within which we have freedom to play.

The notion of playfulness is central to Yaeger's argument in *Honey-Mad Women*. In utilizing ludic metaphors, she seeks to articulate a 'descriptive category that will clarify the way in which the woman writer introduces "free" energy into the "bound" energy of her culture's texts' (207). Yaeger acknowledges, but dismisses, the Freudian conception of play as imitative and normative, of play-as-ritual that enacts and endorses social norms, as a process that sanctions and thus disempowers transgression. She recognizes

[16] Patricia Yaeger, *Honey-Mad Women: Emancipatory Strategies in Women's Writing* (New York: Columbia University Press, 1988), 19.

that gaming may be ideologically complicit, 'part of the nexus of power and constraint' (214) that maintains the *status quo*; but she concludes that awareness of this potential for complicity in gaming does not invalidate its subversive creative capacities. Play in fact draws attention to the flexibility of inherited communal and communicative rules: it shows the manner in which rules can be altered, revised, and invented by consciousness-raising play.

The assertion that consciousness-raising play can effect changes or alterations in (textual and social) game 'rules' *from within* their prescriptive bounds needs further elucidation. A brief look at the later Wittgenstein may be useful here. In the shift from the *Tractatus Logico-Philosophicus* to the work that culminated in the *Philosophical Investigations*, Wittgenstein developed the notion of disparate, incommensurate language-games, each governed by its own set of rules, as the sites of meaning and value constitution beyond which there is no higher sanction. Using the analogy of rule-bound games to suggest the manner in which intersubjective communication takes place, Wittgenstein draws attention to the systematic nature of language operations. This sceptical position is not without difficulty, as it may be taken to imply that the rule-bound nature of socio-linguistic games evacuates autonomy on the part of the human subjects that utilize and are constituted within them. Indeed, Wittgenstein has been charged with conservatism with respect to his view of the situated social subject. If human beings and their morality are constituted in the rule-bound procedures of a socio-linguistic community (as Wittgenstein avers), then how can individuals bring about social change? If existing traditions and communities provide the foundation for critical moral judgement, then how can social subjects ever gain the necessary objectivity and distance to critique them?

In an article defending Wittgenstein against charges of conservatism, Mark S. Cladis considers Wittgenstein's statements in *Philosophical Investigations* about the justifying rules of socio-linguistic practices ('This is simply what I do' or 'I obey the rule blindly'):[17]

His statements on rules belittle autonomy only in that they controvert the autonomy of logic and the isolated individual's ability to follow a

---

[17] Ludwig Wittgenstein, *Philosophical Investigations*, trans. G. E. M. Anscombe (Oxford: Basil Blackwell, 1953), paras. 217 and 218; cited in Cladis, 'Wittgenstein, Rawls and Conservatism', 17.

rule without prior social training. His comments, however, do not touch on practical human autonomy (for example, a senator courageously taking an ethical though unpopular stand on a public issue during an election year) or on critical reasoning (the senator's ability to offer reasons in opposition to those who say, 'This is simply what we do'). [Rules] are not prescriptions for a comprehensive way of life or for grounding moral character. Moreover, to say there are no transcendent justifications for rules is not to say there are no good justifications.[18]

Rules are less prescriptive than procedural. They provide the necessary frameworks within which social subjects can make meaningful choices and register social criticism. It is this last point that interests me most. Cladis argues that, far from being con-servative, Wittgenstein's philosophy can in fact account for and support social evaluation and protest: social subjects have the capacity for internal criticism—that is, criticism from within the procedural rules of plural socio-linguistic practices. Morality may be socially produced, but society is far more than 'a monolithic force that reproduces itself as a seamless moral whole' (17). The heterogeneity of sometimes conflictual social practices, norms, and institutions precludes any simple reduction to a fixed, reproduced moral coding in its members. In fact, it supports protest, which results from the subject's placement in a variety of socio-linguistic communities or language-games.

Radicals and reactionaries speak the same basic language. Their messages divide them. To say that we can all understand each other is only to point out that we are standing on the same basic, sociolinguistic ground. It does not tell us if we are brandishing swords or worse, or what we are standing for. (22)

Positing a common ground of intersubjective understanding, a rule-bound socio-linguistic arena, does not preclude the possibility of contestation of belief between subjects, or necessitate that they all say the same thing or mean the same thing when using the same words.

Ferdinand de Saussure's most enduring bequest to linguistic theory was his definition of the sign as the unit of meaning (and, as I have suggested, his most damaging legacy was his bracketing

---

[18] Cladis, 'Wittgenstein, Rawls and Conservatism', 17–18. Cladis seeks to defend Rawls against the charge of conservatism, and does so by considering the work of the later Wittgenstein, in which he finds many affinities with that of Rawls. Further references to this article will be cited in the text.

of the socio-historic contexts of language use in his focus on the abstract procedures of *langue*). In order to stress the systematic differential constitution of the sign and the rule-bound nature of language, he frequently appealed to ludic metaphors. The lines of his argument, set forth posthumously in *Cours de linguistique générale*, are familiar: difference, rather than identity, is posited as the origin of meaning. Just as the value of an element in a game is not intrinsic to the element itself, but consists in the relations of this element to other elements which are established in the rules of the game; so too is the meaning of a linguistic element not intrinsic but conventional, constituted in the relationship between signifier and signified which composes the sign and that between the multiplicity of other signs from which the sign is distinct. Consider a pack of cards as the metaphorical equivalent of the set of words which make up a language. The value of each card is not immanent and exclusive, but consists in the conventions of play which *are* the game we play with the cards at any given point in time. The same material card, perhaps a three of diamonds, can have an entirely different value in two different games—high in canasta, low in bridge; its meaning inheres in the way the card is played, and this playing is prescribed by the rules, the 'grammar', of the particular game. To play bridge or canasta meaningfully, to understand the value of the cards, requires knowledge of this grammar, or else there is no game, but only the random, non-significatory placement of cards on a table-top. Cards function as signs only when the relationship between signifier and signified (in other words, the value of the card) is fixed and understood by all players in the game. So too in language, in the terms of this analogy, playing the game of communication requires the tacit acknowledgement between players of the rules of relationship which *are* the meaning of each sign used. The transfer of meaning between two or more communicators, like the playing of a particular game, presupposes knowledge of, and conformity with, the grammar or rules of the language which they play in acts of speech or writing.

The fact that speakers in different language systems use radically different signifiers to refer to a common signified (the Afrikaans word 'blom', the French word 'fleur', and the English word 'flower' all refer to the same botanical signified), or that the same homophone can refer to wholly variant signifieds both within a given language and between alternative languages, suggests the arbitrariness of the value-establishing relationship which deter-mines the meaning of a particular sign. Once established, however, this relationship must remain fixed and intersubjectively under-stood if the sign is to function as such—otherwise put, if the sign is to have *meaning*.

This model of meaning and value construction can be extended to the field of morality, with disturbing consequences for those who wish to hold on to the metaphysical convictions of moral absolutism. On such a view, the value of a particular deed or action, its rightness or wrongness, can equally be seen to be arbitrarily established, yet synchronically fixed, in conventions of social interplay. Moral laws, so conceived, are not determined absolutes, externally ordained dictates 'written in stone' like the tablets of Moses and, so inscribed, fixed for perpetuity: the Word. Instead, they are to be regarded as standardized permutations, as simply a conventionally prioritized mode of being. A moral law, then, is never absolute, even if it functions as an absolute within given contexts; its value is intersubjectively fixed, understood as law, while in fact it is only one of an infinite number of alternative modes of acting. (The capacity we have to transgress and challenge moral 'law' will be considered in Chapter 6.)

It is a mistaken leap from the recognition of the convention-bound nature of meaning-construction to the belief that these conventions are rules which govern our behaviour and restrict our freedom with some kind of coercive tyranny, a coercion which we can oppose only by excommunication: self-isolation, alienation from the community and the silent refusal to communicate, radical fragmentation. This misunderstanding originates in the belief that (linguistic) conventions imply the imperious compulsion or pre-scriptive command of incontestable law, in the sense that one *must* perform in such and such a prescribed way. To accept Saussure's proposition that the rules of language are fixed—that is, are pragmatically stable—need not entail resigned acceptance that the game of language is itself fixed. This is only to reintroduce the concept of some shadowy fixer (language, ideology, patri-archy), the idea of tyrannous extra-personal agency which lurks behind so many of the urgent claims in contemporary theory.

Even the most simple game offers the possibility of multiple alternative choices of action, *within* the rules, for each turn of play. There is never only one way to move. Selective play, choice, is essential to our understanding of game-play.[19] If, when we played a game, our playing were merely compulsive, a series of automatic, predictable responses already encoded in the moves of other players or in the rules of the game, or if we ourselves were moved, like pawns, by some extra-personal (metaphysical) player, it would be no game at all. Automatism and passivity are very far removed from what we conceive of as (strategic) play: when we play, we have the ability to rationalize and choose our moves in accordance with the information and circumstances at hand or knowledge accumulated from past experience. We are never merely causal conduits or elements played. Moreover, game rules make possible—indeed, are a necessary condition for—transgressional play: we can choose to deviate from the rules only because there are rules to challenge; this deviancy has meaning only within a field of play constituted by conventions that are understood by players (and frequently spectators too). In every game there is the potential for alternative, rule-breaking play, and our deviance has meaning only in relation to the understood rules of the game. Misplay, misunderstanding, and ambiguity are always present as possibilities in any game.

Of course, the problem remains that our transgressions—willed or inadvertent—may be regarded by other players, by referees and spectators, as punishable deviations. It is in this sense that conventions *can* function in ways that exert a very real constraint on our actions. Yet, if we are to live and communicate with others, we must abandon the utopian imperatives of an ethic of negative freedom which understands liberty as the unqualified capacity for wholly individual choice in disregard of others. The avaricious

---

[19] Of course, there is a sense in which games *are* weighted, if not wholly predetermined: we are dealt a given set of cards, possess a particular set of personal characteristics and qualities. No amount of wishful thinking or hopeful theorizing on my part will change the fact that I hold a three of diamonds in my hand, or the fact that I am a woman, or the fact that I have brown eyes. But this is not to suggest a deterministic philosophy in which responsibility for one's choices and actions are lost to the notion of chance or destiny; see Daniel Dennett, *Elbow Room: The Varieties of Free Will Worth Wanting* (Oxford, Clarendon Press, 1984), 95–8. My 'free play' inheres in the way I play my given hand, the way in which I use and manipulate the possibilities available to me, and in the capacity I have to negotiate new rules, new systems of value determination, with other players in the game (e.g. I cannot change the biological fact of my sex, but the value of womanhood can be (and has been) negotiated in a manner which defines this given in terms other than those of liability). Radically, my free play lies in my ability to abandon the game I am presently playing and choose to play another instead.

indulgence of individual free will, regardless of the needs or desires of others, involves our imposition on their freedom—and, likewise, theirs on ours. Without protocols to order interpersonal exchanges, human interplay would be reduced to an individualistic battle of wills and impulses, in which triumph is accorded to those with greater brute strength, rhetorical skill, or manipulative cunning. Robert Scholes suggests that the social constitution of subjectivity is premissed on respect for others in all our acts of (textual) interplay:

In reading we find ourselves, to be sure, but only through the language of the Other, whose existence we must respect. . . . We must respect the Other in the text because, as human beings, we have a dimension that is irreducibly social. We have been constructed as human subjects by interacting with other people, learning their language and their ways of behaving. Having come to consciousness this way, we have an absolute need for communication. As human subjects we must exchange meanings with others who we recognise as subjects like ourselves, whose desire to communicate we need to respect, in order to confirm our own right to be treated as subjects rather than objects. In every act of reading the irreducible otherness of reader and writer is balanced and opposed by this need for recognition and understanding between the two parties. . . . We need protocols of reading for the same reason that we need other codes and customs—because we desire a framework in which to negotiate our differences.[20]

To live in radical defiance (or ignorance) of the shared protocols that frame our human interactions, destructively impervious to others and radically unobservant of their needs, is hardly what we consider to be a condition of healthy personhood. In fact, a radically solipsistic or autistic divorce or dislocation from others is frequently held to be an indication of debilitating (psychological) illness. This is an idea explored in contemporary fictions like J. M. Coetzee's *The Life and Times of Michael K* (1983), Marie Cardinal's autobiographical *The Words to Say It* (1975), and Janet Frame's *Faces in the Water* (1961). We might note by contrast a number of contemporary fictions, such as Margaret Atwood's *Surfacing* (1972) and Joan Barfoot's *Gaining Ground* (1978), which valorize escape into the 'wilderness', perceived as the only alternative to the repressive prescriptions of familial and social communities, and in doing so, push dangerously close to an

[20] Scholes, *Protocols of Reading*, 51.

advocacy of excommunication. I will challenge the utopian escapism of novels such as these in Chapter 8.

Our freedom as communally situated human subjects is never absolute. It rests in our capacity for calculated choice between a variety of discursive strategies and interpretative sites, choice made in awareness of the consequences of deviant misplay. We have the ability to partake in the constitution of communal rules, by choosing to affirm or ignore their prescriptions; we may even refuse particular communal restrictions by choosing to leave one community of discourse and enter another (to opt out of all communities is suicide, an absolutist expression of self-assertion which is also, paradoxically, radically self-destructive). These are the fundamental premises of pragmatic 'liberal communitarianism': a conception of human subjectivity which understands the subject to be both mediated or defined by a community of others and mediating, in so far as she has a certain capacity to enter into, actively influence, transform, and even leave a variety of self-defining communities.

There is no question that writing (in its broadest poststructuralist sense) can control, and that the conventions and ideological values inherent in language can, and do, shape our behaviour and our beliefs. As we are constantly reminded, language is never innocent. Far from being a neutral medium, it is imbued with the ideological values of dominant social institutions and orders of power, ideological values which we maintain intact by 'playing the game' and adhering to the rules of correct play. In using language, it is argued, we passively reaffirm the potentially limiting values (and identities) which are encoded in the rules of linguistic and moral play. This pessimistic analysis of linguistic operation, which would seem to preclude any possibility of useful contestation, typifies the nihilistic tendencies of poststructuralist theories which turn on a nostalgic yearning for the absolute certainty and existential authenticity which their philosophical allegiances would deny.

But pessimism is not the necessary consequence of a realization of conventional structuration; such a realization can lead to an enlightened awareness of our capacity for self-determination through systematic change. Barbara Johnson reminds us that '[w]hat enslaves is not writing per se but control of writing, and writing as control. What we need is not less writing, but more consciousness of how it works.'[21] Greater awareness of the way in which writing 'works' to control its users is precisely what many contemporary fictions (particularly ostentatiously self-reflexive meta-fictions) attempt to provoke in their readers: a self-reflexive awareness of what it is we do with language and what, in turn, it does to us. This consciousness need not bring with it a despairing vision of extra-personal writtenness, but a recognition of our power as free-playing interpreters. We are players in multiple language-games who can not only break the rules, but make them too. We have the capacity for *creative deviancy*.

The disciplines of linguistics, anthropology, and psychology show us how frequently rules and conventions undergo changes—the meanings of words do not remain constant through time or space; fundamentally different values and conceptions of the good life are held by particular communities or historical eras; customs and manners are the provenance of class and station; a person's moral values or behavioural standards may alter significantly from one context to another (murder, for example, is sanctioned in wartime); the attitudes and beliefs of a single individual may alter considerably in the course of her lifetime. All these changes occur because the understood rules which constitute the meaning of signs, words, and texts are not given for perpetuity, but are contextually created and always open to revision.

Rule changes occur in at least two ways. The first, which may be called 'evolutionary', derive from chance permutations or the unforeseen mutation of existing rules and elemental values which have, as their consequence, the modification of exciting games (systems of signification) or the development of new ones. It is in recognizing this mode of change that many contemporary fictions celebrate the liberating potential of aleatory textual play, inviting readers to participate in the 'chance' construction of textual meaning through the action of (re)combinative play. Contemporary *bricolage* texts, like Georges Perec's *Life: A User's Manual* (1970) and Cortàzar's *Hopscotch* (1963), suggest the proliferation of recombinative possibilities that inhere in the act of reading. The former is composed as a series of digressions, each complete as a narrative in its own right, and the reader is required to 'puzzle' out

[21] Barbara Johnson, 'Writing', in Frank Lentricchia and Thomas McLaughlin (eds.), *Critical Terms for Literary Study* (Chicago and London: University of Chicago Press, 1990), 48.

a coherent order for the story, despite the multiple ways in which the digressions may be sequenced. In the latter, the reader may choose to progress through the book by following the numbered chapters sequentially or by 'hopscotching' between chapters according to a list provided in the table of instructions which prefaces the book. In both books, the various combinations of elements (digressions, chapters) result in radically different apprehensions of the text by the reader. 'Cut-up' texts, popularized in the 1960s by William Burroughs, are constructed using a similar principle of recombinative play, and exemplify another mode for the fictional exploration of change-inducing chance.[22] But evolutionary change is a double-edged sword; its emancipatory capacity is severely circumscribed by the abandonment of personal responsibility to unintentional chance that it entails. In texts such as these, intentionality is abandoned in favour of chance permutation. The belief that rule changes are only ever brought about by chance is a dangerous misassumption. A celebration of chance spontaneity can just as easily become a lamentation of random causality if one holds that all action and meaning are merely the effects of uncontrolled, arbitrary contingency.

The second mode of rule change, which may be called 'revolutionary', is the intentional result of personal agency, the deliberate abandonment of one convention in favour of another. Revolutionary changes may result from repeated transgressional play in which occurrences of deviation finally outweigh those of conformity, supplanting them as the norm. Herein lies the revisionary capacity of free play understood as creative deviance within the bounds of understood convention: it is not only rule-breaking, but potentially rule-making as well. Once conscious of our capacity to change the rules by which we read (and write and live), we are able to challenge or affirm, through our consequent revolutionary (mis)play, the bounds of those conventions which enable us to

---

[22] More extreme examples of the fictional *bricolage* text include A. B. Paulsen's '2', *Tri-Quarterly*, 26 (Winter 1973), n.p.; and Marc Sapporta's *Composition No. 1* (Paris: Seuil, 1962). In the former, the reader is invited to cut, fold, and paste the printed page that comprises the text, according to given directions, so forming a three-dimensional, ten-sided die. On each of the ten faces is a phrase or sentence, and the progressions of the plot are literally left to chance as the reader is urged to play out possible permutations by throwing the die and reading the words which appear on the uppermost face after each throw. Marc Supporta's text comprises an unbound collection of printed pages which the reader is asked to shuffle and deal at random.

construct meanings within community. This, then, is free play, recognition of what Allen Thiher calls our 'rule-bound freedom— how creation takes place within the constraints of law'.[23]

It is the potential of 'rule-bound freedom', of creative deviancy, which many contemporary fictions seek to explore in the analogy they draw between games and writing, a qualified liberty which I would like to extend to the gaming communal subject. In presenting themselves as self-conscious ludic constructs, these texts suggest ways in which we can gain, and productively utilize, 'more consciousness of how [writing] works'. So Thiher:

the writer can view his struggle with language less as a condemnation to defeat than as an agonistic encounter for which he can invent some of the rules. He finds himself in the position to invent some of the rules and make them explicit so that his fiction does not appear to receive its game plan from sources other than itself.[24]

In appealing to the self-same metaphors of textuality which some critics have employed to lament the inauthenticity and writtenness of our being, we can begin to consider ways in which the potentially revolutionary process of textual free play can be fruitfully transposed to the concept of textualized identity; playfulness offers a means of theorizing the creative possibilities available to human subjects within community.

[23] Allen Thiher, *Words in Reflection: Modern Language Theory and Postmodern Fiction* (Chicago: University of Chicago Press, 1984), 61.
[24] Ibid. 156.

3

Feminist Linguistic Determinism

> The problem is as follows: how can a subject transcending
> the given be constituted in the given?
>
> Deleuze, *Empiricism and Subjectivity*

Linguistic creativity has been celebrated by a number of recent feminist theorists, who extol the virtues of creative play in the texts of literature and society. In this chapter I want to look at the way in which feminists have utilized the insights of poststructuralist theory in order to bolster such a position. But the absorption of poststructuralist claims into feminist theory is problematic. What seems to be at issue is a fundamental conflict between the emancipatory impulses of feminism and the deterministic ethos that ostensibly underlies the poststructuralist theories to which many contemporary feminists are attracted. In much recent feminist theory we find an uneasy merging of conceptions of the (female) subject as a political agent *and* as a decentred social construct. In some cases, poststructuralist theories of decentred subjectivity are harnessed to drive forward the liberationist claims of feminism. The reasons for this perhaps unlikely alliance, and the problems which arise from it, are instructive.

The new wave of feminism in the late 1960s and 1970s created a movement in which the acquisition of knowledge was closely aligned with power: it was assumed that the more that women knew about the world and gender relations, the more power they would have to challenge and dismantle the prescriptions of patriarchy.[1] The early manifestos of second-wave feminism stressed the importance to women of increasing their knowledge through

---

[1] See Maureen McNeil, 'Dancing with Foucault: Feminism and Power-Knowledge', in Caroline Ramazanoğlu (ed.), *Up against Foucault: Explorations of Some Tensions between Foucault and Feminism* (London and New York: Routledge, 1993), 147–75. McNeil refers to the women who gave birth to second-wave feminism as 'daughters of the Enlightenment' in so far as they seemed to inherit Enlightenment assumptions about the value of reason and knowledge as tools of power (149).

intensive investigations of the patriarchy and through conscious-ness-raising.[2] Women were to refuse the oppressive constraints of traditional conceptions of femininity, by authorizing their own scripts of being. They were to speak and write their own version of (female) subjectivity, a version conceived in opposition to the implicitly masculine subject of liberal humanism. But the feminist project of disowning the liberal humanist subject and constructing their own conception of 'woman' was limited by the assumption of the identity of all women. As many critics have noted, in this strategic move, feminism merely reproduced its own version of essentialism founded on a generalized, idealized (white, Western, middle-class, heterosexual) 'woman', one that was perhaps as exclusionary as the traditional conception it was attempting to refute.[3] One response to this was the recognition and celebration of difference among women: women might be black, lesbian, working-class, disabled, middle-aged, and so on. The 'woman's movement' fractured into a diversity of groups whose members identified with particular aspects of common experience: black feminists, lesbian feminists, or whatever. But, as Liz Bondi sug-gests, this identity politics has significant limitations. It resulted in the diffusion of the emancipatory feminist impulse into a variety of feminisms to which women belonged on the basis of their *discovered* characteristics of ethnicity, sexuality, age, and so on.

While it challenged misguided assumptions about 'sisterhood' in import-ant and necessary ways, the assertion of multiple identities eclipsed the earlier emphasis on identity as fractured. Reliance upon apparently pre-given categories of class, sexual orientation, race, ethnicity and so on invoked a conception of identity as something to be acknowledged or uncovered rather than constructed, as something fixed rather than changing. Implicitly, therefore, this approach to the issues of the differ-ences among women appealed to a conception of the subject as centred and coherent, that is, to something very close to the liberal humanist model. The chief difference lay in the insistence that there are many, rather than just one, essences of identity.[4]

    [2] See Juliet Mitchell, *Woman's Estate* (Harmondsworth: Penguin, 1974), 61–2.
    [3] See Elizabeth V. Spelman, *Inessential Woman* (London: Women's Press, 1990); and Diana Fuss, *Essentially Speaking: Feminism, Nature and Difference* (London: Routledge, 1989).
    [4] Liz Bondi, 'Locating Identity Politics', in Michael Keith and Steve Pile (eds.), *Place and the Politics of Identity* (London and New York: Routledge, 1993), 93.

Divisive identity politics, then, threatened the efficacy of the feminist emancipatory project: 'the once exhilarating proposition that there is no "essential" female nature has been elaborated to the point where it is now often used to scare "women" away from making *any* generalisations about or political claims on behalf of a group called "women".'[5] Identity politics achieved 'the production of parallel, analogous, but rarely intersecting channels of radical political consciousness'.[6] What woman could speak for, or make claims on behalf of 'women', without assimilating other women's differences into her own totalizing experience? Recognizing the unassimilable nature of women's experiential difference was, in fact, politically enervating.

A return to exclusionary essentialism, however, is not the only response available to those resistant to the divisiveness of identity politics. Another response is the advocacy of a poststructuralist critique of liberal humanism and the positing of a radically de-centred (female) subject. French feminists have been most ready to appropriate some of the insights of poststructuralism. It is simply not enough, they argue, to challenge male canonical authority and the representation of women in mainstream social and literary texts, the revisionary tactics practised by Anglo-American feminism. They propose a radical reassessment of (female) subjectivity using the tools provided by poststructuralist theory and (particularly Lacanian) psychoanalysis. But significant problems surround the contemporary French feminist analysis of subjectivity, most notably the insistence on linguistic determinism. Language processes (which include traditional narrative and communicative strategies) are regarded with deep suspicion, for it is thought that they not only reinscribe the patriarchal cultural norms which marginalize women, but that they also encode the conception of femininity. In other words, the text of femininity is understood to be the creation of phallocentric patriarchal discourse. In 'Castration or Decapitation' (1976), Hélène Cixous explains:

Everything turns on the Word: everything is the Word and only the Word. . . . we must take culture at its word, as it takes us into its word,

[5] Tania Modeleski, *Feminism without Women: Culture and Criticism in a 'Post-feminist Age'* (London: Routledge, 1991), 15.
[6] Edward Soja and Barbara Hooper, 'The Spaces that Difference Makes: Some Notes on the Geographical Margins of the New Cultural Politics', in Keith and Pile (eds.), *Place and the Politics of Identity*, 186.

into its tongue. . . . No political reflection can dispense with reflection on language. For as soon as we exist, we are born into language and language speaks (to) us, dictates its law . . .; even at the moment of uttering a sentence . . . we are already seized by a certain kind of masculine desire.[7]

So conceived, gender is not a descriptive but an evaluative term, and 'woman' is always subordinate and inferior to 'man', the prioritized binary opposite in a signifying system that operates in terms of conceptual oppositions. For Michèle Barrett, gender means 'not simply "difference", but division, oppression, inequality, interiorized inferiority for women'.[8] The poststructuralist feminist claim that language is the medium for gender construction is intimately related to the wider philosophical concerns with the linguistic construction of the subject discussed previously. And the problems raised above with regard to the impossibility of ever being able to articulate a conception of self (or gender) which is not always already written in the terms of the dominant discourse are equally pertinent. How, it is asked, are female subjects to speak of their distinct experience and desires if not in the terms of 'man-made' language, a language internalized as the condition of self-conception and hence constitutive of their very sense of themselves?[9] How are they to attain an 'authentic' voice if their acts of linguistic expression and conscious reflection perpetuate and depend for their meaning on the order(s) of the patriarchy? In *The Daughter's Seduction* Jane Gallop writes: 'it is not the biological given of male and female that is in question . . . but the subject as constituted by the pre-existing signifying chain, that is, by culture, in which the subject must place himself.'[10] According to the Lacanian psychoanalytic theory which Gallop scrutinizes, the subject is divided by her (negative) entry into the signifying chain of language. Femininity, that which is not expressible or comprehensible in the terms of the symbolic order (understood as the patriarchal system of signification that organizes experience), is split off

---

[7] Hélène Cixous, 'Le Sexe ou la tête?', trans. as 'Castration or Decapitation?' by Annette Kuhn, *Signs*, 7/1 (1981), 44–5.

[8] Michèle Barrett, *Women's Oppression Today: Problems in Marxist Feminist Analysis* (London: Villiers Publications, 1980), 112–13.

[9] Deborah Cameron provides a powerful critique of feminist linguistic determinism in *Feminism and Linguistic Theory* (London: Macmillan, 1985).

[10] Jane Gallop, *The Daughter's Seduction: Feminism and Psychoanalysis* (Ithaca, NY: Cornell University Press, 1982), 11–12.

and repressed in the unconscious. Relegated to the realm of the repressed unconscious, the sign 'woman' remains unreadable, and female freedom is theorized as this unreadability. This gives rise to the understanding that '[w]oman is a gap, a silence, invisible and unheard, repressed in the unconscious . . . accessibly [sic] in patriarchal discourse only at the point of contradiction, meaninglessness and silence'.[11] But such a conception has dire consequences for a conception of the female individual as self-determining agent. As Gallop formulates it, 'if patriarchal culture is that within which the self originally constitutes itself, it is always already there in each subject as subject. Thus how can it be overthrown if it has necessarily been internalized in everybody who could possibly act to overthrow it?'[12]

For some feminists, women have traditionally been forced to remain silent in order to evade complicity with the traitorous 'foreign tongue' of patriarchy, to evade construction in terms of the language which would invalidate or marginalize their difference. *Authentic* female experience is incomprehensible; it is 'that which cannot be expressed because it exists outside the realm of symbolic signification'.[13] To speak is thus to act in bad faith. For women to adopt silence as a defensive tactic against putative linguistic subjection is clearly an undesirable act of self-martyrdom. It relegates women to a powerless realm outside the margins of comprehension. It requires, moreover, the denial not only of a speaking voice but also of (linguistic) self-reflection, for even the most intimate thoughts are contaminated by the patriarchal Word. Such a conception is not mitigated by the feminist interpretative tactic of attempting to 'hear' women speak in the gaps and omissions of texts, by attending to the unsettled moments at the surface of the text in which the subtext, the repressed unconscious of the text (or writer), ostensibly resonates. When silence 'speaks' thus, it is of course no longer silent. Once silence is made significant by cognitive apprehension—that is, once it is made able to signify—it is no less subject to interpretative systematization. It is filled with an interpretative voice, raised to consciousness, encoded within

---

[11] Elaine Millard, 'French Feminisms', in Sara Mills, Lynne Pierce, Sue Spaull, and Elaine Millard, *Feminist Readings/Feminists Reading* (Hemel Hempstead: Harvester Wheatsheaf, 1989), 157.

[12] Ibid. 114.

[13] Patricia Waugh, *Feminine Fictions: Revisiting the Postmodern* (London and New York: Routledge, 1989), 8.

the significatory structures it seeks to evade (and yet which give it meaning). Only absolute silence, wholesale expressive opacity, not 'silence' that speaks with or through another voice, can remain immune from apprehension. But if the negative freedom of self-sacrificial silence is inadequate, how are women to express (or know) their individuality? This is a question that Xavière Gauthier asks in 'Is There Such a Thing as Women's Writing?':

As long as women remain silent, they will be outside the historical process. But, if they begin to speak and write *as men do*, they will enter history subdued and alienated; it is a history that, logically speaking, their speech should disrupt.[14]

Gerardine Meaney pushes it even further:

The question remains whether access to history, because it requires the assumption of subjectivity, also requires subjection. If this is so, the option for women in relation to writing and to history is simply between two forms of exile, from articulation and action, or from ourselves.[15]

The response of French feminists such as Cixous and Luce Irigaray to this question is to propose the creation of a new female language and writing, *l'écriture féminine*, one which does not require women to force their experience into a system of reference and classification that endorses and sustains patriarchal values. This female language is one that will 'redress women's exclusion, that will mime the rhythms of women's bodies, permit feminine excess, express women's needs'.[16] This will be a language apart from patriarchal discourse, a language with the potential to create its own meanings. It is a language that will counterpose masculine linearity and 'phallic' closure with the openness of fluidity, tactility, and libidinal impulse. But the call for women to invent their

---

[14] Xaviere Gauthier, 'Is There Such a Thing as Women's Writing?', in Elaine Marks and Isabelle de Courtivron (eds.), *New French Feminisms* (Brighton: Harvester Press, 1980), 162–4.

[15] Gerardine Meaney, *(Un)like Subjects: Women, Theory, Fiction* (London and New York: Routledge, 1993), 99. See also Diana Tietjens Meyers, *Subjection and Subjectivity: Psychoanalytic Feminism and Moral Philosophy* (New York and London: Routledge, 1994).

[16] Patricia Yaeger, *Honey-Mad Women: Emancipatory Strategies in Women's Writing* (New York: Columbia University Press, 1988), 13. A number of critics have been concerned by the biological essentialism which appears to underscore Cixous's account. Toril Moi provides such an argument in *Sexual/Textual Politics: Feminist Literary Theory* (1985; London and New York: Routledge, 1988), 102–6; for a counter-argument defending Cixous against such charges, see Meaney, *(Un)like Subjects*, 52–9.

own language is surely utopian within the terms of a world-view in which linguistic predetermination prevails. If not, if it *is* possible for women to speak (for) themselves without recourse to prevailing ideological discourse, if it is possible for them to construct their *own* original language, then the first presupposition of such theorizing—namely that we are always the unoriginal construct of dominant language systems—does not hold. If it is possible to authorize one's being in the invention of an authentic voice, then the conception of the totalitarian authority of the prevailing symbolic order needs revision. At this point we witness the greatest tensions between poststructuralist/psychoanalytic determinism and feminist emancipatory desire.

The question remains pertinent for feminist theorists: How are women to express the inexpressible? How are they to move from the level of the repressed unconscious to the level of conscious comprehension without betrayal in patriarchal discourse? How are they to maintain the purity of the unsaid when giving it voice? This is a problem which confounds Irigaray's metaphoric programme for the emancipation of women in such well-known tracts as 'When Our Lips Speak Together'. Irigaray advocates an interrogation of the relationship between female sexuality and language with the aim of developing a *different* symbolic order: 'Get out of their [male] language', she urges.[17] But the price which must be paid for such an alternative, such an escape, seems too high. Because wholly other, her theorized women's language can only ever be an unintelligible (if defiant) babble which is readily dismissed by men as meaningless. Its wholesale alterity and anti-systematization preclude comprehension. It maintains women in the realm of excommunication: obscure, incoherent, readily precluded from contribution to social process. It maintains women there, to be sure, for silence, madness, or babble are gestures that will be interpreted as further proof of the weakness and instability with which women have been traditionally associated. Ann Rosalind Jones cautions against 'the risk of paralysis inherent in cultural modes that glorify marginal discourses—silence, hysteria, delirium—and thus leave official structures intact'.[18] Such

---

[17] Luce Irigaray, 'When Our Lips Speak Together', trans. Carolyn Burke, *Signs*, 6 (1980), 70. See also her collection of essays *This Sex Which Is Not One*, trans. Catherine Porter (Ithaca, NY: Cornell University Press, 1985).

[18] Ann Rosalind Jones, 'Inscribing Femininity: French Theories of the Feminine',

a position is utterly self-defeating: men must never be allowed to understand women's language because their comprehension is theorized as unacceptable appropriation, the totalizing imposition of interpretative will-to-power. Women's otherness, precisely in order to remain other, must remain in an incomprehensible (and thus ineffectual) realm of unassimilable distinction. There is a striking parallel here between this separatist school of feminist thought and that of those contemporary theorists who advocate silence, abstention, or marginalization from community and communal conventions in order to escape the 'violence' of comprehensive 'apprehension'. In both cases the appeal of auto-erasure (in excommunicative tactics of silence or babble) is secured only by the use of an emotive rhetoric which gestures threateningly to the purportedly intrusive, or penetrative, consequences of interpretation. In many feminist tracts, for example, intellectual 'penetration' of female minds or texts by men equates with the violation of rape: 'The duplicitous woman is the one whose consciousness is opaque to man, whose mind will not let itself be penetrated by the phallic probings of masculine thought.'[19]

How desirable is an 'escape' conceived of as retreat into an 'opaque' linguistic realm which disallows the possibility of understanding by men or communication with them? This is an exclusionist theory which does nothing to dismantle, but only reifies —solidifies and maintains—a destructive pattern of oppositional thinking by cordoning off a 'wilderness' of experience, an 'other' mode of being and reading, a textual identity and critical stance, which is exclusively female, inevitably feared or dismissed for its otherness.[20] This is surely to condemn women and women writers,

in Gayle Green and Coppélia Khan (eds.), *Making a Difference: Feminist Literary Criticism* (1985; London and New York: Routledge, 1988), 107. A similar critique of Irigaray with respect to the ubiquitous idealization of marginality in contemporary theory is provided by John Carlos Rowe, 'To Live Outside the Law You Must Be Honest: The Authority of the Margin in Contemporary Theory', *Cultural Critique*, 2 (1985–6), 35–70.

[19] Moi, *Sexual/Textual Politics*, 58. Moi is paraphrasing (in order to critique) the argument of Sandra Gilbert and Susan Gubar in *The Madwoman in the Attic: The Woman Writer and the Nineteenth Century Literary Imagination* (New Haven: Yale University Press, 1979).

[20] See Elaine Showalter, 'Feminist Criticism in the Wilderness', *Critical Inquiry*, 8/2 (Winter 1981), 179–205. In this essay, Showalter calls for a critical assessment of those features which characterize the otherness and distinction of women's writing. This she denotes 'gynocriticism', a textual approach which is distinct from the procedures of male scholarship, one which must discover 'its own subject, its own

to remain in what Lillian S. Robinson has termed 'the women's literature ghetto—separate, apparently autonomous, and far from equal', when what is needed is a return to, and *confrontation with*, the prescriptive values encoded in language and the canon.[21] Kate Fullbrook makes a similar point in *Free Women*; she suggests that an attempt to define the absolute distinction of women's values only maintains women 'in a psychological, if purportedly privileged ghetto that locks them outside the making of meaning, culture and history'.[22]

What is the gain for humanity—for women *and* men who quest for individual equality (which turns on the possession of understood self-autonomy)—if personal freedom is theorized at the cost of radical self-alienation, opacity, and textual unreadability? What *value* is there in staking out and defending the sanctity of a (female) linguistic enclave which, because of its exclusivity and incomprehensibility, has forever barred its gates to, and thereby alienated itself from, the crucial political debate about human equality which rages beyond its barricaded boundaries?[23] Feminists who refuse to enter the battlefield of (patriarchal) discourse risk defeat at the hands of an enemy who will accord to their 'subversive' linguistic otherness only the status of inconsequential (because incomprehensible) babble. Further, a strategy of 'silence', however loudly and richly this may resonate in the privileged ears of initiates in the order of abstention from patriarchal discourse, forfeits *any* capacity for potentially revolutionary debate or dialectical engagement.

theory and its own voice' (184), a realm of women's experience beyond and inaccessible to the prescriptions of patriarchal language. While endorsing the importance of surveying women's writing, I question the value of the exclusivity proposed by Showalter. Exiling oneself to a marginalized critical 'wildness' may be more foolhardy than brave. Radical ex-centricity may result in the discreditation and dismissal of one's (incomprehensible) critical readings.

[21] Lillian S. Robinson, 'Treason our Text: Feminist Challenges to the Literary Canon', *Tulsa Studies in Women's Literature*, 2/1 (Spring 1983), 95–6.

[22] Kate Fullbrook, *Free Women: Ethics and Aesthetics in Twentieth Century Women's Fiction* (Hemel Hempstead: Harvester Press, 1990), 3.

[23] The possibility of ascribing *value* to an exclusionist feminist enterprise which wholly dissociates itself from the value-defining terms of social (patriarchal) discourse has recently been challenged by Steven Connor in his chapter 'Feminism and Value: Ethics, Difference, Discourse', in *Theory and Cultural Value* (Oxford: Basil Blackwell, 1992), 158–89.

Linguistic Subversion

> [I]t has been impossible, within humanist and even post-
> humanist discourses, to theorize an agential female subject
> *of* discourse who is not passively and inevitably subject *to*
> discourse.
>
> Robinson, *Engendering the Subject*

One way around the problem may be to think of potentially
subversive (female) discourses not as excluded from and outside
'man-made' language, but rather as a plurality of alternative
communicative sites that exist within and alongside the dominant
(patriarchal) order. We need to conceptualize (female) subjects as
discursive agents not only subject to discourse but as constructive
and productive within it. We do not have to look outside language
for the locus of our self-determining power, hypothesizing an
exclusionary alienation which relies on the uninterpretability of
untranslatable babble or the excommunicative silence of non-
signification. Using language is always more than an act of
reinscription. *In* language we can challenge, question, and even
shape the plural communities within which we are determined:
creative language use is a condition of our partial self-
determination as subjects of/in discourse—an optimistic claim, but
not, I think, a utopian one.

The (early) work of Julia Kristeva provides an entry point at
which to begin a discussion on the emancipatory potential of
subversion from within language systems.[24] In 'The System and
the Speaking Subject', Kristeva charges traditional linguistic theorists with a rigid structuralist approach to language, an approach
which does not take into account the fluidity and heterogeneity of
discursive operations or the psychoanalytical understanding of the
(speaking) subject as a fluid, movable position rather than a
'transcendental ego': 'established as a science inasmuch as it
focuses on language as a social code, the science of linguistics has
no way of apprehending anything in language which belongs not

---

[24] The Bakhtinian foundation of Kristeva's early work, with its stress on the social
context of specific instances of language use, provides more useful insight with
regard to the 'speaking subject' than her later work, which is strongly influenced by a
Derridean negative structuralism which focuses on the determined nature of the
subject.

with the social contract but with play, pleasure or desire'.[25] In this essay she advocates the replacement of traditional linguistics by 'semiology', which 'conceives of meaning not as a sign-system, but a signifying process' (28). Signifying processes or practices, in Kristeva's view, are not wholly constrained by indisputable laws, although they are ordered by interpersonal protocols and situated in 'historically determined relations of production'. Alongside this idea of signifying process, Kristeva advocates a new concept of the 'speaking subject', who is situated within historical and social matrices, yet possesses a capacity for subversion and alteration of systemic protocols through linguistic innovation (or, in her term, 'renouvellement'). Semiology, she announces, 'is ready to give a hearing to any or all of those efforts which, ever since the elaboration of a new position for the speaking subject, have been renewing and reshaping the status of meaning within social exchange to a point where the very order of language is being renewed: Joyce, Burroughs, Sollers' (32).[26]

Kristeva's understanding of language situates meaning in contextual power relationships, not in intrinsic essences, and, most important, it enables her to see language processes as always open to transgression and subversion: language is not a fixed system, but a series of instances of communicative practices in which meanings are mobile and multiple. Kristeva coins the term 'semiotic' to indicate the transgressive drives which function to disrupt the symbolic order of language in which syntax and logic dominate. In her formulation, the semiotic is pre-linguistic, it exists before the hierarchical conceptual structures which engender unity and identity come into being: 'it precedes the establishment of the sign'.[27] It is the energy or pulsions which move through the body of the subject before it is constituted as a subject (for subjective constitution takes place in the realm of the symbolic, which orders the pre-linguistic drives according to social, familial, and biological constraints). The speaking subject, as Kristeva understands it, is structured in the interplay between the semiotic and the symbolic. It is never simply in one or the other. Although the

---

[25] Julia Kristeva, 'The System and the Speaking Subject' (1973), repr. in Toril Moi (ed.), *The Kristeva Reader* (Oxford: Basil Blackwell, 1986), 26.

[26] The 'poetic language' of modernist prose is of particular interest to Kristeva. (The flip side of this interest is the failure of her subversive poetics to deal adequately with more traditional literary forms, e.g. the realist novel.)

[27] Kristeva, 'Revolution in Poetic Language', in Moi (ed.), *Kristeva Reader*, 95.

symbolic dominates (for this is what enables the subject to conceive of itself as a subject), the semiotic disposition in language is always present as disruptive potential: 'Identifying the semiotic disposition means in fact identifying the shift in the speaking subject, his capacity for renewing the order in which he is inescapably caught up; and that capacity is, for the subject, the capacity for enjoyment.'[28]

Following Lacan, Kristeva denominates the symbolic order of social structuration as paternal, the Law of the Father. However, she deviates from Lacanian theory in her designation of the semiotic as maternal, deriving from the pre-oedipal unity of infants with their mothers in a space Kristeva denotes the 'chora'. The chora is 'receptacle, unnameable, improbable, anterior to naming, to the one, to the father, and consequently maternally connoted'.[29] The semiotic is thus maternal, feminine (but not the strict preserve of women[30]). Because it precedes the formation of the symbolic (as a theoretical supposition), the semiotic cannot be represented in or acknowledged by the symbolic. None the less, in practice, it functions within the signifying process of language which constitutes the subject. Kristeva writes:

These two modalities [the semiotic and the symbolic] are inseparable within the *signifying process* that constitutes language, and the dialectic between them determines the type of discourse (narrative, metalanguage, theory, poetry, etc.) involved; in other words, so-called 'natural' language allows the different modes of articulation of the semiotic and the symbolic. . . . Because the subject is always *both* semiotic *and* symbolic, no signifying system he produces can be either 'exclusively' semiotic or 'exclusively' symbolic, and is instead necessarily marked by indebtedness to both.[31]

Kristeva takes an important step towards a theory of revolutionary potential within language by suggesting that although the symbolic

---

[28]   Kristeva, 'The System and the Speaking Subject', 29.

[29]   Kristeva, *Desire in Language: A Semiotic Approach to Literature and Art*, trans. Thomas Gora, Alice Jardine, and Leon S. Roudiez, ed. Leon S. Roudiez (Oxford: Basil Blackwell, 1981), 133.

[30]   According to Kristeva, male writers also have access to the semiotic, particularly through the medium of poetry. Kristeva discusses Mallarmé, Céline, Lautréamont and others in this respect in her thesis for the French *Doctorat d'Etat, La Révolution du langage poétique* (1974); published in English as *The Revolution in Poetic Language*, trans. M. Waller (New York: Columbia University Press, 1984).

[31]   Kristeva, 'Revolution in Poetic Language', 92–3.

is dominant, the semiotic possesses the power to disrupt and unsettle its order. As Gerardine Meaney phrases it, Kristeva 'posits the maternal as a border from which textual terrorism can be launched'.[32] At moments of slippage and condensation, in Freudian terminology, we may note the irruption of the semiotic into the realm of the symbolic. In order to understand how 'corruptions of the symbolic'[33] by the semiotic can take place, we will need to consider another crucial term in Kristeva's account, the 'thetic'.

The thetic constitutes the boundary between the domain of the semiotic and that of the symbolic. It is the moment which establishes a signification, in other words the separation of a subject from an object, the positing of identity and difference: 'that crucial place on the basis of which the human being constitutes himself as signifying and/or social' (117). The thetic break, then, separates the signifier from what was heterogeneous to it; but it always contains a 'semiotic fragment' (99):

> Though absolutely necessary, the thetic is not exclusive: the semiotic, which also precedes it, constantly tears it open, and this transgression beings about the various transformations of the signifying practice that are called 'creation'. . . . [W]hat remodels the symbolic order is always the influx of the semiotic. (113)

(Poetic) transgression thus operates by introducing into the thetic position a stream of semiotic drives which are made to signify: 'all transgressions of the thetic are a crossing of the boundary between true and false—maintained, inevitably, whenever signification is maintained, and shaken irremediably, by the flow of the semiotic into the symbolic' (110). Developing Freudian theory, Kristeva suggests that exchanges or permutations of the symbolic by the semiotic occur through displacement and condensation (metaphor and metonymy) or the passage from one sign system to another (intertextuality or transposition). This process is 'atheological'; poetic language may be complicit with dogma, but it may also 'set in motion what dogma represses' (112).

Importantly, however, Kristeva emphasizes that the thetic is indispensable. When the symbolic fails to be constituted, we find psychosis: 'In the extreme, negativity [the irruption of the

---

[32] Meaney, *(Un)like Subjects*, 99.
[33] Kristeva, 'Revolution in Poetic Language', 111. Further references to this essay will be cited parenthetically in the text.

semiotic] aims to foreclose the thetic phase, which, after a period of explosive semiotic motility, may result in the loss of the symbolic function, as seen in schizophrenia' (119). There can be no language, no signification, without the thetic phase which orders communication and understanding,[34] and from this it follows that without the thetic there can be no conception of oneself as a unified subject: the thetic is a necessary condition for healthy personhood. But this does not mean that each and every act of signification, or self-conception, acts solely from the thetic phase. The semiotic is always present as a repressed, but potentially disruptive, field within the symbolic. The text, and the self as text, 'offers itself as the dialectic of two heterogeneous operations that are, reciprocally and inseparable, preconditions for each other' (116). Throughout her writing, Kristeva stresses the need for the ordering of the symbolic to contain, if never silence, the negativity and death drive of the semiotic. The chora is, she claims, 'on the path of destruction . . . and death' before being ordered by the symbolic (95). In 'About Chinese Women' Kristeva writes passionately about the dangers of relinquishing the (paternal) symbolic wholly in favour of the (maternal) semiotic, a warning which runs counter to the essentialist, separatist demands of some feminists for a unique, distinct 'women's language':

the invasion of her [a woman's] speech by these unphrased, nonsensical, maternal rhythms [the semiotic], far from soothing her, or making her laugh, destroys her symbolic armour and makes her ecstatic, nostalgic or mad. . . . A woman has nothing to laugh about when the symbolic order collapses. She can take pleasure in it. . . . But she can just as easily die from this upheaval, as a victim or a militant.[35]

To wholly eradicate the symbolic order would mean the loss of one's capacity to speak and understand, the loss of one's sense of cohesive selfhood which is structured in that order. Far from liberating the speaking subject, this would be the excommunicative path to psychotic babble or death. What is needed is a subversive opening up of meaning to the 'music' or 'play' of the semiotic. To suggest this is not to relegate playful transgression to the role of an ineffectual irritant within an impermeable social system. It is

---

[34] Kristeva writes: 'Without the completion of the thetic phase . . . no signifying is possible' (ibid. 114).

[35] Kristeva, 'About Chinese Women', in Moi (ed.), *Kristeva Reader*, 150.

rather to suggest that playful transgressions may effect changes in the power structures which generate meanings; they may bring into being *alternative* systems of signification, while never eradicating the need for some system of conceptual ordering as the basis for consciousness and hence subjectivity. Kristeva's textual theory is always political—indeed, like many contemporary theorists following the linguistic turn in philosophical thought, she sees textual or significatory processes as inseparable from, and paradigmatic of, the operations of social law.

What semiotics has discovered in studying 'ideologies' (myths, rituals, moral codes, arts, etc.) as sign-systems is that the law governing, or, if one prefers, the major constraint affecting any social practice is that it signifies; i.e., that it is articulated like a language. Every social practice . . . is also determined by a set of signifying rules, by virtue of the fact that there is present an order of language. . . . One may say, then, that what semiotics had discovered is the fact that there is a general social law, that this law is the symbolic dimension which is given in language and that every social practice offers a specific expression of that law.[36]

Although so often used to support textual readings by feminist critics, the work of Julia Kristeva remains resistant to this exclusive annexation. Her position is certainly less woman-centred than some of her feminist disciples would have us believe. That she denotes the semiotic as feminine is surely not an essentialist or biological claim, but a metaphorical one. To understand the semiotic as literally feminine, as 'the space of privileged contact with the mother's (female) body', is mistaken.[37] The 'feminine' semiotic is intended to represent a subversive space within dominant culture, which in Western society is masculine. Certainly, Kristeva works (sometimes dangerously) within the inherited oppositional structures which order our conceptions—truth/poetry, self/other, feminine/masculine, repressed/liberated—and in so doing, risks perpetuating their divisions. But the application of her theory in her own readings constantly seeks semiotic ruptures in the work of male writers like Céline, Mallarmé, Lautréamont, Joyce, and Artaud, alongside that of female writers. It is deeply mistaken to read Kristeva's theory of the subversive semiotic as a *literal* representation of the lot of women and women alone. Doing

---

[36] Kristeva, 'The System and the Speaking Subject', 25.
[37] Alice Jardine, 'Pre-Texts for the Transatlantic Feminist', *Yale French Studies*, 62 (1981), 228.

so can only result in the bitter disappointment found in critiques of Kristeva by socialist feminists, who fear that her theory has little to distinguish it from traditional views of the female body and that it promotes a vision of women-as-essence which precedes socialization. Jennifer Stone explains:

By privileging the maternal uterus ('*chora*') as the site of production of revolutionary noise, Kristeva was positing the female body outside of social discourse. Traditional Marxism is wary of giving value to an essence which pre-exists social intersubjectivity and it could not endorse a theory which suggested that the pre-constituted female body is able to interrupt social discourses. . . . They disagree with Kristeva's notion of liberation which implies that there is a pre-existent and already fully constituted female subject inside dying to get out.[38]

The danger of locating the feminine in an excluded realm of textual and erotic *jouissance* distinct from (male) socialization is very real. But this is surely not what Kristeva is proposing. She is articulating a vision of disruptive potential contained *within* dominant discursive structures, not excluded from them. The semiotic, *metaphorically* 'feminine' and repressed to be sure, is not distinct from (masculine) discursive practice, but always part of it. And the human subject 'is always *both* semiotic *and* symbolic, no signifying system he produces can be either exclusively semiotic or exclusively symbolic, and is instead necessarily marked by in-debtedness to both.[39]

There are, however, more serious grounds upon which to challenge Kristeva's theory of the disruptive semiotic. Her focus on the psychodynamics of linguistic operation is without any real consideration of the political efficacy of the textual radicalism she promotes. Without articulating how the rebellion of repressed drives might have political efficacy, Kristeva's privileging of erotic textual play may result, as Rita Felski suggests, in a disturbing 'idealization of madness and unreason, as exemplified in the

---

[38] Jennifer Stone, 'The Horrors of Power: A Critique of Kristeva', in Francis Barker, Peter Hulme, Margaret Iversen, and Diana Loxley (eds.), *The Politics of Theory: Proceedings of the Essex Conference on the Sociology of Literature: July 1982* (Colchester: University of Essex, 1983), 42. Stone's critique of Kristeva is centred on the 'fascism' she finds to be the organizing principle of Kristeva's *Powers of Horror* (1982) and also latent in Kristeva's earlier work. See also Ann Rosalind Jones's critique of Kristeva's biological essentialism in her essay 'Julia Kristeva on Femininity: The Limits of a Semiotic Politics', *Feminist Review*, 18 (1984), 56–73.

[39] Kristeva, 'Revolution in Poetic Language', 92–3.

current fascination with the figure of the hysteric'.[40] This in turn can lead to a reificiation of the identification of hysteria and unreason with femininity. In Kristeva's later work very little interest is paid to historicity, to the question of changing social contexts and reader reception. This, as I have noted, is what is at once distinctive and important in her early work. If it is true that certain texts are able to perform functions of radical subversion, how do these revolutionary texts remain immune from social and institutional normalization, a process clearly evident in the contemporary academic appropriation and elucidation of modernist texts? If semiotic disruption is transient and temporary, can it avoid reabsorption and reification by the symbolic order?[41] Rita Felski points to another area of concern *vis-à-vis* the work of Kristeva, the separation of the realms of the private and the social, a separation which fails to ask questions about 'the ultimate relationship between textual and political revolution'.[42] Indeed, Kristeva has established no intrinsic link between radical textuality and social change: 'The subversion of fixed meanings and the unified subject does not in itself necessarily imply anything other than anarchism or relativism and can just as well serve the interests of reactionary irrationalism as the aims of a feminist [or other emancipatory] politics.'[43] Nancy Fraser similarly notes Kristeva's tendency 'to valorise transgression and innovation *per se* irrespective of content', and consequently to dismiss *all* communicative practice as negatively conformist: 'this attitude is not particularly helpful for feminist politics, since such politics requires ethical distinctions between oppressive and emancipatory social norms'.[44] This is a disturbing facet of Kristeva's (later) theorizing: it appears to discredit or disallow any subjective capacity for discernment or

---

[40] Rita Felski, *Beyond Feminist Aesthetics: Feminist Literature and Social Change* (Cambridge, Mass.: Harvard University Press, 1989), 40.

[41] See Judith Butler, 'The Body Politics of Julia Kristeva', *Hypatia: A Journal of Feminist Philosophy*, 3/3 (Winter 1989), 104–18.

[42] Felski, *Beyond Feminist Aesthetics*, 39.

[43] Ibid. 40.

[44] Nancy Fraser, 'The Uses and Abuses of French Discourse Theories for Feminist Politics', *Boundary 2*, 17/2 (1990), 95. Fraser also objects to 'the fact that the semiotic is defined parasitically over and against the symbolic as the latter's mirror image and abstract negation', yielding 'an amalgam of structure and antistructure' that 'leaves us oscillating ceaselessly between a structuralist moment and an antistructuralist moment without ever getting to anything else' (97). Fraser criticizes the strong Lacanian foundation of Kristeva's theory, which produces a subject which is 'split into two halves, neither of which is a potential political agent' (98).

relative assessment of merits (in acts of rebellion and conformity), operating wholly within a binary mind-set that opposes structural conformity and anti-structural transgression as negative and positive respectively. The aim of an emancipatory politics/poetics must surely be the willed creation, modulation, and maintenance of viable alternative communities of discourse and communicative protocols, not the subversion and destruction of *all* structured, interactive communities as intrinsically totalizing. Transgressive energies may in fact be utilized to negative and far from emancipatory ends, while certain interactive communities may provide positive, supportive structures for subjective determination.

While taking on board these criticisms and concerns, it is necessary to recognize the value of Kristeva's work in so far as it begins to articulate the possibility of change-making transgression *within* dominant discursive structures. It offers an alternative conception of revolutionary capacity that does not situate rebellion in a meaningless realm beyond interactive language communities or in untranslatable gestures within them. Provided we recognize that not all subversive rebellion is positive *per se* and that its emancipatory potential lies not simply in systematic destruction but in the renovative restructuring of certain communicative procedures, the notion of the rebellious functioning of the semiotic may in fact be an important feature of an emancipatory politics. Revolution must then be understood as resulting in the development of a greater range of viable alternative communities, or discursive sites, not the wholesale abandonment of all communities and communication. The notion of inherent transgressive potential built into the very structures that may oppress speaking subjects while situating them as social subjects might then be a positively productive one. It offers a conception of the subject which does not reduce it to the passive product of the dominant communicative protocols, but understands both as reciprocally co-constitutive and open to renovation. As long as we recognize the remarkable capacity of existing power structures to absorb and annex subversive energies (witness the bourgeois appropriation of avant-garde art and the consequent devaluation of its revolutionary potential), rule-breaking/making aesthetic play may have revolutionary value.

Communities of Resistance: The Politics of Difference and Identity

> Does inhabiting the inside always guarantee cooptation? . . .
> And does inhabiting the outside always and everywhere
> guarantee radicality? The problem, of course, with the
> inside/outside rhetoric, if it remains undeconstructed, is that
> such polemics disguise the fact that most of us are both
> inside and outside at the same time. Any displaced nostalgia
> for or romanticization of the outside as a privileged site of
> radicality immediately gives us away, for in order to realize
> the outside we must already be, to some degree, comfortably
> on the inside. We only have the leisure to idealize the sub-
> versive potential of the power of the marginal when our
> place of enunciation is quite central.
>
> Fuss, 'Inside/Out'

The move towards a poststructuralist formulation of linguistically
determined subjectivity—and the consequent postulation of a
utopian, but ultimately untenable, escape from signification (and
political efficacy)—is not the only possible response to discredited
identity politics and its fragmentary essentialism. In the preceding
pages I have suggested the incompatibility of (hardline) poststructuralist notions of linguistic determinism and reformist
theories that would articulate a conception of the (female) subject
as a political agent capable of voicing and enacting change. The
hardline poststructuralist account of determined subjectivity sits
uncomfortably with any radical or revolutionary desire, resulting
in a negative theory stymied by its focus on a series of unpalatable
dichotomies: comprehensible entrapment or meaningless authenticity, the betrayal of voice or the freedom of voicelessness,
insider complicity or outsider excommunication. But there are
other ways to conceive of the situation and situatedness of the
human subject. In 'The Spaces that Difference Makes', Edward
Soja and Barbara Hooper offer another response to discredited
identity politics, one which does not limit the placement of the
subject to one or other pole of the inside/outside dichotomy. After
focusing on the negativity of some poststructuralist feminism for
much of this chapter, I will end, more optimistically, by considering the arguments set forth by Soja and Hooper in their essay.

Significantly, they stress the importance of postmodern plurality in any conception of situated subjectivity:

the deeply engrained essentialisms of modernist identity politics have tended to create a competitive exclusivity that resists, even rejects, seeing a 'real' world populated by *multiple subjects with many (often changeable) identities located in varying (and also changeable) subject positions.* Hence modernist identity politics, in its fear and rejection of a fragmented reality, has often tended to create and intensify political divisiveness rather than working toward a multiple, pluralized, and yet still radical conceptualization of agency and identity.[45]

Soja and Hooper promote the development of 'an explicitly post-modernist radical politics, a new cultural politics of difference and identity that moves towards empowering a multiplicity of resistances rather than searches for that one "great refusal" [or great escape], the singular transformation to precede and guide all others'.[46] Their essay brings together two important strands in recent cultural criticism: a stress on the importance of spatiality (and a corresponding critique of historicity) as a constitutive dimension of subjectivity and the celebration of cultural and communal pluralism evident in the work of a variety of post-modernist, black, post-colonial, feminist, and Marxist theorists (among others, they cite Homi Bhabba, Judith Butler, bell hooks, Diana Fuss, Donna Haraway, Edward Said, and Ernesto Laclau). In doing so, it offers a conception of the human subject as one who is empowered to practice subversive politics from a plurality of communal sites and chosen marginalities.

Soja and Hooper stress the importance of the '*disordering* of difference from its persistent binary structuring', urging the necessity of reconstituting difference as the foundation for 'a new cultural politics of multiplicity and strategic alliance among all who are peripheralized, marginalized and subordinated by the social construction of difference (especially in its binary forms)'.[47] In their attempt to re-vision spatiality, they reject the notion of difference as debilitating fragmentation, finding it to offer a plurality of 'new sites for struggle', and join some postmodern cultural critics in suggesting 'how fragmentation, ruptures and discontinuities can be politically transformed from liability and

---

[45] Soja and Hooper, 'The Spaces that Difference Makes', 187 (my emphasis).
[46] Ibid.   [47] Ibid.

weakness to opportunity and strength'.[48] These sites range from the intimate, local contours of the body to the great spaces of global geopolitics;[49] they are real and imagined, metaphorical and material. Crucially, they are not conceived as exclusive, but as a vast array of different, but 'interconnected communities of resistance'.[50] The new strategic spatial politics is one of inclusion: the subversive sites it offers to postmodern subjects are 'combinatorial rather than competitively fragmented and separated communities of resistance'.[51]

Choice is fundamental to Soja and Hooper's outline of a new cultural politics of difference. Their argument at this junction in the essay closely follows that of bell hooks in *Yearning: Race, Gender, and Cultural Politics*, who argues for the subversive potentialities of *choosing* marginality (or marginalities):

As a radical standpoint, perspective, position, 'the politics of location' necessarily calls those of us who would participate in the formation of counter-hegemonic cultural practice to identify the spaces where we might begin the process of re-vision. . . . For me this space of radical openness is a margin—a profound edge. Locating oneself there is difficult yet necessary. It is not a 'safe' place. One is always at risk. One needs a community of resistance.[52]

hooks opts for a marginality that refuses to be displaced and disempowered as 'Other' by the hegemon. This tactic aims to deconstruct both centre and margin, recentring margins as spaces of potential resistance, sites of 'creativity and power'. There is, for hooks, a 'definite distinction between the marginality which is imposed by oppressive structure and that marginality one chooses as a site of resistance, as a location of radical openness and possibility'. Moreover, sites on the margin are inclusive, spaces where we 'move in solidarity to erase the category coloniser/

[48] Ibid. 189, 193.
[49] On the gendered space of the body and its relations to larger urban and global spaces, see B. Colomina (ed.), *Sexuality and Space* (New York: Princeton Architectural Press, 1992); Daphne Spain, *Gendered Spaces* (Chapel Hill, NC: University of North Carolina Press, 1992); Leslie Kanes Weisman, *Discrimination by Design: A Feminist Critique of the Man-made Environment* (Urbana, Ill., and Chicago: University of Illinois Press, 1992).
[50] Soja and Hooper, 'The Spaces that Difference Makes', 189.
[51] Ibid.
[52] bell hooks, *Yearning: Race, Gender, and Cultural Politics* (Boston: South End Press, 1990), 145–9; cited in Soja and Hooper, 'The Spaces that Difference Makes', 189.

colonized'.[53] In short, she advocates the 'centralizing' choice of marginality as a site from which to collaborate with other centralized margins, refusing the passivity of an assigned space.

In refusing the binary of inside/outside (and the unpalatable alternatives it reproduces) and theorizing a plurality of (potentially contestational) chosen communities located within existing structures of power, Soja and Hooper (and the body of cultural critics on whose work they draw) offer a way to conceive of social/linguistic situatedness without reducing it to insider complicity, from which the only escape, or mode of resistance, is outsider excommunication. Human subjects can choose a variety of positions within the existing matrix of social structures. Plural communities offer a range of interpretative and creative strategies from which situated subjects can draw when interpreting the 'texts' of self and plotting meaningful narratives of selfhood. Conceiving subjective situatedness in terms of interconnected communal plurality encourages the cross-fertilization, borrowing, and adaptation of shared interpretative resources between individuals and communities, and thus makes possible the development of new strategies for resistance without passive reinscription of existing norms and protocols. Crucially, Soja and Hooper point to a new way of envisioning the agency of the social subject. In communities of resistance, social subjects exist between enervating inside/outside dualisms in the 'third space' of political choice.[54]

[53] Cited in Soja and Hooper, 'The Spaces that Difference Makes', 191.
[54] Ibid. 192.

4

Rebellion from Within:
Designing Alternatives

[W]ord is a two-sided act. It is determined equally by whose
word it is and for whom it is meant. . . . A word is a territory
shared by both addresser and addressee, by the speaker and
his interlocutor.

Volosinov, *Marxism and the Philosophy of Language*

Here Valentin Volosinov (thought to be a pseudonym of Mikhail
Bakhtin) intends 'word' as both *a* word and as discourse, utterance
(the Russian word *slovo* means both), an understanding which is
crucial to the socio-linguistic work of the Bakhtin school of theorists.
For Bakhtin, 'word' is always a social or 'dialogic' act; it is always
directed outwards from a situated speaker in anticipation of a
response: 'The word in living conversation is directly, blatantly
oriented towards a future answer word. It provokes an answer,
anticipates it and structures itself in the answer's direction.'[1] The
meaning of 'word' is thus situated in the context of its utterance, in
the dialectal play of articulation and response. The contexts in which
words mean are always much more than verbal, involving the status,
historical placement, and relationship between speaker and addressee
and the object or subject of their discourse. 'Word' is thus irreducibly
social, an act of situated communication. 'Language is not a neutral
medium that passes freely and easily into the private property of the
speaker's intentions', claims Bakhtin in *The Dialogic Imagination*;
'the word in language is half someone else's.'[2]

According to Bakhtin, words never simply represent individual
things, ideas, and concepts, but struggle to convey meaning within
the agonistic field of language in which alternatives proliferate: 'no
living word relates to its object in a singular way: between the word

---

[1] Mikhail M. Bakhtin, *The Dialogic Imagination*, trans. Caryl Emerson and
Michael Holquist, ed. Michael Holquist (Austin, Tex.: University of Texas
Press, 1981), 280.
[2] Ibid. 294, 293.

and its object, between the word and the speaking subject, there exists an elastic environment of other alien words about the same object, the same theme.'[3] Language is never unitary ('monologic'), but plural ('polyphonic'), fractured by 'the simultaneous presence of two or more (national) languages interacting within a single cultural system'.[4] Words 'interanimate each other', and the traditional linguistic conception of 'a single, unitary sealed off Ptolemaic world of language' gives way to the realization of 'the open, Galilean world of many languages, mutually animating each other'.[5] The conventional object of linguistic study, *langue*, gives way, on Bakhtin's account to the interrogation of *parole*, the individual acts of utterance which are produced in a plurality of discursive contexts within the structures of *langue*. Intersubjective communication is none the less possible within a multitude of partisan communities made of up human subjects: speaking subjects are able to take up a variety of interpretative and communicative positions within the structures provided by language. We can readily appreciate the value of Bakhtin's understanding of the polyphonic nature of discourse for the account of communication outlined in the preceding chapters: that is, of meaning as constituted within the plural contexts of intersubjective discursive communities.

Bakhtin's rejection of the abstract structuralist approach to language as a fixed, totalizing symbolic system is founded on his realization that such a conception precludes the possibility of meaningful creative agency on the part of human subjects. In bracketing the socio-historic context of discursive use, structuralism effectively theorizes the entrapment of social subjects within the rule-bound system of abstract language: its focus is on the prescriptions of the rules, rather than on concrete instances of discursive gaming. Revealing a negative dependence on structuralism, poststructuralism proceeds by announcing its animosity to all structures, traditions, and norms, understood unequivocally and universally as repressive and totalizing; it is unable to theorize communicative interactions as anything but instances of violence, and intersubjectively comprehensible writing as anything but passive reinscription. Two equally unpalatable alternatives are then proposed as a counter to structural 'subjection': either the specious 'liberation' of excommunicative

---

[3] Bakhtin, *Dialogic Imagination*. 276.
[4] Ibid. 431 n.
[5] Ibid. 68.

exile outside the normative bounds of language or abandonment to unmitigated desconstructive dissolution within them. Fearing the circumscription of meaning in fixed structures of representation, deconstruction abandons itself to the endless dispersals of *différance*, the logical consequence of which is the relinquishment of inter-subjective understanding, for the free-playing mobility of the signifier can never be fixed in the representational contours of the recognizable sign.

We do not need to accept either of these unsatisfactory modes of freedom if we reject the initial poststructuralist premise of wholesale subjection within the fixed structures of language. Instances of understanding can be achieved within shared communicative structures in which subjects are constituted and constitutive: in discursive communities that are local, potentially revisable, and open to modification. A partial but not insubstantial liberty inheres in our capacity for creative language *use*. There is space for subjective agency within communicative praxis.[6] Allon White develops such an argument in 'Bakhtin, Sociolinguistics and Deconstruction', suggesting that the Derridean deconstructive project of a *grammatology* arises from the erroneous severance of verbal mobility and uncertainty from the historical agon of meaning-production, thereby opening meaning to the endless dispersals of *différance*. As a consequence of this failure to account for the situatedness of any given meaning-determination, the deconstructive account of language is as flawed as the abstract systematization of structuralism.

Just as structuralism has an affinity for genres which pertain to monoglossia, deconstruction can be seen as an attempt to grasp the conflicting heterogeneities of language, rewriting its heteroglot difference as precisely the impossibility of a master-discourse, the impossibility of an invulnerable metalanguage. . . . [W]hen we realise that a fundamental

---

[6] Cf. Calvin O. Schrag, *Communicative Praxis and the Space of Subjectivity* (Bloomington, Ind.: Indiana University Press, 1986). In this book Schrag provides a critique of metaphysical and epistemological accounts of subjectivity. In calling into question a pre-linguistic origin for subjectivity, Schrag is far from negative, and aims to provide a 'restorative' account of the subject as constituted in the space of communicative praxis, 'the hermeneutical space of discourse and action' (122). In doing so, he moves towards the articulation of an ethical 'new humanism': 'moral action, as it arises out of the dialectic of conflict and consensus within the space of *ethos*, exhibits an operating intentionality of moral insight and self-understanding that antedates the construction both of value properties and of a monadic ethical subject that entertains them' (202).

form of dialogism exists between speaking and writing, then the project of a *grammatology* is revealed for what it is, a simple metaphysical inversion of the old hierarchy which gave ontological priority to speech over writing. In fact, the relation of written forms to spoken forms in any speech community is an historical question, one which Derrida fails to address because he has a purely *metaphysical* notion of heteroglossia insulated from the transformative and conflictual social arena of speech events.[7]

In contrast to what he perceives as the misplaced thrust of the deconstructive project, White counterposes a Bakhtinian model of meaning-production. Bakhtin, he claims, resists the slide into nihilism or celebratory utopianism, the twin poles of a deconstructive apprehension of conceptual *différance*. Bakhtin's understanding of the contextual, fluid activity of discursive operation maintains both sides of the dialogic equation of meaning-production: structure and slippage, order and transgression, praxis and innovation. A recognition that interpretation is unstable and resists definitive closure, that language is riddled with gaps and omissions and riven by the polyphony of 'alien' voices and traces of other texts need not entail the abandonment of all protocols of reading. Without some system for conceptualization, an ordering communal context, communication and self-conception would be impossible. White continues: '[b]oth poles, the homogenous and the heterogeneous operate to produce meaning, and from this perspective Bakhtin can analyse a whole range of speech events in their historical specificity, according to their social group, context and power relations.'[8]

I have repeatedly suggested that we need not think of discourse as *either* controlled by the transcendental structures of language (for this leads to the positing of an impervious, tyrannical, ideologically circumscribing function for linguistic operation) *or* as wholly resistant to structuration and given over to the unsuppressable movement of the signifier (for this gives lie to the lived experience of communication and understanding of inter- and intra-personal levels). We need to envisage discourse as an activity or practice which occurs within a set of provisionally fixed (if sometimes repressive) and intersubjectively understood communicative protocols, which are open to subversion, transgression, and change. Fundamental to

[7] Allon White, 'Bakhtin, Sociolinguistics and Deconstruction', in Frank Gloversmith (ed.), *The Theory of Reading* (Brighton: Harvester Press and Totowa, NJ: Barnes and Noble Books, 1984), 136–7.
[8] Ibid. 138.

Bakhtin's account is the notion that language cannot be bracketed out of the social matrix in which it operates. He rejects both fields in Saussure's couplet, *langue* and *parole*, as the adequate object of (socio-)linguistic study, because the former focuses on a set of abstract procedures with no scope for the subjective and socio-specific application of these procedures, and the latter focuses on the individual and her use of language without regard for the intra-personal nature of dialogic exchange. Language is above all, for Bakhtin, the historical medium for human interaction and exchange. In short, Bakhtin sees discourse as an agonistic activity performed in a social arena in which the polyphonic plurality of alternative language-games struggle to overcome and destabilize the ostensible unity and control of an authoritarian monologic voice.

In this chapter I want to consider the mistaken conclusions that sometimes arise from a poststructuralist predication of structural determinism and the dangerous consequences of the valorization of anti-structural excommunication. In particular, I am concerned to scrutinize the ethical and political claims made by some post-structuralist theorists with respect to the human 'textual' subject, understood as passively scripted in language. My discussion will focus on a number of experimental contemporary novels whose creative language use is revolutionary, but still intelligible to their readers, in order to suggest the capacity we have for subversive *renouvellement* within the protocols that make intersubjective communication possible. Far from wholly scuttling communicative practice, these are texts that balance the desire for creative expression against the necessity of understood protocols of reading. Finally, against contemporary critical trends, I will suggest the necessity of narrative, understood as a connective activity of interpretation that cuts across the gaps of textual dissolution, as a counter to the abstract notions of deconstructive *différance*. This is fundamentally important when seeking to understand the linguistic constitution of the human subject: personal identity should be understood as constituted in an ongoing process of (self-) narration. This is an idea that will be more fully explored in Chapter 5.

It is Bakhtin's application of his theory to the field of literature, particularly the novel, which is of greatest interest for my discussion. Above all modes of literary production, Bakhtin privileges the novel as the literary genre in which we can observe the workings of the dialogic aspect of language. Most important, he claims that in the dialogic (or polyphonic) structure of the novel we can see how language operates to destabilize ideological norms and conventions encoded in communal and communicative 'law'. According to Bakhtin, the novelistic genre runs counter to the prevailing monologic structure of traditional genres such as epic, myth, and tragedy. The texts in these genres, he claims, are dominated by the authoritarian voice of an author working at all costs to maintain a single voice, a single world-view, and in doing so, to perpetuate a single ideological myth. Characters in these texts may express distinct, antagonistic opinions, but nevertheless, 'an all-pervasive poetic decorum, or the regularities of rhythm and metre, ensure that the effect is one of stylistic (and ideological) consistency and homogeneity'.[9] By contrast, the heterogeneity of voices in the novel, its polyphonic structure, subverts any attempt to reduce its multiplicity to the singular, monologic, ideologically complicit authority of a controlling author. In his earlier writing, Bakhtin attributed to Dostoevsky the creation of the polyphonic novel, contrasting Dostoevsky's work with that of Tolstoy. According to Bakhtin, the characters in Tolstoy's work were still manifestly controlled by the author, whereas, by contrast, Dostoevsky, like Goethe's Prometheus, creates not voiceless slaves (as does Zeus), but rather free people who are capable of standing beside their creator, of disagreeing with him, and even of rebelling against him'.[10] In later works such as *The Dialogic Imagination* and *Rabelais and his World*, Bakhtin extends his analysis of the polyphonic structure of Dostoevsky's writing to encompass all novels. In order to do so, he traces the origin of the novel, which he broadly defines as 'a diversity of social speech types (sometimes even a diversity of languages) and a diversity of individual voices, artistically organized'.[11] He lists as among its classic precursors Socratic dialogue, the crude farce of Roman Atellanae, the satyr play, and in particular Mennipean satire, which arose from direct contact with popular carnival practices. During carnival times the seriousness of official culture is travestied by transgressive celebrations of the nonserious. Carnival is 'a gay parody of official reason, of the narrow seriousness of official truth'.[12] The hierarchy of high and low culture

[9] David Lodge, 'Lawrence, Dostoevsky, Bakhtin', in *After Bakhtin: Essays on Fiction and Criticism* (London and New York: Routledge, 1990), 58.

[10] Bakhtin, *Problems of Dostoevsky's Poetics*, ed. and trans. Caryl Emerson (1929; Manchester: Manchester University Press, 1984), 4.

[11] Bakhtin, *Dialogic Imagination*, 262.

[12] Bakhtin, *Rabelais and his World*, trans. Helene Iwolsky (1968; Bloomington, Ind.: Indiana University Press, 1984), 39.

is inverted, and this is imaged as the subversion of the dominance of the upper parts of the body by the hyperbolic celebration of the lower parts. Grotesque images of lower bodily excess flourish: defecation, ingestion, copulation, as do images of bodily mutilation, disintegration, dismemberment, and decapitation. Bakhtin believes that medieval culture retains the strongest link with the rebellious Mennipean carnival spirit, and finds expression in the work of writers like Rabelais and Cervantes. Carnivalesque literature is characterized by dialogic plurality (heteroglossia), which mixes and incorporates comic verbal compositions, word-play, parody, marketplace billingsgate, street songs, folk sayings (in contrast to the serious languages of classical and high culture, sermon, homily, chivalric romance, etc.); it celebrates abuse and profanity, abnormality and deviance, ridicule and irreverance, and its hugely variant stylistic features included temporal dislocation, circularity, and the rejection of completion and enclosure.[13]

One could be forgiven for mistaking this list of carnivalesque features offered by Bakhtin for a catalogue of the traits evident in much contemporary fiction. And it is not surprising to note that many contemporary critics find a strong resurgence of the Mennipean tradition, the carnivalesque, in (post)modern literature; for contemporary culture is characterized by its loss of belief in, and challenge to, monologic authority (God). Julia Kristeva writes:

> Disputing the laws of language . . . the carnival challenges God, authority and social law; in so far as it is dialogical, it is rebellious. Because of its subversive discourse, the word 'carnival' has understandably acquired a strongly derogatory or narrowly burlesque meaning in our society. . . . In the Middle Ages, Mennipean tendencies were held in check by the authority of the religious text; in the bourgeois era, they were contained by the absolutism of individuals and things. Only modernity—when freed of 'God'—releases the Mennipean force in the novel.[14]

Indeed, many commentators on the contemporary novel, and some novelists themselves, make overtly anti-authoritarian claims for their

---

[13] Ibid. 10 and *passim*:

[14] Julia Kristevea, 'Word, Dialogue, and Novel', in Toril Moi (ed.), *The Kristeva Reader* (Oxford: Basil Blackwell, 1986), 49, 55. Similar claims for the resurgence of the carnivalesque in contemporary writing have been made by Brian McHale in *Postmodernist Fiction* (London and New York: Routledge, 1987), 166–75, and M. Keith Booker in *Techniques of Subversion in Modern Literature: Transgression, Abjection, and the Carnivalesque* (Gainesville, Fla.: University of Florida Press, 1991), 22, 68, and *passim*.

rebellious anti-realist fictions. Some even use motifs and metaphors of the circus, carnival, fiesta, fair, and side-shows to invoke the transgressive energies of the carnivalesque 'mis-rule'. John Barth's *Lost in the Funhouse* (1969), Angela Carter's *Nights at the Circus* (1984), Margaret Atwood's *Lady Oracle* (discussed in Chapter 8), and Gabriel Garcia Marquez's *One Hundred Years of Solitude* (1967) spring readily to mind. But more often than not, contemporary fictions are carnivalesque in spirit and style. They practise a poetics of disruption, fracturing the norms of canonized literature and mimetic realism—consistent characterization, historical narration, description, causal sequence or plot, and so on—in a variety of ways. Several critics have provided excellent accounts of the wide range of these disruptive techniques as they are used by contemporary novelists, and it is not my intention to duplicate their findings here. One of the fullest of these is Brian McHale's discussion in *Postmodernist Fiction*.[15] His catalogue includes the strategy of '*mis-en-abyme*', the nesting of several stories within a fiction, with each embedded story making reference to or mirroring the others, a ploy used by Italo Calvino in *If on a Winter's Night a Traveller* (1979), which is composed of ten cross-referential novels; and fictions in which details and events mirror in miniature the structure of the novel which contains them, a tactic used successfully by Monique Wittig in *Les Guérillères* (1969) and Michel Butor in *Mobile* (1962). 'Transworld migration' is another popular meta-fictional technique: fictional characters move from one ontological realm to another, as Raymond Federman's protagonist does in *Take It or Leave It* (1976) when temporarily taking over the role of the narrator, and Ronald Sukenick does in *Up* (1968) when appropriating fictional characters from other writers' texts into his own fiction. Other meta-fictions utilize what McHale calls 'historic fantasy', the transposing of characters and events from 'real life' into the world of fiction in overtly unhistorical contexts; Thomas Pynchon's *Gravity's Rainbow* (1973) and Robert Coover's *The Public Burning* (1977) provide

---

[15] Other notable recent works which provide detailed consideration of disruptive strategies in contemporary fictions include Patricia Waugh, *Metafiction: The Theory and Practice of Self-Conscious Fiction* (London and New York: Methuen, 1984); Linda Hutcheon, *Narcissistic Narrative: The Metafictional Paradox* (Waterloo: Winifred Laurier University Press, 1980); Christopher Butler, *After the Wake: An Essay on the Contemporary Avant-Garde* (Oxford: Clarendon Press, 1980); and Robert Scholes, *Fabulation and Metafiction* (Urbana, Ill.: University of Illinois Press, 1980).

examples. 'Auto-bio-graphy', the appearance of the author as a character in his own fiction, is a common meta-fictional strategy, and is exemplified at the end of Gabriel Garcia Marquez's *One Hundred Years of Solitude* (1967) or in the cameo role played by Salman Rushdie in his novel *Midnight's Children* (1981). Other meta-fictional texts exhibit the flaunting of anachronism (used effectively by John Fowles in *The French Lieutenant's Woman* (1964), or feature 'non-endings' in which multiple, incomplete, or circular conclusions upset the expectation of closure (examples are Kurt Vonnegut's *Breakfast of Champions* (1973) and Julio Cortàzar's *Hopscotch* (1963)).

The use of these strategies, claims McHale, is intended not only to push beyond the numbingly familiar conventions of traditional fiction, in order to contest the categorical assumptions inscribed in the dominant canon. They are also employed by novelists with the overt aim of effecting a disturbing revaluation of ontological certainty on the part of their readers. They aim to make a reader uncomfortably aware of the unstable 'textual' process which is her own 'reality' by unsettling her confident assumption of ontological stability. Novels which employ such strategies are thought to be at the front line of a revolutionary programme to release textual subjects (in the sense of the *who* reading, writing, and being written, and the *what* of the fiction) from the narrow confines of interpretative strategies which seek to retrieve original meaning and essential identity and from the monologic authority of authorial domination. They celebrate (or commiserate with) the 'textuality' of *all* conceptual constructs, including the texts of self and reality.

The Ethics of Critical Analogy

> The self-eliding author becomes a kind of author, the unreliable character assumes substance in its very lability, while the problematic reader accepts or even enjoys the new status that the very uncertainty may confer.
>
> Beitchman, *I am a Process with no Subject*

It was my earlier contention that many contemporary fictions explore the creative capacity of narrative construction by both reader and writer, despite a theoretical climate in which discursive and textual processes are dismissed, in a variety of metaphorical terms, as traitorous, violent, or passively reinscriptive. In the field of contemporary literary criticism, many critics have misappropriated fragmentary and iconoclastic experimental contemporary fictions in order to vindicate their theories about the desirability of excommunicative rupture. This theoretical enterprise may be misguided and dangerous, particularly when it advocates the wholesale rejection of communal and communicative restraints as the condition for subjective authenticity, for this impels us towards the acceptance of disturbing political and moral consequences.[16] In preceding chapters I have countered the hyperbolic excesses of this theoretical stance by insisting on the need for the intersubjective protocols which enable texts—even rebellious texts—to mean and by stressing the capacity possessed by human subjects for the subversive re-formation of communicative protocols from within the procedural 'rules' of language, and by choosing to be situated on the margins of discourse in communities of resistance.

Many contemporary theorists ostensibly propound an entropic aesthetic of textual dismemberment and self-erasure, yet seek to celebrate the authenticity of the subject-text supposedly so liberated. This stance is deeply at odds with its own claims. Not only does a theory so hostile to canonization construct its own supportive canon, but a theory so vocal about the inherently invidious political nature of discursive operations has become simply another potentially totalizing political discourse (and one that often proceeds according to tactics of intimidation).[17] It is, moreover, deeply paradoxical,

[16] Some recent publications which consider the political and moral claims of literature in relation to ethics include Geoffrey Galt Harpham, *Getting It Right: Language, Literature, and Ethics* (Chicago and London: University of Chicago Press, 1992); Wayne C. Booth, *The Company We Keep: An Ethics of Fiction* (Berkeley and London: University of California Press, 1988); Tobin Siebers, *The Ethics of Criticism* (Ithaca, NY: Cornell University Press, 1988); Martha Nussbaum, 'Perceptive Equilibrium: Literary Theory and Ethical Theory' (1989) and ' "Finely Aware and Richly Responsible": Literature and the Moral Imagination' (1987), 'both repr. in *Love's Knowledge: Essays on Philosophy and Literature* (Oxford and New York: Oxford University Press, 1990), 168–94 and 148–67; J. Hillis Miller, *The Ethics of Reading: Kant, de Man, Eliot, Trollope, James and Benjamin* (New York: Columbia University Press, 1987).

[17] Howard Felperin makes this point in *Beyond Deconstruction: The Uses and Abuses of Literary Theory* (Oxford: Clarendon Press, 1985), 140: 'Deconstruction is indeed proving thoroughly amenable to routinization at the hands of the institution to whose authority it once seemed to pose such a challenge of incompatibility.'

in that independence and autonomy are thought to be realized in the unmaking of monologic identity, in its atomization in the ex-communicative dispersals of extreme eccentricity or the babble of unintelligibility. But what of the (human) textual subject? Radical discontinuity as an escape from community is surely not the gain, but the loss, of self-possession, of meaningful individuality. Freedom, so conceived, is simultaneously excommunication, self-mutilation. And, as Christopher Butler asks, 'If individuals don't have any status for the theory, what sense does it make to speak of them as "dominated" by social structures or of "liberating" them from them?'[18] There is indeed a glaring paradox at the heart of the apparently emancipatory enterprise so heralded. It seems that in order to release the subject (as text), it becomes necessary to annihilate the subject, to dissolve it into the bliss of indefinitely suspended irresolution and meaning-lessness, to announce—and celebrate—the unitary subject's demise in the free play of endless *différance*. Invariably, contemporary experimental fictions resist the self-destruction of ultimate dis-solution; beyond every proclaimed death—be it of author, reader, character, or text—the 'deceased' subject merely casts itself a new mask; its unmaking is only a remaking of identity. These paradoxical rebirths and the disingenuous denial of reconstitution made by those theorists who would annex fragmentary experimental fiction in order to validate the poststructuralist enterprise of subjective discreditation, deserves closer scrutiny. There is something fraudulent in the faked suicide of radical contemporary fictions and the premature obituary of these fictions written by literary theorists seeking to corroborate their political assertions with textual exemplification.

Christopher Nash has suggested of contemporary critical theory that 'in revelling in potent strategies for the disintegration of some of our illusions, we may have to abandoned our larger critical sense in favour of yet more ominous deceptions'.[19] Certainly it appears that many poststructuralist theorists have failed to adequately pursue the ethical consequences which must ensue as a result of their blithe relegation of the (human) subject to the concatenation of endless

---

[18] Christopher Butler, 'The Future of Theory: Saving the Reader', in Ralph Cohen (ed.), *The Future of Literary Theory* (New York and London: Routledge, 1989), 232.

[19] Christopher Nash, 'Slaughtering the Subject: Literature's Assault on Nar-rative', in Christopher Nash (ed.), *Narrative in Culture: The Uses of Storytelling in the Sciences, Philosophy and Literature* (London and New York: Routledge, 1990), 208.

linguistic *différance* and hermeneutic irresolution. Which is not to say that these critics do not invoke 'ethics' in order to lend credence to their self-aggrandizing claims. To the contrary. The immense emotive, rhetorical power of words like 'liberation', 'repression', 'individuality', 'penetration', and 'dominance' is common coinage among poststructuralist theorists. But often 'liberation' remains a vague utopian end, undefined except by contrast with the repressive nature of conventional discursive strategies. The value of (subjective) emancipation, if achievable, and the means by which it is to be maintained in the absence of those 'repressive' discursive structures which confer value, remains unclear. What does it *mean* to talk of textual or subjective liberation? What does it *mean* to say that discursive acts are political (beyond the truism that all intersubjective acts, strictly speaking, are political)? Is it possible to distinguish the political from the polemical in the claims of contemporary theory?

In the pages which follow I will scrutinize the manipulative, or more frequently self-deceptive, nature of the rhetoric in which the theoretical appeal for emancipation is made, a rhetoric modelled on the claims of deconstruction. This rhetoric is characterized by self-congratulatory claims of honesty, openness, and unflinching anti-illusionism, which are set against what are deemed the delusions and naïvety of those mouthpieces of *status quo* conventionalism, traditional mimetic fictions. It implies the heroism and self-sacrifice of its formal and stylistic eccentricity; it announces the valour of its narratives of subversive struggle against the oppression of (metaphysical or patriarchal or logocentric) authority. But perhaps its most disturbing feature is the moral and political intimidation which inhere in both the tacit and explicit analogies it employs.[20]

---

[20] For an excellent discussion of persuasion, argumentation, and the uses of political rhetoric by deconstructionist theorists, see Patrick Colm Hogan, *The Politics of Interpretation* (New York and Oxford: Oxford University Press, 1990), 28–95. Deconstructive rhetoric, suggests Hogan, frequently depends for its effectiveness on the use of 'tacit analogy', which operates by the use of metaphor and ambiguity of which the speaker or reader is unaware, resulting in conclusions being drawn from points of difference as well as from points of similarity. Because tacit, arguments grounded in this kind of analogy remain 'closed to refutation or qualification' (44)—'the most obvious cases may well be those involving tacit analogies of domination or lordship . . . and those involving a daring quest, a conquest, in fact, of the "wilderness" . . .' (44). Examples of such tacit political, religious, and sexual analogizing in deconstructionist writing abound; the authority of logocentric metaphysics is frequently discussed in terms of 'control', 'coercion', 'penetration', 'seduction', and so on.

In a recent interview, Raymond Federman made an emotive claim for the ethical superiority of anti-illusionist fictions such as his own, and those provided by like-minded 'surfictioners'.[21] In the battle against mimetic realism in contemporary literature:

I'm not destroying illusions simply for the sake of destroying illusions. I'm destroying illusions in order that we may face up to reality, and now what passes for reality . . . Unless we constantly question what passes for reality, challenge it, defy it, we will always exist in a falseness, in a system of twisted facts and glorified illusions and we quickly become lobotomized by it.[22]

The metaphorical equation of the circumscription of subjective autonomy by the systematized 'operation' of conventional rationality and the violent cauterization of nonconformist individuality by the invasive wielding of the surgeon's knife in the operation of lobotomy is indeed a powerful one. The equation of madness or eccentricity with desirable freedom and of sane conformity with abhorrent personal delimitation is familiar in literature. Contemporary examples abound: Patrick White in *Riders in the Chariot* (1976), Ken Kesey in *One Flew Over the Cuckoo's Nest* (1962), and Sylvia Plath in *The Bell Jar* (1963) all treat narrators, characters, or protagonists marginalized for their eccentricity and savagely subdued by institutionalized psychological control. The analogy is equally pervasive in contemporary literary, social, and political theory: Michel Foucault, R. D. Laing, and Gilles Deleuze and Felix Guattari provide some of the most powerful examples.[23] But the consequences of a release

---

[21] Federman's term for writers working in the experimental mode he promotes. See his collection of essays, *Surfiction: Fiction Now and Tomorrow* (Chicago: Swallow Press, 1975).

[22] In Tom Le Clair and Larry McCaffery, *Anything Can Happen: Interviews with Contemporary American Novelists* (Urbana, Ill.: University of Illinois Press, 1983), 42.

[23] Philip Beitchman, in *I Am a Process with No Subject* (Gainesville, Fla.: University of Florida Press, 1988), 218, observes that modernism 'in general is permeated by and preoccupied with questions of insanity and theatricality', and continues on the former quality: 'Madness is quintessentially the absence (and also the plethora) of work, of book, of memory, and of continuity that is so anguishing today; and schizophrenia, restlessly seeking and spiralling ever outward, compelled by its own inner logic and necessity and endemic refusal of accountability, its incessant "and then . . . and then," serves as an apt symbol, once it has been demedicalized, of a model for desire, availability, and functional endlessness in some of the most effective and influential texts of our times'. Beitchman's somewhat confused account is thoroughly permeated with references to the thought and writing of Michel Foucault, *Madness and*

(whether personal or textual) into the 'madness' of wholesale nonconformity, although frequently touted as desirable, are rarely explored by those who champion it. This is hardly surprising; the power of the appeal to the liberation of insanity lies not in the positive value of madness *per se*, but rather in the invidious negativity of its metaphorical opposite, psychological domination and control. The desirability for human subjects of wholesale release from normative rationality, so often equated with insanity or excommunication, needs evaluation.

One of the principal ways in which Federman and other contemporary experimental writers actualize their ideal of 'destroying [lobotomizing] illusions' is by heightening their reader's awareness of textual materiality, of the ways in which fictions work to construct the identities of reader, writer, and characters in a text. In drawing attention to the way in which the material 'solidity' of the text is in fact shot through with gaps and spaces, some contemporary fictioners challenge the solidity of all the identities to which we accord the metaphysical certainty of 'full presence', not least the personal identities we construct in our narrative acts of introspection. The format of conventional novels—a cover-bound series of consecutively numbered pages, neatly justified and arranged into easily digestible blocks of uniform type—is so familiar that we are encouraged to imagine that a direct translation of meaning occurs, through the neutral text, from author to reader. This illusion is thought by some to encourage essentialist notions of language, which have been called into question by contemporary philosophers and theorists, for whom epistemological scepticism, indeterminism, and relativity ensure that no text or language is ever 'innocent'. Words, it is claimed, like all the signs we interpret in our apprehension of meaning, are not simply neutral vehicles which carry pre-existing truths; language is more than an inert medium for the communication of realities which lie beyond it. We are never able to short-cut the mediating circuit of signification and contemplate thought directly—a circularity alluded to in the uroborus structure of a number of contemporary fictions and given its most economical treatment perhaps in John Barth's

Civilisation: A History of Insanity, trans. Richard Howard (New York: Vintage Books, 1965); it also directs the reader to Gilles Deleuze and Felix Guattari, *Anti-Oedipus: Capitalism and Schizophrenia*, trans. Robert Hurley, Mark Seem, and Helen Lane (New York: Viking, 1977), and R. D. Laing, *The Politics of Experience* (New York: Random House, 1967).

'Frame-Tale' in the collection of stories *Lost in the Funhouse* (1969). For many poststructuralist theorists, linguistic mediation is insidious, contagious, doubly deceptive, for its apparent neutrality; it is a violation of a pre-conceptual purity. Signs, according to Jonathan Culler, 'arrest the gaze, and by interposing their material form, affect or infect the thought'.[24]

Culler's metaphorical derogation of signing in the equation of its functioning with the contagion of disease (infection) typifies what I have called the 'rhetorical intimidation' employed by many post-structuralist critics. Instances in which the processes of reading, writing, and speaking are metaphorically equated with violation, dismemberment, submission, infelicity, and illness abound in contemporary theory. Michel Foucault, for example, urges us to conceive of discourse as 'a violence which we do to things'.[25] Sandra Gilbert and Susan Gubar aver that for the woman writer under patriarchy, '[t]he body of her precursor's art, and thus the body of her own art lies in pieces around her, dismembered, dis-remembered, disintegrated'.[26] Etienne Balibar and Pierre Machery assert that the writer is only ever a 'material agent, an intermediary inserted into a particular place, under conditions he has not created, *in submission* to contradictions which by definition he cannot control'[27] And Derrida writes that 'infelicity is an ill to which *all* [speech] acts are heir'.[28]

Consider the challenge to grammatical conventions which is made in the Pretext to Federman's novel *Take It or Leave It* (1976):

Syntax, traditionally is the unity, the continuity of the words, the *law* which *dominates* them. It reduces their multiplicity, *controls* their violence. It fixes them into a place, a space, *prescribes an order* to them. It *prevents* them from wandering. Even if it is hidden, it *reigns* always on the horizon of words which *buckle* under its *mute exigency*.[29]

[24] Jonathan Culler, *On Deconstruction: Theory and Criticism after Structuralism* (London: Routledge and Kegan Paul, 1983) 91.

[25] Michel Foucault, 'The Order of Discourse' (1970), repr. in Robert Young (ed.), *Untying the Text: A Post-Structuralist Reader* (Boston, London, and Henley: Routledge and Kegan Paul, 1981), 67.

[26] Sandra Gilbert and Susan Gubar, *The Madwoman in the Attic: The Woman Writer and Nineteenth-Century Literary Imagination* (New Haven: Yale University Press, 1979), 98.

[27] Etienne Balibar and Pierre Macherey, 'On Literature as an Ideological Form', in Young (ed.), *Untying the Text*, 95.

[28] Jacques Derrida, 'Signature Event Context', *Glyph* I (1977), 190.

[29] Raymond Federman, *Take It or Leave It* (New York: Fiction Collective,

The controlling, prescriptive domination of syntax, so described, is an affront to the values of democratic self-sovereignty which have such immense value in modern culture; the ordering restraint of grammatical law is approbative precisely because it threatens to violate the separateness and sanctity of individuality. Federman claims that in this novel, the monologic law of syntax gives way to the contextual situation of material production: 'syntax is abolished once and for all,' he claims. Syntax in *Take It or Leave It* 'ingratiates itself / to the constraint of the paper / its format / its dimensions / its margins / its edges / its consistency / its whiteness', and subordinates itself to the 'hazard / fatality which determines what will happen / next: the unpredictable shape of / typography' (8th page). One cannot help but question why ingratiation to the 'constraints of the paper' is in any way an improvement on a condition of submission to the dominance of syntactical law. Federman still requires a means of ordering his text and of communicating his rebellion if it is to remain a narrative structure that signifies. He is just proposing an *alternative* way of doing so, a way that self-consciously seeks to expose and challenge traditionally uncontested features of narrative organization.[30]

The novel which follows this revolutionary manifesto proceeds to bend and break the customary linear 'horizon of words' in presenting a polyphony of 'words / without order / where all elements are positive' (7th page). Sentences, phrases, words, syllables, and letters all 'occupy' the space of the pages, unbound by the controlling laws of syntax; words run backwards, vertically, diagonally, in circles, in squares, in numerous shapes and patterns, or gather in apparently random clusters which seem devoid of symbolic or iconographic purpose. Such typographic deviance is not unique to the work of

1976), 5th page (my emphasis); references hereafter in the text. Pages in the novel are unnumbered, but for the purposes of my discussion I will refer to their position as sequentially bound.

[30] See Peter Brooks, *Reading for the Plot: Design and Intention in Narrative* (1984; Cambridge, Mass., and London: Harvard University Press, 1992). Brooks argues that plotting ('the logic and dynamic of narrative, and narrative itself a form of understanding and explanation' (10); 'the logic and syntax of those meanings that develop only through sequence and succession' (113)) endures even the most radical postmodern anti-narrative suspicion: 'If the novels of Joyce and Woolf and Proust and Gide, and then Faulkner and Robbe-Grillet, cannot ultimately do without plotting insofar as they remain narrative structures that signify, they plot with irony and bad conscience, intent (in their very different ways) to expose the artifices of formal structure and human design' (113–14).

Federman; it has been used to varying effect in novels such as Steve Katz's *The Exagggerations* [*sic*] *of Peter Prince* (1968) and William Bain's *Informed Sources (Day East Received)* (1969) and in the work of critics such as Derrida, Mas'ud Zavarzadeh, and Ihab Hassan.[31]

Rebellion from Within: Errant Typography and Spacey Texts

Commenting on the novels of Katz and Bain, Joel Roth has suggested that the 'errant type arrangement' they employ 'pulls the reader in as an active participant and makes reading a creative act rather than passive absorption of information.'[32] This is certainly the case in *Take It or Leave It*, where the reader is forced to grapple with a mass of subversive textual elements in the struggle to impose coherence on the deviant pages of the book. Federman utilizes the full potential of the typewriter keyboard in his novel, with the idiosyncratic, unexpected use of punctuation marks, brackets, asterisks, dollar signs, and so on, in addition to the use of a variety of languages, fonts, numerals, italics, and upper- and lower-case letters. The effect of this unorthodox invasion of signs in the conventionally alphabetical domain of the novelistic page is to bring about a revaluation of those signs—letters, words spaces—whose signing capacity has been so masked by familiarity in standardized texts as to achieve the illusion of unmediating transparency. In doing so, it may encourage a revaluation of all the processes of signification which constitute the meanings and ontologies we perceive. But these signs never stop functioning *as* signs; their meaning is established by repetition and in terms of the new textual conditions set out in the Preface, conditions which sanction (and make explicable) their deviance. They offer alternative forms of, not an escape from, signification. The text does not invalidate the activity of signings; rather, it asks us to consider how signing works. The values of signs are determined by a different ordering context, but they still continue to mean.

The dizzying display of acrobatic verbosity in *Take It or Leave It*

[31] See e.g. Mas'ud Zavarzadeh, 'Critic as Conservator', *Poetics Today*, 3 (1982), 47–63; Ihab Hassan, *Paracriticisms: Seven Speculations on the Times* (Urbana, Ill.: University of Illinois Press, 1975); and Jacques Derrida, *Glas*, trans. John P. Leavey, Jr., and Richard Rand (Lincoln, Nebr.: University of Nebraska Press, 1986).

[32] Joel Roth, 'Excerpt: Typography that Makes the Reader Work', *Journal of Typographic Research*, 3 (Apr. 1969), 194.

makes a mockery of the standardized fictional format. As the novel progresses and the voices within it begin to jostle with one another for dominance and narrative control, so the number of typefaces increases, competing with each other for the reader's attention. Just as the material text is fractured by the manipulation of the white space of the page, the physical dislocation of words, and the disorientation caused by the use of a variety of fonts and point sizes, so too is the narrative flow repeatedly obstructed and disrupted. Events are constantly re-evaluated by the ploy of dissonant repetition whereby details are often changed significantly in each retelling (a strategy compounded by temporal shifts, perspectival changes, and the alternation of narrators). We are frequently enjoined to ignore previously recounted details and actions. It is impossible to secure the 'truth' with certainty; we are prevented from suspending disbelief and abandoning ourselves to the 'reality' of the fictional heterocosm. Essential information is only briefly sketched in the novel, or is omitted altogether, while seemingly trivial details are treated to lengthy articulation. Narrative progression is constantly interrupted as the narrator digresses to pontificate on a variety of topics from literature, through politics, to death. In fact, the narrator actually disappears for a time, leaving the telling of his tale to his protagonist, only to re-emerge several chapters later in order to reclaim the story and deride his temporary successor's narratorial incompetence. Chronology is hopelessly jumbled as characters from the past and the future or from other narrative frames and alternative worlds descend (literally!) into the fictional present. This radical ontological migration, the disconcerting appearance of trans-world identities, results in an unsettling shift of narrative frames and reader perspectives, which has its parallel in the convolutions of the type. The carnival of the sign, of the text, is unashamedly celebrated. As the narrator proudly asserts, this is a story 'which unloads in all directions and without respect for logic and with rather crooked means it is impossible to follow a straight line' (294th–295th pages).

But follow it we do. Meaning is far from forfeited in the multifarious free play of the fragmented text; ordering (and ultimately reductive closure) still take place, even if the locus of order has been displaced from an omnipotent author to a subjective reader-as-author. But even this last assertion is questionable; for the text is more than a random collection of marks which the reader patterns according to wholly subjective whim. The reader's capacity to 'make' the text is still constrained by the author's prior placement of signs and by an understanding of the protocols of reading which enable the words and text to signify, to function *as* words and text. The terms of Federman's (and our own) free play are made clear in his Pretext, where the (new) protocols that enable textual signification to proceed are clearly established. Indeterminism and ambiguity, active reader involvement and authorial absenteeism—these are the conditions of the text's, and our, play. Our interpretative creativity is *sanctioned*, we are invited (more, *told*) to make up the pages and impose our own meanings on signs as we read. The possibility and the productivity of interpretative plurality are written into the new, but none the less organizational, reading conventions set out in the Pretext. Federman declares, for example, that in his novel 'the pages become syntax' (7th page)—typography, then, is to replace grammar as the method of organization. Once this is understood, the atomized text is easily assimilated by the reader, even if this assimilation takes place as a narrative of disorder or discontinuity. The conventions which organize textual play need not be as explicitly stated as they are in Federman's novel, but are implicit in all texts; they are prior to, and the condition of, reader creativity, regardless of how active or passive this is.

In *A Future for Astyanax*, Leo Bersani gives voice to a recurrent motif in the (pseudo-) political claims of contemporary literary criticism, namely that the conventions of mimetic realism in fiction sustain and perpetuate undesirable ideological myths which falsely represent reality and the status of human subjects to its naïve, complacently accepting readers. This false ideological representation, it is claimed, induces the mistaken belief of the subject in her personal freedom and in the purposive order of her environment. Bersani proposes that the nineteenth-century realist novel 'has trained us to be compulsive pursuers of significant design in fiction', and that 'the realistic novel gives us an image of social fragmentation contained within the order of significant form'.[33] Novels such as *War and Peace* and *Middlemarch*, he argues, functioned to sustain misleading Victorian political and philosophical beliefs by 'providing [them] with strategies for containing (and repressing) order within significantly structured stories'.[34] He develops this idea in *The Freudian Body*:

[33] Leo Bersani, *A Future for Astyanax: Character and Desire in Literature* (London: Marion Boyars, 1978), 52, 66.

[34] Ibid., 63. Similar claims are made for the 'totalizing' effect of Eliot's novel

The realistic novel, for all its apparent 'looseness' . . . is an extremely tight and coherent structure: it encourages us to believe in the temporal myth of real beginnings and definitive endings, it portrays a world in which events always have a significance which can be articulated, and it encourages the view of the self as organized (if also ravaged) by dominant passions or faculties. These ordered significances of realistic fiction are in fact the mythical denial of that society's destructively fragmented nature.[35]

Bersani's claims are representative of the suspicion and mistrust displayed by many contemporary theorists towards what is deemed the deceptive, repressive nature of mimetic realism or other conventional literary modes. The Victorian realistic novel, charged with naïve and dangerous literalism, has borne the brunt of this attack: through its mimetic re-presentation of an ordered reality in teleological causal narratives which portray the actions of psychologically rounded and consistent characters, nineteenth-century realist fiction is responsible, it is argued, for deceiving readers into misrecognizing the chaotic fragmentation of phenomenological reality and the subjection of their social constitution. In other words, the dogma of realist theories of literary representation, founded on essentialist concepts such as transcendence, unity, originality, closure, and authority, is thought to sustain and endorse repressive social and political structures while propagating misconceptions about subjective freedom. Significant design in fiction, then, lulls the reader into a sense of false security, and dishonestly encourages aberrant assumptions with regard to the 'significance' of the external world and the 'organization' of the inner self. It fosters an illusory belief in mythical notions such as self-coherence and meaningful progression. And more, in order to do so, it contains and represses by marginalizing, subordinating, or excluding alternative modes of writing and being which do not conform to its hierarchical structures of organization.

The deviation from typographic norms in experimental meta-fiction may show the manner in which rule-bound rebellion can

by J. Hillis Miller 'Optic and Semiotic in *Middlemarch*', in Jerome Buckley (ed.), *The Worlds of Victorian Fiction* (Cambridge, Mass., and London: Harvard University Press, 1975), 125–45; and Colin McCabe, *James Joyce and the Revolution of the Word* (London: Macmillan, 1979), 4–29. For a discussion of the claims of Miller and McCabe in this regard, see David Lodge, '*Middlemarch* and the Idea of the Classic Realist Text', in *After Bakhtin*, 87–99.

[35] Leo Bersani, *The Freudian Body* (New York: Columbia University Press, 1986), 82.

proceed for meta-fictional novelists who situate their resistance to conformity *within* the novelistic form itself. Furthermore, it provides a useful means of considering the success and the failure of the revolutionary enterprise of textual authenticity. In light of the metaphorical equation of text and self, the meta-fictional project of typographic deviance has far greater import than that of mere playfulness: it aims not only to draw attention to the material constitution of the text, but to expose also the materiality of the conceptual medium, thought, wherein self (as text) is written.

The derogation of print conventions is common in contemporary literary criticism. Ronald Sukenick, for example, formulates his attack on type conventions as follows:

We badly need a new way of thinking about novels that acknow-ledges their technological reality. We have to learn how to look at fic-tion as lines of print on a page and have to ask whether it is the best arrangement to have a *solid block of print* from one margin to the other running down the page from top to bottom, except for the occasional paragraph indentation. We have to learn to think about a novel as a concrete structure rather than as allegory, existing in the realm of experience rather than in the realm of discursive meaning, and available to multiple interpretations or none.[36]

The conventional 'arrangement' of the novelistic page has certainly been rethought by many contemporary writers, who, in acknow-ledging the 'technological reality' of the text, aim to fragment the page, to expose its porosity, and to call attention to the gaps and spaces which riddle the apparently 'solid block of print'. Brian McHale has argued that postmodern novelists' use of unexpected blank space in their texts disrupts the expectations of spacelessness usually associated with prose-writing, thereby foregrounding the materiality of the page, the arena in which type conventions *contain* meaning: 'the functional invisibility of space in prose fiction is what distinguishes prose from verse, with its conventions of unjustified right margin and stanza breaks. Spacing is the sign of verse; prose, the unmarked member of the pair, is identified by spacelessness.'[37]

Contemporary fiction is notable for its 'spaciness'; unorthodox, invasive gaps are evident in a variety of places in many novels— between chapters, paragraphs, sentences, words, and even letters. In

[36] Ronald Sukenick, *In Form: Twelve Digressions on the Act of Fiction* (Car-bondale, Ill.: Southern Illinois University Press, 1985), 206.

[37] McHale, *Postmodernist Fiction*, 181.

Kurt Vonnegut's *Wampeters, Foma and Granfalloons* (1975), for example, the disintegration of illusory 'spacelessness' is achieved in flagrantly graphic terms. Short paragraphs are severed from each other by apparently gratuitous white space, several line-lengths in depth, and the disruption of paginal solidity so achieved is further heightened by the use of very large, bold typeface for the first letter of each paragraph. Russell Hoban has made extensive use of the ploy of spaciness in his fiction; his *Kleinzeit* (1974) consists of a series of very short chapters, some only half a page in length. The chapters in his novel *Medusa Frequency* (1987) are similarly brief, with the first chapter having only eight lines, chapter 19 only ten lines, and chapters 22 and 28 only eight and twenty-four lines respectively. Angela Carter's *The Passion of New Eve* (1977) and Richard Brautigan's *The Abortion: An Historical Romance, 1966* (1973) make similar use of extremely short chapters which strikingly foreground the blank space of the page. The invasive, unexpected introduction of space into the previously solid novelistic page has been taken to its limit by writers such as Eugene Wildman in *Montezuma's Ball* (1970), B. S. Johnson in *Housemother Normal* (1971), Ronald Sukenick in *Long Talking Bad Conditions Blues* (1979), and Alasdair Gray in *1982, Janine* (1984), all of which contain completely blank pages.

Ronald Suckenick's *Out* (1973) begins in a deceptively ordinary manner: the layout of the first chapter, chapter 10 (the chapters are numbered regressively) conforms to conventional prose format, with words filling each page in a single block of justified type. However, with each subsequent chapter, the invasion of space becomes more pervasive. Pages are broken up into smaller and smaller sections of type, and as the novel progresses, the expanse of white space between each cluster of words increases. These forced breaks are not syntactic, but proceed according to a rigid numerical design: in the second chapter, chapter 9, nine lines of type before a single line space, which is followed by another nine-line block of type and another single line space, to the chapter's end. In the following chapter, chapter 8, each block of type is only eight lines deep, and is separated by a double line space; in chapter 7, units of seven lines of print are separated by triple line spaces. This pattern continues throughout the novel, so that, as we move through the numerical regression of the chapters, pages are increasingly dominated by white space. The final chapter, chapter 0, features only a single '0' on an otherwise empty page, and is followed by several blank pages.

We cannot read *Out*, with its ostentatious flouting of the conventions of prose spacelessness without asking important questions about the constraints imposed on fiction by conformity to the standardized format. But the questions we ask are less to do with the possibility of escape from formal dictates than of the degree to which a writer is bound to accept any *given* set of formal regulations and the capacity she has to transgress them while still producing a readable text. The disruptive strategies used by Sukenick in *Out* strikingly reveal the problems which confound poststructuralist programmes of revolutionary 'release' from the requirements of iterability and recognition which are the conditions for communication. *Out* fails to escape the constraints of its own making: the novel's liberating dissolution is itself rigidly controlled, its fragmentation stylized and soon established as merely an alternative means of ordering, not an escape from order. If the value of its enterprise is to be understood, its innovative form must be given significance as design. Not even the silent expanse of the white pages at the novel's end manage to circumvent what is finally only another imposition of order; their meaning is bound, literally and conceptually, within the covers of the book and to the pattern of the preceding pages. *Out* evidences the inevitability of conceptual closure, where the condition for meaningfulness is, ineluctably, the imposition of design.[38]

[38] Sukenick's radical format has been rationalized by several critics, who suggest that it functions as a visual representation of increasing psychological vacuity on the part of the novel's characters and narrator (McHale, *Postmodernist Fiction*, 183) or, alternatively, as the typographic rendition of the narrative journey 'from the clutter and hassle of the East to the pure space of an empty California beach' (Jerome Klinkowitz, *Literary Disruptions: The Making of a Post-Contemporary Fiction* (Urbana, Ill., Chicago and London: University of Illinois Press, 1975), 13. Such rationalizations typify the (inevitable?) critical tendency to reduce literary formal experimentation to readily explainable iconicity. We are comfortable with such (essentially aesthetic) reductions; iconographic literature has long been established within the 'literary' canon (consider the poems of George Herbert, e.g., or, in fiction, the experimental pages in Laurence Sterne's *Tristram Shandy*). Form is secondary, merely the confirmation or expression of the 'meaning' of a work. The work of writers such as Sukenick is certainly amenable to such analysis. But this is not the whole picture. As I have suggested, these writers are particularly concerned to reverse this prioritization, to stress the priority of form in determining meaning: 'The truth of these pages is on top of it, not underneath or over at the library' (Sukenick, *In Form*, 212). Form, in these terms, is constitutive of textual meaning, not merely an expression of it. The viability of the wholesale prioritization of form over content in literature is dubious, a point to which I shall return.

Conceptual Self-sundering

> Every 'I' implies immediately a 'you'—real, fictive or even
> ideal—to whom the speech act is directed. For every emitter
> there is a receiver. . . . A monologue is strictly impossible, for
> even when I speak to myself I am split into two selves and
> thus there is an emitter and a receiver.
>
> Carroll, *The Subject in Question*[39]

Unfamiliar typography and intrusive spaciness are used to striking
effect in Federman's *The Voice in the Closet* (1979). In a radical
deviation from the self-effacing transparency of standardized typography, the novel's unconventional format ostentatiously announces
its status as artefact. But the novel does far more than merely reiterate
the ploy, so often used in contemporary meta-fictions, of flaunting its
own made-up status through the use of disruptive typography. It not
only flaunts its artifice, but probes the necessity of significant form,
revealing the specious limits of an idealistic dream of wholesale
release from formal constraints.

The Voice in the Closet alternates twenty pages of visual text with
twenty pages of verbal text. The first page of the visual text features a
single vertical line on an otherwise empty page; on each successive
page a new line is added at right angles, so that by the fourth page a
square has been formed. The procedure is repeated over the next four
pages, within the area delimited by the borders of this square,
resulting in the formation of another square within the first. This
process is continued to the end of the book, at which point five boxes
within boxes occupy the previously empty paginal space. The words
which constitute the verbal text flow across each alternate page
separated only by a single letter space, without the organizing
presence of paragraphs, sentences, punctuation, or capitalization
(except for the pronoun 'I').

The text is an autobiographical fiction in which the protagonist,
the 'real' Federman, 'the actual me', struggles vainly to assert
independence from Federman-the-narrator's retelling of him(self).
Federman-the-narrator, claims the protagonist, 'pretends to invent'

---

[39] Carroll is, of course, summarizing the claims of Emile Benveniste. The
notion that a private language is impossible is more rightly attributed to the
later Wittgenstein.

his autobiographical self as a 'virtual being' in the (re)writing of his life. 'Me' wishes to convey the unmediated actuality of his being, to recount, without the circumvolutions and distortions of narrational rewriting, the horrific story of his childhood escape from the Nazi death camps which claimed the lives of the rest of his Jewish family. His impossible desire is to exist meaningfully as a subject, authentically untold. He wishes to be free from Federman's (his own) conceptual articulations, and to realize 'the reality of [his] past' unsullied by the distortions of narrative (re)telling:

a split exists between the actual me wandering voiceless in a temporary landscape and the virtual being federman pretends to invent in his excremental packages of delusions a survivor who dissolves in verbal articulations unable to do what I had to do admit that his fictions can no longer match the reality of my past (eleventh page)

The Voice in the Closet thus confronts the post-Cartesian philosophical dilemma of 'misrecognition' in the reflexive act of self-conceptualization, the fundamental psychic split between the 'I' who experiences being ('the actual me') and the 'I' ('federman') who recognizes that experience by rewriting it as meaningful narrative in the temporal linear sequence of conceptualization: the split which is at once both the condition of self-identification and that which prohibits self-identity (the unity of 'me' and 'federman' in an authentic 'I'). The problem of self-narrativization, of reflective introspection, is one persistently posed by contemporary theorists. Many contemporary autobiographies, such as Breyten Breytenbach's *The True Confessions of an Albino Terrorist* (1984), Philip Roth's *The Facts* (1988), and Janet Frame's autobiographical trilogy *To the Is-land* (1982), *An Angel at My Table* (1984), and *The Envoy from Mirror City* (1985), stress the fictionality of the act of remembering one's life-story—a tactic which unsettles conventional assumptions about the factuality of autobiography and, even more disturbingly, challenges the assumption that we can ever, with impunity, truthfully conceptualize our own life-story. There always exists a gap, temporal and conceptual, between the I who is telling and the I who is told, even in the telling of oneself to oneself. Derrida expresses the impossibility of speaking authentic (in other words, certain and singular) selfhood, of conceptualizing one's self in language and yet remaining uncontaminated by the dialogical and dialectical processes of linguistic meditation:

As soon as I speak, the words I have found (as soon as they are words) no longer belong to me. . . . As soon as I am heard, as soon as I hear myself, the I who hears *itself*, who hears *me*, becomes the I who speaks and takes speech from the I who thinks that he speaks and is heard in his own name; and becomes the I who takes speech *without ever cutting off* the I who thinks that he speaks.[40]

The pain of the torturous self-sundering which inheres in the act of conceptualizing oneself in communal language is all the more powerfully portrayed in Federman's novel for the implicit, perhaps audacious, analogy drawn between the 'violence' of the conceptual cleavage of the 'I', 'dissolve[d] in verbal articulations', and the atrocities of dismemberment—the severance and dissolution of social, familial, psychic, and physical identities—which were inflicted in the Nazi concentration camps.

It is impossible for 'the actual me' to escape from 'federman's' narrative (re)constructions: they are the condition of his meaningful being. This is the paradox of (re)cognized selfhood—we at once both write (as 'I') and are written as a character in (as 'me') our own narratives of personal identity. Although we desire to escape the limitations and partiality of our conceptual narrations, we depend on these for our very perception of who we are. Such an analysis of identity is, of course, the familiar rhetoric of poststructuralism, and opens the door to a host of seemingly insoluble problems, some of which were discussed in previous chapters. Not least of these is the implication of the extra-personal violation of communicated selfhood towards which Federman's text gestures: if 'me' is recognizable only as the subject of another's thought (albeit that this thinking other may be a past or alternative 'I'), then my intuition of myself is always tainted by otherness. I am always the mutilated victim of my own reflexive questing, framed in the language of others. I am forever condemned to endure the torturous deceptions of my own (as another's) thought processes. So Derrida again: 'The speaking subject discovers his irreducible secondarity, his origin that is always already eluded'.[41]

The pronominal space denoted by 'I' in *The Voice in the Closet* is the location of both the 'survivor' and the perpetrator of textual violence. It is simultaneously I-he who wanders 'voiceless in

[40] Jacques Derrida, *Writing and Difference*, trans. Alan Bass (1967; Chicago: University of Chicago Press, 1978), 177–8.
[41] Ibid. 178.

temporary landscapes' and I-he who 'invent[s] . . . excremental packages of delusions . . . fictions [which] can no longer match the reality of my [his] past'. In the conflation of narrator and character in the pronominal space of 'I', introspection becomes a kind of narcissistic masochism: Federman, I-he, in thinking (of) self is inescapably implicated in the (self-)deception he describes. The text is equally deceived and deceiving in its disconcerting lability, which prohibits settlement into the contours of formal familiarity or consistent characterological identity. It is 'words in regress without destination', the dubious 'historic fiasco' of 'faulty memory', a fraudulent narrative which obscures the 'hysterical screaming' of the past (15th page). The poststructuralist paradox of introspective thought, the misrepresentation of self to self in the language of others, seems unavoidable here: both text and textualized selfhood are shattered, yet brought into being, in language.

The echoes of Samuel Beckett in Federman's onslaught on the narrative 'subject'—text, narrator, character—denoted by the pronominal 'I', are unmistakable.[42] An extract from *The Unnamable* reveals the correspondence between Federman and Beckett's concerns: 'I never spoke, I seem to speak, that's because he says I as if he were I, I nearly believed him, do you hear him, as if he were I . . . there is no name for me, no pronoun for me, all the trouble comes from that.'[43] A few pages later, Beckett's narrator continues, 'No sense in bickering about pronouns and other parts of blather. The subject doesn't matter, there is none.'[44] But how is writing to proceed when '[t]he subject doesn't matter', when, with the wholesale dismemberment of the subject by and in language, there remains only 'the terror-stricken babble of those condemned to silence'?[45]—a question of great importance, with consequences that extend far beyond the arena of literature. Claims for the politically insidious nature of textual processes are frequently made by contemporary

---

[42] Federman is, of course, a noted Beckett critic.

[43] Samuel Beckett, *Three Novels: Malloy, Malone Dies, and the Unnamable*, trans. Samuel Beckett (New York: Grove Press, 1955), 497.

[44] Ibid. 500. Compare this with Beckett's comment on *The Unnamable* in 1956: 'there's complete disintegration. No "I", no "have", no "being". No nominative, no accusative, no verb. There's no way to go on.' Cited in John Fletcher, *The Novels of Samuel Beckett* (London: Chatto and Windus, 1972), 194. Of course, after his eight-year silence Beckett *did* go on, seeking a way out of the impasse of silence or suicide through the stylistic innovations of his later novels and plays. See Fletcher, *Novels of Samuel Beckett*, 195–233.

[45] Beckett, *Three Novels*, 492.

critics—and hotly disputed.[46] Leo Bersani, for example, suggests that the

> mythologizing of the human as a readable organisation is a fundamental political strategy, and the eagerness with which both literature and psycho-analysis have contributed to that mythology may be the surest sign of their willingness to serve various types of orders interested in the shaping of the human as a precondition for predicting and controlling it.[47]

Fearful invocation of these manipulative ideological 'orders' is rife in much contemporary theory. Bersani's overt politicization of textuality as the site of the ideological reproduction of hierarchical and gender stereotypes follows the precedent set by a legion of anti-authoritarian theorists. Richard Crosman, for example, writes of 'an ideology of society that is authoritarian and hierarchical';[48] and James Kavanagh writes similarly: 'if society uses apparatuses of force to confront overt rebellion, it uses apparatuses of ideology to form members of its various classes into social subjects who are unlikely to ever consider rebellion.'[49] Derrida suggests that 'there is always a police tribunal ready to intervene each time a rule . . . is invoked in a case involving signatures, events, or contexts';[50] and Geoffrey Hartman insists that

---

[46] See Hogan, *Politics of Interpretation*, for a discussion of the claims and counter-claims made for the political value of applied poststructuralist theory, to whose self-aggrandizing rhetoric of liberation he is less than sympathetic. His book is an important extension of the debate on interpretative politics. See Gerald Graff, 'The Pseudo-Politics of Interpretation', in W. J. T. Mitchell (ed.), *The Politics of Interpretation* (Chicago and London: University of Chicago Press, 1982), 145–158. Graff asks, 'Are political arguments relevant in literary theory and, if so, under what conditions?' (147). The Mitchell anthology collects together a series of essays concerned with the political nature of our acts of interpretation which were published in the September 1982, December 1982, and March 1983 issues of *Critical Inquiry*. Important essays in this collection include Walter Benn Michaels, 'Is There a Politics of Interpretation?' (335–46); E. D. Hirsh, Jr., 'The Politics of Theories of Interpretation' (321–34); and Gayatri Chakravorty Spivak, 'The Politics of Interpretations' (347–66). See also Jim Merod, *The Political Responsibility of the Critic* (Ithaca, NY: Cornell University Press, 1987), and Alan Kennedy, *Reading Resistance Value: Deconstructive Practice and the Politics of Literary Criticism* (Basingstoke: Macmillan, 1990).

[47] Bersani, *Freudian Body*, 83.

[48] Richard Crosman, 'Do Readers Make Meaning?', in Susan Rubin Suleiman and Inge Crosman (eds.), *The Reader in the Text: Essays on Audience and Reception* (Princeton: Princeton University Press, 1980), 154.

[49] James Kavanagh, 'Ideology', in Frank Lentricchia and Thomas McLaughlin (eds.), *Critical Terms for Literary Study* (Chicago and London: University of Chicago Press, 1990), 308–9.

[50] Jacques Derrida, 'Limited Inc. abc . . .', trans S. Weber, *Glyph*, 2 (1977), 205.

any attempt to establish an objective hermeneutics is 'an act of defensive mastery' which 'involves technocratic violence'.[51] Beyond proclaiming their menace, such metaphorical rhetoric fails utterly to define the nature of these controlling orders or to suggest how shattering the myth of the organized, 'readable' subject might in any way liberate us from their power. Even more important, it fails to explain the value of this shattering of the readable subject-text: why should it matter at all if the subject who is to be liberated no longer matters—*can* no longer matter because its liberation necessarily entails its devaluation, the utter dissolution of its identity?

Bersani's argument, like that of other poststructuralist critics, hints at an impossible and paradoxical escape which is itself only a reinscription of domination: 'By initiating a designifying mobility within a text, the author's silent, insistent voice undoes that security of statement by which we can so easily be seduced, and possessed.'[52] It seems to me that this is no more than a trade-off or relocation of the site of domination—from the seduction of possessive textual statement to the silent insistence of authorial voice. The dream of escape from the coercive designs of formal significance, when pushed to its limit must entail the annihilation of the subject-text with either resignation to the wholesale fragmentation of non-communicative babble or a suicidal submission to silence.

Narrative Creation

It is a mistake, however, to assume that the entire generation of contemporary writers is simply content (or condemned) to reiterate this self-flagellating intuition of linguistic despair and inauthenticity or to wallow in the paradox of the communication of communicative impossibility. Many contemporary novelists remain singularly resistant to such self-destructive defeatism. For these, writing is more than a Sisyphean labour, more than an act of obdurate stoicism; it is never simply the endurance of the unbearable task of writing, the unbearable fate of being. Certainly, many contemporary fictions begin with the doubt—epistemological and ontological—which is their philosophical and literary inheritance (a doubt, it must be said,

[51] Geoffrey Hartman, 'Literary Criticism and its Discontents', *Critical Inquiry*, 3 (Winter 1976), 218, 217.
[52] Bersani, *Freudian Body*, 67.

which they are remarkably capable of both recognizing and conveying). But they have moved beyond the narcissistic paralysis of self-reflexive agony. Contemporary writers, after all, continue to write. Many have recognized the creative potential of narration, its power to order experiential chaos into comprehensible narratives of reality and identity, its power to invent and maintain communal values which make interactive human lives meaningful and purposeful. Although these writers can never claim the innocence of ontological certainty, they are not, content to woefully lament the sceptical realization that consciousness, like writing, entails deception, mediation, repression, and the falsification of reality. They have moved on, instead, to explore the regenerative nature of their art. Their literary enterprise is one of replenishment, not exhaustion, as further consideration of *The Voice in the Closet* suggests.[53]

Despite their apparent freedom from grammatical restraints, the words comprising the verbal text of the novel are carefully organized within a rigidly formatted design. On each page the words are shaped into a perfectly justified square, echoing the framed boxes portrayed in the visual text and consistent with the narrative concern with concentration camp incarceration and conceptual enclosure. A character in a later Federman novel, *The Twofold Vibration* (1982) describes *The Voice in the Closet* as

perfect squares of words on pages with no punctuation, no interruptions, it was like a long delirious verbal disarticulation without beginning or end, just boxes of black words prisoner of their own form. . . . a long syntactical disarticulation, without beginning or end, as it should be, but in the right place, I hope, yes, just words, words abandoned to deliberate chaos and yet boxed into an inescapable form, you'll see, boxes of words.[54]

This oxymoronic description—'syntactical disarticulation', 'deliberate chaos'—suggests the paradoxical impasse of (narrative) conceptualization I have just discussed: the necessity of limiting form which enables the realization of meaning and identity, while at the same time always precluding the possibility of achieving formless textual autonomy. Federman's words remain 'prisoner of their own form'. In

---

[53] I refer to John Barth's oft-cited essays 'The Literature of Exhaustion', 1967, repr. in Malcolm Bradbury (ed.), *The Novel Today: Contemporary Writers on Modern Fiction* (London: Fontana, 1977), 70–83; and 'The Literature of Replenishment', *Atlantic Monthly*, 245/1 (1980), 65–71.

[54] Raymond Federman, *The Twofold Vibration* (Bloomington, Ind.: Indiana University Press and Brighton: Harvester Press, 1982), 115–16.

exchanging one type of enclosure (or enclosure of type), that of the traditional page format, for another type of enclosure, his own equally circumscribing design, he does not find freedom in *The Voice in the Closet*, but admits only to the necessity of 'inescapable form'.

Such an admission could not be further from a poststructuralist celebration of radically transgressive, hence formless, emancipation. The very form of Federman's novel draws attention to the boxing and containment of the subject (text and character) by the (de)signs which strive to articulate them. Words can no more escape the framing conventions which are the condition of their communicative function than can the 'actual me' exist as an autonomous identity disengaged from its narrating self or the medium of narration, language. The impossibility of a (meaningful) utopian escape into formlessness is brilliantly portrayed on the fifteenth page of the verbal text. Here the 'actual me' makes his most desperate bid for essentiality, his most strident demand for an independent voice: 'I will set out of my reversed role speak in my *own voice* at last even if I must outstretch myself to the unattainable' (my emphasis), only to immediately acknowledge the unattainability of this ideal. It is impossible to sever the umbilical cord which binds him to the narrating I, 'federman', without surrendering to the bloodless suspension of voiceless non-being, to the endless postponement of his beginning:

but suppose fatigued and disgusted he [federman] abandons me will I ever be able to become the essential and not remain a special event on the edge of the abyss stalled words in regress without destination an historic fiasco within his hysterical screaming obscured by faulty memory yes suppose he gives up dies one morning among millions of unfinished moments in the middle of a word will I remain suspended from his blood lifeless voice within a voice without a story to tell my beginning postponed by federman's absence.

The dream of attaining his 'own voice' is a cruel fantasy, for without 'federman', the 'actual me' is voiceless, lifeless, 'without a story to tell'. Unless communicated and read, he has no meaningful being, he has no perceivable existence in the silences between the words of the narrating I, his speaking and spoken self:

now then				I forever been
where to	now	don't even say why		but you
you ask		how		I
skip	never before spoken		yet what	for me	no

The visual impact of these unexpected inter-verbal spaces is very powerful, particularly in their marked deviation from the pattern of verbal solidity established on the previous pages. These gaping holes in the hitherto dense weave of the text vividly portray the protagonist's dependence on the narrator who speaks both the voice and the story he would claim as his unspoken own. There is no escape from the taint of otherness and the constraints of communication into the essentiality of an unmediated 'me', unless into the mindless oblivion of the blank page. Freedom equates here to the silence of self-obliteration or the pathological babble of formless nonsense and misrecognition. We all exist as 'virtual' beings, caught within the closets, the boxes and enclosures, of articulation; we are all caught within the concentration camps of our intellections. The self-torturous post-Cartesian dilemma of endlessly mediated conceptuality adopted and then eschewed by some contemporary theorists and novelists in manifestos of subjective dissolution is unmitigated by a myth of pre-linguistic authenticity or excommunicative escape. This amounts, finally, to a suicidal fantasy of paradisal reclamation, a fantasy which is, paradoxically, the most fundamental expression of Romantic narcissism. We see here the impasse of poststructuralist theory: a futile narcissism born of a metaphysics of loss, one which contrasts only the (irretrievable) pure plenitude of unnarrativized essentiality with the failure of conceptual narrativity to encapsulate the mobility of nomadic being; an exhausted headbanging which seeks to escape the contours of its own defining skull. Victory is indeed bitter when the worth of the liberating enterprise is underwritten by the martyrdom of the subject it would liberate.

But it appears to me that the initial premiss of wholesale extra-textual constitution upon which this self-defeating account turns is discredited by the remarkable resistance to fragmentation of the subject, characterological and textual. Much contemporary theory, in its stress on the corruption and infection wreaked by the communicative structures of significant design (typographic, linguistic, psychological, political), wholly disregards the generative creativity of narrative (de)signing, the capacity of interpretation and narrativization to shape and order those silent potentialities which gain voice and identity only in (as) formal constitution. This is a grave omission. Again and again the subject is reaffirmed and reconstituted in the very processes of contemporary experimental fictions, fictions that are able to recognize and agonize over their own constitutional dilemma. Federman's novel is a case in point: certainly, 'me' is constrained by the form of F/federman's prescripted and recognizable narrative; but unspoken, he must remain speechless; unwritten, he has no story to tell. Until 'subjected' in language, he has no meaningful being. The activity of self-narration *creates* for him an identity, one which is certainly problematic, but an identity which none the less can recognize and confront the problematics of its own constitution: speaking/writing himself offers some capacity for self-constitution. The hyperbolic advocacy of excommunicative fragmentation as a means of attaining subjective authenticity and the theoretical call for the endless subversion of meaning in the free play of (linguistic) difference are finally unrealized in those contemporary fictions in which the overriding desire to communicate makes it impossible to accept the consequences of poststructuralist dissemination. In anticonventional acts of rebellion, these fictions do not escape the limitations of communication, but are invariably reformed in, and as, significant, signifying alternative or marginal textual communities.

On the model proposed in previous chapters, our interpretative freedom is never absolute, but resides in our ability to challenge and even change, *within* language, the communicative conventions, or protocols of reading, which determine the interpretation of textual meaning, and by metaphoric extension, the meaning of our own narratives of selfhood which are constituted within the variety of communal contexts within which we exist. Within language, as a condition of its productive operation, there always exists the disruptive and creative potential of irreducible otherness: the semiotic (Kristeva), the polyphonic (Bakhtin), the centralized margin (Soja and Hooper). As the radical, but readable, novels discussed in this chapter suggest, within the boundaries of language and literary convention there is significant scope for transgression. It may not be possible (or desirable) to escape the intersubjective protocols of readable (de)signing, but we are able to instigate their reformation by choosing to situate ourselves at rebellious sites on the margins of conventional readability and communication, where the polyphonic voices of plurality may contest the authority of established discursive protocols. *Contra* the claims of some deconstructive critics, rebellious and experimental fictions such as those discussed in this chapter have in no way opted for outsider excommunication, but have wilfully situated themselves at plural sites of resistance, (de)signing altern-atives on the margins of community and communication.

5

The Posture of Textual Dissemination

For many contemporary theorists and philosophers, introspection entails not the unmediated discovery of a unified and self-transparent self, but the division of the introspective subject into reflecting subject ('I') and reflected object ('me'). The 'I' which observes and the 'me' being observed can never cohere into a transcending self; they are always divided in the very act of self-conscious observation. This is, of course, the familiar position of Benveniste, Lacan, and Derrida. So conceived, the self I imagine myself to be is always imaginary, a discursive construct fraught with hermeneutic uncertainty. It is subject to the radical temporality of *différance* which renders pure presence, true meaning, impossible of discovery. Selfhood is always less (and more) than the discovery of permanent presence; it is a textual process fragmented by gaps and omissions, riven by repressed drives and desires. I can only ever (mis)recognize the (mis)represented image of myself constituted in the symbolic realm of 'reality'. I can never truly know the foundational presence which is my 'real' self. But why should I seek to know myself as a fixed, permanent presence? This is surely to look for the wrong thing entirely. The discovery of a transcendental self is hardly desirable, even if it were possible, for this must limit me to the given contours of the unchanging, permanent form I discover. In the lamentation of the loss of the permanent presence of an immanent self, discredited metaphysics and determinism are reconstituted with a vengeance, as unattainable desire.

For Lacan and the many poststructuralists who adhere to the notion of the conceptually divided subject, self-scrutiny reveals not the presence of self, but the absence of its realized loss (not mere lack) in the (mis)recognition of the specular image of oneself as textual subject. 'I' is only another temporal language construct located in the space between a speaking self and a spoken representation of self. So Derrida avers: 'What is called the speaking subject is no longer the person himself, or the person alone, who speaks. The speaking subject discovers his irreducible secondarity, his origin that is always already eluded . . . on the basis of an organised field of speech.'[1] Conjoined with this notion in contemporary theory is an understanding of the intersubjectivity of all speech acts. There is no private language. Even the most personal internal 'monologue' is in fact dialogic and diachronic in its functioning: 'As soon as I speak', writes Derrida, 'the words that I have found (as soon as they are words) no longer belong to me.'[2] For many contemporary theorists, because knowledge of oneself is always mediated by the terms of social discourse, self-perception is always corrupted or defiled by the language of others, or the language of oneself as another. (But why? Why not simply changed, or even improved?) Unmediated awareness of selfhood is deemed impossible.

Although dismissal of Cartesian claims of self-reflexive certainty is the familiar rhetoric of poststructuralist theory, it is hardly original to contemporary thought, as Peter Dews (following Dieter Heinrich) and Andrew Bowie have recently argued.[3] The notion of the absence of any pre-predicative, pre-reflexive ground of (self-)certainty was contemplated by philosophers in the eighteenth century, although the logical consequences for subjectivity of such thinking were dismissed as untenable at the time. Fichte, for example, argued that in the absence of any self-certainty, existence would be no more than a state of permanent misrecognition and a condition of infinitely regressive self-fragmentation. This, he claimed, was wholly incommensurate with his experience of being human. If we are to deny the unity of the self, argued Fichte, the knowledge of which is immanent and prior to conceptualization, the logical consequences are quite insupportable. Without self-certainty, he wrote:

There is nowhere anything lasting, neither outside me, nor within me, but only incessant change. I nowhere know of any being, not even my own. There is no being. *I myself* know nothing and am nothing. There

---

[1] Jacques Derrida, *Writing and Difference*, trans. Alan Bass (1967; Chicago: University of Chicago Press, 1978), 177–8.

[2] Ibid. 178.

[3] Peter Dews, *The Logics of Disintegration: Post-Structuralist Thought and the Claims of Critical Theory* (London and New York: Verso, 1987). Dews acknowledges his debt in this analysis to Deiter Heinrich's essay 'Ficht's Original Insight', trans. R. D. Lachterman, in *Contemporary German Philosophy* (University Park, Pa.: Pennsylvania State University Press, 1982), 15–22. See also Andrew Bowie, *Aesthetics and Subjectivity: From Kant to Nietzsche* (Manchester: Manchester University Press, 1990).

are only *images*: they are the only things which exist, and they know of themselves in the manner of images. . . . I myself am one of those images; indeed, I am not even this but only a confused image of images.[4]

For Ficht, as for many of his contemporaries, this is an unacceptable misrepresentation of our most intimate intuitions of self-substantiality. This led to Fichte's development of the notion of the 'self-positing subject', of an I that is self-grounded, absolute, or unconditionally posited, an I that is capable of self-determination.[5]

Where poststructuralists differ in their thinking from earlier thinkers in this sceptical tradition is in their acceptance, and even celebration, of a vision of subjective uncertainty and fragmentation. The endless misrecognition and interminable displacement of one's self, which is logically presupposed in a poststructuralist theory of textualized subjectivity where language is deemed prior to (conceptual) being, is hailed as emancipatory. It appears to offer freedom from the transcendentalist essentiality which would bind one to the predetermined characteristics of a fixed selfhood or the tents of an external moral law. For poststructuralists, the notion of selfhood unbound by the strictures of characterological fixity and cohesive unity need not be perceived negatively, as a sentence to an interminable condition of unmitigated desire and unfulfilled frustration, but rather as a release from enthralment to an illusory, restrictive 'metaphysics of presence'. In terms of a metaphor of self as text, selfhood is ceaselessly rewritten in the interpretative activities of one's own and others' acts of intellection, and is never reducible to a single interpretation; no intentional origin can be ascertained to restrict the plenitude of self as the product of conceptual *différance*. Meaning, value, identity: these are not fixed givens, latent and waiting to be discovered, but made and re-made in our activities of interpretation. The free play of hermeneutic indeterminacy, argue these theorists, is to be celebrated.

In the terms set forth by Roland Barthes, whose later work embraced poststructuralist theory, the subject must no longer be conceived of as *lisible*, as a discrete book which 'closes on a signified'; it is not pleasurable 'work' which can be read as a self-sufficient entity, transparently conveying the immanent meaning of a

---

[4] Johan G. Fichte, *The Vocation of Man* (La Salle, Ill.: Open Court, 1965), 89; cited in Dews, *Logics of Disintegration*, 31.
[5] See Frederick Neuhouser, *Fichte's Theory of Subjectivity* (Cambridge: Cambridge University Press, 1990).

certain identity whose origin and end are firmly transcribed between its covers.[6] The subject, rather, is *scriptible*, a 'blissful . . . text', fractured by repressed desire, a text which

practices the infinite deferment of the signified, is dilatory; its field is that of the signifier and the signifier must not be conceived of as 'the first stage of meaning,' its material vestibule, but, in complete opposition to this, as its *deferred action*. Similarly, the infinity of the signifier refers not to some idea of the ineffable (the unnameable signified) but to that of a plaything.[7]

And so with the subject understood as linguistic construct. When idealized as a discrete 'work', the subject offers itself as a cohesive centre of intentionality, a transcendental signified whose meaning is constant and immutable, and in doing so, limits its possibility and potential to the mere vehicle of a priori 'authorial' intention. However, the subject conceived of as a dilatory 'text' is denied the closure of meaning, the delimitation of possibility, and the certain assumption of transmitted intentionality. It is the product of the perpetual deferrals wrought by (conceptual) discourse and the unending differential movement of interpretation. As such, it has 'no other origin than language itself, language which ceaselessly calls into question all origins'.[8]

Subjective essentialism, on Barthes's account, is countered by the potentiality of revisionary supplementation in the acts of 'reading' which constitute the narratives of 'reality' and selfhood we invent in reflexive interpretation.[9] The endless activity of interpretative reading which is our self-reflexive being is for poststructuralists a liberating activity of extension and revision. It is a fertile supplementation of alternative possibilities, which releases the subject (as text) from the poverty of servitude to a fixed concept of self (and originary intention). The celebratory notions of fertility and freedom are to be found everywhere in poststructuralist theory (they are almost as ubiquitous as the fear and threats of metaphysical intimidation which are used, equally pervasively, to urge the desirability of this

---

[6] Roland Barthes, 'From Work to Text', in *Image-Music-Text*, trans. and ed. Simon Heath (New York: Hill and Wang, 1977), 158.
[7] Ibid., emphasis original.
[8] Barthes, 'Death of the Author', in *Image-Music-Text*, 146.
[9] See Derrida on supplementation in *Of Grammatology*, trans. Gayatri Chakravorty Spivak (1967; Baltimore: Johns Hopkins University Press, 1974.), 141–64.

fertility and release). Consider Barthes's comments on the 'generative idea' he would convey in the use of the word 'text' as opposed to the closure of the 'work':

Text means tissue; but whereas hitherto we have taken this tissue as a product, a ready-made veil, behind which lies, more or less hidden, meaning (truth), we are now emphasizing, in the tissue, the generative idea that the text is made, is worked out in a perpetual interweaving.[10]

Or consider Derrida's oft-cited affirmation of interpretative 'freedom' in his challenge to metaphysics in his influential essay 'Structure, Sign and Play':

There are . . . two interpretations of interpretation, of structure, of sign, of freeplay. The one seeks to decipher, dreams of deciphering, a truth or an origin which is free from freeplay and the order of the sign, and lives like an exile the necessity of interpretation. The other, which is no longer turned towards the origin, affirms freedom and tries to pass beyond man and humanism, the name of man being the name of that being who, throughout the history of metaphysics or of ontotheology— in other words, the history of all his history—has dreamed of full presence, the reassuring foundation, the origin and end of the game.[11]

For Derrida, Barthes, and others, the subject, as text, is released into the perpetuity of intertextuality as the meeting-point of all texts, interpretations, and significations that precede and follow it, all those 'others' which it presupposes and all those which reach ahead of it into posterity. Otherwise put, identity, as text, 'is not an isolated entity, it is a relationship, an axis of innumerable relationships'.[12] 'I' is never complete, but always becoming, 'an empty "place" where many selves come to mingle and depart'.[13]

But where do we draw the line between a fertile, potentially

[10] Barthes, The Pleasure of the Text, trans. Richard Miller (London: Jonathan Cape, 1976), 63. We might note the dangerous, and to my mind, mistaken, elision of 'truth' and 'meaning' in this passage. Truth, as an unquestionable absolute, is an unrealizable (and unnecessary) category; we may assign truth status to a variety of meanings, according to the context of their utterance and/ or interpretation.

[11] Derrida, 'Structure, Sign and Play in the Discourse of the Human Sciences', in Richard Macksey and Eugenio Donato (eds.), The Structuralist Controversy: The Language of Criticism and the Science of Man (Baltimore: Johns Hopkins University Press, 1972), 264–5.

[12] Jorges Louis Borges, 'A Note on (towards) Bernard Shaw', in D. A. Yates and Y. E. Irby (eds.), Labyrinthes (New York: Penguin, 1970), 249.

[13] Ihab Hassan, The Right Promethean Fire (Urbana, Ill., Chicago, and London: University of Illinois Press, 1980), 202.

liberating infinity of meaning and the unchecked profusion of multiple and meaningless (self-)interpretations? Surely the concept of meaning (or meaninglessness) is obsolete, a mere metaphysical remainder, in an existence where the 'origin and the end of the game [of interpretation]' is forever denied? So argues Peter Dews:

[J]ust as the regress of reflection renders the phenomenon of consciousness inexplicable, so—on Derrida's account—there could never be an emergence of meaning: there would be nothing but an unstoppable mediation of signs by other signs. The majority of Derrida's interpreters have, of course, resisted this implication of his position: Derrida is portrayed as merely suggesting that meaning is far more insecure, elusive, undecidable than philosophers had previously imagined. Yet the logical consequence of his argument is not the volatization of meaning, but its destruction.[14]

And one might add that personhood, if understood as wholly constituted in processes of poststructuralist textual dissemination, must also logically be defunct. When extreme epistemological scepticism is turned on subjectivity on the basis of the equation encouraged by the metaphor of the self as text, the consequence is a devastating annihilation of ontological certainty. It results not in the liberation of a previously restrained subjectivity, but in the abolition of any possibility of coherent personhood whatsoever. As Dews suggests, '[t]he insistence on infinite regress—if it were coherent—would ruin *any* possibility of presence or meaning.'[15]

The serious moral and ethical implications for notions of responsible agency evoked by the conception of a centreless subjectivity which is fragmented in the attempt to attain self-knowledge are of central importance in contemporary thought. As such, they are also a dominant concern in contemporary fiction. To open up the notion of subjectivity to the endless free play of supplementary possibility, stressing the inherent failure of any attempt to retrieve undisputed meaning or certain personhood, raises severe moral questions. If my identity is not fixed and continuous, if I am not ready-made but only constantly re-made, how can my actions and relations have any guarantee of consistency? How can I be held responsible for my actions if the self who performs them is never me, an intentional agent of causal determination, but always only a misrecognized

---

[14] Dews, *Logics of Disintegration*, 30.
[15] Ibid., 248, n. 73.

other? How is friendship or relationship of any kind possible if the self I believe myself to be today, now, is different from the self I thought I was yesterday, then?

A return to the metaphysical notion of a fixed, self-transparent self, however is not our only option if we are to dispute the claims of a poststructuralist account of subjectivity, although this counter-claim is frequently made. From the metaphysical viewpoint, the predicated absence of a foundational self threatens to bring about the utter collapse and devastation of frameworks of meaning and value, a collapse which can only be averted, it seems, by the reaffirmation of a wholly present self-identical self. So argues William Barrett, who concludes his strident attack on the pervasive 'nihilism' of twentieth-century culture which he finds particularly manifest in deconstructive literary theory by insisting that 'the deconstructionists would have us give up the notion of the self altogether; we have simply to learn to "desubstantialize" our thinking. And this desubstantialization they see as one of the primary tasks of our culture.'[16] Barrett suggests further that in a world thus 'desubstantialized' devoid of the security of an objective ground for meaning, all interpretations are equally valid—'with the deconstructionist, in short, we are in a world of total relativism, where anything goes'.[17] Appalled by the vision of indeterminism and monadic isolation which he infers as the logical consequence of deconstructionism, Barrett conjures up a centre of substantiality whose loss, he claims, is at the root of the 'spiritual dispersion' and alienation of modern society: 'ultimately this alienation will be healed only if the universe is believed to have some meaning in harmony with our own spiritual and moral aims—which means, in effect, the discovery, or rediscovery of God.'[18]

One cannot help noting that such a critical move, which counters the threat of relativistic dispersal by invoking a centre or principal of fixity, can be performed endlessly, *will* be performed endlessly, unless we rid ourselves of our need to assign a centre of transcendent authority, an absolute principle or entity with which to allay the panicky fear of infinite regress. We will always be able to note the point at which an argument or interpretation, however assertively it proclaims emancipatory 'openness', in fact opts for closure in the

[16] William Barrett, *Death of the Soul: From Descartes to the Computer* (Oxford: Clarendon Press, 1987), 131, 128.
[17] Ibid. 129.
[18] Ibid. 90–1.

assertion of its own 'truth', and at this point triumphantly proclaims our inescapable need for closure. It is precisely this sterile thrust and counter-thrust, in which the next move is always the discovery of a transcendental ground for certainty (however assiduously hidden), a point at which we can observe the cessation of regress, which needs revision. As long as we continue to think of *the* self as the guarantor of all meaning, as the permanent presence necessary for achieving the identity of (past) intention and (present) interpretation, then the poststructuralist appeal to metaphors of textualized identity will remain hopelessly problematic. For in these essentialist terms, the self-transparent self is the necessary base of responsible agency upon which the edifice of morality is built. Given this mistaken premiss, it seems to follow that the wholesale discreditation of the possibility of textual resolution or a coherent liberal humanist subject must also entail the rejection of any possibility of personal agency or morality.

Poststructuralists, it would seem, have moved too fast, too far, sweeping the human subject along in the wake of their textual dissemination. Language is not purely differential and arbitrary; it functions systematically too. This is why we can, and do, communicate. The play of difference is never total; it can never wholly obliterate the opposing principles of order, connection, and continuity which are integral to linguistic functioning and which make communication possible. This is not to suggest a return to the structuralist notion of an all-pervasive systematization of language and behaviour or an essentialist notion of linguistic transparency and subjective immanence. No; it is indisputable that ambiguity, transgression, intentional confusion, and misunderstanding are potentialities in any inter- and (intra-) communicative act. The operations of language, and hence of the constitution of textual (and personal) meaning, lie somewhere in between these two extremes, between the rigidity of stucturalist systematization and the atomistic meaninglessness of poststructuralist linguistic relativism.

Strategic Silence

> Behind the appeals for silence [in art] lies the wish for a perceptual and cultural clean slate. And, in its horatory and ambitious version, the advocacy of silence expresses a mythic project of total liberation. What's envisaged is nothing less

than the liberation of the artist from himself . . . of the
mind from its perceptual and intellectual limitations.

Sontag, 'The Aesthetics of Silence'

I suggested in the introduction that, instead of conceiving self as a
perpetually fractured, dispersed poststructuralist text, selfhood may
be fruitfully considered as a narrative written and interpreted in
social language. Narrative meanings are not fixed for perpetuity, but
none the less afford coherence; they are, like the plots that underpin
them, 'intentional structures, goal-oriented and forward moving'.[19]
My dispute with the poststructuralist equation of self and text is not
with the trend which understands selves as linguistic constructs, but
with the invalid poststructuralist assumptions of dissolute textuality
which are applied, without due regard, to the human subject conceived as text. It is the initial poststructuralist premiss, which rejects
communicative structures as oppressive, opting instead for the empty
liberation of endlessly dispersed, unsituated meaning, that remains
questionable, and invalidates the conclusions which are too often
drawn regarding the nature of human subjectivity.

The analogy between the conceptual 'text' of personal identity and
the material text of the fictional book has resulted in the burgeoning
growth of a previously minor fictional genre, that of 'meta-fiction'.[20]
Meta-fictions are characterized by self-reflexive scrutiny, where the
overt problematization of their own textual processes allows us to
explore the nature of our ostensibly 'textual' intellections. According
to Linda Hutcheon, a notable commentator on the genre, in self-
reflexive fictions, '[t]he act of creation becomes paradigmatic of all
human acts of constructing ordered visions'; and further '[t]he novel
is not a copy of the empirical world, nor does it stand in opposition
to it. It is rather a continuation of that ordering fiction-making
process that is part of our normal coming to terms with experience.'[21]

[19] Peter Brooks, *Reading for the Plot: Design and Intention in Narrative*
(1984; Cambridge, Mass., and London: Harvard University Press, 1992), 12.

[20] For a discussion of the fictional precedents for the genre of meta-fiction,
see Robert Alter, *Partial Magic: The Novel as a Self-Conscious Genre* (Berkeley,
Los Angeles, and London: University of California Press, 1975). Alter traces the
'history' of the genre in his discussion of Cervantes, Sterne, and Diderot, outlines reasons for the 'eclipse' of this fictional mode in the nineteenth century,
and offers suggestions for its resurgent popularity in the twentieth century.

[21] Linda Hutcheon, *Narcissistic Narrative: The Metafictional Paradox* (Waterloo: Wilfred Laurier University Press, 1980), 87, 89. Other notable contri-
butions to the debate about and classification of this genre include Wenche

A character in John Barth's short story 'Bellerophoniad' suggests the same with more succinct wit: 'Art is as natural an artifice as Nature; the truth of Fiction is that Fact is fantasy; the made-up story is a model of the world.'[22]

Is it really possible to eliminate all divisions which would maintain the ontological and epistemological distinctions between art and nature, fact and fiction? How far, we might ask, can we push the equivalence between fictional characters—who, as the mute construct of (reader and writer) interpretation, are denied, by virtue of ontological separation, any right of speech or dialogic interaction which might influence the interpretation of their characterological identity—and human subjects, who are constituted in (but who also crucially, constitute) language? The wholesale translation of poststructuralist notions of textual *différance* to the concept of the human subject, encouraged by contemporary theory and seemingly affirmed in recent meta-fictions, brings with it a host of problems and complexities, not least the consequences for morally responsible personhood which it evokes. Attempts to subsume all notions of subjectivity under the rubric of textuality are too simplistic, particularly textuality as narrowly and erroneously conceived as that of some recent theory.

Are we truly 'authored' *by* language, simply subjected in the procedural operations of communicative rationality? Is our existential condition truly one of hopelessly mediated inauthenticity? Susan Sontag writes that because art is '[p]racticed in a world furnished with second-hand perceptions, and specifically confounded by the treachery of words the artist's activity is cursed with mediacy'.[23]

Ommundsen, *Metafictions? Reflexivity in Contemporary Texts* (Melbourne: Melbourne University Press, 1993); E. J. Smythe, *Postmodernism and Contemporary Fiction* (London: Batsford, 1991); Matei Calinescu and Douwe Fokemma (eds.), *Exploring Postmodernism* (Amsterdam and Philadelphia: John Benjamins, 1987); Brian McHale, *Postmodernist Fiction* (London and New York: Routledge, 1987); Patricia Waugh, *Metafiction: The Theory and Practice of Self-Conscious Fiction* (London and New York: Methuen, 1984); Charles Caramello, *Silverless Mirrors: Book, Self and Postmodern American Fiction* (Tallahassee, Fla.: University Press of Florida, 1983); Alan Wilde, *Horizons of Assent: Modernism, Postmodernism and the Ironic Imagination* (Baltimore: Johns Hopkins University Press, 1991). See also ch. 4, n. 15.

[22] Cited in Hutcheon, *Narcissistic Narrative*, 45.

[23] Susan Sontag, 'The Aesthetics of Silence', (1967), repr. in William J. Handy and Max Westbrook (eds.), *Twentieth Century Criticism: The Major Statements* (New York: The Free Press, 1974), 454. Further references to this essay will be cited parenthetically in the text.

If this despairing intuition pervades all contemporary artistic endeavour, why then do contemporary novelists continue to write? If one recognizes that no writing is exempt from the systematization and otherness which invalidates its claims of originality, then surely one must abstain from utterance; rather than accept the sentence of slavery (or the slavery of the sentence), one must instead be silent. So concludes Sontag, who finds a new element in contemporary art, 'the quest for a consciousness purified of contaminating language' (465). This aesthetic quest finds expression in individual artworks as self-negation, as 'the appeal (tacit or overt) for its own abolition—and ultimately for the abolition of art itself' (454). A number of contemporary writers may be seen to advocate the negative aesthetics of silence in the use of blank pages and white spaces in their fictions, as discussed in the previous chapter. Fictions in which the verbosity of the text literally dissolves into the silence of blank space includes Eugene Wildman's *Montezuma's Ball* (1970), Ronald Sukenick's *Long Talking Bad Condition Blues* (1979), and Alasdair Gray's *1982, Janine* (1984). Others perform alternative tactics of self-erasure: words are actually crossed out, overlaid with other words, or otherwise rendered almost unreadable (the works of Raymond Federman and Ronald Sukenick provide numerous examples). But when this advocacy of textual martyrdom is transferred to the notion of the human subject as the text, the results are insupportable, and far from emancipatory. If the conceptual activity of 'writing' one's narrative of selfhood amounts to no more than the traitorous violation of personal authenticity and submission to the 'treachery of words', then the ingenious escape which Sontag writes of, the 'advocacy of silence', is truly in one's 'own abolition': unconsciousness, death. Sontag suggests as much in noting the 'exemplary suicide of the artist (Kleist, Lautréamont)' (457).

Or perhaps, equally unpalatable, an alternative escape from the 'inauthenticity' predicated in a condition of normative rationality may lie in unintelligibility, incoherence. Sontag notes this tendency in (post)modernity. She writes of an apparent paradox: 'in the era of the widespread advocacy of art's silence, [we find] an increasing number of works of art babble', works that 'cultivate a kind of ontological stammer' and express the idea 'that it might be possible to out-talk language, or to talk oneself into silence' (468).[24] Sontag

---

[24] Sontag notes, but does not endorse, this textual tactic: 'This is not a very promising strategy, considering what results might be reasonably anticipated

lists Stein, Burroughs, and Beckett as exemplary employers of the tactic of babble to defy the perfidy of linear syntax and verbal signification without succumbing to the void of silence. A number of contemporary writers appear to adopt this strategy; Donald Barthelme, Steve Katz, and Richard Brautigan all fill their pages to overflowing with words seemingly written only for the sake of writing, words perhaps written to keep silence at bay.

Silence or babble; death or irrationality? So baldly stated, post-structuralist freedom from textuality and textual intellection is surely untenable and, I would argue, is seldom seriously entertained. Despite misleading bluster about the desirability of wholesale textual (personal) indeterminism and the value of an excommunicative exile from the rule-bound bindings of signification in the wilderness of non-communication, most contemporary theory in fact maintains a balance between such a stance of (meaningless) martyrdom and an essentially Romantic endorsement of the creative subject and the creative enterprise. The extract from Barthes's *Pleasure of the Text* cited above continues thus:

we are now emphasising . . . the generative idea that the text is made, is worked out in a perpetual interweaving; lost in this tissue—this texture—the subject unmakes himself, like a spider dissolving in the constructive secretions of its web. (63)

Here 'the subject unmakes himself', 'dissolving' in verbal secretions which are none the less 'constructive'; the idea of dissolution remains 'generative', and finally, 'the text is made'. In seeking to dislocate the identity and locus of the self, Barthes succeeds only in securing for the textual subject another location and another role: self as extra-linguistic product gives way to self as the agent of textual construction. Identity, thus reconstituted (relocated), is then masked by linguistic paradox; rationalization is ostensibly denied in the irresolvable vacillation of semantic opposites: absent presence, produced producer, written writer. To speak of subjectivity as Barthes does here, as an activity of writing or as a process of interpretation may well 'free' the subject from the essentialist bindings of authorial intention, releasing it into the dialectic of verbal production. However, although the sovereignty of selfhood is challenged by Barthes, creative subjective presence is not abolished.

from it. But perhaps not so odd, when one observes how often the aesthetic of silence appears alongside a barely controlled abhorrence of the void' (468).

Rather, it is reconstituted as the site of fictive self-production. The subject, so conceived, vacillates precariously between the roles of (passive) textual product and (active) producer of the text.

What is significant is that the concept of subjective production espoused by Barthes still implies the notion of a producer. We may indeed say with poststructuralists that 'language is prior to being', but language presupposes a producer of language, a writer or speaker who utilizes it. Of course, this producer may disappear on utterance or some time after writing; she may be lost, dead, uncontactable, or otherwise unable to confirm intention. All that may remain of her is her linguistic signs, signs which beg (for) interpretation. But the speaker or writer is none the less irrefutably necessary as the instigator of the production process, an instigator absent perhaps, but always re-made, reimagined in readings which follow. Returning to the Barthes extract, we find implicit in its logic an agent of activity: 'the subject' of this textual unmaking which is yet making, an ambiguous 'himself' who is both made *and* unmade in 'its' verbal web. In moving towards metaphors of textual creativity, Barthes firmly retains, as a necessary component of his production equation, the figure of the creating subject.

The overt poststructuralist rhetoric of emancipation and radical revisionism, which promises the usurpation of existing structures of rationality in the unregulated free play of *différance*, is thus conjoined with the tacit reinscription of Romantic creative idealism in theoretical tracts such as that of Barthes. It is precisely the paradoxical nature of this stance which appeals to the writers of innovative, anti-realist contemporary fiction. It enables them to adopt a stance of self-dissolution while in fact stressing the originality and ingenuity of their individual creativity—in short, their personal value and political purpose. Dissolution or silence in such fictions is no more than a posture: it is the pretence of dissolution, the affectation of silence, intentionally and tactically conceived as a mode of signification.

In *Silverless Mirrors*, Charles Caramello has argued convincingly that 'while postmodern writers cannot fail to reflect the dissolution of identity endemic in our historical moment, nor, given their poetics, to exacerbate that dissolution', they remain 'more equivocal' in their enterprise of textual fragmentation than is commonly supposed.[25] He suggests that postmodern (American) fiction exhibits a

---

[25] Caramello, *Silverless Mirrors*, 28–9. Caramello works on the premiss, which I would sustain, that in postmodern American fiction 'the problematics of the

profound ambivalence towards poststructuralist theory. The fiction appears to have

> invested in a writing that cuts intertextually through the body of the self and of the book, a writing that dismembers both bodies and that remains, therefore, exterior to them. *But this fiction also remains nostalgic, if not for a writing that can be grounded in the self and in the book, then for precisely the self and the book that this writing has dismembered.* (15; emphasis original).

I agree with Caramello's observation regarding the ambivalence of much postmodern fiction towards theories of dismembered textuality and subjectivity. However, I find this ambivalence to be not contrary to, but consistent with, an ambivalence already latent in so much poststructuralist theory, a theory which is unable to accept the logical consequences of its own hardline position. In their meta-fictional problematization of this theory, postmodern fictions only amplify and give form to those ambiguities which inhere in the paradoxes of a poststructuralist thought: subject as decentred and agential, textual meaning as recoupable and endlessly deferred. Further, in developing the metaphor of textualized identity offered by many contemporary theorists, this fiction seeks not to invalidate, but to legitimize, the importance of narrative creativity in the constitution of human subjectivity.

In *The Pleasure of the Text* Barthes writes of interpretation that it is an act in which 'perhaps the subject returns, not as illusion, but as fiction. A certain pleasure is derived from a way of inventing oneself as *individual*, of inventing a final, rarest fiction: the fictive identity'.[26] Considering this ambiguous 'return' of the subject, can we not say that in claiming to annul the concept of subjectivity, Barthes in the above extract (and the fiction which ostensibly endorses this theoretical position) succeeds only in (re)locating it in creative language, releasing it into a newly defined site of fictive production? And more, that the subject is not merely (inevitably) reconstituted (as 'oneself') in the physical bindings of the book and the conceptual space of the mind, but is reconstituted as the author of

self converge with the problematics of the book' and that the two problematics are not only 'mutually entailing' but also 'structurally homologous' (20–1). I would, however, extend this analysis to encompass postmodern fiction in general, not merely that produced in America. Further references to this book will be cited parenthetically in the text.

[26] Barthes, *Pleasure of the Text*, 62 (emphasis original).

an activity which readmits notions of personal identity: the lost subject regains meaningful being as fictive *individual*. Further, in this transfer of definition from produced 'written' object to productive 'writing' subject, theory and fiction both enact a tacit reaffirmation of the narrative enterprise.

The ambiguity inherent in the subjective problematics explored in contemporary fiction results from the dualistic opposition of two intuitions which I have repeatedly contrasted: the desire for absolute interpretative freedom (of texts and selves as texts) and the fear of anarchic meaninglessness in the absence of regulation which this seems to entail. Contemporary fiction seeks, on the one hand, to expound and to celebrate the emancipation of self and/as text from conformity to prescribed dictates in accordance with the celebratory proclamations of poststructuralist theory, and on the other hand, to maintain notions of the discrete book and intending author in the face of the debilitating disintegrations of identity and meaning which this emancipation appears to postulate as its necessary condition. Sontag's analysis of Rilke's writing may be extended to all texts which *articulate* the treachery and contamination of the linguistic medium in which they are constituted: 'Rilke's remedy lies halfway between exploiting the numbness of language as a gross, fully installed cultural institution and yielding to the suicidal vertigo of pure silence' (467). Hence the paradoxical nature of contemporary fiction's self-reflexive interrogation, which, according to Caramello, 'hesitates in accepting the findings of this investigation: it attempts to revive the book and the authorial self it has found to be defunct' (p. x). Stymied by the irresolvable opposition of dissolute freedom and bound writtenness, it is no wonder that we constantly confront the paradox of textualized subjectivity which haunts the fictions that Caramello observes. The individualistic novelty and self-reflexive narcissism of so many meta-fictions, which are characterized by revolutionary formal and stylistic techniques and self-concerned introspection, sits uncomfortably with their overt protestations of their own lack of originality and inescapable inauthenticity. Despite a putative insistence on the final impossibility of articulating presence or communicating meaning, many contemporary experimental novels actualize their material and conceptual identity precisely in their *understood* rebellious anti-narrative stance. These texts claim to negate selfhood, but in fact assert their own demise in fictional bodies and material acts whose radical individuality only serves to confirm, and even draw attention to, their own communicating presence.

This paradoxical equivocation is also implicit in our sceptical stance. From such a critical perspective, it is little wonder that Caramello's response to these fictions is one of perplexity: 'I see no way out of the paradox that we treat *as* literature that which denies its status as literature, that we qualify it as *a* literature precisely on the grounds of that denial' (48). Nor is it surprising that the 'way out of the paradox' for critics like Caramello is finally to reinstate a metaphysical notion of an absolute concept or principle, here denoted Silence:

> We must continue to ask, however, if Joyce, Beckett, and the post-modern writers who succeed them do not also wish to comprehend intertextuality as a concept and as a metaphysic, to comprehend 'writing' *as* the absolute absence of a Book, the absent absence of the Word, or in a word, *Silence*. We must ask, that is, if they do not still yearn for the centres of self and world that do not hold (44; emphasis original)

Ihab Hassan, in an early book, *The Literature of Silence*, is similarly bemused by the simultaneous yet conflicting desire exhibited in contemporary literature which appears to both affirm and deny the possibility of its own meaning, seeking to assert and to annihilate its own presence: 'Literature, turning against itself, aspires to silence, leaving us with the uneasy intimations of outrage and apocalypse. If there is an avant-garde in our time it is probably hell-bent on discovery through suicide. . . . Is this the future then, all vagrancy and disaster for all who profess the Word?'[27] And, like Caramello, Hassan resolves this dilemma in an inane affirmation of the meta-phorical paradox which enables him to have things both ways: inauthentic writing gives way to the alternative signification of authentic silence, the writer adopts a pose of voicelessness in which she still somehow manages to communicate: 'the imagination renounces its ancient authority, finding its apotheosis not in the romantic idea of the damned poet but in the ironic attitude of the

---

[27] Ihab Hassan, *The Literature of Silence: Henry Miller and Samuel Beckett* (New York: Knopf, 1967), 3. Further references to this book, will be cited parenthetically in the text. Hassan develops further the notion of a paradoxically vocal 'silence' as a metaphor for the subversive, negative, apocalyptic, alienated, and alienating tactics of postmodern literature in his later book, *The Dismemberment of Orpheus: Toward a Postmodern Literature*, 2nd edn. (Madison: University of Wisconsin Press, 1982).

wordless author binding a sheaf of blank pages' (3). Further, this principle of silence now offers a centre which will control and contain the threat of dispersion: 'Clearly, the silence at this centre of anti-literature is loud and various. . . . The point is this: silence now develops as the metaphor of a new attitude that literature has chosen toward itself' (8). For Hassan, rebellious textuality is thus trans-figured as a metaphorical plenitudinous silence in which the author finds not his death ('suicide') nor his fragmentation into anarchic 'apocalypse' or madness, but rather his apotheosis in the figure of the rebellious author 'binding a sheaf of blank pages'. The act of 'binding' prevents the disintegration of the text into meaninglessness, and 'wordless[ness]' simply becomes an alternative form of significa-tion. Anti-literature such as that Hassan discusses is not silent, but finds its voice in a symbolic, signifying *posture* of silence. The theoretical renunciation of voice is a symbolic act which leaves intact the possibility of vocalization, while maintaining the moral superior-ity of that renunciation.

Clearly, Hassan's theory in *The Literature of Silence* retreats, like the fiction which Caramello comments on, into the equi-vocation of paradox: the only authentic voice is voicelessness; the only valuable writing is unwritten; the only true book is no book at all. But his claims, like so many postmodernist rhetorical para-doxes, are self-defeatingly nonsensical. What does it *mean* to speak of 'multivocal silence' or 'plenitudinous lack' or 'absent presence'? Is this critical position, as Caramello suggests, the inevitable result of the confrontation with a postmodern fiction, 'torn between a commitment to the integrity of the authorial self . . . and a post-structuralist deconstruction of the intending subjectivity' (23–4), a fiction forced, by the conflict of allegiances (to book and text, self and self-abolition), into the compromised corner of ambiguous prevarication? I think not. This is theory that wants to have things both ways. It wants to alienate itself from the ideological 'form' of language, its prescriptive categorization and confining rationality, yet it wants this strategic alienation to have understood value. In other words, these theorists and novelists seek to communicate the worth of their purposive alienation and for this to be rationally comprehended.

In short, silence as a textual tactic is still, is always, an act of signification. Silent expanses in texts (as in any discourse) are framed by words, or the expectation of them. They are the spectral other of language, and they mean only in relation to it. This is so clearly the case in those fictions, mentioned above, that utilize blank pages. These gaps, or omissions, function only in relation to the words which frame them, or as iconic representations of something (a blizzard in the case of Sukenick's *Long Talking Bad Conditions Blues* and the narrator's unconsciousness in Gray's *1982, Janine*). Susan Sontag acknowledges this paradox at the heart of the revolutionary writer's appeal to the efficacy of silent self-negation:

'Silence' never ceases to imply its opposite and to depend on its presence: just as there can never be 'up' without 'down' or 'left' without 'right,' so one must acknowledge a surrounding environment of sound or language in order to recognize silence. . . . A genuine emptiness, a pure silence are not feasible—either conceptually or in fact. If only because the artwork exists in a world furnished with many other things, the artist who produces silence or emptiness must produce something dialectical: a full void, an enriching emptiness, a resonating or eloquent silence. Silence remains, inescapably, a form of speech (in many instances, of complaint or indictment) and an element in a dialogue. (458)

The theoretical ambivalence and continual resort to the mystification of paradox which is observable in contemporary fiction and theory is less evidence of a desperate dilemma of 'torn' loyalties than a masterful exploitation of the dual impulses which are implicit in the textual metaphors employed so abundantly in contemporary theory. These metaphors, as I have suggested in considering the claims made by Barthes in *The Pleasure of the Text*, appeal precisely because they harbour two conflicting, seemingly mutually exclusive, expressions of human desire. On the one hand, they appear to endorse a defiant rejection of the confinement and limitation deemed unavoidable in structures of cohesive presence and obedient conformity to communicative restraints. On the other hand, they maintain a nostalgic yearning for (and ultimately an affirmation of) the securities and certainties that are conferred by the discredited structures and conventions of language. The liberation of silent self-erasure is thus always complicit with the structuring presence of the language it seeks to negate. The poststructuralist critical manœuvre which reads the auto-erasure of tactical gestures such as silence or babble in contemporary fiction as evidence of the efficacy of human sunderance from the communicative protocols of the social text is thus guilty of perpetrating a gross illusion of an impossible subjective freedom. *Only* in the absence of consciousness and coherent language—in death, in madness—can this absolute freedom be achieved. And at what an implausible cost to meaningful subjectivity.

Identity Creation: Personhood as Narrative

> A person's identity is not to be found in behaviour, nor— important though this is—in the reactions of others, but in the capacity *to keep a particular narrative going.* The individual's biography, if she is to maintain a regular interaction with others in the day to day world, cannot be wholly fictive. It must continually integrate events which occur in the external world, and sort them into an ongoing 'story' about the self.
>
> Giddens, *Modernity and Self-identity*

In *The Literature of Silence,* Ihab Hassan makes an important observation: 'the paradox of art employing art to deny itself is rooted in the power of the human consciousness to view itself both as subject and object' (13). This conceptual split, the human capacity to view ourselves as both the subject and the object of conscious scrutiny, is precisely what many contemporary theorists evoke to reveal the desperate situation of our existential inauthenticity. Yet Hassan seems to find something redemptive in this condition of self-sunderance: he deems it to be the source of our creative *power.* In other words, he finds 'the power of the human consciousness' to exist in the intuition of our fundamental psychic split. The failure of self-reflexive introspection to achieve the identity of unmediated being does not bring despair on Hassan's account, but necessitates and enables the (re)writing of narratives of personal meaning and identity. The gap between a pre-linguistic experiential self and its entry into conceptual textuality always leaves open a space for revision and change. This revisionary writing releases us from slavish commitment to the wholesale writtenness of characterological consistency. Herein, as Hassan suggests, lies the *power* of self-consciousness and of art. Personhood understood as narrative activity is less a condemnation to suicidal silence or the madness of endless dispersal than a recognition and an endorsement of our capacity to be creative in our readings and writings of the narratives of self. Such a notion stands in direct opposition to nihilistic claims of perpetual dissolution or of the debilitating infection of otherness resulting in self-betrayal and alienation, which characterizes a hardline poststructuralist conception of self-consciousness. Self-reflective acts are also, *always*, acts of identity-creation.

The idea that our sense of selfhood inheres in a creative act of self-constituting narration has been advanced by a number of theorists in recent years, notably Jonathan Glover in *I: The Philosophy and Psychology of Personal Identity*, Alasdair MacIntyre in *After Virtue*, Charles Taylor in *Sources of the Self*, and Anthony Giddens in *Modernity and Self-Identity*.[28] This notion has significant appeal to contemporary writers, in both its implicit endorsement of the fictional vocation and its provision of a means to counter the nihilistic atomism of contemporary thought without recourse to metaphysical essentialism. Although he abandons the traditional metaphysical model of a discrete and permanent self, Glover retains the notion of personal continuity, contending that 'the idea that we are not so deeply integrated as we assume does not simply follow from the abandonment of the ego. . . . Metaphysics is not the only basis for integration' (139). Life lived as the unintegrated, temporary manifestations of multiple unfixed selves would, Glover insists, be meaningless: 'Without the ego, the episodes of a life can seem like a heap of stones'.[29] But the ego need not be an absolute; it can be

[28] Jonathan Glover, *I: The Philosophy and Psychology of Personal Identity* (Harmondsworth: Penguin, 1988); Alasdair MacIntyre, *After Virtue* (London: Duckworth, 1981); Taylor, *Sources of the Self: The Making of the Modern Identity* (Cambridge, Mass.: Harvard University Press, 1989), esp. 3–110; Anthony Giddens, *Modernity and Self-Identity: Self and Society in the Late Modern Age* (Cambridge: Polity Press, 1991). Further references to Glover, *I*, will be cited parenthetically in the text.

[29] This observation lies at the heart of his rejection of Derek Parfit's argument for 'survival' as an alternative to cohesive identity, elaborated in *Reasons and Persons* (Oxford: Clarendon Press, 1984). Parfit argues that we cannot talk of a present self, but only of selves that were, selves that existed in different (past) stages of our lifetime. Accordingly decisions made regarding 'me' will always be like decisions made about another person, a past self no longer identical to the self performing in the present. Parfit's argument evokes radical, unacceptable consequences for our notions of personal accountability. He demands abandonment of the traditional model of causal intentionality which underwrites notions of moral responsibility and endorses the values of justice and desert: how can I be held responsible for actions, decisions, and promises made by a self no longer me? Glover finds this morally unacceptable: 'On this view, both deserts and commitments seem as fugitive as our past selves' (103). It is this moral indignation which leads him to hypothesize the alternative model of narrative self-creation. See also Charles Taylor's comparable critique of Parfit's position in *Sources of the Self*, 49—51, and that of Patrick Grant in *Literature and Personal Values* (London and Basingstoke: Macmillan, 1992), 1–2.

a narrative construct open to interpretative revision, an activity of conceptual connection and interpretation (in Barthesian terms, the 'interweaving' of past selves), a structure of intention.

Identity-creation, as defined by Glover, relies heavily on memory, through the agency of which a sense of personal continuity is achieved through time. In suggesting the importance of remembrance, Glover writes of the *recognition* of one's personal identity as one might describe the writing or reading of a novel, as a narrative and interpretative process in which past significations, events, and actions are assimilated into the present interpretative moment: 'Both the history and the emotional content of the story [of my life] so far make intentions about the next part more intelligible' (140).[30] Loss of memory or the capacity for intentional projection, on such an account, would have devastating effects for the maintenance of a sense of cohesive selfhood: 'Coherence needs sequences of actions, planned as part of integrated projects' (ibid.). Instantaneous apprehension of selfhood is impossible, for a sense of one's self is achieved through time as a series of interconnected experiential moments, sequentially ordered—plotted—in the restrospection of memory. Accordingly, for Glover, our sense of who we are is synthesized in the narrative assimilation of past subject positions that is achieved through the interpretative interconnections of memory, a 'process of involuntary comparison [which] locates present experience in the context of past history' (26). The upsurge of critical interest in the genre of auto-biography, particularly with respect to its 'fictional' status, has been significant in recent years, and reflects a growing awareness of the narrative nature of even 'truthful' self-reflection and remembrance.[31] The question of autobiographical veracity has been playfully ex-ploited by many contemporary writers and novelists. In Philip Roth's *The Facts: A Novelist's Autobiography* (1988), the autobiography is prefaced by a letter from Roth to one of his own fictional characters, Zuckerman (thereby eliminating the distinction between the 'real' world inhabited by the author and the 'fictional' world inhabited by his characters), as follows:

---

[30] On the importance of memory to a sense of cohesive selfhood, see Mark Freeman, *Rewriting the Self: History, Memory, Narrative* (London and New York: Routledge, 1993); Anthony Paul Kerby, *Narrative and the Self* (Bloomington and Indianapolis: Indiana University Press, 1991); and Richard Wollheim, *The Thread of Life* (Cambridge, Mass.: Harvard University Press, 1984).

[31] See Freeman, *Rewriting the Self*, and Introduction, n. 32.

Memories of the past are not memories of facts but memories of your imaginings of the facts. . . . It isn't that you subordinate your ideas to the force of the facts in autobiography but that you construct a sequence of stories to bind up the facts with a persuasive *hypothesis* that unravels your history's meaning.[32]

And in Carol Shields's fictional autobiography *The Stone Diaries* (1993), the narrator questions the possibility of autobiographical truth throughout—'Her autobiography, if such a thing were imaginable, would be, if such a thing were ever to be written, an assemblage of dark voids and unbridgeable gaps' (75–6); 'And the question arises: what is the story of a life? A chronicle of facts or a skilfully wrought impression?' (340). A number of contemporary fictions explore the crucial importance of memory and the construction of a functioning narrative of selfhood as fundamental aspects of psychological health. The titular hero in Russell Hoban's *Kleinzeit* (1974) has to learn to 're-member' himself, to integrate past and present in a wonderful celebration of narrative creativity in the face of illness and death. In Toni Morrison's *Beloved* (1987) the importance of 'rememory' and 'disremembering' (words coined to describe *willed* acts of remembrance and forgetting) are central: the novel urges the importance of claiming responsibility for, and power over, one's own narrative of selfhood by wilfully integrating or excising memories of the past in the continuing narratives of the present.

Glover's version of narrative self-identity bears many resemblances to that proposed by MacIntyre in *After Virtue*. MacIntyre propounds the notion of 'a self whose unity resides in the unity of a narrative which links birth to life to death as narrative beginning to middle to end'.[33] The actions and speech acts of a subject, according to MacIntyre, are intelligible only when situated in the meaning-determining contexts of her ongoing life narrative and, crucially, the ongoing historical narratives of her community: 'An action is a moment in a possible or actual history or a number of such histories' (199). Against this notion, he counterposes Sartre's existentialist claim (as argued by his protagonist, Roquentin, in *La Nausée*) that to present a life in the form of a historical narrative is to falsify the lived

---

[32] Philip Roth, *The Facts: A Novelist's Autobiography* (1988; repr. Harmondsworth: Penguin, 1989), 8.

[33] MacIntyre, *After Virtue*, 191. Cf. Taylor, *Sources of the Self*, who suggests similarly that 'we grasp our lives in a narrative' (47). Taylor's conception of selfhood will be discussed in more detail in Chapter 6. Further references to *After Virtue* will be cited parenthetically in the text.

experience of alienation, fragmentation, and dislocation. Life, as Sartre's character recognizes it, comprises a series of unintelligible, disconnected moments that are retrospectively ordered and connected, in bad faith, as a fictional (auto)biography.[34] A number of contemporary literary theorists, following this kind of reasoning, have roundly dismissed the enterprise of narration as falsification, and even as ideologically complicit in the reductive assumption that all processes of narrative ordering reduplicate and reinscribe repressive conventions (this is, for example, the line taken by Leo Bersani, as discussed in Chapter 4). Such theorists hypothesize a 'liberated' postmodernity that is radically fragmented and disparate, a postmodernity providing no communal home(s) for nomadic agents condemned to the normlessness of anomie, one for which contemporary fragmentary anti-narratives provide a laudable model (so with Thomas Docherty, discussed in Chapter 7). But we must ask, with MacIntyre, what life experienced as a series of discrete, disconnected moments, without the ordering and patterning of narrative or the rational frameworks provided by particular socially embodied traditions, would be like. Surely the theoretically exalted condition of anti-narrational, excommunicative, experiential dissemination would result in radically disabling dislocation and unintelligibility both for and between social agents, a condition of schizophrenic dislocation and lack of a sense of selfhood or meaningful being that is far from redemptive. It is impossible to imagine such a condition, for the intelligibility of actions and events is conditional on their placement within specific narrative structures and intersubjective communicative contexts that enable them to mean: 'the characterisation of actions allegedly prior to any narrative form being imposed on them will always turn out to be the presentation of what are plainly the disjointed parts of some narrative' (200). The narrative apprehension

---

[34] Mark Freeman provides a thoughtful discussion of *La Nausée* in *Rewriting the Self*, 81–111. He concludes by suggesting that Roquentin's intuition of the 'authentic' but agonizing untidiness of ongoing present moments and the bad faith of recollective narrative ordering is mistaken, for it ignores the 'narrative' aspect of self-conscious being: 'To live without narrative, it would appear, is to live in an essentially meaningless perpetual present, devoid of form or coherence; it is to experience the world as disconnected and fragmented, as an endless series of things that happen. This, Roquentin had suggested, was the reality of our existence; anything else was to be understood as a product of our imagination. But what he failed to see is that the very project of living itself is no less imaginative and no less bound to narrative than the alleged fictions that we create when we reflect upon or write about our lives' (110).

of actions, events, utterances, and experiences is fundamental to healthy personhood; we regard as significantly and tragically disabled those who are unable to perform the connective task of narrative ordering in the conceptualization of themselves and the world about them.

MacIntyre introduces some important qualifications to the idea of narrativized selfhood. Significantly, he asserts that individuals are never wholly in control of their self-narratives, a qualification which makes clear his communitarian leanings. We cannot simply write ourselves as we choose; our (self-)narrativizations are always bound to the contexts or 'settings' in which we, as social beings, are embedded. MacIntyre's term 'settings' is relatively inclusive, denoting an institution, a social practice, or 'a milieu of some other human kind' (192). I would like to suggest its broad equivalence with the term 'communities' as defined earlier: as the diverse, protocol-bound communal contexts in which speaking subjects are situated by chance or choice. MacIntyre insists that it is impossible to

characterize behaviour independently of intentions, and we cannot characterize intentions independently of the settings [communities] which make those intentions intelligible both to agents themselves and to others. . . . [A] setting has a history, a history within which the histories of individual agents not only are, but have to be, situated, just because without the setting and its changes through time the history of the individual agent and his changes through time will be unintelligible. Of course one and the same piece of behaviour may belong to more than one setting. (192)

This last point is vitally important, and echoes the claims made in earlier chapters with regard to the subject's situation in, and mobility between a variety of different interpretative or discursive communities. In the above citation MacIntyre not only suggests that self-narrativization is always contextually situated (in other words, that it is bound to one or more intersubjective social 'settings'); he also offers an explanation of how plural contextualization renders the interpretation of a text, an action, or a person intelligible without precluding uncertainty and ambiguity in that interpretation or the possibility of revision. Any given action or event may be interpreted and characterized in a variety of different ways, according to the contextual setting of the action and the site of interpretation. We are able to read and understand a text, an action, or a person as a cohesive, intelligible narrative without foreclosing the possibility of other, equally valid, interpretations of that text, action, or person. In other words, there may well be a number of settings or communities in which a text is intelligible to its readers, albeit that the meaning of the text may be conceived of as different from one setting to the next. The intelligibility of an action, event, word, or utterance is not commensurate with some absolute fixity of its meaning or the retrieval of pre-given, indisputable actorial or authorial intention. It is dependent on its specific placement in a particular socio-historic setting or settings, that is, in terms of the ongoing narrative of a particular agent or discursive community.[35]

What MacIntyre, like Glover, is advocating is a conception of 'the agent not only as an actor, but as an author' (198)—of persons who not only do things, but authorize the doing of them—a surprisingly liberal affirmation, perhaps, given MacIntyre's status as a pre-eminent communitarian. It is fallacious to suggest (as do some of his liberal opponents) that MacIntyre's communitarianism wholly evacuates *any* notion of subjective agency or personal choice. Quite clearly, his conception of the human agent as self-narrating author is intended to overcome such a deficiency, although a communitarian stress on the fundamental constitutive importance of intersubjective attachments and communities remains. On the other hand, McIntyre's conception of self-authorization in no way equates to existentialist fiat or essentialist autonomy. Selfhood cannot simply be founded on the psychological (dis)continuity of the individual self, but is intrinsically correlative, part of the stories of other selves who are also and always part of ours:

what the agent is able to do and say intelligibly as an actor is deeply affected by the fact that *we are never more (and sometimes less) than the co-authors of our own narratives*. Only in fantasy do we live what story we please. In life, as both Aristotle and Engels noted, we are always under certain constraints. We enter upon a stage which we did not

[35] In fact, it is the very possibility of there being more than one perfectly adequate way of reading a text—of identity, of action, of value—which accounts for the 'tragedy' of our existential capacity to choose. It is never simply a case of discovering *the* meaning of a text or choosing to act in accordance with *one* determinate principle value or being *one* consistent person. MacIntyre suggests that in any given situation there may be several perfectly viable ways of reading or doing or being: 'By choosing one I do nothing to diminish or derogate from the claims upon me of the other; and therefore, whatever I do, I shall have left undone what I ought to have done' (208).

design and we find ourselves part of an action that was not of our making. Each of us being a main character in his own drama plays subordinate parts in the dramas of others, and each drama constrains the others. (199; my emphasis)

Our capacity for self-authorization is never absolute; we are always subject to 'certain constraints': constraints imposed by other subjects with whom we commune and communicate and the contextual constraints of our community settings. Wholesale personal freedom, the prerogative to be whatever we want whenever we choose, is always limited by the traditions, the conventions, the codes of reference—in short, the protocols—of the (con)textual communities in which we write and in which we have meaning. But equally, we are never merely the wholly inauthentic, written characters in these communities whose rich diversification constitutes the social text. We have the capacity, within constraints, to order and interpret our own narratives of personal continuity, within and between a variety of communal contexts. Of course, as subjects in existing inter-subjective communities, certain possibilities 'seem already foreclosed and others perhaps inevitable' (200), for certain personal attributes and attachments are pre-given: 'I inherit from the past of my family, my city, my tribe, my nation, a variety of debts, inheritances, rightful expectations and obligations. These constitute the given in my life, my moral starting point' (204–5). Our inheritances are never static and immobile, but fluid and correlative; they modulate, supplement, and interanimate one another. Once again, an analogy with the fictional process is useful: just as within a fiction, framed by the expectation of an ending and bound by a variety of formal and linguistic protocols, it is possible for a reader to make an indefinite number of meaningful interpretations, so too for the human subject existing in plural communities; teleology and unpredictability coexist with the possibility of attaining intersubjective understanding.

There is no present which is not informed by some image of some future, and an image of the future which always presents itself in the form of a *telos*—or of a variety of ends or goals—towards which we are either moving or failing to move in the present. Unpredictability and teleology therefore coexist as part of our lives; like characters in a fictional narrative [and the readers of that narrative] we do not know what will happen next, but nonetheless our lives [and interpretations] have a certain form which projects itself towards our future. . . . If the narrative of our individual lives is to continue intelligibly . . . it is always the case both that there are constraints on how the story can be told [and interpreted] *and* that within those constraints there are indefinitely many ways in which it can continue. (200–1)

MacIntyre's version of narrative selfhood thus firmly endorses a communitarian conception of embedded personhood while maintaining what might appear to be a liberal vision of the human subject as capable of self-scrutiny, accountability, and (partial) self-determination. In short, he promotes the idea of selfhood as a co-authored narrative constituted in the context of communal significations and interpretations: 'the story of my life is always embedded in the story of those from which I derive my identity' (205).

In *Modernity and Self-Identity* Giddens similarly utilizes the metaphor of narration to articulate a conception of self-identity which involves more than mere persistence over time (a traditional philosophical condition for object identity). Selfhood, as he conceives it, presumes reflexive awareness and biographical continuity; it is not a given or a distinctive trait possessed by an individual, 'but something that has to be routinely created and sustained in the reflexive activities of the individual'.[36] As cited in the previous epigraph, a person's identity is 'in the capacity *to keep a particular narrative going*'.[37] The similarity between Giddens' concept of narrative self-identity constituted in the self-reflexive monitoring of agents within social structures and MacIntyre's notion of selfhood narrated in social contexts or settings is not surprising. The self-reflexivity of human agents is, for Giddens, a fundamental capacity, one he affirms again and again in his writing: 'nothing is more central to, and distinctive of, human life than the reflexive monitoring of behaviour';[38] 'human beings reflexively monitor what they do as an intrinsic part of what it is that they do';[39] '[h]uman beings in all societies routinely reflexively monitor their actions and thereby processes of reproduction.'[40]

---

[36] Giddens, *Modernity and Self-Identity*, 52.

[37] Ibid. 54.

[38] Anthony Giddens, *New Rules of Sociological Method: A Positive Critique of Interpretative Sociologies*, 2nd edn. (Cambridge: Polity Press, 1993), 120.

[39] Giddens, *Social Theory and Modern Sociology* (Stanford, Calif.: Stanford University Press, 1987), 99.

[40] Giddens, 'Structuration Theory: Past, Present and Future', in Christopher G. A. Bryant and David Jary (eds.), *Giddens' Theory of Structuration: A Critical Appreciation* (London and New York: Routledge, 1991), 207. Giddens avers that in our present conditions of modernity (he views postmodernity as a condition yet to be realized) the reflexive (re)ordering of system reproduction is almost pervasive: 'modernity is marked by the tendency routinely to incorporate

The most significant aspect of Giddens's work, for present purposes, is his well-known 'structuration theory', developed in his numerous publications over the past two decades, and now the subject of a considerable body of secondary literature. Giddens's theory is complex, and anything more than a brief discussion of it is beyond the scope of this work. What is vitally important, however, is that it comprises one of the most sustained contemporary accounts of human agents as the bearers of power as 'transformative capacity': structural transformation is to be viewed not merely as evolutionary consequence but as actualized intentionality.[41]

Structuration theory rejects the claims of both positivism and subjectivism, and as an 'ontology of social life',[42] rather than as an epistemological inquiry, it attempts to avoid the dualisms of agency and structure, voluntarism and determinism. Structuration theory takes issue with both structuralism (in its functionalist, Marxist, and modern forms) and philosophies of action. According to Giddens, in his 'new introduction' to the second edition of *New Rules of Sociological Method*, varieties of structuralism treat human agents 'as if they were inert and inept—the playthings of forces larger than themselves',[43] and in *Studies in Social and Political Theory* he claims that constructivist structuralist philosophies view the reproduction of social relations as the outcome of mechanistic operations, 'rather than as an active constituting process, accomplished by, and consisting in, the doings of active subjects'.[44] Philosophies of action, by contrast, pay little or no attention to structural formation, focusing instead only on the problematics of production, viewing human beings as purposive agents, without adequate focus on structural analysis and the 'problems of constraint, power and large-scale social organization'.[45] According to Giddens, structuration theory is an attempt to attend to the deficiencies in both the structuralist and the actionist accounts: 'social structure is both constituted *by* human

---

new information about conditions of action, as a means of altering or reorganizing those conditions' (ibid.). See Giddens, *Modernity and Self-Identity*, for a discussion of the developed character of institutional reflexivity in modernity and its parallels with the reflexive project of the self.

[41] See Giddens, *The Consequences of Modernity* (Cambridge: Polity Press; Stanford, Calif.: Stanford University Press, 1990).

[42] Giddens, 'Structuration Theory', 203.

[43] Giddens, 'New Rules', 4.

[44] Ibid. 128.

[45] Ibid. 4.

agency, and yet at the same time is the very *medium* for this constitution',[46] in other words, through the co-determining processes of 'the *duality of structure*'.[47] Importantly, 'structure', as Giddens defines it, is not synonymous with 'group' or 'organization', which *have* structural properties. It refers not to the descriptive analysis of organizational relations or interaction, 'but to systems of generative rules and resources' and the maintenance and transformation ('production' and 'reproduction' in his terminology) of these through time. Structures are to be understood not only in terms of the limitations and constraints that they impose on agents (although these are acknowledged), but also as the very medium within which human beings are 'enabled' (Giddens's term) as reflexive, intentional agents. Crucially, structures are not simply reproduced by unintended and mechanistic feedback (through what Giddens calls 'homeostatic causal loops'),[48] but also by self-regulation through feedback that is affected by agents' knowledge and reflexive self-regulation: 'structures only exist as the reproduced conduct of situated actors with definite intentions and interests.'

Every act which contributes to the reproduction of structure is also an act of production, a novel enterprise, and as such may initiate change by altering that structure at the same time as it reproduces it—as the meanings of words change in and through their use.[49]

Action is thus conceived by Giddens as reflexively ordered rational conduct performed by human agents through the medium of language, where language is understood as 'a fragmented and diverse array of practices, contexts and modes of collective organisation', not as a closed, monolithic system.[50] This idea bears closely on the notion of multiple discursive communities within which subjects are constituted *and* that are constituted by speaking subjects, which was developed in earlier chapters of this book. Moreover, in a manner that parallels some of my earlier observations, Giddens regards the insights of Wittgensteinian

---

[46] Ibid. 128–9.
[47] Ibid. 125–33 and *passim*. In his new introduction to the 2nd edn. of *New Rules*, 1–15, Giddens attempts to answer some of the most common objections to the notion of the duality of structure.
[48] Giddens, *Studies in Social and Political Theory* (London: Hutchinson; New York: Basic Books, 1977), 115.
[49] Giddens, *New Rules*, 134.
[50] Giddens, new introduction, 8.

philosophy with regard to 'differences' mediated in the praxis of a plurality of rule-bound language-games to be of more enduring importance than the poststructuralist emphasis on the differential operation of signifiers or discourse.[51] This is not to suggest that he wholly dismisses the insights of poststructuralist theory; he is particularly concerned to endorse the poststructuralist introduction of temporality (and spatiality) into textual and social analysis, providing the concept of structure is not wholly abandoned in favour of the endless movement of supplementation.[52] However, Giddens argues that the structuralist and consequent poststructuralist notion that the elements of *langue* have identity only through their differential placement within an overall system serves to sever the relations and references of language to the objects and events in the world, resulting in the failure to generate an adequate account of reference. This tendency to 'retreat into the code' has thus resulted in a great deal of attention being paid to the 'internal organisation of texts, in which the play of signifiers can be analysed as an internal affair'.[53] In particular, he questions the Derridean prioritization of 'writing' over speech, insisting on the importance of theorizing 'the process of *using* words and phrases in contexts of social conduct':

> Meaning is not constructed by the play of signifiers, but by the intersection of the production of signifiers with objects and events in the world, focused and organized via the acting individual. . . . [S]peech—or rather talk—recovers a priority over other media of signification. Talk, carried on in day-to-day contexts of activity, is the fundamental 'carrier' of signification, because it operates in saturated behavioural and conceptual contexts.[54]

He notes, furthermore, that the ambiguous meaning of 'writing' as noun (that which is written) and verb (the act of writing), its close linkage in contemporary theory with the interpretative act of

---

[51] Giddens, 'Structuration Theory', 205. See his critical discussion of the post-Wittgensteinian social theory of Peter Winch in *New Rules*, 50–7 and his argument with post-structuralism in *Social Theory and Modern Sociology*, 73–108.

[52] Giddens, 'Structuration Theory', 95–8. Roy Boyne challenges Giddens's interpretation of Derrida in 'Power-Knowledge and Social Theory: The Systematic Misrepresentation of Contemporary French Social Theory in the Work of Anthony Giddens', in Bryant and Jary (eds.) *Giddens' Theory of Structuration*, 52–73; see esp. 65–9.

[53] Giddens, *Social Theory and Modern Sociology*, 85.

[54] Ibid. 91–2.

'reading', and the contemporary fascination with authorship, has sometimes resulted in texts being portrayed as if they wrote themselves. The consequence is often an unsatisfactory relegation of the author to the 'role of a shadowy adjunct'.[55] Giddens's objections to this aspect of poststructuralist thought may be readily anticipated, for it threatens to evacuate any notions of agency and intention. What is missing in the poststructuralist account, he insists, is an interpretation of the agent and agency (rather than the subject and subjectivity alone): '"Subjects" are first and foremost agents.'[56]

My brief, selective accounts of MacIntyre's and Giddens's writing glosses over much, and ignores even more. However, the ideas which these theorists articulate with respect to the human subject as an accountable, reflexive narrative agent who exists and has the power to 'transform' *within* the context of particular social settings or structures—that is, communities—is particularly relevant to the discussion of subjectivity pursued so far. The model of contextually determined self-narration that is elaborated by theorists such as Glover, MacIntyre, Giddens, and Taylor offers narrativization as the fundamental, necessary—and potentially redemptive, because revisionary or transformative—condition of human existence. It challenges and rejects the (post)structuralist notion which condemns the theorized subject to endless vacillation between the unpalatable 'alternatives' of inauthentic writtenness and meaningless dissemination within language structures. Significantly, this model attempts to retain the value of the human agent and the activity of narrative creativity; the narrative subject is not only made up in, but makes up, communal (cont)texts of value and meaning. We are not only constructed, but also construct, in language. This is not to suggest that there is an 'I', an essential, and pre-existing ego, which resides behind and co-ordinates the numerous subject positions adopted by individuals, an 'I' that retrospectively falsifies the narrative of her life; but rather to suggest that personal identity *is* the process of continuing narrative modulation and assimilation. The activity of self-narrativization may be endless, an activity of perpetual revision which always admits the possibility of change and reinterpretation, and never stabilizes into the unmoving stasis of certainty. But it

[55] Ibid. 94. Giddens acknowledges the value of the poststructuralist concerns with the 'disappearance of the author' in achieving a reconsideration of naïve accounts of traditional literary criticism (ibid. 106–7).
[56] Ibid. 98.

affords a sense of accountable self-identity through time. In developing the notion of self-identity in this direction, we may consider the situation of subjects in plural communal and communicative contexts not as a hopeless condition of loss and endless deferral, but as a fundamental human condition, one which enables us to function as purposive, intentional moral agents. Absolute personal freedom may not be possible as anything more than a utopian ideal, but relinquishing such an ideal need not entail resignation to a mandate of 'writtenness' and numbing conformity or meaningless escape. If we realize the creative, revolutionary potential of narration, rather than endlessly lament its deficiencies—the splits, absences, and gaps which characterize communication in its broadest sense—a measure of freedom is possible *within* the protocols that facilitate intra- and inter-personal readability in the communicative contexts we inhabit.

I have argued that some contemporary theorists, following the general linguistic turn in philosophical thought from epistemology to hermeneutics, have mistakenly appropriated inconoclastic, self-reflexive contemporary fictions to endorse and promote what are at times dubious political ends, ultimately advocating abstention from community in the reification of outside/inside dualisms. The application of conceptions of inauthentic and reinscriptive textual process to notions of the human subject has resulted in deterministic scare-mongering, with a concomitant invocation of the desirability of rule-less free play and the endless dispersal of meaning, conditions which open-ended, purportedly anti-narrational contemporary texts are called on to exemplify. Such theorizing is disingenuous. Many contemporary fictions do not celebrate the dissolute bliss of excommunicative, anti-narrational escape, but exemplify the power of situational choice: the power of choosing to be situated on the margins, yet still within communities of radical discourse; the power of calculated deviancy that can be creative or destructive. In Part II I will consider the strategic narration of three contemporary authors and their novelistic protagonists. These texts are concerned less with the problems of inauthentic writtenness than with an exploration of the possibilities and problematics of narrative creativity (and destructivity) and a simultaneous enquiry into the transformative possibilities of (self-)narrativization utilizing the wide variety of interpretative and communicative strategies available to subjects situated in a range of positions within community. They alert us to the possibility of alternative readings and interpretations in the texts of fiction and the metaphorical texts of selfhood. The (readable) rebellious strategies of these contemporary fictions point to the possibility of a politics of empowered difference, and with it a radical reconception of subjectivity.

Part II

THE EXPLORATION OF THE SUBJECT IN THREE CONTEMPORARY FICTIONS

6

A Deviant Narrative:
John Banville's *Book of Evidence*

The 'you' is the real 'I', the one perceived by others. . . .
Our little shard, our little divine shred of identity, so precariously held, is altogether lost as we join the oneness of the
audience.

Weldon, *The Cloning of Joanna May*

Maps of Self

If texts (and selves understood as texts) are to remain readable, and,
for that matter, if their novelty, deviation, or revolutionary intentions
are to be understood and function as significant, potentially revisionary acts, they must conform to certain intersubjective requirements of referentiality and expectation which make possible the
communication of their meaning and the value of their challenging
intentions. To make the radical assertion that, in order to evade
appropriation, one must wholly abandon oneself or one's text to the
exile of what I have called excommunication is clearly untenable. As
Jacques Derrida writes (in one of his softline statements) in *Of
Grammatology*, rebellious acts or narratives cannot 'destroy structures from the outside. They are not possible and effective, nor can
they take accurate aim except by inhabiting those structures.'[1] Yet the
freedom promoted by some contemporary theorists (often citing
Derrida's more hardline pronouncements) rests on precisely this
fallacious fiction of heroic exile or self-erasure.

These theorists persist in urging the freedom of an excommunicative aesthetic credo of silence, babble, and exile, often in the
name of a political enterprise which would delegitimate and abolish
the authority of dominant social power structures. Philip Beitchman,

[1] Jacques Derrida, *Of Grammatology*, trans. Gayatri Chakravorty Spivak (1967;
Baltimore: Johns Hopkins University Press, 1976), 24.

for example, hails as exemplary the 'madness' of deviant contemporary experimental texts which 'refuse permanently *any accommodation* with the social structures in which they are obliged to operate . . . [and] aim not towards amelioration but toward abolition of the social order' (my emphasis). He continues, in a tendentious expression of left-wing solidarity: 'the statement they [subversive texts] make is radical, uncompromising, unacceptable. Like a proletariat, "with nothing to lose but its chains," they seek not to make us over and better but to destroy what or the way we are.'[2] Loss, absence, emptiness, denial, destruction, abolition, homelessness, emptiness, exile, oblivion—again and again in contemporary criticism, textual process is characterized in terms of negativity and loss. A keynote in Roland Barthes work is the valorization of the non-identity of textual (and authorial) self-erasure. The 'text' (as opposed to the conventional 'work'), he asserts, is 'that neutral, composite, oblique space where our subject slips away, the negative where all identity is lost, starting with the identity of the body writing'.[3] In a similar manner, Charles Scott finds something redemptive in a postmodern language in which 'words might leave one without the book that they seem to compose, or with a non-word (e.g. *différance*) to which the words seem to give place'.[4] How viable are these purportedly revolutionary claims? What is the liberating value of a revolutionary enterprise which seeks, in the words of Beitchman, to 'destroy what or the way we are'? How redemptive, how meaningful, is the 'neutrality' of textual or personal non-identity? What is the worth of an aesthetic that leaves us without books, or a language that leaves us only with 'non-words'? What is the value of an act of deviance which is not understood as a purposive action at all?

I have already noted my concern with the ubiquitous application of the hyperbolic claims of some aspects of deconstructive theory to conceptions of personhood under the apparent sanction of an analogy which equates self-reflexive intellection with textual process. My dispute is not with the trope *per se*, for the metaphorical equation of

[2] Philip Beitchman, *I am a Process with no Subject* (Gainesville, Fla.: University of Florida Press, 1988), 279.
[3] Roland Barthes, 'Death of the Author', in *Image-Music-Text*, trans. and ed. Simon Heath (New York: Hill and Wang 1977), 142.
[4] Charles Scott, 'Postmodern Language', in Hugh J. Silverman (ed.), *Postmodernism: Philosophy and the Arts* (London and New York: Routledge, 1990), 33.

self and text may provide a useful means of conceiving personhood, when 'text' is understood as a creative narrative process, not simply a site of dissolution. This equation would then seek to understand selfhood as a narrative of continuity written, and read with a degree of interpretative licence, in terms of the expectation of intelligibility held by oneself and the others with whom one coexists and communes. It is only a short distance, however, from an acknowledgement of the intersubjective, linguistic constitution of personhood to a despairing vision of the human subject as an inauthentic social text, constituted and subdued by the violent authority of the word. The conclusions that are too readily drawn via the metaphor of textual identity are mistaken. What is most disturbing about this metaphorical leap are the moral and political implications which seem to follow as a logical consequence of claims about the wholesale extrapersonal linguistic determination of personhood. Such accounts stress the need to escape what they deem the restrictive 'orders' of metanarrational and communicative control, encouraging an impossible and ultimately insidious dream of subjective emancipation through tactics of displacement and exile—insidious because the revolutionary dream is itself a (potentially repressive) fiction of value which manipulates our (post)modern yearning for the freedom of unqualified self-authorization. But escape from the normative structures of intersubjective communicative rationality equates with politically ineffectual abandonment to irrationality. When human beings eschew, or remain outside, the frameworks of communal protocols, their behaviour may be deemed unreadable, unintelligible, and, as such, empty political gestures. Alasdair MacIntyre, in expounding his theory of narrative personhood (see Chapter 5), writes of the bafflement we experience when we attempt to understand (to read) such apparently senseless or unintelligible behaviour:

this kind of bafflement does indeed occur in a number of different kinds of situations; when we enter alien cultures or even alien social structures within our own culture, in our encounters with certain types of neurotic or psychotic patient (it is indeed the unintelligibility of such patients' actions that leads to their being treated as patients; actions unintelligible to the agent as well as to everyone else are understood—rightly—as a kind of suffering).[5]

[5] MacIntyre, cited in Michael Sandel (ed.), *Liberalism and its Critics* (1984; Oxford: Basil Blackwell, 1987), 131.

MacIntyre's stress on the importance of community and the need for interpersonally understood 'protocols' of (moral) behaviour is well known. Human actions, he claims, are 'readable' only within a communal framework of shared moral understanding. This is an idea developed by Charles Taylor at some length in his recent account of subjectivity, *Sources of the Self*.[6] Taylor argues that there can be no such thing as truly horizonless selfhood; the pathological consequences for the human subject of such a displacement are too great. He asserts that a sense of placement within frameworks or horizons of communal meanings is a fundamental condition of healthy personhood: 'doing without frameworks is utterly impossible for us; otherwise put, . . . the horizons within which we live our lives and make sense of them have to include . . . strong qualitative distinctions' (27). Furthermore, 'living within such strongly qualified horizons is constitutive of human agency, . . . stepping outside these limits would be tantamount to stepping outside what we regard as integral, that is, undamaged personhood' (ibid.). Elsewhere, Taylor claims that if we were to escape from the 'commonality of shared self-understanding' then 'we would break down as persons, be incapable of being persons in the full sense'.[7]

Taylor develops his argument by appealing to our intuitions with regard to orientation in physical space, suggesting that physical placement (a sense of where we are) is analogous to moral orientation (a metaphorical sense of 'placement' in relation to frameworks of communal value and the vision of the good life they define), and that both are fundamental to a sense of healthy—that is, undamaged—personhood.[8] For Taylor, moral orientation, like physical orientation, is not simply an optional stance, but an intuition intrinsic to

---

[6] Charles Taylor, *Sources of the Self: The Making of the Modern Identity* (Cambridge, Mass.: Harvard University Press, 1989). Further references to this book will be cited parenthetically in the text. In particular see chapter 2, 'The Self in Moral Space'.

[7] Taylor, 'What is Human Agency?', cited in William Corlett, *Community without Unity: A Politics of Derridean Extravagance* (Durham, NC, and London: Duke University Press, 1989), 29.

[8] Many contemporary fiction-writers develop the analogy between physical displacement and psychological disorientation, often utilizing images and motifs of mazes, labyrinths, and puzzles to do so. In the stories collected in Jorge Luis Borges's *Labyrinthes* (1962) and John Barth's *Lost in the Funhouse* (1968) and in Georges Perec's *Life: A User's Manual* (1970; first published in English in 1987), the disorientation felt by the characters parallels that experienced by readers who must struggle to find their way through the seemingly disjointed convolutions of the texts.

being: 'To know who you are is to be oriented in moral space' (28).
Asking *who* I am, like asking *where* I am, is a question always already
there, 'an absolute question [which] always frames our relative
ones' (47). By contrast, some poststructuralist theorists claim that a
sense of 'mapped' moral orientation, like narrative orientation,
is an illusory artifice which categorically restricts the prerogative
of individual liberty. Leo Bersani, for example, opines that the
conventional realist novelist, in presenting fiction with an ordered
teleological structure, falsely portrays 'the human as a readable
organisation', and in doing so, 'makes an important contribution to
the viability of the society which he can also violently criticize, by
providing that society with what may be termed maps of self'.[9] Maps
of self, with their implied commitment to established patterns
of behaviour and the constraints on characterological spontaneity
imposed by limitations of moral conformity, are precisely what many
contemporary theorists so adamantly disavow in their advocacy of
disorientation and dissolution. Steven Connor suggests in *Postmodernist Culture* that 'the means to orient oneself spatially may be
precisely what are missing from the postmodern world'.[10] More
correctly, perhaps, what the postmodern subject lacks is access to the
one undisputed map, or a singular means of (moral) orientation. The
absence of all maps of meaning and value would herald a disabling,
relativistic dis-location in which notions of morality, or responsible
agency, are meaningless. But this is surely not the case in postmodernity. Rather than a lack of maps, postmodern subjects have
access to a wide range of them. A plurality of possibilities for
mapping does not amount to displacement, even if it does foster
uncertainty and open up possibilities of contestation.

Positing the existence of orienting frameworks—that is, communal maps of intelligible behaviour—need not necessitate their
objective constitution, if we hold on to the notion of plurality. Nor
need they entail coercion or conformity to determined dictates.
Communally framed subjects are not simply the helpless victims of
systematic violence. Choice within frameworks (maps) and, to a
degree, choice between frameworks (maps) always remain possible.
Having a map or knowing in which direction North lies does not

[9] Leo Bersani, *The Freudian Body* (New York: Columbia University Press,
1986), 83.
[10] Steven Connor, *Postmodernist Culture: An Introduction to Theories of the
Contemporary* (Oxford: Basil Blackwell, 1989), 227.

determine the road a traveller opts to take within a demarcated landscape (although it may certainly influence the choices she makes). Moreover, our knowledge of the lie of the land does not make inevitable or imperative a certain path or passage through it (although it may make the choice of a certain path more likely). There is always more than one way to travel. Just as a person may belong to a variety of determining communities that frame her interpretations, so a traveller may be in possession of several maps or guidebooks, each offering alternative or even contradictory advice for the traveller. Some may be outdated, printed before the construction of a new highway or the demolition of a forest which has radically changed the landscape; others may be concerned only with population distribution or the placement of waterways or with rail and bus routes; some may be detailed, specific survey charts, others vague and unclear; different guidebooks may contain conflicting recommendations, or have been written to promote a particular purpose or serve a specific need. A traveller may, of course, opt to take a known route, ignoring the other possibilities for travel within a familiar landscape; or she may choose to take a back road, a little travelled route towards her intended destination. She may find that the way she chooses is blocked or unpassable, or that the demands of fellow-travellers urge her to go in ways contrary to her own desires. In finding her way and selecting her paths, a traveller must assimilate and choose between various forms of guidance, compare a variety of mapped possibilities for travel, and heed circumstantial and contextual restraints. This does not in any way preclude the possibility of misreading the maps she has at hand, or using an outdated one, or mistakenly taking the wrong path, or choosing to detour via the back roads. Our subjective freedom (always qualified by our partial and retrospective knowledge, the demands of other travellers, the limitations of our physical capabilities, and the obstructions in the landscape) inheres in the choices we make with regard to which maps we will use, when, and what paths we will travel, out of a plurality of options—not in throwing all maps to the wind and striking out into the wilderness alone.

We need moral and discursive 'maps' (and a belief in their credibility in the majority of cases, a claim which does not preclude the possibility of error, redundancy, or mutability) to provide the sense of placement which enables us to make purposive choices and act with intention. This is not to say that there is ever only one map, or that some maps are *intrinsically* better than others; the maps we have at hand may well prove to be (with the benefit of hindsight) outdated, faulty, or inadequate to our purpose; but the assurances of placement they give at the moment we consult them and our expectations and assumptions that in most cases the information they give us will be true are necessary to our sense of meaningful, purposeful progression. To have some sense of who I am requires that I place my self-conception in relation to the expectation of personal continuity and moral intelligibility held by myself and others, cohabitants in a variety of mapped, situated communities. It requires that I place my actions and intentions within the moral and discursive frameworks of a number of intersubjective communities. It requires also that I orientate my present narrative of self in relation to the 'others' who are the past and future subject positions I inhabit— in other words, in terms of my own narrative of self-continuity and progression. Otherwise put, I know and write myself as a narrative of personal continuity governed by certain intra- and inter-subjective expectations, expectations which may or may not be fulfilled, although in the majority of instances they are, this being what makes 'me' recognisable or 'readable' to myself and others. To function as a moral agent without some sense of placement and of cardinal points of shared value is impossible. And to exist as a comprehensible subject outside or beyond a determining community, in the terms of whose conventions and language I define my own meaning and identity, is similarly impossible. This would be like trying to read a novel (or understand a language) without some understanding of the conventions, shared expectations, and referential value of the linguistic elements which comprise its meaning. We cannot begin to think of purpose or meaning or value in a wholly unmapped landscape—geographic, psychic, or textual.

Terms such as 'frameworks', 'maps', and 'conventions' run counter to the values of personal autonomy and individual freedom which have such high currency in post-Romantic Western society; they seem to imply the intrusive presence of extra-personal imperatives which restrict the free movement of the individual. Much has been written on the difference between earlier (other) cultures and our own in this regard. It is frequently noted, for example, that the increasing value placed on personal liberty and moral autonomy in contemporary Western culture is a consequence of the secular dissolution of theistic belief in an ordained, cosmic map of order.[11] Post-theism is hardly new, but the modern sense of dislocation and lost certainty seem to have reached an apex of doubt in contemporary society, where even the integrity of the 'god' of the self-reflexive subject has been radically undermined. The renunciation of faith in the orderings of external (or immanent) authority and communicative rationality ostensibly brings freedom, but it is a freedom tainted with fear and a disturbing sense of meaninglessness. Released from enslavement to given codes of conduct into the wilderness of hermeneutic and ethical indeterminacy, modern Westerners are thought to engage in a perpetual quest for meaning in textual and cultural landscapes emptied of the securely defined signposts mapped out for earlier (other) cultures. The price of contemporary freedom from charted conformity (from the authoritative moral map of the Bible, for example) may be insecurity and loss of direction, a sense of purposelessness, as Taylor suggests: 'the world loses altogether its spiritaul [sic] contour, nothing is worth doing, the fear is of a terrifying emptiness, a kind of vertigo, or even a fracturing of our world or body space' (18). The sense of purposelessness, disorientation, and vertigo diagnosed by Taylor is the consequence of radical displacement, of refusing accommodation within *any* community, of denying all responsibility to any communal protocols; it need not be the consequence of an expanding horizon of alternative sites for meaning-construction and a diversity of means of mapping. Communal plurality does not necessitate radical displacement or schizophrenic fragmentation. The equation of subjective authenticity and nonconformist madness or irrationality, so pervasive in contemporary theory, results from a mistaken assumption that any accommodation within communities of rational discourse amounts to entrapment. All too often the devastating psychic fragmentation of schizophrenia, in which personal continuity and the ties of community are absent or abandoned, are paraded as an honest, desirable alternative to institutional control and totalizing rationality. This,

[11] Mark C. Taylor, has recently provided an analysis of postmodernity in theological terms which equates the desacralization of the book and the self with the loss of faith in God. In EЯRING: *A Postmodern A/Theology* (Chicago: University of Chicago Press, 1984) he writes: 'God, self, history, and book are, thus, bound in an intricate relationship in which each mirrors the other. . . . The echoes of the death of God can be heard in the disappearance of the self, the end of history, and the closure of the book' (7–8). See also Anthony Cascardi, 'Secularization and Modernization', in *The Subject of Modernity* (Cambridge: Cambridge University Press, 1992), 125–78.

quite simply, is a blithe, irresponsible refusal to acknowledge the crippling conditions and consequences of a state of personal dissemination and displacement experienced by the schizophrenic. As Donald Kuspit notes in considering Jameson's, Baudrillard's, and Deleuze and Guattari's advocacy of postmodern schizophrenia as a counter to the evils of capitalist ideology, '[f]rom a psychiatric point of view, [this argument] involves a preposterous misunderstanding and misappropriation of the concept of schizophrenic pathology—a facile application of it to advanced capitalist society'.[12]

In elaborating his theory of personhood in *After Virtue*, Alasdair MacIntyre suggests that it is contextualization through the connective, associative strategies of narrativization within communal and communicative protocols that provides the means for personal/moral orientation and for our understanding and identification of intelligible (and morally culpable) behaviour:

> We identify a particular action only by invoking two kinds of context, implicitly if not explicitly. We place the agent's intentions . . . in causal and temporal order with reference to their role in his or her history; and we also place them with reference to their role in the history of the setting or settings to which they belong. In doing this, in determining what causal efficacy the agent's intentions had in one or more directions, and how his short-term intentions succeeded or failed to be constitutive of long-term intentions, we ourselves write a further part of these histories. *Narrative history of a certain kind turns out to be the basic and essential genre for the characterisation of human actions.*[13]

This analysis is, I believe, essentially correct, but with one proviso— that the 'genre' of 'narrative history' understood by MacIntyre to be characteristic of intelligible, intentional human actions is a genre governed by certain understood linguistic and narrative conventions. If, in fear of the restrictions imposed by mapped communities, we jettison those conventions which render our narratives readable to ourselves and others, and opt instead for the poststructuralist freedom

[12] Donald Kuspit, 'The Contradictory Character of Postmodernism', in Hugh J. Silverman (ed.), *Postmodernism: Philosophy and the Arts* (London and NY: Routledge, 1990), 60, 268 n.

[13] Alasdair MacIntyre, *After Virtue* (London: Duckworth, 1981), 194 (my emphasis). MacIntyre elaborates: 'we render the actions of others intelligible . . . because action itself has a basically historical character. It is because we all live out narratives in our lives and because we understand our own lives in terms of the narratives that we live out that the form of narrative is appropriate for understanding the actions of others' (197).

of wholesale textual indeterminism and fragmentation, what is the consequence? What happens, in other words, if we bring to MacIntyre's model of narrativized personal identity the philosophical and theoretical claims about the necessity of escape adumbrated by some contemporary literary theorists? How, indeed, are we to write and live meaningful narratives of selfhood, how are we to maintain the notion of morality, in the absence of a sense of placement in a mapped community, and without those intersubjective conventions which enable intelligible orientation?

Diminished Responsibility: Disavowing Agency

> [His] overriding passion is a need to dramatize himself, to show himself as *other*—and this passion cannot be reduced to moral or exemplary terms. . . . [His] guilt does not issue in remorse or contrition. The guilt retains a residue of anxiety, but in a confessional act it is strangely robbed of its moral quality and becomes instead . . . a dramatic occasion.
>
> Goodheart, *The Cult of the Ego*[14]

John Banville's novel *The Book of Evidence* brings into sharp relief many of the concerns discussed above.[15] Significantly, it opens to scrutiny the posture of 'unreadable' alienation from communal protocols that is advocated by some (readable) contemporary theorists, revealing the moral consequences of such posturing in its masking of intention. Posture here implies both (theoretical) stance and pretence; it implies the wilful situation of the theorists at a site of calculated deviance within community while feigning excommunication (and irresponsible detachment) from the constraints of rational placement. As I have suggested, the paradox that underpins the poststructuralist account is that the purpose and productivity of its negative aesthetics (escape and exile) can be secured only by appeal to the very kinds of normative insider values it so vehemently decries as restrictive: the worth of individuality, the desirability of personal autonomy, and so on. The value of its anti-normative deviance can be comprehended only when framed by the inter-

---

[14] Goodheart refers here to Rousseau in *The Confessions*.
[15] John Banville, *The Book of Evidence* (London: Secker and Warburg, 1989). Further references to this book will be cited parenthetically in the text.

subjective protocols that facilitate meaningful communication. Some contemporary critics, while gesturing towards an unarticulable, inexpressible utopia of excommunicative freedom, beyond or without language and rationality, in fact remain within the boundaries of rational communication, for these provide the means for the comprehension of their claims. Comprehended, interpreted, and recuperated as meaningful narratives (and, moreover, narratives of emancipatory value), such critics only pretend to the dissolute condition of excommunicative irrationality that they valorize. Rather than escaping all community, they have situated themselves at contestational marginal sites within the communities they seek to critique.

In our courts of law, approbative actions are those perceived as being deviant from intersubjectively understood norms of 'right' behaviour. The game of justice proceeds according to intersubjectively understood rules (ones which are quite clearly provisional, local, and revisable[16]) which provide the horizon for agency of social conformists and rebels alike. Certainly these rules may be prescriptive and repressive, and the utilitarian goods they proclaim to endorse may well restrict individual prerogative and run counter to individual belief; but they are, none the less, a necessary condition in the attribution of moral culpability. We do not assign blame in cases where a transgressive individual has no comprehension of the norms by which to gauge her conformity or deviance, or in cases where the accused has no coherent sense of selfhood. Central to our attribution of blame and punishment are notions of intentionality, responsibility, and, crucially, coherent personal identity. Individuals who are (or were) not able to understand expectations of 'right' behaviour when breaking communal laws are not deemed guilty of willed transgression. Individuals who have no sense of themselves as intentional, coherent agents are not held responsible for their actions, but are understood to be possessed of a disorientating, disabling incapacity for self- or moral evaluation. Persons who are unable to connect their present manifestation of self with past manifestations of self are believed to be not responsible for actions they may have performed in the past. It is for this reason that our courts of law allow for the plea

---

[16] The taking of life in the context of war, e.g., is an action not subject to the same approbation as the taking of life in the context of peace; behaviour deemed legally or morally 'right' behaviour may differ significantly from one culture or age to the next; laws are clearly revisable in so far as legal precedents may be (and frequently are) retrospectively overturned.

of not guilty on grounds of (temporary) insanity. This legal dispensation suggests how fundamental to notions of justice are the possession by individuals of a coherent sense of selfhood and a sense of moral orientation and the capacity for moral evaluation it engenders.

To reiterate: some contemporary theorists (and the novels they appropriate) purport to a condition of unintelligibility and personal dislocation in what remain, ultimately, readable and often politically motivated theoretical narratives. This may seem a critical manœuvre of minor moral consequence, and perhaps it is—until we push the theoretical equivalence of textual processes and human intellection, or textual deviance and human transgression, via the equation of self as text. If intentionally deviant textuality, posturing as excommunicated and irrationally unmapped, is deemed laudable, might not it be understood to endorse the adoption of similarly intentionally deviant postures of excommunication and irrationality in human subjects (as texts)? Might not the posture of excommunication, masking the intentional deviance of a subject, be used by that subject to disavow her responsibility to the communal protocols she clearly understands and seeks to disrupt? What happens when the intentional, understood act of deliberately situating oneself in opposition to communal protocols, while pretending no understanding of communal constraints (the very constraints that render one's deviant act meaningful), takes the form of a radically destructive, conventionally approbative act, like that of murder? These are questions with which Banville's novel confronts us. In short, *The Book of Evidence* forces us to consider the ethical consequences of a theoretical posture of excommunicative irresponsibility.

The Book of Evidence is an autobiographical fiction in so far as it comprises the selective life-story of its narrating protagonist, Freddie. Freddie writes from his prison cell, where he has been incarcerated for the murder of a housemaid, Josephine Bell. In exchange for a shortened prison sentence, his attorney has negotiated with counsel a plea of guilty to the lesser charge of manslaughter, thereby avoiding the necessity of a protracted trial and thus inadvertently preventing Freddie from having his 'say' in court. His narrative, addressed to the reader in lieu of the judge and jury he never had the chance to regale with 'his story', purports to give a truthful account of the circumstances that resulted in, and immediately followed, the murder. The life-story Freddie tells is one of deprivation and personal misery, fraught with references to an unhappy childhood, a thwarted career, and an unsuccessful marriage—a life in which he has been consistently dealt a raw deal. Apparently lonely and unloved, the boy Freddie finally found his vocation as a statistician, a calling in which he was both talented and successful. Soon after, however, he married (unhappily), and set aside his career to live the life of an itinerant in southern Europe with his wife and autistic son. Here he ran into debt, and foolishly borrowed money from a shady loan shark who, when repayment was unforthcoming, threatened the life of his wife and child. Freddie opted to return home in the hope of cajoling his aged mother into coming up with the outstanding sum. Soon after his return to Holyhead, Freddie recalls that he decided to visit an old, wealthy friend, Binkie Behrens, with whose daughter, Anna, he had once had an affair. There was an ulterior motive to the visit: the Behrens's home housed a number of artworks on public display, and Freddie intended to steal one of the paintings (no doubt, the valuable painting would do much to accommodate his debtors). With this in mind, on the way to the Behrens's house, he stopped and purchased a hammer and some string. Having successfully lifted his chosen painting from the wall (*Portrait of a Woman with Gloves*), Freddie was interrupted in his felonious endeavour by the appearance of a housemaid. Enter Josephine Bell. Flustered and afraid that she would raise the alarm, Freddie took Josephine hostage, dragging her across the Behrens's lawn to his rented car. He then drove to a secluded location, where he bludgeoned Josephine (almost) to death with the hammer. Leaving her to die in the abandoned car, Freddie caught the train back into Holyhead, where he called on the hospitality of an old family friend, Charlie French, who, ignorant of his murderous actions, took him in. The only sensation which Freddie recalls feeling at the time of the killing was a sense of immense numbness and isolation; he felt (and feels) no remorse. Freddie stayed in Charlie's home for over a week, while the police tried to hunt him down. During this time he claims to have anticipated his impending arrest with some pleasure, eagerly following the daily newspaper reports on police progress in the case, and making no attempt to escape. He looked forward to the public notoriety he would enjoy as a result of his crime. At this point in the story, Freddie's recollections draw near to the narrative present in which he writes: he tells of his arrest, of being forced to sign a fabricated confession (once again this prevents him from having 'his say'), of his sentencing, imprisonment, and bitter disappointment at having been denied the right to tell his version of events in court.

Such is Freddie's story. While openly admitting his actions, Freddie denies his culpability for the crimes of kidnap and murder of which he is accused. In doing so, he swings between precisely the two positions which I have suggested form the extremist poles of the contemporary debate about situated subjectivity: he proclaims, on the one hand, the inauthenticity of determined being, and on the other, the madness of exiled excommunication. He finds in both stances a means of denying personal responsibility for his actions. And yet neither stance is an adequate representation of his existential condition: his is only a posture of a-responsible inauthenticity and a posture of insanity. In such posturing, Freddie seeks to mitigate responsibility for his chosen act of destructive deviance. In the former condition he can claim to be merely the subject of external authorization (which is, paradoxically, his status as a character in Banville's fiction), condemned to act out a predetermined narrative, or simply to be the passive victim of cosmic causality. In the latter condition he presents himself as an alienated outsider, the insane inhabitant of a 'crystal bubble' (115) of solipsism, radically excluded from a community of others who would judge him according to their own rules of play—rules from which, by virtue of his exclusion and lack of comprehension, he claims to be exempt.

We soon realize, however, that Freddie himself authorizes the 'evidence' we read. As exclusive autobiographical narrator, he has selective control over the 'facts' we are told. He does not passively record events; his narrative is not merely the product of chance or contingency. Moreover, the (text of) self which Freddie narrates in the course of his (re)presentation of 'the evidence' does not lack narrative coherence nor is it fragmented by the dissolution and discontinuity expressive of insanity; the readable self he (re)presents is selective and selecting, an agent with the capacity for choosing deviance, a capacity he expresses in a most radical, destructive form. Freddie claims to be the written product of external determinants in self-aware terms which make very evident his own selective role as a self-authorizing writer who is eminently capable of rhetorical manipulation. There are clear parallels between Freddie's self-abnegating authorial stance and the negative aesthetics of self-abolition evident in those contemporary texts and authors who so strenuously proclaim their own self-erasure or gesture towards the resonance of their silence. Like Freddie, these texts and writers persistently deny their own originality and authenticity in the creative, innovative medium of fiction; and Freddie's self-narrative is, if nothing else, a masterful fiction.

Far from establishing Freddie as the passive victim of extra-personal control, his (act of) narration reveals his monomaniac insistence on, and possession of, self-authority. The story(telling) does not confirm Freddie's absence of self so much as proclaim his creative presence; the narrative functions less as an assertion of passive writtenness than as an expression of his capacity for deviant (self-)creation. At the outset, the novel is established as the written transcript of the speech which Freddie proposed to make when called to give evidence in court at the trial for the murder of which he is accused: 'My Lord, when you ask me to tell the court *in my own words*, this is what I shall say' (3; my emphasis). By framing his address within the conventions of the law (and perhaps of religion— 'My Lord' is suggestive of prayer or confession), Freddie hopes to secure the veracity of his speech, to accord to his story the status of history. From the first, he is at pains to establish the pious credibility of his narrative, to convince his juror-readers that what follows is incontrovertible fact, a truthful account of the events and circum-stances which led to, and culminated in, his killing of Josephine Bell.

The belief in the possibility of reclaiming truth or factual evidence (which is the basis of our courtroom procedure, as it is the conven-tional foundation of the genre of autobiography) is a myth which Freddie utilizes for his own purposes. He points towards the inherently partial, subjective nature of all (re)telling, saying, 'Do you swear to the tell the truth, the whole truth and nothing but the truth? Don't make me laugh' (7). Yet, at the same time, he deliberately exploits the expectation of factuality and truthfulness conferred by the imaginary courtroom setting in order to further his deceptions. By introducing his narrative as unmediated history, as *The* (the definite article implies that this is the single, one and only account) *Book* (biblical intonations are evident again) of *Evidence* (the word itself implies objective truth and factual assessment), Freddie seeks to deny his creative role as narrator. He insinuates that he is merely an a-responsible reporter on events, a retrospective chronicler. By stress-ing that his evidence is spoken—the text is ostensibly the written transcript of his defence speech—and, moreover, spoken under oath (or in the confidentiality of the confessional), he aims to exploit the assumption of truthfulness and spontaneity which are conventionally associated with direct speech. This is fact, he would have us believe, not fiction.

But Freddie's 'truthful', spoken account is constantly undercut by references to its own textuality and to the artifice of its own constitution. This is, after all, a *book* of evidence, a fictional reconstruction of events, or perhaps, as we become increasingly aware, even of pure imaginative fantasy. In overtly self-reflexive references to his role as writer, Freddie teasingly alludes to the fictional identity, the imaginative status, of the witnesses he 'calls'. He situates himself as ontologically prior to the characters whose testimonials he so blatantly authors. This is most evident in his naming of the characters. His mother's stablehand, for example, is first introduced as 'Joan or Jean—I'll compromise, and call her Jane' (49), but on the following page this name is rejected as artistically unsuitable: 'Jane—no, I can't call her that, it doesn't fit' (50). Of the melancholy taxi-driver who ferries him to the Behrens's house he says, 'I had better give him a name'—it is Reck, I am afraid—for I shall be stuck with him for a while yet' (90).[17] Ironically, it is Freddie's desire to assert authorial dominance by drawing attention to his creative *power*—his capacity to situate, circumscribe, name, and control the representation of himself and the other characters through narrative strategies of naming and description—which also undercuts the validity of his claims that he is the powerless product of some other determining authority. Drawing attention to his role as author and inventor of the characters—and the self—who populate his tale is a means of asserting his imaginative power and prowess, but in doing so, he also discredits his claim to the lack of creative selfhood which is the basis of the defence he would construct.

Freddie's self-aware occupation as inventive writer is made very clear in his frequent allusions to the verbal constitution of his address. On the second page of the novel he writes of his need to 'get a dictionary', and several pages later he flaunts the fruit of this acquisition, writing of 'that state of floating ease, of . . . balanic, ataraxic bliss', adding 'yes, yes, I have got hold of a dictionary' (19–20). He is supremely aware of the capacity of language to construct truths (or lies) and fictions of identity, as is evident in his tribute to the artistry

---

[17] See also the naming of the cowboy, Randolph (13); the dog, Patch (46); and the home help, Madge (174).

of the 'confession' fabricated for him to sign by the policeman, Cunningham, soon after his arrest:

Oh, well-named Cunningham! Behind the mask of the bald old codger a fiendish artist had been at work, the kind of artist I could never be, direct yet subtle, a master of the spare style, *of the art that conceals art*. I marvelled at how he had turned everything to his purpose, mis-spellings, clumsy purpose, mis-spellings, clumsy syntax, even the atrocious typing. Such humility, such deference, *such ruthless suppression of the ego for the sake of the text*. . . . it was an account of my crime I hardly recognised, and yet I believe it. He had made a murderer of me. (202–3; my emphasis)

'The ruthless suppression of the ego for the sake of the text', so artfully managed by Cunningham, is ultimately what Freddie fails to accomplish. His overwhelming selfishness and his egoistic desire for recognition as the author make him unable to effectively disguise his artifice (behind either a façade of anonymity or the fragmentations of stylistic incomprehensibility). He is unable to write in a style 'that conceals art'. His monologic disclosure testifies to his need to control and possess the characters (and the self) that he portrays: no witnesses will be called except those he conjures up with his pen; no voices will be heard except those he chooses to let speak; all facts given are those that he elects to tell. And yet the final paragraph of the novel is a wry acknowledgement of the limitations of his authorial power, a statement about the inevitability of contestation, by the 'evidence' of readers, of other writers and alternative accounts, of 'his story'. The evidence he presents is, he finally admits, a fiction—only one possible fiction is an unlimited field of alternative inventions. It is not the truth, but merely a fiction posturing as such. Of his testimony (the book we read), Freddie writes:

I have asked Inspector Haslet to put it into my file, with the other, official fictions. He came to see me today, here in my cell. He picked up the pages, hefted them in his hand. It was to be my defence, I said. He gave me a wry look. Did you put in about being a scientist, he said, and knowing the Behrens woman, and owing money, and all that stuff? I smiled. It's my story, I said, and I'm sticking to it. He laughed at that. Come on, Freddie, he said, how much of it is true? It was the first time he had called me by my name. True, Inspector? I said, All of it. None of it. Only the shame. (219–20).

The importance of an authorizing, authoritative role to Freddie becomes clear towards the end of the novel when he records learning that his celebrity appearance on the stage of justice has been denied him due to his lawyer's plea-bargaining. He will never give evidence in court, a state of affairs which he bitterly resents:

> I'll plead guilty, of course—haven't I done so all along?—but I do not like it that I may not give evidence, no, that I don't like. It's not fair. Even a dog such as I must have his day. I have always been myself in the witness box, gazing straight ahead, quite calm, and wearing casual clothes, as the newspapers will have it. *And then that authoritative voice, telling my side of things, in my own words.* Now I am to be denied this moment of drama. (182; my emphasis)

Denied the opportunity of courtroom histrionics, his 'moment of drama', Freddie's selfish desire for authority is transferred from the judicial stage to the page of his testimony—the novel we read. He actively seeks to influence the way in which we, as substitute jurors and judge, read him (the self he fictionalizes). Both 'performances', courtroom theatrics and textual testimony, are activities of self-representation, of imaginary self-construction. Freddie is the character he dramatizes, the persona he intends. There is no access to a 'true', unrepresented self; the represented self is finally the only self that we, and others, can apprehend and respond to. In realizing, as he does, that we are what others perceive us to be or, more precisely, that we are what our interpreted language and behaviour makes us appear, Freddie must be held responsible for the self he projects. He is not simply a written product, but also a productive writer who seeks to actively influence and challenge the way in which others read his narrative.

The Hidden Arranger of all These Things

So, Freddie claims himself to be the pawn of extra-personal determination. It is this which enables him to admit to the act of murder with such bare-faced complacency. Responsibility and guilt have no meaning in a cosmos denuded of free will; apology is futile, and defence impossible, when actions are performed without choice. He thus says to his 'judge':

> I used to believe, like everyone else, that I was determining the course of my own life, according to my own decisions, but gradually, as I accumulated more and more past to look back on, I realised that I had done the things I did simply because I could do no other. Please do not imagine,

my lord, I hasten to say it, do not imagine that you detect here the insinuation of an apologia, or even of a defence. I wish to claim full responsibility for my actions—after all they are the only things I can call my own—and declare in advance that I shall accept without demur the verdict of the court. I am merely asking, with all respect, whether it is feasible to hold on to the principle of moral culpability once the notion of free will has been abandoned. (15–16)

Life, asserts Freddie, is 'a prison in which all actions are determined according to a random pattern thrown down by an unknown and insensate authority' (16); 'the whole damn thing is chance, pure chance' (19). The world is 'unpredictable, seething . . . a swirl of chance collisions' (18). This persistent denial of motivated self-authorization is a repeated motif in Freddie's evidence; it is the bass register maintained throughout the orchestration of his defence. He imagines himself as 'a clockwork toy' (124), one whose actions are not premeditated but prescribed. '[T]he hidden arranger of all this intricate, amazing affair' (161) is perpetually evoked. Finding a discarded pullover in the boot of his rented car with which to replace his own blood-stained one immediately after the murder, Freddie remarks on the 'deceptive casualness [of] the hidden arranger of all these things' (111). It is a comment which could stand as a summary of his proclaimed philosophy of determined being. But the ironic tone of so much of his self-description (he lampoons, mocks, and parodies the self he describes throughout) suggests that, far from being the written subject of some 'insensate authority', he is in fact able to maintain an objective authorial distance from the 'inevitable' self he describes: 'inevitable, mind you, does not mean excusable, in my vocabulary. No indeed, a strong mixture of Catholic and Calvinist blood courses in my veins' (98).

If all actions are unmotivated, simply knee-jerk responses to an unknowable string-puller's commands, then there can be no answer to the question 'Why?' To ask 'Why are you living like this?', as Charlie French does of Freddie soon after their reunion, is pointless:

The question is wrong, that's the trouble. It assumes that actions are determined by volition, deliberate thought, a careful weighing-up of the facts, all that puppet-show twitching which passes for consciousness. I was living like that because I was living like that, there is no other answer. (38)

Freddie argues that questions regarding motivation are themselves nothing but habit, a learned response, the mere 'puppet-show twitching' of a justice system structured around a myth of purposive intentionality. That we ask them at all is yet another example of the illusion of purposive volition whereby we imagine meaningful being, and upon which our moral beliefs and our legal and judicial systems of blame and punishment, have their foundation. Following his arrest, the police interrogator who questions Freddie comes up against a blank wall when framing his question 'Why did you do it?' (196). To ask such a question of one who views his life as contingent reflex devoid of deliberation, and who looks back on his actions with 'an amnesiac's numbed amazement' (55), is futile. The only answer that can be given is the chilling answer that Freddie gives: 'I killed her because I could, . . . what more can I say?' (198)

There are, Freddie insists, no turning-points. There is no moment at which motivated choice can in any way enable one to deviate from the path inexorably mapped out for the duration of one's life. Things simply are; events simply happen; and on to this 'ceaseless, slow, demented drift of things' (135), we impose our illusionary frame-works of purpose and meaningful action. At one point on the long train journey returning from southern Europe, as the sun was rising, Freddie tells us at the felt 'a gust of euphoria, or something like euphoria' (23), but he is quick to dismiss any possible meanings or symbolic value which his readers may surmise of this epiphanic moment:

> I was at a turning point, you will tell me, just there the future forked for me, and I took the wrong path without noticing—that's what you will tell me, isn't it, you, who must have a meaning in everything, who lust after meaning, your palms sticky and your faces on fire! . . . I do not believe such moments mean anything—or any other moments, for that matter. They have significance, apparently. They may even have value of some sort. But they do not mean anything. (24)

The train journey, this movement of meaningless moments, is, Freddie would have us see, analogous to the journey of (his) life—perpetual motion in which, as Freddie will later assert, 'there are no moments' (135). Life, rationalized thus, is a pathetic, purposeless process of existential 'drift' (37); we travel along our predetermined path without the capacity to actualize the possibilities of other, alternative routes, whose lost potential we can only lament in futile retrospection. Musing on missed opportunities, Freddie surmises that the pain of life is not in what is done, but in what remains undone, all the 'secret paths' we fail to take until, finally, we realize 'it is too late' (171). He writes:

The myriad possibilities of the past lay behind me, a strew of wreckage. Was there, in all that, one particular shard—a decision reached, a sign-post followed—that would show me just how I had come to my present state? No, of course not. My journey, like everyone else's, even yours, your honour, had not been a thing of signposts and decisive marching, but drift only, a kind of slow subsistence, my shoulders bowing under the gradual accumulation of all the things I had not done. (37–8)

Yet, in the description of the train journey home, the narrative objectivity of Freddie's self-ironic perspective is very evident. As elsewhere, he self-consciously watches himself perform, and tran-scribes this performance in the selective terms of his narrative, mediating the 'faculty' of the actions and events—the evidence—narrated to his reader. Throughout the novel he remains the supreme artificer, formulating his fictional material with care and deliberation, manipulating the distance between self portrayed and portraying self, which never fuse in the spontaneity of comprehended, incontrovertible identity. ' I am a sort of floating eye', he tells us, 'watching, noting, scheming' (64). In the two passages cited above, for example, he mocks the clichéd ingredients of the pregnant 'moment' of choice and the conventional expectations of a decisive turning-point this engenders; he parodies the stereotypical symbolism of the dawn and the journey—this was no moment of rebirth, we must realize, but a regressive return enacted by a stooped, broken victim of cruel circumstance.

Before abandoning his career for the pursuit of pleasure in sunnier climes, he was, Freddie tells his reader, a statistician, a brilliant young scientist in the field of probability theory. (This claim is radically challenged in the final paragraph of the novel, cited above, in which we learn that even the most seemingly commonplace 'truths' of Freddie's narrative, such as that regarding his vocational status, are fictions.) He took up science, he maintains, 'in order to find certainty', or rather, 'in order to make the lack of certainty more manageable' (18). He hoped, through the procedures of rational investigation, to find a way

of erecting a solid structure on the very sands that were everywhere, always shifting under me. And I was good at it, I had a flair. It helped to be without convictions as to the nature of reality, truth, ethics, all those big things—indeed, I discovered in science a vision of the unpredictable, seething world that was eerily familiar to me, to whom matter had always seemed a swirl of chance collisions. (18)

'[R]eality, truth, ethics, all those big things' are, according to Freddie, no more than the arbitrary inventions of our intellections, the artificial constructs of our language. They have no metaphysical validity as immutable grounds for certainty. Concepts of value— goodness, badness, right, and wrong—are merely conventions imposed on a neutral world in the same way that we impose meaningful moments on the random flux of eternity, or erect illusive structures of scientific solidity on the perpetually shifting sands of experience:

Evil, wickedness, mischief, these words imply an agency, the conscious or at least active doing of wrong. They do not signify the bad in its inert, neutral self-sustaining state. Then there are the adjectives; dreadful, heinous, execrable, vile, and so on. They are not so much descriptive as judgmental. They carry a weight of censure mingled with fear. Is this not a queer state of affairs? It makes me wonder. I ask myself if perhaps the thing itself— badness—does not exist at all, if these strangely vague and imprecise words are only a kind of ruse, a kind of cover for the fact that nothing is there. Or perhaps the words are an attempt to make it be there? Or, again, perhaps there is something, but the words invented it. (54–5)

These blatantly anti-metaphysical assertions, the speculation on the 'ruse' of scientific (and moral) objectivity, and the predication of the capacity of words to invent even those seemingly unchallengeable 'big things' that we credit with absolute presence—'reality, truth, ethics'—make very evident Freddie's epistemologically insecure twentieth-century identity. Moral values, so conceived, are never absolute, but are structured in terms of difference, in terms of the conceptual opposites they invoke, not an inherent quality they define. Language is never neutrally descriptive, but is always prescriptive, judgemental, and ideologically complicit.

Freddie is shrewd enough to realize that it is no good denying the actual act of murder, as the weight of evidence confirming his guilt is simply too great. Instead, he declares that our moral repugnance is itself misplaced, that in judging his actions to be 'heinous' or 'execrable' we are imposing an arbitrary framework of value on a purely neutral occurrence, on an action performed unavoidably in accordance with his true nature, faithful to his given potential: 'I killed her because I could.' His defence, then, is not the crude formulation of a denial, but a sophisticated challenge to the obligatory nature of moral law. The authority and objective status (in so far as it transcends and regulates subjective desires) of social morality is thus repudiated by evoking the radical scepticism of moral indeterminism whereby moral values are understood as only ever being expressions of individual preference. How can we judge an individual's actions to be 'evil' or 'wicked', Freddie implies, simply because these fall outside the invented boundaries of arbitrary defined social 'good'?

In order to claim non-culpability by means of this radically subjective antinomian argument, as Freddie seeks to do, it is necessary to establish oneself as truly an outsider (as an individual in the most extreme sense), as one who does not belong to the community of shared values within whose terms one is (unfairly) judged. If we make an appeal for exemption from intersubjective morality on the grounds of our right to unconstrained personal choice, and if we hold that moral values are no more than individualistic projections on an otherwise neutral existence, then our appeal must carry as its necessary condition the solipsistic isolation of the individual and her exclusion from an understanding of commonly understood rules of moral play. Subjective autonomy, so interpreted, equates with unconstrained personal autonomy, unbound, absolute existential freedom. But surely we are not limited to the two alternatives (if alternatives they are) of either individualistic relativism or wholesale extra-personal determination. Is it not possible to construct a model of subjective morality, of free-playing self-narration in community, which still maintains responsibility (and culpability) with regard to the values inscribed in intersubjective conventions? Further, rather than using metaphors of textuality and notions of conceptual materiality to lament the paradoxical impasse of entrapment between a dream of impossible freedom and an existential condition of determinism (writtenness), can we not instead recognize the way in which narrative models of self-construction provide a means of escaping this impasse and envisioning the human condition as one of responsible, articulate(d) agency within community?

Healthy Personhood and the Communal Matrix

I have already suggested that a model of narrativized selfhood such as that proposed by Charles Taylor in *The Sources of the Self* or Alasdair MacIntyre in *After Virtue* may provide us with a means of countering the reductive, extremist positions of either an existentialist advocacy of unregulated free play or the reactionary conservatism which seeks to reintroduce metaphysical absolutism as a counter to the relativism of asocial individualism. Taylor suggests, for example, that '[w]e find the sense of life through articulating it. . . . Discovering here depends on, is interwoven with, inventing. . . . [W]hat meaning there is for us depends on our powers of expression', and '[m]y sense of myself is of a being who is growing and becoming. . . . My sense of self understanding necessarily has temporal depth and incorporates narrative.'[18] Such a model rests on the supposition that we do exist as moral beings not in isolation, but rather in community and, importantly, that the communal relations which constitute our moral being are achieved within the terms and conventions of intersubjective discursive practices.[19] So conceived, an individual is defined in the space of communicative praxis. Taylor asserts that '[a] self can never be described without reference to those who surround it'; 'I am a self only in relation to certain interlocutors' (35, 36). Our placement in the matrix of community, in 'webs of interlocution', is, for Taylor, fundamentally linguistic (36). Induction into personhood requires initiation into a defining community (or number of them) through adoption of that community's shared language (or another common system of communication). There is no such thing as a private language, because acts of signification always presuppose, indeed necessitate, an other.

For Taylor, non-significatory, amoral existence is inconceivable if one has a 'healthy' sense of one's (communally defined) selfhood; indeed, a condition of wholesale social exclusion is 'pathological' (35). A similar intuition shapes the latter half of Freddie Montgomery's narrative in The Book of Evidence. If he is to succeed in claiming exemption from social law, he must prove himself to have been situated outside communal frameworks of (linguistic) value at the time of the murder. This is why it becomes imperative that he

[18] Taylor, Sources of the Self, 18, 50. Further references to this book will be cited parenthetically in the text.

[19] Taylor's analysis of socially situated selfhood appears to owe much to the social theory of the self set forth by G. H. Mead. Karen Hanson, in The Self Imagined: Philosophical Reflections of the Social Character of the Psyche (New York and London: Routledge and Kegan Paul, 1986), discusses Mead's social philosophy in relation to notions of subjectivity and community set forth by Descartes, Ryle, Sartre, and Wittgenstein. Hanson both challenges and develops the model of selfhood given by Mead in order to substantiate her proposition that the self is not an essential essence, but a 'fantasy' (fiction) constituted in and through social contextualization.

convince his juror-reader of his (temporary) insanity in order to sustain his non-culpability. By appealing to a condition of dislocated madness, Freddie intimates that at the time of the murder he was simply unable to recognize or understand communally defined rules of (moral and linguistic) play; he was in an unhealthy state of excommunication. When detailing events that occurred after the murder, Freddie deliberately describes his actions in terms of the absence of rules, or his failure to understand them. Soon after the murder, he informs his reader, he entered a public toilet in order to wash the blood from his hands, but rather than use the men's toilet, he chose to enter the women's instead, for, as he writes, 'there were no rules after all' (125). Later, while awaiting capture at the home of Charles French, he claims, 'I was in another country now, where the old rules did not apply' (173).

An appeal for moral exemption such as Freddie's can have validity only if he is shown truly to be an alienated outsider, one who is without an understanding of communal rules of 'fair play'. He must promote his condition as one of pathological excommunication or radical solipsism, in which, without comprehension of interpersonal conventions of 'right' behaviour, or devoid of the ability to recognize and respect others, his transgressions of social law are unmotivated and blameless. From the first, Freddie works to portray his exclusion from society, an exclusion explicitly detailed in terms of language and articulacy. In effect, he seeks to convince us of his (temporary) insanity at the time of the murder. According to the self-portrait he sketches, Freddie is, and always has been, alienated, isolated, an 'outsider' (19). He explicitly draws to the attention of the 'court' his life of exile in southern Europe, implying that his role is that of the archetypal isolate: 'Ibiza? Ischia? Mykonos perhaps? Always an island, please note that clerk, it might mean something' (8). He is, in his own words, nothing more than a 'poor lost wandering creature' (129). Communicative failure characterizes all his relationships and interactions with others; those with Daphne, his wife (9), his mother (41), Charlie (139), and even his autistic son (146).

We must ask, however, to what extent this alienated identity is deliberately invoked. To what extent is it a role of solipsistic insularity wilfully adopted, deliberately fostered and portrayed by Freddie in his (self-)narrative as a means of denying culpability? All his descriptions serve to reinforce this isolated self-characterization: he does not belong anywhere. In an apparently innocuous descriptive vignette, for example, he recounts walking through the city one night and passing the doorway of a crowded pub: 'A kind of slow amazement came over me, a kind of bafflement and grief, at how firmly I felt myself excluded from that simple, ugly, roistering world. That is how I seem to have spent my life, walking by open, noisy doorways, and passing on, into darkness' (217). In detailing his journey home, Freddie speculates that fellow train-travellers 'might [have been] looking in from another world' (25), and on reaching Holyhead, the city of his upbringing, he recalls that the landscape of 'home' appeared utterly foreign. Looking about him, he saw 'scenes he hardly recognized' (30); he remarks with self-pity: 'My world, and I an outcast in it' (129). Again, this isolation is described as linguistic in kind. It is the speech of his 'fellow countrymen' (27) that is so totally alien to him: 'The voices, that was what startled me first of all. I thought they must be putting on this accent, it sounded so like a caricature' (27). As he tellingly says of those around him, 'I don't understand these people. I have said it before. I don't understand them' (129). Imprisonment, Freddie suggests towards the end of the novel, only confirms his condition of existential isolation; it is 'an official and outward definition of what had been the case, in my case, all along' (202). It is the physical externalization of the solipsistic isolation that he would suggest is his given lot, lifelong exile. In prison he lives in 'a state of virtual quarantine' (145), a state which recalls the chosen island exile of the preceding years. Here he is separated by a window of glass from his visitors, who 'exist in a different element' (145); all communication from 'outside' is mediated, like the daylight which filters into the prison, 'as if something had been done to it, before it is allowed to reach us' (4).

It is in his description of the murder itself that Freddie's appeal to the solipsism of radical autonomy and the excommunication of madness is most evident. The self that Freddie narrates appears to be alienated to a pathological degree, exhibiting a condition of wholesale severance from any community, external or internal. He is ostracized from those around him, lacking the ability to understand their morality or the language which defines it; moreover, he is unable to reconcile the inner community of interrelated past subject positions he has inhabited, past 'selves' whose narrative interweaving, through the processes of memory, composes a sense of sane personhood. In other words, the existential condition which Freddie describes is that of the absolute isolation of insanity, an insanity which is defined, moreover, explicitly in linguistic terms. Freddie went to the Behrens's household, he tells us, not with the intention to kill, but to steal a painting—*Portrait of a Woman with Gloves*. His description of the abortive theft, and the events which followed, are shot through with images and references to the pathologically excommunicated self that Freddie would portray: he is imaged as a being lacking the capacity for intersubjective communication. Immediately before, during, and after the murder, he tells us, he abstained, or was prevented, from communicating with others (see 93, 94, and 98–9). We learn that after finally managing to lift the painting from the wall, our protagonist scampered about on his knees 'talking to [him]self' (110); soon after, he seems to have completely lost his capacity for speech, and to have resorted to 'uttering little squeaks of distress' (110). As he frog-marched his hostage towards the rented get-away car, Freddie recollects that '[s]he said nothing, or if she did I was not listening' (111).

The pages in which Freddie describes the murder itself abound with references to his inability to communicate and his failure to understand the words and actions of others or the circumstances in which he found himself. In the instant before he struck Josephine with the hammer, he recalls '[h]e could not speak' (113). He narrates how, after striking the fatal blows, he left the car briefly, only to find himself utterly alone, lost in an unrecognizable landscape: 'the road in both directions was empty, and I had no idea where I was' (114). He was, we are told, 'mute and amazed' (115). On returning to the car, he shut himself inside, refusing to open the windows, 'afraid of what might come in' (115); he then drove away 'soundlessly' through a 'strange' landscape, 'as if in a crystal bubble' (115). This image of enclosure behind glass echoes the description of the prison cited earlier; it is a repeated motif in Freddie's narrative, a perpetually evoked metaphor for the existential condition Freddie would promote: a life lived hermetically sealed within the 'crystal bubble' of solipsism.

Freedom as Excommunication?

I have argued that wholesale freedom, absolute individuality, can only exist in the absence of social language and a narrative of self-continuity. Freedom, in these terms, requires, *is*, severance from some defining community—severance not only from external others, but from a community of internal others whose narrative relationships through time constitute one's (sane) story of selfhood. Absolute freedom (in contrast to the qualified liberty of interpretative free play) is not simply the refusal or inability to recognize the rules which enable one to play or commune meaningfully with others, but also the absence of any sense of consistent personal continuity or communal belonging whatsoever. In order to claim exemption from communal law, Freddie must prove himself to have been wholly free in this absolute sense at the time of the murder—that is, excommunicated from society and without a coherent internal story of self-identity. This is exactly what he attempts to convey. Consider his description of his flight though the countryside with the young woman dying (silently) on the back seat of his car:

I stared through the windscreen in dreamy amazement. I might have been a visitor from another part of the world altogether, hardly able to believe how much like home everything looked and yet how different it was. I did not know where I was going, I mean I was not going anywhere, just driving. It was almost restful, sailing along like that, turning the wheel with one finger, shut off from everything. It was as if all my life I had been clambering up a steep and difficult slope, and now had reached the peak and leaped out blithely into the blue. *I felt so free.* (116; my emphasis)

I felt so free. The freedom Freddie invokes in this description is the wholesale existential freedom so frequently touted as the only alternative to the extra-personal writtenness of ideological determinism. It is an impossible freedom—impossible, that is, within the terms of what we recognize as 'healthy' personhood. The claim of absolute self-determination is incompatible with the comprehension of (sane and moral) personal identity. The capacity for free play in our interpretation of moral meaning and self-identity is impossible without a comprehension of the defining conventions that make interpersonal fair play—and deviance—meaningful. *Comprehension* of communal conventions, however, in no way commits us to absolute compliance with them or to blind belief in their prescriptions. I have already stressed the need for us to maintain a distinction between the notions of understanding and belief. Moreover, human beings are situated within many defining communities, never only one. Our sense of selfhood is compounded by loyalties and allegiances to the conventions of many different communities, some of which we enter into wilfully, others of which we are born into or are contingently situated. The interplay of multiple communal allegiances in conjunction with our partial liberty to move and choose between a variety of communal sites is what constitutes our qualified personal freedom. Freddie's absolute freedom, however, amounts to the excommunicated freedom of insanity, of wholesale exile: 'With a gulp of demented laughter I drove on . . . and I was free' (118).

Throughout the section detailing the events of the murder, Freddie's account of his release into the freedom of insanity is charted by the progressive dissipation of his articulateness—his ability to speak, to hear, and to understand. After delivering the murderous blows, Freddie drove blindly through the countryside, finally bringing the car to rest 'in the midst of a vast and final silence' (118). A last attempt to communicate on the part of the dying victim fails; even her final word is misheard, its meaning clarified only much later. Freddie recounts how he watched her, with complete detachment and utter passivity; he recalls his sensation of dehumanized alienation: 'I can't remember feeling anything, except a sense of strangeness, of being in a place I knew but did not recognize. . . . I thought: *I am not human*' (119; my emphasis). In the hours and days that followed the murder, Freddie recalls, he continued to drift through a nightmare of discontinuity—aloof, detached, and unresponsive, as if trapped, to utilize his persistent metaphor, 'in a crystal bubble' (115). There was '[n]ot a soul to be seen' (126) on the railway siding where he waited for a train shortly after deserting the car and his dying victim. When a train finally pulled into the station, the passengers seemed unreal, 'propped up in the wide windows like manikins' (126; again, Freddie's isolation is imaged as separation from others by glass). Throughout this time, he tells us, he floated 'in dreamy detachment, as if I had been given a great dose of local anaesthetic' (128).

At this time, Freddie constantly stresses, he was insane. The days spent at Charlie's house awaiting capture were, he reflects, 'the strangest period of my life' (149). But he is equally concerned to emphasize the temporary, lapsed nature of this spell of madness. In fact, as he tells it, he regained his sanity within a few days of the crime; after floating 'freely' for a short time, he returned again to the solid ground of recognized self-identity: 'I had come back to myself' (159). But reintegration in the community whose values his insane actions have so violently transgressed proves impossible. Venturing beyond the glass, back into the 'reality' of the world beyond Charlie's home, following his 'recovery', only reaffirms his otherness. He has been irredeemably alienated from 'normal' community by the radically deviant act he has committed (163–7). Early in his narrative, Freddie disassociated himself from the 'initiated crowd', those whose ability to be sympathetic and compassionate is born, he suggests, of a mysterious 'universal principle', the knowledge of which is 'the badge of their fellowship' (49), a knowledge which he claims not to possess. Again and again, throughout his story, Freddie stresses his exclusion from 'the community of men', self-piteously asking, 'when was I ever part of *that* gathering?' (193; emphasis original). Representatives of this 'fellowship' gather outside the courtroom after his sentencing:

They shook their fists, they howled. One or two seemed about to break from the rest and fly at me. A woman spat, and called me a dirty bastard. I just stood there, nodding and waving like a clockwork man, with a terrified fixed grin on my face. That was when I realised, for the first time, it was *one of theirs* I had killed. (211; emphasis original)

The sense of separation and alienation Freddie would convey to his juror-reader is not simply the result of exclusion from this united community of others (individuals only 'seemed about to break from the rest', but chose instead to stay with the crowd). He is, he insists, also alienated from himself. The deep sense of dislocation and division which characterizes his relationship with others is, he would have us realize, only an externalized projection of his own deeply divided, fragmented psyche. Freddie's solipsistic realm, the 'crystal bubble' of his mind, does not, it appears, enjoy the sovereign rule of a discrete, unified self. He contrasts his sense of (postmodern) selflessness with the apparent (Romantic) self-possession of others:

when I was young I saw myself as a masterbuilder who would one day assemble a marvellous edifice around myself, a kind of grand pavilion, airy and light, which would contain me utterly and yet wherein I would be free. Look, they would say, distinguishing this eminence from afar, look how sound it is, how solid: it's him all right, yes, no doubt about it, the man himself. Meantime, however, unhoused, I felt at once exposed and invisible. How shall I describe it, this sense of myself as something without weight, without moorings, a floating phantom? Other people seemed to have a density, a thereness which I lacked. . . . They would speak of whole peoples as if they were speaking of a single individual, while to speak even of an individual with any show of certainty seemed to me foolhardy. (16–17)

Self-reflection for Freddie is less a matter of Cartesian certainty than of (post-)Freudian inner conflict. He describes himself as 'bifurcate' (95), distinguishing between 'that stern interior sergeant' (17), a controlling super-ego, and 'that other, terrible creature [which] chafed and struggled, lusting for experience' (172), a subversive source of animal drives that he nicknames '[Billy?] Bunter' (29). For much of his life, Freddie tells us, Bunter has been restrained, subdued, and silenced by the sergeant. But on the day of the murder a profound change of internal constitution occurred; Bunter, previously mute, gained a voice, gained control: 'I felt that I was utterly unlike myself,' writes Freddie:

> That is to say, I was perfectly familiar with this large, somewhat over-weight, fair-haired man in a wrinkled suit sitting here fretfully twiddling his thumbs, yet at the same time it was as if I—the real, thinking sentient I—had somehow got myself trapped in a body not my own. But no, that's not it, exactly. For the person that was inside was also strange to me, stranger by far, indeed than the familiar, physical creature. This is not clear, I know. I say the one inside me was strange to *me*, but which version of *me* do I mean? No, not clear at all. But it was not a new sensation. I have always felt—what is the word—bifurcate, that's it. Today, however, this feeling was stronger, more pronounced than usual. Bunter was restive, aching to get out. He had been shut up for so long, burbling and grumbling and taunting in there that when he burst out at last he would *talk and talk and talk.* (95–6; emphasis original)

The murder, then, claims Freddie, was consequent on the eruption of this repressed, forcefully muted *alter ego*, a pervasive other who inhabits his tormented physical body, not the rational deed of that 'real, sensate, thinking I' that he more readily designates 'me'. But, as he acknowledges, his muddled argument is far from clear: indeed, which version of this multiple self is *truly* 'me', the conformist subject or the repressed other? It is only with the release of Bunter and the refutation of controlling reason that Freddie experiences what he believes to be personal liberty. Only thus is he truly '[him]self':

> Ever since I had reached what they call the age of reason I had been doing one think and thinking another, because the weight of things seemed so much greater than that of thoughts. What I said was never exactly what I

felt, what I felt was never what it seemed I should feel, though the feelings were what felt genuine, and right, and inescapable. Now I had struck a blow for the inner man, that guffawing, fat, foulmouth who had been telling me all along I was living a lie. . . . *To do the worst thing, the very worst thing, that's the way to be free.* I would never again need to pretend to myself to be what I was not. (124; my emphasis)

The psychoanalytic drift of the argument is clear. In Kristevan terms, Bunter might be thought to represent the semiotic, the reservoir of repressed drives and desires contained and controlled by the construction of the subject at the level of the symbolic order. Bunter's explosive ascendance then suggests the irruption of the semiotic into the symbolic, and the transgressive consequences of this 'burst[ing] out' the radical subversion of the rules of the symbolic order. We are forced to consider the consequences of a blithe prioritization of the irrational 'reality' of the semiotic over the artificial constructs of the symbolic. In Chapter 3 I suggested that the danger of Kristeva's theory of the semiotic, taken literally as the model for subjective emancipation and operating wholly within a binary mind-set that opposes structural conformity and anti-structural transgression as negative and positive respectively, is the tendency to valorize transgression and subversion, across the board, over the 'repressive' rationality of the symbolic. Without paying attention to the nature and content of subversive action, such theorizing may result in a dangerous idealization of madness and unreason, and an advocacy of lawlessness that is far from positive or redemptive.

In suggesting the primacy of his repressed (semiotic) other, Bunter, Freddie appears to advocate an existentialist credo of unqualified personal liberty: freedom that eschews the constraints imposed by the maintenance of a continuous and (reasonably) recognizable or readable personal identity; freedom as excommunication, an unwillingness or inability to register the needs and desires of others; freedom as anarchic and (self-)destructive.

Calculated Deviance: Doing the 'Worst Thing'

It becomes clear, however, that Freddie's antinomian argument is founded on an understanding of (if not a belief in) the moral values of the society he *chooses* to neglect. Despite his claims of excommunication and his inability to understand others, it is evident that his actions are those of radical, willed deviance, not those of an amoral incomprehension of the intersubjective norms of 'right' behaviour. They are an expression not of determined automatism, but of his very human capacity for calculated transgression: his ability to misplay in a purposeful flouting of understood conventions of fair play and his capacity to choose to be situated at a site of radical deviance. He clearly understands the moral values of his society, but chooses to reject them. He chooses to situate himself on the margins of understood moral conventions, in a rebellious community that rejects conventional law. He defines himself in terms of this rejection, as a rebel who defiantly refuses to comply with convention. To the very end, he still understands himself in terms of others, having merely traded one community ('normal' society) for another (the community of social rebels or that of prison inmates). Ironically, the freedom that Freddie claims to have gained is still wholly conditional on social arbitration, and will remain so for as long as it is to have value, be understood, *as* the rebellious expression of individual free will. He suggests, in the passage cited above, that freedom lies in our ability to 'do the worst thing'; yet what is 'worst' but a statement of value which understands that there are other, better modes of being and doing? Freedom as he perceives it is still wholly inscribed in the terms of social morality; it has meaning only as the capacity to choose to transgress rules which are communally understood (if not believed in).

The deviant liberty which Freddie exercised in murdering Josephine Bell was not that of a pathologically irrational, dislocated, unmapped being, but that of a rational, rationalizing moral agent. His use of the moral qualification 'worst' suggests that he recognized, understood, and chose to violate the moral codes of the society in which he exists. He elected to assert his identity as an individual rebelling against the recognized distinctions between 'better' and 'worse' actions. In his egotistical desire to assert his individuality, Freddie chose to commit an act which would situate him as deviant—a choice made in full awareness of the game rules which would demand retributive punishment.

I am claiming, then, that Freddie wilfully adopts his identity as a deviant on the margins of communal morality. He engages in an activity of self-narrativization, adopting and manipulating a range of narrative strategies; he is in fact the manipulative writer of his (readable and read) self. Moreover, he is *aware* of his narrative ability

for self-production; Freddie understands that he is, like Binkie
Behrens and like us all, a 'self-made man' (200). It is precisely
because he is aware of his ability to invent his social identity through
external representation, and because he understands that (socially
defined) moral behaviour may involve the repression of his 'worst'
desires, that Freddie's appeal for exemption from retributive sentencing cannot stand.

Paradoxically, it is Freddie's egotism ultimately which prevents
him from sustaining a believable fiction of non-culpable self-dissolution.
I have already discussed how eager he is to establish the temporary
nature of his spell of madness and his subsequent return to rationality;
his vanity requires us to admire his intelligence, not pity his insanity.
His overwhelming desire to appear witty and authoritative undercuts
the fragmentation he would portray. This need is the impetus behind
his monologic domination of the narrative and his urgent demand for
the right to tell his story 'in his own words'. He is driven by desperate
longing for others to respect, and even fear, the authority of the self
he authors. The sustained performance which is Freddie's narrative
reverberates with expressions of this egotism. Unexceptional conformity affords little notice or recognition from those around him, so
he seeks to draw attention to himself through the most repulsive of
morally deviant acts. Early on in the novel he writes of the stardom
he believed would follow his arrest and imprisonment for murder,
describing in detail the role of fame and notoriety he intended to
assume:

Somehow I pictured myself a sort of celebrity, kept apart from the other
prisoners in a special wing, where I would receive parties of grave, important people and hold forth to them about the great issues of the day,
impressing the men and charming the ladies. What insight! they would cry.
What breadth! We were told you were a beast, cold-blooded, cruel, but
now that we have seen you, have heard you, why—! And there am I,
striking an elegant pose, my ascetic profile lifted to the light in the barred
window, fingering a scented handkerchief and faintly smirking, Jean-
Jacques the cultured killer. (5)

The most striking feature of this imaginary projection is the dramatic
imagery in which it is couched: 'the cultured killer', elegant, charming, impressive—this is the star role Freddie wrote and hoped to
enact. He clearly imagined and intended this performance to be the
consequence of his crime, as the following statement of intentionality

reveals: 'I was *fully intending* to conduct my own defence, and *already saw myself* making brilliant and impassioned speeches from the dock' (201; my emphasis).

It becomes increasingly evident that the whole sordid affair was carried out intentionally by Freddie, who not only 'fully intend[ed]' his actions in self-interested anticipation of the fame they would ensure, but also 'saw [him]self' doing them in imaginative expectation of the attention they would bring. He is a self-conscious actor of the notorious persona perceived (read) by others. This is most clear in his description of the kidnap of Josephine Bell, an episode which Freddie outlines as if it were a scene from a play, complete with an appreciative audience. Dragging his captive to the car, Freddie enjoyed the sensation of being 'exposed' and 'look[ed] at', and looked forward to future spectators 'who would soon be crowding around me in fascination and horror' (112). It is for this reason that Freddie does not attempt to cover his tracks or even leave the vicinity after committing the murder: he wanted and expected to be discovered. He knew what he was doing; he knew the consequences of his actions. He awaited his arrest with impatient anticipation, eagerly imagining his impending stardom (161). We learn that while waiting for the police to track him down he read the daily papers avidly, scouring them for details about himself and the mounting police search—'It was strange to be the object of so much meticulous attention, strange, and not entirely unpleasant' (173). When the arrest finally occurred, Freddie believed that he had at last achieved his longed-for recognition: 'I had never in my life been so entirely the *centre* of attention' (193; my emphasis).[20]

The imagery used by Freddie in his description of the arrest is significant. It was, he recounts, staged like a film (189), played out like 'a grotesque kitchen comedy' (191), one in which not only he and the police, but Charlie French too, performed their clichéd roles to the hilt.

Is that really necessary, Inspector? [Charlie] said [as Freddie is hand-cuffed]. It was such a grand old line, and so splendidly delivered, with just the right degree of solemn hauteur, that for a second I thought it might elicit a small round of a applause. I looked at him with renewed admiration. He had thrown off that infirm air of a minute or two ago,

---

[20] Similar expressions of his eager anticipation of attention occur elsewhere in the narrative (189, 190, 205). His disappointed realization that this is not to be the case is voiced several times (5, 194, 210).

and looked, really, quite impressive three [sic] in his dark suit and silver wings of hair. Even his unshaven cheeks and tieless collar only served to give him the appearance of a statesman roused from his bed to deal with some grave crisis in the affairs of the nation. Believe me, I am sincere when I say I admire his expertise as a quick-change artist. To place all faith in the mask, that seems to me the true stamp of refined humanity. (190–1)[21]

In paraphrasing Yeats's dictum, '[t]o place all faith in the mask', Freddie lays bare his understanding of the interpretative interplay of human existence: we are the masks we adopt, he acknowledges; we are the selves we narrate, and are perceived by others to be. Behind the *posture* of excommunication exists a communally responsible agent. According to Freddie, in the drama of life, appearances are the only 'truths' available to us: 'This is the only way another creature can be known', he avers, 'on the surface, that's where there is depth' (72). The manner we adopt, the image we project, the self-conscious masks and disguises we wear, all these are 'no less plausible . . . than [our] real self' (178): personal identity is a social narrative that we and others read. On the surface, at the level of the narrative, on the interface of interpretation—this is where the game of life is played.

Freddie's awareness of his own (and others) histrionic capacity, of his ability to play (pretend) the hapless, fragmented self that he is in public, is very evident in his repeated, almost obsessional, use of dramatic imagery. His descriptions of others, as well as those of himself, continually draw attention to the staged nature of person-hood, the constructed quality of projected and perceived subjectivity; motifs of masks, disguises, and role-playing abound.[22] Freddie is

---

[21] For other instances in which Freddie admiringly gives details of Charlie's histrionic prowess see pp. 35, 36, 37, and 133–4. Other characters are equally well endowed with the ability to act; see e.g. the description of Freddie's father (28), the actors who populate Charlies' favourite bar (66, 128), and the 'cow-boy' Randolph (13).

[22] Examples of Freddie's self-aware fictionalization are abundant in *The Book of Evidence*: dressed in Charlie's clothes, he wears a 'new mask' (172); attempt-ing to remove the painting from the wall of the Behrens's exhibition room, Freddie images himself to be 'like the villain in an old three-reeler, all twitches and scowls and wriggling eyebrows' (110). Realizing that he has fallen foul of the men whom he has attempted to blackmail, Freddie describes his predicament as material for 'a third rate film' (10), a 'supporting feature' into which he and his co-star Randolph (another master dissembler, 13) have stumbled. He de-scribes his mother's funeral as a 'brief, hackneyed little drama' (100); a bus trip into the city is said to be 'faintly theatrical' (127), played out like a stage show

quite clearly adept in the art of role-playing. He prides himself on his ability to impersonate, remarking near the beginning of his narrative, 'I have always been a good mimic' (12), and relating how, in order to pass the time in prison, he amuses fellow inmates and his counsel 'with tales of prison life, fleshing them out with impersonations' (169).[23] Freddie's most sustained impersonation and successful fictional elaboration is his self-narrative. His narrative recollections reveal his self-aware habitation of a succession of subject positions or personae: he writes of himself as 'playing at being a blackmailer' (14) and 'playing at being relaxed' (64). Unrecognized by Charlie at their first meeting after many years of separation, Freddie recounts how he delighted in the sensation of anonymity; it was like 'being in disguise' (34). He recalls how, at a dinner party thrown by Charlie, he 'pos[ed] as Charlie's factotum', providing a disturbing analysis of the unfixed, illusory nature of self-identity:

I even invented a history for myself as I went along, I mean I—how shall I express it—I fell into a certain manner that was not my own and that yet seemed, even to me, no less authentic, or plausible, at least, than my real self. (My real self!) (178)

As this passage suggests, Freddie recognizes that it is the self he pretends (and intends)—the posture that he wilfully adopts—which is the self that others perceive *as* him and whose actions others will finally judge as his. What condemns Freddie is that he *knows* this. He acknowledges—even flaunts—his skilful capacity to fictionalize various modes of being, to write and act a variety of positioned selves. The self who is perceived, who performs—this is the self, finally, who is guilty of murder.

---

in which each of the passengers 'has a role of sorts to play' (128). Landscape, too, is imaged in theatrical terms: the countryside looks 'like a hastily painted backdrop' (114); a long shadow across the lawn at Coolgrange is 'like a fallen stage-flat' (57); the back room of a pub is 'like a stage' (163); street life in the city is 'a rackety little scene' (194).

[23] The ease with which Freddie 'fleshes out' characters, animates them in acts of creative imagining, is particularly evident in his imaginary construction of a life and history for the woman in the painting *Portrait of a Woman with Gloves*. 'There is no she, of course,' he says. 'There is only an organisation of shapes and colours. Yet I try to make up a life for her' (105). This stands in direct contrast to the 'failure of imagination' he experiences in relation to Josephine Bell, his inability to 'make her live' through imaginative reconstruction of her reality (215–16).

The Weight of the Evidence

It was my earlier contention that in his *Book* Freddie appeals to both excommunicated insanity and determined writtenness in order to deny his responsibility for the murder he has committed. But the cumulative weight of the *Evidence* suggests that neither condition is an adequate expression of his existential condition. Excommunication? Hardly so. Freddie is well versed in the protocols of intersubjective communication; he is a (self-)narrator who consciously manipulates the possibilities of his craft, fully aware of the rules of narrative play. His deviant position on the margin of social morality is chosen in full understanding, even eager anticipation, of its consequences. He is not without comprehension of the meaning of the words 'good' and 'bad', 'better' and 'worse', meanings invented by and constituted in an intersubjective discourse that shapes his understandings (though not his beliefs). In fact he characterizes his rebellious behaviour in these terms, defining himself as a self-styled transgressor, one who has chosen the freedom of radical individuality by doing what he *knows* to be 'the worst thing'. In an act of supreme egotism he has written (re-membered, intended) a self-narrative which he hopes will situate him away from 'the crowd', but still within reach of their understanding. Significantly, this self-narrative is plotted. It possesses the sequential continuity imposed by (past) remembrance and (future) intentionality; it is not the perpetual present of unreadable, anti-narrative incoherence expressive of truly excommunicated irrationality.

And what of writtenness? In a passage cited earlier, Freddie claims that the unfolding of events which constitute his life narrative are the result of the careful orchestration of 'the hidden arranger of all these things'. He shunts his responsibility (and blame) on to an extra-personal determining force that orders his actions. Yet who is this mythical determiner but Freddie himself—Freddie Montgomery the 'self-made man', the arch fictioner, the master performer, who is responsible, ultimately, for the deviant actions of the individual he pretends (and intends) to be?

It is imperative, as a corollary to recognizing our capacity to situate ourselves in communities of marginal resistance, that we acknowledge our responsibility for the moves we make. These deviant moves may be constructive, providing new maps for moral orientation, and revisionary, invoking the reassessment and adaptation of our current meaning-making maps. But equally, they can be destructive. This destructiveness is particularly insidious in cases where claims of irresponsible excommunication, or escape from the [constraints] of intersubjective rationality, are employed as a means of masking the radical will-to-power of a rebelling individual. This is precisely what Freddie does, pretending either irrationality or determinism in order to evade responsibility for an action performed in anticipation of its consequences. It is also the tactic used by some contemporary critics who laud the revolutionary capacity of excommunicative deviance *per se*, who pronounce on the desirability of madness, or the value of disintegration, while remaining very firmly, and rationally, in control of their own rebellious narratives. My point is this: we cannot evade culpability for our intentional positionality by evoking one or both of the demons of determinism and excommunication. Responsibility for actions is an unavoidable condition of our subjective capacity for choice in and between communities of discourse, whether our chosen actions are destructive and/or potentially constructive.

7

Speaking (for) One's Self:
J. M. Coetzee's *Foe*

A person who becomes silent becomes opaque for the other
person; somebody's silence opens up an array of possibilities
for interpreting that silence, for imputing speech to it.

Sontag, 'The Aesthetics of Silence'

A New Self at Every Moment?

There persists in some contemporary theory the idealistic dream for,
or deceptive invocation of, the unconditional liberty of an autonomous 'I', an 'I' whose authenticity is unlimited by expectations of
narrative continuity and the constraints of identity realized through
time. What theorists in this mould are keen to discover (or encourage)
in the contemporary fiction they analyse is a move towards the
release of the previously bound 'identities' of traditional narrative
(the identities of characters, readers, authors, and texts) into a state of
existential emancipation which is uncircumscribed by expectations
of continuity or referentiality. In their wishful insistence on the
possibility of escape from conventional narrative restraints, these
theorists appear to avoid (or evade) the consequences for notions of
morality and agency which are encouraged by the provocation of
unlicensed interpretative liberty. The assumptive optimism of such
claims is quite insupportable. It promises the unattainable by imagining that we can meaningfully deny or escape frameworks of meaning
altogether, encouraging the belief that we can simply side-step the
(potentially restrictive) enclosures of convention and still retain the
value of this strategic move.

Here is Thomas Docherty in *Reading (Absent) Character*:

if I am a new self at every moment, at every saying of 'I,' then why fix
myself in one named self—for every different self, if discreteness and
individuation is to be maintained, there must be a different name; and
more radically, why retain the notion of a self at all? Why not become so

fully liberated as to be able to assume whatever personality and name I wish at any moment; why not become a series of disconnected manifestations of different 'selves,' none of which need ever relate to themselves nor any previous manifestation of a self? . . . Another way of regarding this would be to say that the notion of the coherent and unified self has been replaced with that of the surface subjectivity: we have not a series of 'selves' as such but rather a series of instants of subjectivity, a series of instantiations of the 'I'.[1]

There are many inconsistencies in this passage which invalidate or detract from the viability of its schismatic assertions. In what authority, for example, does the compulsive 'must' in the first sentence originate? This unequivocal directive sits uncomfortably in an anti-authoritarian manifesto which challenges the power of totalizing command. More important, who is the 'I' evoked in the second sentence who is able to wishfully rename himself or herself 'at any moment', 'assum[ing]' those 'manifestations' of self it desires? This seems to imply an intentional (certainly wishful), presumably author-itative 'true' self behind the willed (re)presentations of selves it performs. Docherty argues that the traditional notion of character-ological continuity begins, in the fiction he analyses, to 'concede place to a continuity merely of surface style', which ostensibly achieves a condition of moral neutrality, a 'kind of irresponsibility and loss of self' (for both readers and characters) in the wake of characterological 'dehumanisation' (76). This accords dangerously with the assertions of Freddie Montgomery, protagonist in John Banville's *The Book of Evidence* (see previous chapter). Docherty's blithe advocacy of characterological and personal 'irresponsibility', 'dehumanization', and 'loss of self' and the abandonment of the constraints of communal rationality is no more than a posture of excommunication behind which he orchestrates and maintains a narrative of intentionality and totalizing desire. We must then ask, if the (human) textual subject is to be so fully liberated as to have no responsible or coherent conception of selfhood, for whom does this dehumanization and neutrality have value? For whom does Docherty's rebellious narrative have value? What is its worth if the liberated,

[1] Thomas Docherty, *Reading (Absent) Character: Towards a Theory of Charac-terization in Fiction* (Oxford: Clarendon Press, 1983), 75–6. Further references to this book will be cited parenthetically in the text. My dispute with Docherty should be conceived as a dispute with all those theorists who posit an impossible, ultimately undesirable poetics of textual fragmentation, a theoretical stance of which he is so clearly representative.

'neutral' individual has no sense of self, no voice with which to speak, because she has been 'released' from her bounds of recognizability and communicative rationality which give her, and her utterances, meaning? How viable is a poetics of textual and personal freedom in which, denied the stability afforded by a sense of moral or communal orientation, selves are deemed to enjoy neutral, positionless, amoral—but none the less meaningless and irrational—being? In short, we must ask what it would be like to be truly outside any community—silenced, without a voice or a discursive site from which to speak—rather than simply to pretend such debilitating exile.

The Assimilative Power of Reading

Docherty expresses the libertarian wish for 'fully liberated' selfhood, a desire which can only be achieved, he claims, in the loss of 'coherent and unified' selfhood, the fracturing and dispersal of a *readable* self into a 'series of instants of subjectivity' which *must* resist interpretation in order to remain free. But Docherty still wants the radically fragmented texts (and liberated subjects) he promotes to *mean*; that is, for their rebellion to have understood, and hence intersubjective, value. In order to resist dissipation into the utter meaninglessness of a series of moments or subject positions truly resistant to interpretation, Docherty maintains the presence of a self which resides behind these temporal manifestations of 'surface' subjectivity, a self whose individuality is secured in the activity of pretended dissolution, one which adopts the intentional posture of unintelligibility. My discussion in the previous chapter of John Banville's *The Book of Evidence* suggested the moral consequences which may result when an intending subject opts to exercise his will-to-power masked by the posture or pretence of excommunicative self-dissolution. The fragmented texts which Docherty valorizes resist true excommunication: that is, the wholesale abstention from (meaningful) signification. Although these fictions are shattered into a series of (written) subjective moments, they are still interpretable by readers —indeed, they must be if their radicalism is to be understood. They desire to exist as wholly autonomous, but withstand the meaninglessness of excommunication. They are rebellious within the bounds of communicative and communal convention, for only thus can they mean.

The limitations and fallibility of an emancipatory poetics such as that proposed by Docherty become very evident when we scrutinize his argument with regard to the process of characterological naming in literature. Docherty notes that one way in which an author maintains the illusion of control over her characters (and hence readers) in traditional fiction is by naming them. Following Derrida, he suggests that the act of naming is a fundamental political act of dominance.

To give a proper name to an object, especially, perhaps, to a fictional character, is to distinguish that character-object from the rest of its environment; moreover, it also distinguished the speaker from that object, making the speaker the subject of the act of nomination, and making the object, or character, occupy the position of subservient object, 'apprehended' by the naming subject. In phenomenological, if not political, terms the subject has primacy here, for the object's existence gains in status and distinction with the *separative act of comprehension* and nomination, and hence becomes dependent upon the subject performing the act. (43; my emphasis)

Docherty's fast rhetorical footwork obscures the deceptive drift of his argument. This deception lies less in what he says than in what he omits to say. Certainly, *all* 'separative act[s] of comprehension' (not simply the act of nomination) are essentially 'political' in so far as they involve subjective 'imposition' of meaning and the conceptual delimitation of the apprehended object-character into the recognizable lineaments of a perceived, distinctive, named form. What Docherty omits to mention, however, is the indisputable fact that 'separative' comprehension also secures for the character-object an identity—an *individual* identity, moreover—one which is known and has value *as* individual precisely because of its comprehended distinction from another. Docherty wants freedom, freedom as the faculty—or the right—of the individual to 'become so fully liberated as to be able to assume whatever personality and name [she] wish[es] at any moment'—in other words, to be as she chooses without the delimitation of possibility that results from characterological consistency, from named apprehension. But how can we talk of individual freedom if (the written and read fiction of) individuality is disallowed because comprehension of it curtails the possibility of that individual to be (an)other?

In mainstream realist fiction, argues Docherty, characterological identity is commonly established by the linking of a given name to a catalogue of reiterated descriptive qualities (distinguishing traits, physical features, and so on). Names thus function as fixed, recognizable signs which, on recurrence, refer the reader to unified, unchanging characters (except for predictable changes like ageing or maturation or ones which are otherwise causally justified) who are 'apprehended' as the sum of their described parts and histories. In other words, the site of nomination, as it occurs in the realist text, designates a space in which the reader is encouraged to recognize characterological continuity and depth—the presence of permanent selfhood. In this manner, it is argued, naming functions as a means of totalization and control of the named subject. Here is Leo Bersani:

> the names of people and places contain and promise fixed, coherent possibilities. To say a name is to totalize an existence. Even empty of content, the name confronts us with the prospect of a conceptual unity behind a world of bewilderingly fragmented phenomena.[2]

It is the mistaken appropriation of hyperbolic claims like this which provide, in part, the impetus behind Docherty's formulation of a contemporary poetics which rejects conventional naming and narrative strategies. Bersani's claim remains vague. With what would he oppose the nominal totalization he diagnoses? Namelessness? The abolition of language's referential function? Is he suggesting the desirability of the 'bewilderingly fragmented phenomena' of an uncomprehended, unnamed Reality over the deceptive fixity and order of a named (and thus comprehended) fiction of 'reality'?

This would seem to be what is implied by Docherty, who, with the ostensible endorsement of theorists like Derrida and Bersani, encourages a move away from consistent characterological representation towards a dislocative 'surface stylishness' of phenomenal fragmentation which denies both depth and continuity and which seeks to subvert the 'totalizing' project of 'fixing' character (and reader) in the enclosures of a consistent, named, locatable identity. He advocates the literary equivalent of existentialist freedom, where 'I am a new self at every moment, at every saying of "I" ', a polymorphous, chimerical being, 'a series of discontinuous manifestations of different selves' (75–6). Docherty goes further. It is not enough, he contends, to simply forgo the naming of characters in fiction, as Natalie Saurrate does in *Portrait d'un inconnu* (1947) or Beckett does

---

[2] Leo Bersani, *Balzac to Beckett: Center and Circumference in French Fiction* (New York: Oxford University Press, 1970), 3.

at the end of *The Unnamable* (1955). In these fictions the assumptions of referentiality and consistency which underlie the conventions of naming still operate. Readers are directed from a recognized sign or verbal constellation—be it a name, a pronoun, or the description of a familiar trait—to the illusory full presence of a character somehow imagined to be residing in, or given by, that sign. The illusion of characterological depth is as readily sustainable in the use of anonymous, but consistent, signification as it is in the use of proper names. It is equally evident in the fixation of pronominal referents or consistent behavioural descriptions in the text. According to Docherty's analysis, if contemporary fiction is to escape the tyrannous control of authorization and reader 'apprehension', it must shatter the assumption of coherence nurtured by logocentric notions of referentiality which read recognized textual configurations as the repositories of essential presences. Readers must never be allowed to 'apprehend' characters under a single, repeated sign or verbal constellation or a set of recognizable traits. The potential totalitarianism of the reading process must be thwarted by the wholesale abandonment of characterological consistency. If fiction is to be neutral and sustain its neutrality through the act of reading, it must present only a series of disparate surface subjectivities (which may or may not be named) which never cohere into consistent, readable personalities: characters must be 'dehumanized' (77).

For Docherty, the freedom of the reader of fiction is as much at stake in this debate as that of the fictional character. The dissolution of depthful character into the fragmented instantiations of surface stylishness 'implicates the reading ego in the dissolving process' (79), because the reader is unable to 'settle' into the fixed perspective of a consistent observing 'I'. The reader is forced to adopt a series of observational perspectives which are not reducible to the singular point of view of a dominant 'I' (eye). In discussing the bewildering use of proper names on Ronald Sukenick's novel *Out* (1970), Docherty writes:

Out must be assimilated in a discontinuous manner, and the reader's own response to a particular event or situation in the text is precluded in the manoeuvre of the narrative which moves the reading ego from one *locus* instantly to another; the *locus* in which the reader creatively reads at one point has nothing to do with the succeeding *loci* which are available and which should ostensibly contain the space for the reader's reaction to the previous event, located in the same name: the change of name thus has a serious effect on the involved reader. (79)

Stranded inside a text like *Out*, without the illusion of complicity with am omniscient or authoritative narrator to guide our way, confronted as we wander in the realm of the 'unmapped' text by an apparently random array of events and characters, how do we read? The same might be asked of any number of fragmented contemporary texts which work against the reduction to a singular reader (or authorial) perspective: the work of Donald Barthelme, Julio Cortázar, Angela Carter, Thomas Pynchon, or Salman Rushdie. Docherty asserts that such strategies of discontinuity effect a desirable 'shattering' of the reader, who is never able to stabilize into a secure identity; she is apparently lost in an unmapped textual wasteland which precludes a sense of location and forbids settlement. In making these claims, he is not alone. William Spanos, for example, like Docherty, approves of radical reader displacement in his analysis of some recent texts which function, he avers, to

perform a Heideggerian 'de-struction' of the traditional metaphysical frame of reference, that is to accomplish the phenomenal reduction of the spatial perspective by formal violence, thus, like Kierkegaard, leaving the reader *inter esse*—a naked and unaccommodated being-in-the-world, a dasein in the place of origins, where time is ontologically prior to being.[3]

All well and good—but to what end this 'phenomenal reduction'? Beyond vaguely intimating the virtue of the unpositioned, apolitical neutrality which presumably characterizes the unsettled and 'unaccommodated' reader of 'de-structed' texts, the viability of such displacement is nowhere established. Spanos, like so many contemporary theorists, is unwilling (or unable) to offer suggestions as to how the 'naked and unaccommodated' reader should (and frequently does) progress through the disorientating labyrinths of 'de-structed' texts. Moreover, Spanos's use of metaphor renders the desirability of this project of textual and reader fragmentation more than a little questionable: how desirable is the 'reduction' of identity by 'violence' or the 'stripping' and 'eviction' of the reader here implied?

I am only too willing to concede that the narrative ploys of a novel like *Out* encourage the reader to adopt a series of limited (because

---

[3] William Spanos, *Martin Heidegger and the Question of Literature: Towards a Postmodern Literary Hermeneutics* (Bloomington, Ind.: Indiana University Press, 1979), 121.

transient) perspectival positions which are not reducible to the 'totalizing' viewpoint of omniscience. But the conclusion that this has a 'serious [and, it is implied, destructive] effect' on the reading ego, as Docherty insists, does not follow from this premiss. By contrast, the strategic value of such tactical play is that it urges the reader to recognize and exercise her assimilative *power*, not her dissolute non-identity.[4] Confronted by the inconsistent and often confusingly polymorphic nature of the text, a reader reads a novel like *Out* by inventing connections between disparate textual elements and providing the connectives missing in the text.

'[W]hat we are faced with in the recent experimental novel', writes Docherty, 'is a more subversive activity of what we may call the "decentralization" of the self, not only of the characters in the fiction, but also by implication of the reader' (80). This does not appear to me to be the case at all. On the contrary, the identity of a reader of a text like *Out* is consolidated in the exercise of assimilative power which is the *reading* of that text: she gains status and identity as a co-creator, empowered with the faculty of partial meaning-determination. Such texts invite the reader to recognize the creative potential of her localized readings, not the alleged powerlessness of her 'decentred' identity. The difference between the reading of *Out* and that of a more traditional mimetic fiction is merely that in the former the reader is perhaps far more aware of her creative assimilative faculty than she would be when reading the latter (although of course it is in operation in both).

Characterological Writtenness

Docherty's analysis of authorial placement in fiction follows a similar pattern to his discussion of fictional characters. In much the same

---

[4] It is appropriate to talk of narrative 'strategy' and 'tactical ploys' when discussing novels such as *Out*, because these novels are deliberately conceived as acts of revolutionary rebellion which will *force* readers to adopt new roles and attitudes to their acts of reading. It is no small irony that this overtly *positioned* political stance and its revisionary aims are encouraged on a platform of alleged neutrality which advocates the desirability of unpositioned reading/being. The duplicitous nature of these claims to neutrality are very evident in the passage here cited, which marshals linguistic force to further its weighted, imperious claims. The passage abounds in coercive directives—insisting, e.g. that the reader 'must' assimilate *Out* in the manner it prescribes, a process which 'preclude[s]' the individualistic response which 'should' arise in conventional reading situations.

way as the suspension of naming in itself fails to subvert the referential assumptions which underlie conventional reading, he observes, the revolutionary desire to avoid authorial domination is not served by the apparent absence of the author from the text or a wishful, premature announcement of authorial 'death'. All too often, commonly in those modernist novels which aspire to 'impersonality', authorial absence amounts only to an act of ventriloquism: the author slips behind the mask of (one or more) seemingly impartial narrator(s). Thus hidden, the authoritative act of power is all the more insidious, for its seemingly absent originator appears to be innocuous, blameless, literally beyond our approach. One way in which contemporary experimental novels reveal this deceptive illusion of writerly deportation is in portraying and parodying the impossible fantasy of characterological independence: characters in this mode appear to enjoy an existence which is independent of their author-narrator's determination; they seem to be able to function with free-will in ways that ostensibly 'shock', 'deceive', or 'surprise' their creators. But readers are always reminded of the dependence of these fictional characters on the authors who write them and thus who determine their actions and existence. Frequently, the purpose of this metafictional strategy is interpreted as a challenge to readers to consider and revise illusory assumptions about their own autonomy, to recognize that they too may be the 'written' product of discursive operations. John Fowles, in *Mantissa* (1982), has pushed the metafictional strategy of characterological independence to its limit. The novel brilliantly exposes the paradoxical dream of unwritten writtenness, of fictional characters who claim independence from the fictions in which their meanings are constituted. Similar ploys are used by Sukenick in *Up* and Federman in *Double or Nothing*.

Three common-sense, but crucial, points are worth making with regard to the debate concerning the writtenness of fictional characters by their determining authors and their purported mirroring of the inauthentic 'textual' condition of human beings inscribed in social language. All concern the difference between human beings and fictional characters, a distinction which is often overlooked when metaphors of textuality are employed to scrutinize the human condition. The first is in relation to the impossibility of a fictional character's freedom from *authorial* prescription; the second concerns the impossibility of a fictional character's freedom from *readerly* assimilation or apprehension; the third recalls ideas discussed in previous chapters with regard to the capacity of human beings to be creative and productive within the bounds of the discursive systems in which they are constituted. First, a fictional character is, by definition, the imaginary product of authorial invention: she *is* written in ways that are fundamentally different from the 'writtenness' of social subjects constituted in discursive process. To talk about the possibility of a fictional character existing independently of the author's act of inscription or the reader's act of interpretation is, in a fundamental sense, nonsensical. Of course, a character may 'live on' on the page long after the author has relinquished responsibility for, or consciousness of, that character. How that character is interpreted by a (later) reader may certainly be very different from the way the author intended. She may appear to possess qualities and attributes other than those intentionally scripted by the author—which is to say that an alert reader may perceive sub-textual traits, motivations, or beliefs within a character which are other than, or even contrary to, those overtly given or intended by the author at the time of inscription; or a reader can impose her personal values and desires on the textual characters and events she interprets. Recognizing this amounts to no more (and no less) than acknowledging that the possibility for alternative interpretation is always written into any given text. In the terms of psychoanalysis, this is a recognition that a fictional character may embody or represent an author's (or reader's) unconscious desires or needs. This is not to say that characters can ever wilfully choose to usurp or reject their written constitution, for their existence depends on a writer or reader's conception of them. Human beings are composed of blood and bone, textual characters of ink and paper—a fact which is brought home to the eponymous character in Alasdair Gray's *Lanark* (1981):

'Everything you have experienced and are experiencing . . . is made of one thing'
'Atoms,' said Lanark.
'No. Print. Some worlds are made of atoms but yours is made of tiny marks marching in neat lines, like armies of insects, across pages and pages and pages of white paper.'[5]

This brings me to my second point. Quite simply, a *read* character can never be wholly free in the sense that Docherty demands. It can

[5] Cited in Brian McHale, *Postmodernist Fiction* (London and New York: Routledge, 1987), 179.

never resist interpretation. If discontinuity is so radical as to render the project of interpretative reading impossible, so that a text is not identifiable as a conglomerate of meaningful 'marks' on paper which are intended to be deciphered, but remains unread as inky scribbles, a fictional character would have no meaning as a character whatsoever. She would remain an unassimilable, unassimilated collection of disparate, unread textual elements. Her 'freedom' is utterly worthless unless she is interpreted by a reader. A fictional character only means if read, if imaginatively conceived, and for this reason will always be the ontologically inferior 'subject' of readerly empowerment. The crucial difference between human beings and fictional characters is this: human beings are certainly 'read' by others (and themselves), but they occupy the *same* ontological level as their human interpreters, and thus possess a dialogic capacity to controvert or challenge the interpretations of those who read them.This is certainly not the case with fictional characters, who exist inan inferior ontological realm, a world of 'print' in Gray's words, without the capacity to actively influence the readings of their interpreters. In Chapter 4 I discussed Bakhtin's theory of dialogic meaning-production in the social arena, stressing the idea that meaning is the interactive product of social subjects. There is no such dialogic interplay between fictional characters and their readers: fictional characters are the mute constructs of a one-way process of reader interpretation.

A third difference between 'subjected' fictional characters and human beings lies in the ability of the latter, through transgressive play or reflexive monitoring, to actively change the rules of the discursive systems within which they are determined, and in doing so, alter the way in which they are read by others and themselves. This claim finds support in the work of writers like Alasdair MacIntyre, Anthony Giddens, and Charles Taylor, who utilize metaphors of narration to suggest *not* that human beings are wholly determined fictions or fictional characters, but rather that they posses a degree of freedom in their capacity for self-reflexive, interactive narration. Moreover, I have argued, with recourse to theorists like Robert Scholes, Marilyn Friedman, Edward Soja, and Barbara Hooper, that human beings are the inhabitants of multiple determining interpretative communities of discourse, between which they have the capacity to move with a certain amount of freedom. Fictional characters do not possess the freedom or ability for self-reflexive, chosen movement between the determining interpretative communities they inhabit (except at the ontologically inferior level of the fictional realm). It is a gross error to seek to understand our human constitution by reducing it, by metaphorical comparison, to the prescripted nature of a novelistic character. We are *not* like fictional characters in this very basic sense: human beings may indeed be 'written' by language, but they also possess the ability to read, interpret, and change their communities in language, and to influence and change other readers and interpreters in their communicative interactions. The character in a novel, by contrast, has no such creative (and potentially revisionary) power, existing *only* as a written and read entity.

Muriel Spark's novella *The Driver's Seat* (1970) brilliantly refutes the possibility of wholly autonomous characterological freedom. In the novella, the protagonist, Lise, sets out on a quest to find a man who will kill her, with the proviso that the killing must take place in the manner she decrees (this desire to orchestrate her own death is, like any suicidal impulse, the most bitterly ironic expression of existential freedom). She chooses Richard, a rehabilitated sex offender, to perform the deed, believing that she can harness the 'drive' of his repressed desire to reach the destination of her carefully scripted death. All proceeds according to Lise's plan until, in the final paragraphs of the novella, Spark, apparently absent until this moment from her heroine's self-written text, steps in to assert the authorial determining power which Lise had mistakenly imagined to be her own. Lise's emancipatory script is over-written (over-ridden?) as her murder takes place in terms wholly other than those she had chosen. Against her demands, Richard ignores her insistence that he bind her ankles, and rapes her before plunging in the knife that will end her life. In the portrayal of this most fundamental violation of her character's selfhood, Spark cruelly ridicules any claims to characterological self-authorization. Lise, at the novella's end, is entirely bound within the constraints of Spark's bleak vision; she is firmly located as the deluded victim of both sexual and authorial violence.

Reader Authority

For Docherty, it is not enough, to simply pretend to remove the author from the text while maintaining the author's power to over-write meaning and control narrative progression. Such apparently self-abnegating authorial impersonalization is understood as a devious ploy to retain manipulative control behind a façade of authorial absence. Instead, suggests Docherty, just as the conventional illusion of characterological unity must be shattered into a series of 'surface subjectivities', so too must an equivalent 'decentralization' of the authorial self take place if we are to escape writerly domination. The author must not be allowed to rest in the stable identity secured for her by a consistent narrational voice or voices; she must be dissolved into fragmentary 'stylishness', into the dissolute bliss of vocal irresolution in a plethora of unassailable narrative 'subjectivities':

the removal of one coherent narrator (either the narrator's total removal as a character or the fragmentation of the narrational function into a number of contradictory and therefore discontinuous and incoherent voices), result[s] in an in-forming of the reader with the voices (or words) of a number of characters, and it is the reader who is left to impersonate, to lend a voice to the characters. Thus *the reader gains authority over the creation of a world.* . . . The way to the *authoritative self* seems to be in the indirect mode of impersonation of other voices. (66; my emphasis)

There seems to me to be a basic inconsistency in the argument for textual liberation put forward by Docherty, which is manifest in the above passage. On the one hand, he suggests that the subversive tactics of 'dehumanizing' fragmentation in experimental contemporary fiction results in 'what we may call the "decentralization" of the self, not only of the characters in the fiction, but by implication of the reader [and, as suggested above, of the author]' (80). Moreover, he would have it that this disorientating 'loss of self' results in texts which are 'morally neutral' and readers who are free to enjoy a kind of 'irresponsibility' (76). In such fiction, he claims, the reader is set free to drift without anchorage; there are no frameworks or orientating maps by which to place the reading ego, the author, or the characters. On the other hand, Docherty maintains precisely the opposite stance: the fragmentary stylishness of experimental fiction enables the reader to fix for herself a very precise, central location and role, that of the 'authoritative self'. Appropriating the space emptied by the exile of the tyrannical author of conventional fiction, 'the reader gains authority over the creation of a world'. The textual and characterological 'liberation' which Docherty announces seems to me to be no more than a statement about the transferral, not eradication, of authoritative power. Under this new constitution, the reader is now given licence to perform the appropriation of characterological and authorial voice, to 'impersonate' both, and to write (some) meaning for character and author in the act of her subjective interpretation. Far from readerly 'irresponsibility', what is here announced is the reader's considerable responsibility for the creation of meaning.

Docherty attempts to evade the implications of this implicitly *self*ish assertion of reader control by suggesting that traditional, positioned reading now becomes chimerical ecstasy (or in his term, 'ex-stasis'), an empathetic impersonation of multiple, contradictory textual positions, a conceptual occupation of diverse, irreconcilable selves which never stabilize or cohere: 'one is never an isolated self "here," for the self is always located not in this present hermetic situation, but in another manifestation of itself, another person' (82). Further, 'the reader impersonates many positions, and in-forms his or her subjectivity by losing identity as a nameable self, and becoming a series of discrete eyes and "I"s' (86). Under closer scrutiny, this is insupportable. The claim of the loss of nameable selfhood for a reader sounds suspiciously like the manipulative 'anonymity' of apparent authorial impersonalization which Docherty himself criticizes as no more than the insidious ventriloquial occupation of narrator/characters by an author only pretending to be absent from the fiction she writes. Just as a controlling authorial presence persists behind the anonymous (but consistent and referential) descriptions and pronominal designations to be found in those fictions which forgo naming *per se*, so too does the controlling, comprehending reader persist behind the 'multiple selves' which she 'in-forms' in the process of reading. The reader does not 'becom[e] a series of discrete "I"', but *performs* them; she enacts a series of (perhaps unnamed) impersonations behind which she, as actor, persists—the empowered reader whose presence is confirmed and consolidated, not lost, in the in-formative act of reading.

Declining to name a reader is not identical with denying her a coherent (narrative of) personal identity. The reader of experimental fiction may indeed be 'unnamed', perhaps even 'unnameable', but her presence persists behind the façade of anonymity and the personae she performs and in-forms in the act of interpretation. She is situated in the (authoritative) role of textual apprehender; her identity is constituted in the connective conceptual process which *is* reading. Reading is never instantaneous, but a process of assimilation that (necessarily) takes place through time. The reading of a text involves retrospection, expectation, and the creative *narrative* assimilation of past and future textual elements: the apprehension or imposition of a plot. This narrative activity is precisely that involved in our apprehension of a (more or less) coherent narrative of personal identity. Existing in time, we are always elsewhere and other than the imaginary self we perceive, and continuously invent a story of growth and development (a narrative of personal identity) that links the legion of sometimes contradictory 'I's or subject positions we remember and anticipate. To recall a comment by Charles Taylor cited earlier, 'My sense of myself is of a being who is growing and becoming. In the very nature of things this cannot be instantaneous. . . . My self understanding necessarily has temporal depth and incorporates narrative.'⁶ This is precisely the case in our interpretation (reading) of fictional texts. Regardless of how fragmented, bewildering, and disorientating a fiction appears to be, our reading of it always involves the assimilation of its disparate parts into some form of subjective meaning: we fill in gaps, make connections, imagine or invent omitted detail. Otherwise put, we read it *as narrative*. We impose a beginning, and project an ending. We recognize textual signs, and attribute meaning to them. Failure to do so means that the text is not read, but rejected as meaningless or as something other than fiction. Narratives remain singularly resistant to wholesale fragmentation into the non-sense of unintelligible babble.

If, as Docherty contends, the reader of experimental fiction experiences an unsettling personal and perspectival fragmentation into a multiplicity of subjective 'I's and eyes, then we cannot help, in the very act of reading, but re-member these disparate manifestations of self, just as we gather together fragmented linguistic and typographic elements in the comprehensive, 'apprehensive' act of narrative reading. We impose meaning and invent continuity where we find it to be lost or absent—this *is* the narrative nature of interpretation. Moreover, in this process of narrative invention, we gain a voice: the voice of inventor, of meaning-maker, a voice of

---

⁶ Charles Taylor, *Sources of the Self: The Making of the Modern Identity* (Cambridge: Cambridge University Press, 1989), 50.

authority and control. As long as we continue to speak of fiction in terms of reading and interpretation (and how else can we speak of it?), we must forgo the impossible textual (personal, authorial, characterological) 'freedom' offered by Docherty. His claims for liberation from the constraints of identity in experimental fiction are ultimately untenable. If texts are to be truly liberated, Docherty's thesis amounts to no more than a self-destructive injunction for texts (and self as text) to remain unintelligible, beyond the 'separative acts' of comprehension.

Quite simply, reading is never apolitical or 'irresponsible'; it is always a narrative activity of appropriation and control licensed under the auspices of our subjective creativity.[7] As long as we continue to perform the interpretative acts which constitute all conceptual activity, we will continue to make the objects/characters/texts we apprehend into the 'subjects' of our interpretative narratives, dependent on our reading for their comprehended identity. In reading, we gain power to speak for, and through, the selves and characters for whom we invent narratives of personal continuity, fictions of presence. To recognize this is to acknowledge a formulation of textual freedom such as Docherty's for what it is: a supremely egotistical manifesto of readerly propriety. Paradoxically, despite its claims to the contrary, it expresses a fundamentally Romantic desire for wholly independent, creative selfhood, a desire for the reader to wrest authority from the once dominant author or narrator of mainstream realist and modernist fiction. (I have suggested, in Chapter 5, that this Romantic impulse is paradoxically inherent in the poststructuralist call for textual dissemination.) This is an expression of readerly will-to-power which is all the more insidious for its pretence of neutrality or absence. Docherty's claims make evident the thoroughly *selfish* nature of so many contemporary theoretical treatises, in which the 'death of the author' announces the coronation of a new authorizing centre, not its abolition: control is appropriated by the reader behind a self-serving mask of lost selfhood or impersonality.

---

[7] See Geoffrey Galt Harpham, 'Getting It Right: The Story of Creation' in *Getting It Right: Literature, Language, and Ethics* (Chicago and London: University of Chicago Press, 1992), 157–219, for a comprehensive discussion of the competing claims of contemporary theorists and writers with regard to the (a)political status of narratives.

Interpretative Will-to-power

J. M. Coetzee's novel *Foe* seems to me to offer valuable insight into the issues I have raised so far in my discussion: the utopian impossibility of ever achieving neutral, free being for any (textual) identity *comprehended* within the communicative frameworks of narrative and language; the crucial need for dialogic interaction on the part of situated social subjects if they are to prevent the totalizing colonization of their plural spaces or voices; the wholly unsatisfactory (because suicidal or pathological) condition of silence or self-mutilating denial of voice which would be necessary to escape the interlocutory narrative construction of (textual) identity; and, finally, the inherently political nature of the positioning that occurs in the readerly occupation of characterological and authorial voice.[8] *Foe* is a typical contemporary novel in so far as in it Coetzee appears to willingly abdicate his role as sole authority for meaning and identity construction, issuing an open invitation to his readers to enter into and co-write the somewhat opaque, fragmented text. The novel is a masterly portrayal of tactical authorial withdrawal, a four-stage manœuvre in which the controlling figure of the writer and his authorizing voice become increasingly difficult to locate. As the novel progresses, empty textual spaces and characterological silences proliferate, and the reader is called upon to occupy and fill these in order to comprehend the novel's meaning. Meaning finally rests in the occupation of the narratorial voice by an involved reader of the text, a voice with which, to use Docherty's terminology, she 'impersonates' or 'subjects' characters and action, 'in-forming' them with readable presence. The political ramifications of vocal appropriation are not only formally foregrounded, but are explored on the diegetic level of the text.

Foe is a rewriting of Defoe's *Robinson Crusoe*. Of the numerous differences between Defoe's work and Coetzee's subsequent revision, one significant deviation concerns Coetzee's explicit description of Friday's blackness. While Defoe's Friday is tawny in colour and has a small nose, 'not flat like the Negroes', Coetzee's Friday is 'black: a Negro with a heady of fuzzy wool'. This variation encourages us, as numerous critics have noted, to read *Foe* as an 'allegory of

[8] J. M. Coetzee, *Foe* (1986; Harmondsworth: Penguin, 1988). Further references to this book will be cited parenthetically in the text.

contemporary South Africa', despite its eighteenth-century setting.[9] Coetzee's frequent structuring of his novels around relationships of power and powerlessness (in *Foe* between man and woman, master/mistress and slave) has been read as an allegorical means of exploring and criticizing the injustices of colonial exploitation and subjugation of the indigine, a process in which white South Africa (until recently) was so complicit.[10] The silence of Coetzee's Friday, ostensibly due to the amputation of his tongue either by slave-traders or Cruso [sic], is typically read as symbolic of the denial of (political) voice to black South Africans by white colonists.

Another of Coetzee's striking revisions in *Foe* is the addition of a female castaway as one of the inhabitants of Cruso's island: Susan Barton. Cruso and Susan are finally rescued from the island by a passing ship, and although Friday runs away when he sees the ship's crew, he is tracked down and forcibly 'rescued' too. Cruso dies before the trio reach their destination, England. Here Susan settles into temporary lodgings with Friday, in the home of Daniel Defoe ('Foe'), the famous writer, who at that time is hiding from his creditors. For much of the narrative present, Susan attempts to write the retrospective story of their time as castaways, but she is hampered in this endeavour by the partiality of her memory and knowledge and her recognition that if the truth is told, life on the island was mundane, rather than exciting—hardly the material for a riveting castaway tale. She enters into an imaginary correspondence with the absent Foe, in which she ponders the problems of writing 'truthful' fiction. Later in the novel, Foe actually appears on the scene, having apparently cleared his debts, and attempts to wrest control of the island narrative from Susan. He seeks not only to pen the tale, but to elaborate and 'fictionalize' events and circumstances to bolster the rather boring nature of the 'real' story. The struggle between Foe and Susan for control of the historical narrative invites allegorical reading

---

[9] Robert M. Post, 'The Noise of Freedom: J. M. Coetzee's *Foe*', *Critique*, 30/3 (Spring 1989), 145. For a discussion of the relationship between Coetzee's novel and the work of Defoe, see Gayatri Chakravorty Spivak, 'Theory in the Margin: Coetzee's *Foe* Reading Defoe's *Crusoe/Roxana*', *English in Africa*, 172 (1990), 1–23.

[10] See Stephen Watson, 'Colonialism and the Novels of J. M. Coetzee', *Research in African Literatures*, 17 (Fall 1986), 370–92; and Derek Attridge, 'The Silence of the Canon: J. M. Coetzee's *Foe*, Cultural Narrative, and Political Oppression', in Karen Lawrence (ed.), *Decolonizing Tradition: New Views of Twentieth Century 'British' Literary Canon* (Urbana, Ill.: University of Illinois Press, 1992), 212–38.

within the terms of another oppressed/oppressor polarity: Susan (woman) struggles with Foe's (men's) attempt to appropriate her story, to subordinate it to the canonical contours of his(s)tory. Having escaped the (patriarchal) realm of Cruso's island, Susan has usurped the narrative authority accorded by Defoe to his male protagonist, and ostensibly controls the narrative for much of Coetzee's book. This aspect of the novel, read as an allegory of female appropriation of the (phallic) pen of masculine writing, has received much critical attention.[11]

It is ironic, but perhaps not surprising, that Susan, herself a victim of Cruso's misogyny and Foe's desirous (patriarchal) plotting, is also guilty of victimization perpetrated on her subordinate other, Friday, the silenced black slave. Susan vehemently resists Foe's attempts to 'father' her tale, while at the same time she seeks to impose her language (and customs) on the silent Friday: she wishes to make him speak *her* language. History confirms the accuracy of Coetzee's observation: too often the oppressed (seek to) become the oppressor. Frequently the means of oppression lies in the imposition of the language of the colonizer, and the cultural values it encodes, on those she would subdue (the now infamous 1976 uprisings in Soweto originated in the desire by schoolchildren to be taught in their own tongue, not the language of their white, Afrikaans 'masters'). Towards the end of the novel, Susan and Foe become lovers, a gesture which signifies, perhaps, the prospective mutual 'parenting' of the island story, the fruitful union of antagonistic genders. Disturbingly, however, at this junction in the novel they acknowledge complicity in the mutual domination of (the still silent and uncommunicative) Friday, confirming their desire to 'descend into [Friday's] mouth' and 'to make Friday's silence speak': 'tomorrow . . . [to] teach him *a*' (152). They seek to appropriate his silence, to speak for him. (In this reading I am less optimistic than some critics, who interpret Susan and Foe's pledge to teach Friday their language as a pledge on their part to empower him.[12]) So ends the third section of the novel, ambiguously balanced between putative sexual parity and what is

[11] See Peter E. Morgan, '*Foe's* Defoe and *La Jeune Née*: Establishing a Metaphorical Referent for the Elided Female Voice', *Critique*, 35/2 (Winter 1994), 81–96; and Brian Macaskill and Jeanne Colleran, 'Reading History, Writing Heresy: The Resistance of Representation and the Representation of Resistance in J. M. Coetzee's *Foe*', *Contemporary Literature*, 33/3 (Fall 1992), 432–57.

[12] Macaskill and Colleran, in 'Reading History, Writing Heresy', write: '[Friday] can trust that they will continue to give him words' (450).

perhaps an indictment, but also a reinscription, of racial oppression and colonial appropriative lust.

But the novel does not end here. The third section is followed by a concluding short, surreal five-page section. In this, Susan, who has dominated the telling of the tale so far, no longer speaks, but is spoken by a new, anonymous narrator. This unnamed narrational 'I' has variously been seen as 'Coetzee himself',[13] the 'voice of poetic imagination'[14] or as the irrational voice of a dreaming, or now insane, Susan.[15] I will suggest otherwise in my reading of *Foe*, claiming that the unnamed narratorial 'I' offers an overt invitation for the reader to enter the undefended territory of the 'vacant' pronominal space and, in doing so, to enact the appropriation of characterological voice in an act of readerly colonization. The narratorial 'I' (readerly eye/'I') enters into the room which contains the lifeless bodies of Foe and Susan, and finds a sheaf of pages from Susan's island adventure manuscript. Reading these, the 'I'/eye slips into the manuscript at the same point at which the reader entered the novel, with Susan's introductory words '[w]ith a sigh, with barely a splash' (155). The 'I' then dives into the (narrative) wreck and swims amongst the flotsam she discovers, eventually finding the still living body of Friday, whose clenched teeth she attempts to open. What issues from the mouth of Friday is a stream of bubbles, a soundless scream. To the end, Friday remains voiceless, the subject of interpretative will-to-power.

In this final section the reader is asked to recognize the political stance that is involved in any act of reading, the subjective imposition of a readerly voice on the undefended (because without the right of reply) sites inhabited by characters and narrators in any work of fiction. Crucially, the reader is thus impelled to recognize that, unlike fictional characters, human beings are more than the mute victims of interpretation. The possibility of subjective freedom inheres in the possession of a speaking voice and the exercising of a capacity for dialogic interaction with one's (potentially oppressive) interpreters. *Contra* those theorists who posit freedom in communal escape and tactics of silence, Coetzee seems to urge the indispensable necessity of situated speech: *to be free we must speak.*

---

[13] Jane Gardam, 'The Only Story', *The* [London] *Sunday Times*, 7 Sept. 1986, p. 49.

[14] Denis Donoghue, 'Her Man Friday', *New York Times Book Review*, 22 Feb. 1987, p. 27.

[15] Post, 'Noise of Freedom', 152.

Throughout the novel we are asked to recognize the way in which dominant power systems seek to subdue and control their subjects (and servants) by speaking (for) them. The novel focuses on the attempts by Susan to comprehend the silent Friday and to subject him to her language. Susan's (unsuccessful) attempts to comprehend Friday, to render him readable, and thereby subject him to the authority of her (and her society's) language and values amount to an attempt to domesticate and control him; throughout the novel she attempts to coerce him into performing acts of communication with the aim of circumscribing and delimiting his personal autonomy. Susan's efforts are analogous to those performed by the reader: we, like Susan, who tries to imagine the 'true' story of Friday's life, perform the inventive apprehending activity of characterological interpretation. Susan's frustrated question is ours too: 'How will we ever know the truth?' (23). Perplexed by Friday's impenetrability (and ultimately that of other characters), we too attempt to authorize his being, to write his life and imagine his identity, in our reading of him. This is made very evident in the final section of the novel, in which the reader is literally invited to enter into the mouth of Friday and speak for him.

The first section of the novel is spoken by Susan. It takes the form of a first-person monologue, an autobiographical fragment, in which she purports to tell the 'true' story of her year as a castaway on some unlocatable island which is inhabited only by the mysterious Cruso and his silent servant Friday. The overt intertextual appropriation by Coetzee of Defoe's *Robinson Crusoe* results in significant ironic resonance, underscoring the politics of appropriative textual 'apprehension' which is a dominant thematic concern in *Foe*. Moreover, the avowal of (subjective) truth from the mouth of a female witness suggests the possibility of alternative interpretations of events on the island to that of the famously solipsistic, masculine perspective provided by Defoe's hero. Susan's tale, told after her rescue from the island and return to England, is addressed to Foe, a novelist who enjoys repute for his skilful ability to convert real-life 'confessions' into saleable fictional commodities (48). The format of the first section, then, is a familiar one—a conventional 'traveller's tale' (7)— which affords a recognizable framework for the orientation of writer, reader, and characters. Susan is firmly positioned in the fiction in the role of (first-person) narrator; her credentials and credibility are established in the traditional manner, by assigning her a name and placing her within the terms of historical heritage and patriarchal lineage (10). The author, Coetzee, although not overtly present in the text, is none the less unproblematically implicated as the ventriloquial director who speaks through the narrator, Susan (who in turn speaks through, and for, the characters in her tale). Readers also enjoy secure placement in this section, situated as the auditory subjects of the narrational address, a space shared with Foe, to whom the narration is ostensibly directed. We take our place as dutiful listeners to a traveller's tale, and, in concurrence with the conventions which govern this traditional form of fiction, we willingly suspend our disbelief, prepared to accept the veracity of our teller's tale (and her 'reality' within this ontological realm) for the duration of the narrative.

Perhaps the most disturbing aspect of island life which Susan recounts was the silence of its human inhabitants. This was 'an island where no one spoke' (35), a realm devoid of all but the most minimal communication. Although both her fellow castaways, Cruso and Friday, are silent, their silences are entirely different: whereas Cruso's is selective and partial, Friday's has been inflicted on him and appears complete. Cruso chooses silence, and wields it with a master's power. He uses his selective silence to withhold information, as a means of maintaining privacy and even of attaining a certain kind of self-creation. Without recourse to the 'full story' of Cruso's life, Susan is compelled to imagine a history and an identity for him on the basis of the fragmented pieces of the past that he elects to tell. Confounded by the multiplicity of Cruso's devious narrations and the gaps and silences of his omissions, Susan is unable to confidently place or 'totalize' his identity under the sign of his name. He is still credited with a stable identity, however; in her words, he is still 'this singular Cruso'—it is just that, through choice, wilful evasion, or forgetfulness, the exact contours of his self remain indistinct, despite Susan's (and our) intrusive probings. Susan's comprehension of Cruso is simply a matter of subjectively filling in the gaps of his partial narrative: Susan *co*-writes Cruso's identity with guidance and material provided by Cruso himself, but she never wholly authorizes him while he is alive. Following Cruso's death, which ensures that he no longer has a dialogic right to reply to her assumptive interpretations, she gains full power to write him as she desires. He no longer occupies the same ontological realm as Susan (that of lived human life), and hence is unable to influence her writing of him; he now becomes a scripted character in the story she writes. Her will-to-power, to control and manipulate the characters she represents through narrative, is made explicit in the final paragraph of the novel's first section. Here, with the accent of propriety, Susan tells the captain of the ship which rescues them from the island, 'it is I who have disposal of all that Cruso leaves behind, which is the story of his island' (45).

The absolute speechlessness of Friday, who has 'no understanding of words or power of speech' (39), gives rise to a wholly different situation. He appears to remain free from interpretative apprehension in the libertarian sense that Docherty urges, because his exile from discursive community renders him unintelligible. He presents no 'coherent and unified self', but only a series of 'surface subjectives' which invite interpretation. He exists, to utilize the spatial metaphors developed earlier, in an unmapped wilderness outside the bounds of moral and communicative convention. Friday remains meaningless *unless* Susan appropriates the space of his silence and imaginatively speaks for him. This she does. In the absence of any understood, intentional signification on the part of Friday, Susan invents for him a narrative of meaningful personal identity, a fiction of unified, coherent selfhood. In this activity there is no dialogic, mutual co-authoring of identity, as there is in the case of her 'reading' of (the living) Cruso, but total writerly empowerment on the part of Susan. In effect, Susan authors and authorizes Friday in her appropriation of his voice.

Ontological Hierarchies

The format of the second section of *Foe*, although different from that of the first, is none the less equally familiar in the subservient placement it allocates to the reader. It is structured as a series of letters written by Susan, now resident in temporary lodgings in London, to the absent writer Foe. We move from our position in the first section as ostensibly passive readers of a monologic chronicle, the traveller's tale, to a seemingly equally passive role as readers of a series of first-person, present-tense letters reporting on the day-to-day life of Susan and Friday. In this familiar narrative format, writer, characters, and reader all occupy conventionally recognizable, stable locations in the text. That is, we still perceive an organized series of frameworks, an ordered textual ontological hierarchy: of a writer who frames the narrator, who, in turn, frames the characters of the fiction.

In this second section Susan again enjoys dominance as the controlling narrator of the story we read; for, although we may recognize her 'written' identity as a character in Coetzee's fiction, we suspend this awareness, and, in accordance with fictional convention, confer on her the authority which is conventionally granted to the figure of story-teller. As is the case in the first section, the reader is not invited to move into the narrational space as active co-creator of narrative meaning. The space of perspectival authority, the 'I' (eye), is apparently fully occupied by the letter-writing Susan. Instead, the reader is relegated, with Foe, to the space of mute addressee, the position of a silently reading (listening) 'you'. The reader is thus written into the text as the silent eavesdropper or interceptor of Susan's letters, unable to enter into creative dialogic exchange with the writer. The reader is, it seems, without a voice. Significantly, Susan's 'communication' by letter is entirely one-way: the absent Foe does not (cannot) reply. His presence appears to be purely nominal, simply a name that functions to justify Susan's scribblings. Susan continues to write, however, no longer even pretending that her 'letters' are addressed to him: 'To whom am I writing? I blot the pages and toss them out the window. Let who will read them' (64). The unnamed 'who' that will read (or rather that Susan would will to read), is the reader of Foe, now placed in the empty space of listening 'you' which has been vacated by the apparently dispensable Foe.

In both the first and second sections, Susan pointedly stresses the subordinate role she would assign to the silent Friday, who is without voice to challenge her authority. In writing of island life, she describes him as Cruso's servant—he was 'obedient to his master' (22); his deference was 'like that of a dog who heeds but one master' (21).[16] Following the death of Cruso and Susan's return to England, she appropriates his vassal: 'His master is dead, now he has a mistress,' she proclaims. Friday is hers: 'mine to set free' (99). Susan

[16] For other descriptions by Susan of Friday's servile role see pp. 23, 24, 26, and 37. For examples of her use of animal imagery to suggest the mute, irrational, inhuman status of Friday, see p. 98 (he is like a gelded stallion); p. 70 (he is 'like an animal wrapt entirely in itself'); p. 77 (she finds herself speaking to him 'as an old woman talks to cats'); pp. 41–2 (she treats him 'as we treat a frightened horse'); p. 80 (he is likened to a dog); p. 59 (he is like a spider 'sitting . . . alone at the heart of his web, which to him is the entire world').

believes that the removal of Friday's tongue was an act of domination performed in order to enforce his 'eternal obedience' (98) and 'to prevent him from ever telling his story' (23). But Friday's tongue is symbolic of a far more radical mutilation; he does not merely lack the capacity for speech—his exclusion from signifying community is total. He cannot (or will not) communicate in any way; it is clear that he performs no alternative activity of signification. Friday's tongue-lessness is thus the physical manifestation of his excommunication, his utter solipsistic isolation. If in this radical silence there is a certain libertarian power and freedom, that of absolute independence, it is a freedom purchased at a self-defeating, self-destructive cost. Although free from communicative rationality and its determinations, such a radical incapacity to signify precludes the possibility of any meaningful or comprehended selfhood. Friday remains unbound by the language (and hence the prescriptions) of others. He is free, yes, but the price of this freedom is that he remains wholly outside the dialogic community which Susan describes as 'the world of words in which you, Mr Foe, and I, and other people live' (60).

Her inability to penetrate Friday's silence terrifies Susan. Through-out the novel she will try to initiate him into a community of signification and intersubjective value within whose terms she (and we) can comprehend—and subdue—him. This interpretative will-to-power, to authorize, is the impetus behind Susan's attempts to 'civilize' and 'educate' Friday, and thereby to eliminate, by assimila-tion into her own cultural and linguistic framework, his otherness. In a parody of the colonial zeal with which Western civilization tried to subject black Africa, Susan wishes to '[bring] home to him [Friday] some of the blessings of civilisation and make him a better man' (22). In a telling moment of uncharacteristic openness, Susan admits to her knowing abuse of language and education as a means of empower-ment: 'I tell myself I talk to Friday to educate him out of darkness and silence. But is that the truth? There are times when benevolence deserts me and I use words only as the shortest way to subject him to my will' (60).

Alone in Foe's house, with only Friday for company, Susan becomes increasingly desperate to shatter the blank wall of his unresponsive silence and teach him the communicative skills which will help to alleviate the monotony of her isolated existence. But Susan fails in her attempts to teach Friday to 'understand meanings' (56). She is unable to make him understand the representational function of words, and he remains utterly aloof from any common referential framework which would make the transfer of meaning possible. This is superbly exemplified in the episode in which Susan tries to elicit the 'truth' from Friday by using a range of alternative means of signification, all of which fail: drawings, gestures, facial expressions. Susan ponders this:

after years of speechlessness the very notion of speech may be lost to him. When I take the spoon from his hand (but is it truly a spoon to him, or a mere thing—I do not know), and say *Spoon*, how can I be sure he does not think I am chattering to myself as a magpie or an ape does, for the pleasure of hearing the noise I make, and feeling the play of my tongue, as he himself used to find pleasure in playing his flute? (57)

Upon hearing Friday play an endlessly repetitive six-note 'tune' on his flute, Susan resolves to communicate with him through music: 'it occurred to me that if there were any language accessible to Friday, it would be the language of music' (96). She learns the tune, and whenever he plays it, she 'answers' by mimicking him, for a while believing that their monotonous duet is a form of 'conversation' (97). It is not long, however, before she is disillusioned, realizing that the simple mimicry of sounds is meaningless, mere parroting, without a shared referential context within which those sounds function as recognized and recognizable signs: 'But alas, just as we cannot exchange forever the same utterances—"Good day, sir"—"Good day"—and believe we are conversing, or perform the same motion and call it love-making, so it is with music: we cannot play the same tune and be content' (97). Friday remains insensible and unresponsive to Susan's music. She is bitterly disappointed upon realizing that this attempt to induce him into her community has also failed. Her frustration is described in a passage which makes very clear her will to force Friday's subservience: 'I had to hold back an urge to strike him . . . and thus rudely teach him he was not alone on this earth (98).

As the section progresses, Susan's desire to possess and control is increasingly manifest. Her appropriative lust finds expression on both a material and a textual level. She describes her occupation of Foe's house in terms which make explicit her desire to sequestrate all that belongs to Foe, including his authoritative status as a writer. She writes to him: 'I have your table to sit at, your window to gaze through. I write with your pen on your paper, and when [the letters] are completed they go into your chest. So your life continues to be lived, though you are gone' (65). Susan's occupational avidity is not limited to a desire to colonize Foe's house or penetrate the realm of Friday's silent self-possession through tactics of domestication. It manifests itself most strikingly in her aspiration to usurp Foe's position as writer and authorize her own story: 'I sat at your bureau this morning', she writes to him, 'and took out a clean sheet of paper and dipped pen in ink—your pen, your ink, I know, but somehow the pen becomes mine when I write with it, as though growing out of my hand' (66–7). Is this a parody, or perhaps an endorsement, of feminist aspirations to appropriate the masculine pen?

Through the medium of Susan's deliberations as she tries to write her story, Coetzee conducts a self-reflexive debate on the nature of the fictional enterprise—a favourite meta-fictional ploy in contemporary fictions. Susan is forced to re-evaluate her previously held convictions regarding the truth status of historical narratives (and this must include autobiography) and to contemplate the necessity (inevitability) that all retelling involves a fictionalization of 'truth'. Listing the events which occurred on the island, she muses: '[a]re these enough strange circumstances to make a story of? How long before I am driven to invent new and strange circumstances. . . . Alas, will the day ever arrive when we can make a story without strange circumstances?' (67). She continues to ponder the artifices of fictionality and the right of the (historical) writer to indulge them: 'But what shall I write? You know how dull our life was, in truth' (81); 'I ask myself what past historians of the castaway state have done—whether in despair they have not begun to make up lies' (88). History, she recognizes, is always a partial, and politicized, reconstruction.

In particular, Susan's meta-fictional speculations force her to contemplate the role of the reader, who cannot, she realizes, simply be relegated to a position of naïve, unquestioning acceptance. No story is complete and impervious to interpretative supplementation; there are unanswered questions in any tale. Narratives, like the language that composes them, are by nature partial, selective, and open to interpretative revision. By claiming their narratives to be unchallengeable 'truth' or 'history', traditional, logocentric modes of discourse seek to subordinate the active, questioning capacity of their readers under an illusion of textual completion, effacing or papering over gaps and omissions in the assertion of full (semantic) presence. But in Foe the reader's attention is deliberately drawn to the obvious preponderance of empty spaces and unsaids in Susan's tale, a common meta-fictional ploy which prevents the reduction of the novel to the status of mere mimetic reportage. There are 'touches of mystery' (83) throughout the book, not least the unexplained mutilation of Friday. Susan writes:

> On the island I accepted that I should never learn how Friday lost his tongue, as I accepted that I should never learn how the apes crossed the sea. But what we can accept in life we cannot accept in history. To tell my story and be silent on Friday's tongue is no better than offering a book for sale with pages in it left empty. Yet the only tongue that can tell Friday's secret is the tongue he has lost! (67)

Susan's comment can be read as a (postmodern) realization of textual incompletion. Only the impossible tongue of unmediated full presence can speak the full truth. The narrating 'I' is always an eye with limited vision. The omniscience of an all-encompassing perspectival position is a mimetic, metaphysical fallacy; it postures as the all-seeing eye of God. All books, all histories, and all selves, contain 'empty pages' of unwritten possibility. These are the unwritten pages of an alterity, ignored or eliminated in the partial, discretionary activity of narration. These are the unacknowledged supplements to any text, supplements which potentially challenge authorial dominance. Here, then, is another reason for Susan's fear of Friday's silence. It is an analogic expression of all those papered-over textual spaces into which another version of history (or herstory) might be written. It represents the 'empty pages' which a contestational reader can fill with her own (potentially subversive) writings, the spaces in any text which are beyond the directives of authorial control.

Dehumanization

In the third section of Coetzee's novel, the narrative style undergoes another change, now taking the form of a limited, first-person narration which is again performed by Susan. The limited, first-person voice is traditionally far less powerful in its assertion of narrational authority than the autobiographical monologue and letter formats which have been used in the two preceding sections. In limited first-person mode, the partiality of the narrator is stressed; the authority of perspectival objectivity commonly conferred on a third-person omniscient narrator and the commanding tone granted to the speaker in an uninterrupted monologic address are absent. The use of a limited, first-person narrative style opens up a space for entry into the text by an involved reader. The illusion of the narrator's ontological supremacy, sustained in more commanding narrational modes, is abandoned. The reader now adopts an ontologically superior role; placed above, or at least alongside, the narrator, we are invited to read her ironically, and to judge the validity of her truth claims in the sceptical context of our own knowledge or contextual understanding.

In the first three sections of *Foe*, then, we can discern a steady undermining of traditional narratorial authority or, otherwise put, an increasing endorsement of the reader's creative involvement in the writing of the text. Susan makes overt claims of factual validity in the first section, emphatically rejecting the embellishments or fictionality, as a means of disallowing the reader's subjective mediation of *her* story. In a similar manner, the series of letters which compose the second section function to render the reader voiceless. The reader is a silent eavesdropper, and, like the absent Foe whose position of subordinate 'you' she shares, is without the right to reply. Nevertheless, there is a reduction in narrational authority from the first to the second section, which is manifested as Susan's gradual realization that fictionalization—selective invention and creative omission—is a necessary (and inevitable) element in the writing (and reading) of *any* truth or history. This opens up a space for doubt and the possible controversion of represented 'facts': the reader, Susan reluctantly acknowledges, has the ability to ask questions about, and invent answers for, the unexplained 'mysteries' in her (any) story. As eavesdropper, the reader is not yet allowed to actively intervene (as will be the case in later sections), but there is a recognition of her capacity to entertain her own, possibly contentious conclusions about the contents of the 'letters' she intercepts.

In the third section of *Foe*, the space of doubt opens even further; the ironic reader is far better situated to challenge Susan's narratorial credibility. In the first two sections, Susan appears to occupy a position of ontological dominance over the characters she writes— Foe, Cruso, Friday, all characters in her story—and, by implication, enjoys a similarly superior stance with regard to the reader who shares with Foe the subordinate status of mute addressee, 'you'. The third section introduces a radical change, which effectively levels this hierarchy: a collapse of ontological frameworks. Although Susan continues to narrate, Foe reappears on the scene, which means that he is now *in the same ontological framework*. Both now exist as ontological equivalents, as overtly fictional characters in the fiction of Coetzee. Foe is no longer invented and circumscribed in the writing of *Susan*; both he and Susan are exposed as paper constructs in the fiction written by Coetzee and interpreted by the reader. On the substantive level of the narrative, Foe is now more than a nominal space functioning in the inferior role of dispensable addressee; he now has a voice and being with which to interrupt, challenge, and question Susan's previous narratorial authority. The existential equality of these two characters is substantiated in the battle of wits that now occurs as they vie for possession of the island story.

Foe insists that the narrative of island life as told by Susan 'is too much the same throughout' (117), that it lacks sufficient excitement and adventure to make a saleable fiction. As he perceives it, '[t]he island is not a story in itself. . . . We can bring it to life only by setting it in another story' (117). He would incorporate in his alternative fiction details of Susan's life before and after she became a castaway, and interrogates her about events which preceded the island 'episode': about the loss of her daughter, Susan's journey to Bahia to look for her, the nature of her life in the years that she remained in this Brazilian port, and her departure from Bahia as mistress of the captain of the ship from which she would become a castaway. He proposes a story which has

five parts in all: the loss of the daughter; the quest for the daughter in Brazil; abandonment of the quest, and the adventure of the island; assumption of the quest by the daughter; and reunion of the daughter with the mother. It is thus that we make up a book: loss, then quest, then recovery; beginning, then middle, then end. (117)

Susan emphatically rejects Foe's plans to alter her story (and to invent new details—like the final two episodes he proposes), wishing to retain authority in what is essentially her self-narrative:

The story I desire to be known by is the story of the island. You call it an episode, but I call it a story in its own right. It commences with my being cast away there and concludes with the death of Cruso and the return of Friday and myself to England full of new hope. . . . Taken in all, it is a narrative with a beginning and an end, and with pleasing digressions too, lacking only a substantial and varied middle. (121; my emphasis)

What is at stake here, what Foe threatens to usurp in his rewriting, is the illusory authority which Susan has enjoyed in the two previous sections—her uncontested power to authorize herself and others. She insists that her omissions from her story are the deliberate expression of her freedom of choice, of her right—authority—to withhold the information she does not care to divulge (in much the way Cruso earlier chose to withhold details of his life narrative): 'It is still in my power to guide and amend. Above all, to withhold. By such means do I still endeavour to be father to my story' (123).[17] Susan's passionate defence of her right and capacity for self-authority, articulated in the comparison of her narrative omissions with the wholesale abstention from self-narration of Friday, is also a damning indictment of the so-called freedom of excommunication. She says to Foe of Friday:

Friday has no command of words and therefore no defence against being re-shaped day by day in conformity with the desires of others. . . . No matter what he is to himself (is he anything to himself?—how can he tell us?), *what he is to the world is what I make of him.* Therefore the silence of Friday is a helpless silence. . . . Whereas the silence I keep regarding Bahia and other matters is chosen and purposeful: it is my own silence. (121–2; my emphasis)

This passage is a crucial expression of the issues of textual politicization with which I am concerned in this chapter. The capacity for conceptual signification (the ability to speak or, as Derrida would have it, write) is the capacity for (self-)authoritative *power*, a capacity qualified, but not refuted, by the binding demands of conformity to communal conventions of intersubjective referentiality. This power is not simply the faculty to 'subject' others through a selfish rewriting of their narratives of identity ('re-shap[ing them] in conformity with

---

[17] This lust for (patriarchal) authorial control is expressed again a few pages later: 'I was intended not to be the mother of my story', writes Susan, 'but to beget it' (126). The desire of fictional characters to invent themselves in the act of writing is a common motif in contemporary fiction. Frequently in feminist fiction, this desire equates with the desire to appropriate the traditionally male-dominated role of writer. Isadora Wing, the heroine in Erica Jong's *Fear of Flying* (St Albans: Panther, 1973) declares: 'What I really wanted was to give birth myself' (52). With regard to the desire for sexual possession, it is worth noting that when Foe and Susan first make love, she insists on adopting a position which she perceives as the expression of the (patriarchal) power of sexual and textual domination (clearly aligned here with the power of creativity): 'I coaxed him till he lay beneath me. Then I drew off my shirt and straddled him . . . "This is the manner of the Muse when she visits her poets" I whispered, . . . "She must do whatever is in her power to father her offspring"' (139–40).

. . . [one's own] desires'), reducing them to the subordinate status of invented characters in our 'apprehensive' fictions ('he is to the world what I make of him'). No. The power to speak (or to choose not to speak) is also the power to contest, challenge, and possibly revise the interpretations of others; it is the ability to defend one's own narrative of selfhood against the interpretative will-to-power of others. Friday's refusal or inability to enter into the dialogic arena of communicative power-play by remaining wholly outside the bounds of meaningful signification amounts not to freedom, but to a loss or relinquishment of potentially revisionary power.

In this third section we witness a disturbing 'dehumanization' of Susan. No longer does she enjoy the secure ontological status, held in the earlier sections, that is accorded to a coherent character whose 'reality' we accept for the duration of the novel. The reader is encouraged to recognize the awful irony of Susan's claims to discrete, self-determining, unwritten being, given her status as a written character in Coetzee's fiction:

> if I were like a bottle bobbing on the waves with a scrap of writing inside,
> . . . if I were a mere receptacle ready to accommodate whatever story is stuffed into me, surely you would dismiss me, surely you would say to yourself, 'This is no woman but a house of words, hollow, without substance'? I am not a story, Mr Foe. (130–1)

Susan is, after all, no more than a verbal construct; she may have 'substantial' (133) presence—as marks on the page—but she remains meaningless until 'subjected' in Coetzee's act of writing and ours of reading. She is only 'real' in the ontologically inferior realm of the novel where she is subject to authorial prescription and readerly apprehension.

As the section proceeds, Susan is plunged into deeper and deeper existential crisis; she becomes a familiar figure to readers of contemporary fiction, a character increasingly aware of her own precarious writtenness, of her dependence for meaning on the writing (and reading as writing) of the author and readers. She is a fictional character dehumanized. This crisis is exacerbated by the continuing migration of characters between ontological frames.[18] Not only does *Foe* challenge Susan's authority by intruding on her world and wrestling with her for authoritative power, but fictional identities of

---

[18] McHale discusses the meta-fictional tactic of frame-breaking or ontological migration in *Postmodernist Fiction*, 99–101, 134–7, 197–8, and *passim*.

his construction begin to populate her world as well. So it is with the disturbing arrival of Susan's 'daughter', a character whose identity is penned by Foe. He has engineered her appearance in order to secure the 'reunion of the daughter with the mother', in accordance with *his* proposed 'end' to Susan's story. When the young woman first materializes, Susan refuses to acknowledge her, steadfastly dismissing her parental/nominal claims and insisting that far from being 'mothered' by herself, the child has in fact been 'fathered' by Foe. She says to the child:

I do not know who told you that your father was a brewer from Deptford who fled to the low countries, but the story is false. Your father is a man named Daniel Foe. . . . Just as it was he who told you I was your mother, I will vouch that he is the author of the story of the brewer. He maintains whole regiments in Flanders. . . . [W]hat you know of your parentage comes to you in the form of stories and the stories have but a single source. (90–1)

Previously, Susan had asserted her existential independence: she was self-authored and in control of her own narrative of identity, possessing a 'substantial' presence. She scornfully dismissed the other characters in Foe's fictions—like his 'regiments in Flanders' in the passage above—because of their dependence for existence on his writing. Unlike them, she contends, she and Friday are *real*, independent of Foe's writings; they do not 'fall into an enchanted sleep whenever he [the writer, Foe] absents himself, [but] . . . continue to eat and drink and fret' (66). But by the third section this self-assurance has gone. The debate established at the beginning of the novel regarding the problematic status of historical fact and fictional fantasy is further developed here, as the boundaries between apparent reality and assumed illusion begin to waver. Susan is forced to question the 'reality'—her own and that of her world—which she has previously assumed as fact. She says to Foe of his characterological inventions, 'if these women are creatures of yours, visiting me at your instruction, speaking words you have prepared for them, then who am I and who indeed are you?' (133). She is no longer able 'to trust in [her] own authorship', and in a statement of overwhelming self-doubt pleads with Foe for affirmation of her identity:

In the beginning I thought I would tell you the story of an island and, being done with that return to my former life. *But now all my life grows to be a story and there is nothing of my own self left to me.* I thought I was myself and this girl a creature from another order speaking words you made up for her. But now I am full of doubt. I am doubt itself. Who is speaking me? Am I a phantom too? To what order do I belong? And you: who are you? (133; my emphasis)

'And you: who are you?' Susan's identity crisis equally implicates the reading 'you'. Indeed, we may find ourselves asking: who speaks *us*, to what order do *we* belong? In observing Susan's fall from the self-possessed position of authoritative command to the devastating disorientation engendered by wholesale dispossession ('nothing of my own [is] left to me') and writtenness ('all my life grows to be a story'), we are asked to consider the factuality of our own 'order' of reality and the unwritten essentiality we accord to our own selves in our daily (if not theoretical) existences. But the introspection this provokes in the reader results less in despairing empathy with Susan than in the realization of the difference between our existential condition as human beings possessed of the dialogic capacity for co-authorization and hers as wholly written novelistic character. Unlike Susan, who is unable to talk *with* the novelist and readers who write her (who exist in 'another [ontologically superior] order'), we do have some capacity—if we speak—to enter into dialogic exchange with those who read us (and who inhabit the same 'order', the communities in which we have meaningful being). In this manner we are perhaps able to influence or change their interpretations of who we are. Power and the potential for qualified liberty reside in the possession of a (contestational) voice and a space from which to speak, within community.

By the end of the third section, Susan has been forced to abandon her pretensions of ontological superiority and authorial control, saying to Foe, 'my daughter is substantial and I am substantial: and you too are substantial, no less and no more than any of us. We are all alive, we are all substantial, we are all in the same world' (152)— that is, the world constructed by Coetzee's fiction. All but Friday inhabit this 'same world', the realm which Susan has previously referred to as 'the world of words in which you, Mr Foe, and I, and other people live' (60), a world in which inhabitants can speak to each other. The co-inhabitance of Susan and Foe in this common signifying community, the order of 'reality' written by Coetzee and the reader, is marked at the end of the section when they make love. Although this union is not without a certain degree of possessive manœuvring, it connotes, by and large, their ontological equivalence. (It also suggests some resolution to the gendered opposition between Susan and Foe.) Foe is no longer the absent, exiled character whose home and career Susan seeks to appropriate, but her partner in this creative act. But Coetzee introduces an uneasy note into this scene of apparent reconciliation between Susan and Foe. The dialogue which accompanies their consummation amounts to a pact of collusion, a statement of their co-opted power to interpret (read, write) the meaning of the silent Friday, who is exiled from their 'world of words'. Foe says to Susan:

In every story there is a silence, some sight concealed, some word unspoken, I believe. Till we have spoken the unspoken we have not come to the heart of the story. I ask: Why was Friday drawn into such deadly peril [when scattering petals on the ocean perilously perched on a log of wood] given that life on the island was without peril, and then saved? . . . I have said the heart of the story . . . but I should have said the eye, the eye of the story. Friday rows his log of wood across the dark pupil— or dead socket—of an eye staring up at him from the floor of the sea. He rows it and is safe. To us he leaves the task of descending into that eye. Otherwise, like him, we sail across the surface and come ashore none the wiser. (141)

'Or like a mouth', replies Susan, contributing her endorsement to this pact of (colonial) appropriation, 'it is for us to descend into the mouth. . . . It is for us to open Friday's mouth and hear what it holds' (141–2). Foe agrees: 'We must make Friday's silence speak, as well as the silence surrounding Friday' (142). Having apparently dislodged one binary hierarchy, that between man and woman in the portrayal of sexual/textual equivalence, Coetzee merely replaces it with another: the empowered, speaking white characters (Susan and Foe) pledge to maintain their dominance over the powerless, silent, black Friday by appropriating his voice.

Descending into the 'I'

In the short fourth section of the novel we witness the final disintegration of Susan's narrative authority. The reader is encouraged to perform precisely the impersonating 'descent' into the eye or 'I' of authorizing control which is discussed by the two protagonists above: 'To us he leaves the task of descending into that eye.' Susan and Foe are now voiceless and unnamed, merely referred to by third-person pronouns ('she', 'he') in the narrative of another writer, an unidentified observing 'I' (eye) who comes across their lifeless bodies. We are not given any clue, however, as to the identity of the mysterious narrating 'I' who replaces the 'dehumanized' Susan. It hovers without introduction (compare the very particular placement of Susan as narrator in terms of her name and history; 10) and without fixity, sliding from one perspectival and temporal viewpoint to another. It seems impossible to locate this 'I' in time or space—unless, that is, we appropriate it as our *own* reading perspective. In this final section of *Foe*, I suggest, the unnamed pronominal space denoted by 'I' has been left open to the reader to enter and fill, to self-consciously inpersonate (in Docherty's term) in the act of subjective ventriloquism which *is* interpretation. In other words, the reader must actively *occupy* this authoritative space: she must perform a subjective descent into the eye ('I') of controlling perspective, into the mouth of narratorial authority.

I am suggesting that the fourth section of the novel can be read as an allegory of the subjective 'descent' which is performed by (writing) readers in any act of textual interpretation. Of course, this activity of meaning-imposition occurs in all acts of reading, but in this typically postmodern section of *Foe*, which is flagrantly and self-reflexively discontinuous and devoid of an authoritative narrator, our own authorizing role is overt. With the fragmentation and dislocation of the narrative voice, the passive receptivity of conventional reading gives way to the active imposition of meaning (this is clearly evident in the numerous, varied interpretations of this section by critics). In order for these (any) fictional characters to have meaning, the reader must 'subject' them to the 'separative act of comprehension'. Until so subjected, these characters may have 'substantial' presence as ink on the page of the novel, but they are without meaning. Until read, until animated in the creative conceptual process of interpretation, they remain dry and lifeless, mere paper constructs: 'They [Susan and Foe] lie side by side, not touching. The skin, dry as paper, is stretched tight over their bones. Their lips have receded, uncovering their teeth, so that they seem to be smiling. Their eyes [I's] are closed' (153).

To us, his readers, Coetzee 'leaves the task of descending into that eye', the task of '[speaking] the unspoken' in the colonizing manner outlined by Susan and Foe at the end of the previous section when discussing their proposed appropriation of the voice of Friday: we must speak for Friday, and indeed for all the characters in this and other novels. We must inform the silences, concealed sights, and unspoken words to be found in every story with our own voice: 'We must make [their] silence speak, as well as the silence surrounding [them]' unless we are 'to sail across the surface and come ashore none the wiser'. Confronted by the mystery of a character like Friday, who epitomizes the gaps of possibility in all fictional constructs, we must '[try] to find a way in' (157); 'it is for us to descend into that mouth' (141) and speak (for) him. Unspoken, Friday remains in the limbo of silence, 'a place where bodies are their own signs' (157), substantial but meaningless.

With a meta-fictional flourish, Coetzee returns us, in the final pages of *Foe*, to the novel's beginning. The unnamed narrator of the fourth section comes across and reads the first page of Susan's traveller's tale: 'With a sigh, making barely a splash, I slip overboard. Gripped by the current, the boat bobs away, drawn south toward the realm of the whales and eternal ice. Around me are the petals cast by Friday' (155). This is, of course, also the point at which the reading 'I' entered Coetzee's novel so many pages earlier, and was confronted with the first-person voice of Susan's recollection. Here, then, at the end of the book, there is a bewildering conflation in the shifting space of the unnamed 'I' of the voice of the reader, the narrator, and Susan. In order to impose meaning, we descend into that 'I'/eye, a descent in which we were in fact implicated at the beginning of the novel.

Speaking (for) Oneself

In the changing narrative modes which constitute the four sections of *Foe*, we discern a progressive discreditation of authorial power and a corresponding promotion of the reader's creative co-authorial role in the determination of textual meaning. Coetzee offers us a mini-synopsis of the historical development of the novel as it has recently been theorized: we move from the secure (but subordinate) placement of reader and characters of conventional narrative techniques (in the first and second sections) to the 'freer' (but more unstable) positions of existential uncertainty experienced by readers and characters of more recent fiction (in the third section) and finally to the radical displacement of authorial voice and the active readerly appropriation of that voice, which are common in present-day meta-fiction (in the last section). It is Thomas Docherty's contention in *Reading (Absent) Character* that the unsettling discontinuities which characterize many contemporary fictions (exemplified in the final section of *Foe*) effect a 'serious' and disturbing shattering of the reading ego. This is, quite simply, untrue. It is his further claim that the textual, characterological, and authorial decentralization he defines is politically desirable in so far as it precludes the occupation of a fixed (and potentially judgemental or dictatorial) position by the reader. This is not merely untrue, but disingenuous. Reading is never neutral; it is always political, always potentially an act of colonization. It is grossly misguided (or manipulative) to claim that we can dismiss the implicitly political nature of all reading by adopting textual strategies that shatter characterological identities into multiple, instantaneous 'surface' positions in a text. This serves less to dissolve reader identity, as Docherty suggests, than to consolidate reader authority and identity in an interpreting 'I'. Fictions and fictional characters, if they are to have any *meaning* at all (which is not to deny the substantiality of their unread physical *presence*), must be 'subjected' by an apprehending reader. This secures for the reader a position of ontological dominance and priority over the read subject, who depends on her for meaningful identity.

Let me be clear. Coetzee is not simply endorsing the blithe equation of human beings with fictional characters in *Foe*. The novel encourages us to recognize the difference between the characters of fiction and human subjects. The economy of interpretative dominance and mute subjection that operates in the reading of fiction does not wholly accord with the operations of intersubjective communication. The vitally important difference between our apprehension of silent, undefended fictional characters (silent, that is, unless spoken/written by reader or author) and our communication with other, vocal human beings is too easily obscured by metaphors which reduce human beings to textual process. We read and interpret others (and ourselves) *like* texts, but human beings are not texts. Human beings, unless physically or mentally incapacitated, always have recourse to the co-creative faculty of intersubjective speech (or some other form of mutually understood signification): they occupy the same ontological order as, and can communicate *with*, those who interpret them, offering resistance or encouragement to the way in which they are 'read' by others. Fictional characters cannot co-authorize their selfhood in this manner; they are merely given ventriloquial voice *by* their readers, and are unable to enter into the dialogic exchange which characterizes the relationships of human beings. Human interplay takes place within communal arenas of contestation and debate, in which subjects vie for authority in exchanges of interpretative will-to-power.

This is not to suggest some egalitarian ideal of communal intersubjective co-operation where human subjects co-exist in agreement and mutual consensus. Far from it. Hierarchical relations of power, held in place by the (learned or inherited) rhetorical skill and verbal dexterity of particular individuals or institutions and sustained by the active suppression and silencing of others, will always pertain. What I am suggesting is that, within shared referential frameworks or signifying communities, hierarchical constitution, like subjective status, is negotiable and potentially open to change and revision— provided, that is, that we recognize and claim the authoritative power of potentially contestational voices. To abstain or suffer exile from membership in a signifying community, remaining silent or incomprehensible, is to relinquish or lose one's power to negotiate revision and reinterpretation. This is the fate of the silent Friday, who is wholly authorized by Susan's colonizing voice. In the figure of Friday we may begin to see the destructive consequences for human subjects of rhetorical claims which encourage the self-martyrdom of auto-erasure and silence as a means of attaining unmediated personal and textual authenticity. The 'freedom' of Friday's (willed or inflicted) exile from discursive community is bought at the cost of a radical solipsistic alienation which, paradoxically, does nothing to prevent him from being read and written by others. In fact, it encourages others to 'invent' him and 'speak for' him in their attempts to comprehend him. He is exiled to an inferior 'order', where his meaning is the product of others' interpretative will-to-power as they appropriate and descend into his eye/'I'. Excommunicated, and without the dialogic capacity to enter into debate or discussion with others, he does not gain authenticity and escape writtenness, but is relegated to a subservient position as a character written in the narratives of communicating others.

The danger of a theory of contemporary poetics such as that proposed by Thomas Docherty is that it wilfully ignores the inescapably political nature of reading by suggesting the possibility of a release from referential frameworks and the escape of the reader into positionless fragmentation deemed necessary to evade perspectival totalitarianism. In doing so, it mistakenly encourages the abandonment of our responsible capacity for partial determination of self and others through (contestational) communication in favour of unfixed, 'surface irresponsibility'. In terms of the analogy between reading and (responsible) self-narration which I have developed in my analysis of *Foe*, our reading of the (moral) narratives of selfhood—our own and that of others—must be recognized as entailing a positioned and positioning stance. Our narratives are never neutral, but are socially constituted and *constituting*. In this way, our communicative interactions are always responsible for meaning- and value-determination. Within the many communities to which we belong, we have a capacity for movement and contestation which is never absolute, but conditional; we have the power and responsibility to (re)define, through intervention, challenge, and debate, the communal frameworks which define our meaning. Only *within* a framework of shared signification do we have the potential authority to co-write our meaning and our narratives of selfhood. The 'freedom' offered by Docherty is untenable: it is to be purchased only at the unacceptable cost of incomprehensibility, the loss of readable subjective meaning.

The possibilities of contestation and challenge arise only within language, within and between the variety of discursive and interpretative communities in which speaking subjects are situated. Only *in* language do we have the power to negotiate our interpretative differences as members of plural communities that interanimate and modify each other. Silent, we are subjected *by* language, remaining victims of a colonizing tongue. Without voice, we remain mute subjects of other speakers' interpretative will-to-power: we must speak (for) ourselves.

8

Communal Contestation:
Margaret Atwood's *Lady Oracle*

The re-birth of feminism inspires and/or coincides with a
proliferation of first person fictions by women inventing
themselves as writers. Or is it the other way round?

Sage, *Women in the House of Fiction*

[T]extual experience represents one of the most daring
explorations the subject can allow himself, one that delves
into his constitutive process. But at the same time and as a
result, textual experience reaches the very foundation of
the social—that which is exploited by sociality but which
elaborates and can go beyond it, either destroying or trans-
forming it.

Kristeva, *Revolution in Poetic Language*

A Surprise within the Rules

After an abortive attempt to escape what she deems the repressive
conventions and expectations of her rational everyday existence, the
protagonist in Renata Adler's *Pitch Dark* resigns herself to determination within them, surmising that the best one can hope for is
'under conscious pressure, a surprise within the rules'.[1] Kate's
personal dilemma is her entrapment between, on the one hand her
desire for the affirmation and 'placement' afforded by her relationship with her lover Jake and, on the other hand, a sense of lost
spontaneity and thwarted individuality that characterize their affair,
which has become 'boring, . . . droning, and repetitive' (6). Her
relational entrapment echoes her sense of entrapment in communal
and communicative structures that appear to leave no scope for the
expression of individuality or deviance, demanding only the unrequited boredom of conformity. The dangers of boredom, suggests

[1] Renata Adler, *Pitch Dark* (London: Hamish Hamilton, 1983), 68. Further
references to this book will be cited parenthetically in the text.

Kate, threaten to corrupt all our relationships, all our habitualized, convention-bound interactions with others. The consequences of this realization of the insidious power of habitual boredom extend far beyond the realm of the personal: 'The real danger lies, I think, in this: that boredom has intimately to do with power. One only has to think of hypnosis, of being mesmerized. Monotony, as a literal method of enthralment. . . . Deliberate, pointless boredom is a kind of menace, and a disturbing exercise of power' (107).

In search of autonomy and a sense of selfhood that is not dependent on conformity with the expectations of those around her, Kate leaves the security of her ordered North American life and travels to rural Ireland, where she struggles for orientation in an alien landscape of perpetually shifting horizons. Here, without the securities of her everyday life and denuded of the repetitions and routines which order her rational being, she finds herself adrift in what is truly the nightmare wasteland of postmodernity, in a state of almost pathological self-dissolution. Struggling to traverse this terrain of uncertainty, fleeing the repercussions of some vaguely intimated crime she fears she may have committed, Kate is an exile, a refugee outside shared bounds of understanding. Displaced in an alien communal setting whose values and norms she cannot understand, she is unable to comprehend the behavioural (or language-) games played by those who surround her. The ambiguous elements of the interpersonal play she experiences in Ireland are, at best, the sources of comical miscommunication, and at worst, the site of treachery, intimidation, and deception. She opts to return to the stifling security of her rule-bound American life.

Kate thus contrasts the authority of intersubjective communal determination with the pathology of excommunicative (self-) dissolution, and finds both wanting; she perceives her existential choice as being one of only two equally unacceptable alternatives: the numbing stasis of conformity or the delirious, frightening fluidity of an escape from rationality, from the 'conscious pressures' of intersubjective intelligibility. The sense of loss involved in her resigned acceptance of the former is appalling. Towards the end of the second section of the novel, we are presented with a horrific metaphor for the condition of habitualized, prescribed existence which Kate deems the only alternative to the disorientating conditions of communicative exile experienced in Ireland. It is a vision of existential purposelessness, of somnambulistic adherence to paths and patterns of learned behaviour where habit and ritual enforce a route whose origins and meanings have long been lost. Kate describes the actions of 'the shrew, the poor unevolved, benighted shrew, which will keep jumping high in the air in the place where an obstacle, a rock perhaps, once was but no longer is'. She then ponders

all those places where, though the obstacles have long been removed, one persists either in the jump or in taking the long way round. It seemed such an unnecessary jolt or expenditure of time and energy. And yet, if you have acquired a profound aversion for just such a place simply because of an obstacle that once was there, or even an incapacity to discern that the obstacle no longer exists, or an indifference as to whether it exists or not, or even if turning back dejected has become for you the path itself, or if you have a superstitious need to treat the path as if the obstacle still remained, or even a belief that the discovery that the obstacle is gone is itself a punishable offence, if any of these things is true for you, then you are lost. (82)

Refuting the possibility of willed transgression or productive revision within rule-bound procedures, Kate abandons herself to a philosophy of loss; change, as she perceives it can never be more than 'a surprise within the rules'.

In Chapter 3 I suggested that for many feminist writers communicative rationality seems to require abandonment to the prescriptive norms of 'man-made language', masculine literary conventions, and patriarchal communal structures. From a deterministic feminist perspective, the assumption of (linguistic) subjectivity requires subjection to the 'law of the father', and writing and speaking involve no more than the passive reinscription of patriarchal dictates. Echoing the call for the negative freedom of a poststructuralist aesthetics of excommunication, feminist rebellion is then theorized as an escape from communal and communicative strictures: freedom lies in the pre-linguistic plenitude of non-articulateness prior to social subjection in the symbolic order, or the fluid, unmapped realm of an idealized 'female language', or the bliss of non-linear subjective dissolution.

Many contemporary fictions by women valorize escape into a 'wilderness' beyond the repressive prescriptions of familial and social communities and the constraints of patriarchal language. In *Surfacing* (1979) Margaret Atwood seems to endorse the project of escape from patriarchal discourse through the recovery (or invention) of a distinctly female language.[2] The novel's protagonist 'escapes' to the non-linguistic natural world of the uncivilized Canadian outback, following the devastating self-mutilation of an abortion performed on the instruction of her former lover (who functions here as an embodiment of death-inducing patriarchy). The heroine's spiritual quest in the untamed wilderness has been interpreted by a variety of feminist critics 'as a search for feminine discourse: her escape from, and challenge to, the patriarchal social order she has previously accepted as the norm. . . . [Atwood] depicts her protagonist gradually becoming "silenced" in her inability to find expression through the dominant structure of society.'[3]

Surfacing certainly appears to invite such a reading. Moving deeper and deeper into the wilderness, the protagonist finds conventional language increasingly invalid as a means of expressing her emotions and experience. At one point she says of language, 'I couldn't use it because it wasn't mine' (109); later she observes that '[l]anguage divides us into fragments, I wanted to be whole' (146). This realization leads the protagonist to abandon her companions in a final push to achieve oneness with nature, an abandonment which is interpreted by Sue Spaull in the following manner: 'She sets forth on her final journey to the "wild zone", the place beyond language, beyond the Symbolic Order where boundaries cease to exist. . . . Atwood's deliberate omission of full-stops in the subsequent sentences serves to reinforce the protagonist's sense of fluidity, her loss of personal identity.'[4] But the novelist hesitates to accept the seductive appeal of the radical self-erasure, the 'loss of personal identity', which must accompany her protagonist's wholesale rejection of language and the self-definition it makes possible. In the final pages of the novel, the protagonist prepares to return to civilization in the company of a new lover, strengthened and wiser, we are assured, by her wilderness experience. At the end of *Surfacing*, then, Atwood seems to reject the enticement of an exclusionist feminism which promises freedom from dismembering patriarchal discourse at the cost of the loss of readable selfhood. Excommunication, escape from (patriarchal) communicative rationality, fails utterly to procure meaningful

[2] Margaret Atwood, *Surfacing* (1979; London: Virago, 1984). Further references to this edition will be cited parenthetically in the text.
[3] Sue Spaull, 'Margaret Atwood: *Surfacing*', in Sara Mills, Lynne Pierce, Sue Spaull, and Elaine Millard, *Feminist Readings, Feminists Reading* (Hemel Hempstead: Harvester Wheatsheaf, 1989), 114.
[4] Spaull, 'Margaret Atwood', 116.

self-identity and (self-)constitutive agency for female subjects: it does nothing at all to diminish, but in fact panders to, the perception of women *as* silent or irrational and incapable of serious constitutional engagement.

Unconscious Subversion

Surfacing concludes somewhat ambivalently with the recognition by its protagonist of the need to remain in community while fearing the possible encroachment of that community on the preserve of her individuality. It ends with the protagonist's immanent return to community (patriarchal civilization), but fails to provide an account of how her experience of the 'wilderness' of her silent otherness will help her to maintain her sense of individual value and distinction in the face of the crippling patriarchal definitions she sought to escape in the first place. In *Lady Oracle*, however, Atwood provides precisely such an account.[5] In this novel, Atwood not only parodies the mistaken aspirations of her heroine's yearning for deathlike excommunicative escape, but offers an alternative means of challenging patriarchal prescriptions by engaging in discourse in acts of creative narration. Writing, the active utilization of linguistic creativity, provides Joan, the novel's narrating protagonist, with the contestational means of disputing and changing the communal codes which constitute what has become for her an unacceptable interpretation of 'femininity'.

Joan is a clandestine writer of Gothic romances, a fact she has kept hidden from the unsuspecting eyes of her academician husband Arthur, anticipating his disapproval.[6] She realizes that her books would be dismissed by Arthur and his socialist intellectual circle as trash: 'Worse than trash, for didn't they exploit the masses, corrupt by distracting, and perpetrate degrading stereotypes of women as

---

[5] Margaret Atwood, *Lady Oracle* (1977; London: Virago Press, 1982). Further references to this edition will be cited parenthetically in the text.

[6] For a discussion of Atwood's use of the Gothic genre in *Lady Oracle* see Susan J. Rosowski, 'Margaret Atwood's *Lady Oracle*: Fantasy and the Modern Gothic Novel', in Judith McCombs (ed.), *Critical Essays on Margaret Atwood* (Boston: G. K. Hall, 1988), 197–207. For feminist discussion of the Gothic genre, see the collection of essays edited by Juliann Fleenor, *The Female Gothic* (London: Eden Press, 1983), and Eugenia C. DeLamotte, *Perils of the Night: A Feminist Study of Nineteenth-Century Gothic* (New York: Oxford University Press, 1990).

helpless and persecuted?' (34). Despite Joan's insistence that her novels 'dealt in hope' and 'offered a vision of a better world, however preposterous' (35), the fact remains that she herself has been a victim of the 'degrading stereotype' perpetrated by her own escapist fictions. During the years of her marriage she has maintained a surface appearance of ideal femininity which matches that of her fictional heroines: beautiful, thin, uncomplicated, and endearingly incompetent.[7] Beneath this mask of perfection, however, Joan has maintained a complex hidden life, from which Arthur was excluded. When a blackmailer eventually threatened to divulge Joan's duplicity (or multiplicity) to Arthur, she planned her own fake death in a staged drowning accident, and flew to Italy: 'I planned my death carefully. . . . At first I thought I'd managed it' (7). Joan hoped to abscond from the confusions and complexities of her life of multiple identities by faking her accidental death, but had absolutely no intention of truly ending her life—in fact, the impetus for her willed disappearance lies in her desire to be reborn, to 'begin again', only this time with the 'self-control' which has eluded her all her life (10). Pretending death was an attempt to gain self-possession, to attain the power of self-definition unhampered by the interfering mediation of those who control her life: 'I pretended to die so I could live, so I could have another life' (315).

Joan tells her story from the rented villa in the Italian village to which she fled following her supposed death. It is the same village in which she and Arthur once enjoyed a holiday, and to avoid recognition by the villagers, she cuts off her waist-length red hair, dyes it mud-brown, and dons a pair of dark glasses. She then settles down to finish her latest romance novel, *Stalked by Love*. Atwood enters familiar feminist territory in drawing attention to the irony of Joan's self-victimizing reinscription of patriarchal myths of femininity in her Gothic romances. Joan's novels might, as she defends them, offer her readers a ready means of escape from the drudgery of their everyday lives into imaginary realms of other-worldly perfection, but they also reinforce a degrading myth which generates the felt need for that escape—a myth of female persecution, flight and/or

---

[7] In a telling statement about her (culinary) incompetence, Joan writes: 'My failure was a performance and Arthur was the audience. His applause kept me going' (210). Arthur's demands for subservient failure are not limited to the kitchen. Her tendency towards absent-mindedness, e.g., becomes a characterological 'given' in the eyes of Arthur and his friends: 'it was expected of me, and I added to my repertoire of deficiencies' (212).

escape, and finally rescue by a man. In this scenario the heroine's rescue is her prize (or compensation) for conformity to male ideals of appearance and behaviour. In the same way, punishment by death or madness (or both) is the inevitable end for those female characters who refuse to comply with the stereotypical demands of femininity. But if the rescuer in these novels is always a man, so too is the persecutor: the persecuted heroines of Joan's Gothic romances flee both from and into the waiting arms of men. Men are both villains and redeemers, a paradox which is deeply rooted in the experiences of Joan's past and one which she finds increasingly difficult to reconcile. 'Was every Heathcliff a Linton in disguise?' she asks with bemusement. It is a question which resonates throughout *Lady Oracle*.

While rumours flourish about the nature and cause of her death, in the sanctuary of her Italian hideaway Joan settles down to finish *Stalked by Love*. While working on the book, Joan ruminates on her past. Much of *Lady Oracle* is in fact recollective, Joan's memories of childhood and married life being interwoven with action and events in the Italian present. The boundaries between past and present are often blurred, and the complexity that results is further compounded by the integration into *Lady Oracle* of extracts from Joan's own novel, *Stalked by Love*. (The interpolated sections of Joan's writings are differentiated from the main body of Atwood's novel by the use of italics.) One formative childhood memory amalgamates the daffodil-carrying figure of a male flasher witnessed as a child with a middle-aged, tweed-coated man who rescued her when she was blindfolded and tied to a wooden post by malicious peers. She recalls her bemused conflation of the two men: 'Was the man who untied me a rescuer or a villain? Or, an even more baffling thought: was it possible for a man to be both at once?' (64). The same irreconcilable duality characterizes all the men in Joan's life: her father, a wartime executioner who has a life-saving role as an anaesthetist in civilian life; her first lover (Count) Paul, a bank clerk by day and romance novelist writing under a feminine pseudonym by night; the Royal Porcupine, with whom she has an affair while married to Arthur, whose crazy life-style and mannerisms are a mask to hide the suburban stolidity of his *alter ego* Chuck Brewster. So too with Arthur, whose patina of banner-waving, emancipatory politics disguises a prescriptive Calvinistic determinism as repressive as any of the governmental and institutional structures he claims to disavow. 'Every man I'd ever been involved with', comments Joan, 'had two selves' (292). Not surprisingly, duplicity is fundamentally characteristic of the male characters she pens in *Stalked by Love*.

Self-duality or, more correctly, self-multiplicity is a reiterated motif in *Lady Oracle*, and is by no means only the preserve of male characters. Joan is herself split, multiple, a condition she laments, yearning for wholeness. Throughout her marriage she has pretended passive conformity to Arthur's expectations, repressing a disparate amalgamation of 'hidden selves, . . . other lives' (286) behind her mask of wifely acquiescence. During these years, she indulged the romanticism forbidden her by Arthur's contempt by enacting elaborate escapist fantasies behind her locked bedroom door (23). Throughout this time she wrote and published her romance novels under the name Louisa K. Delacourt, hiding her manuscripts from Arthur and pretending employment at a variety of fictitious jobs in order to explain both her income from the books and her absences from home while writing them (208, 213). While Arthur watched television, Joan secretly practised automatic writing in the locked bedroom (219). These journeys in to the nether realms of her psyche result in a collection of obscure scribblings, later to be published to much acclaim (and to Arthur's dismay) as the best-selling sequence of poems 'Lady Oracle'. The collection of poems is Joan's first subversive rewriting of romance conventions; they contain many of the required elements and plot details of the genre, but subvert and transgress the expected endings: 'There were the sufferings, the flights, the looming death, the sense of being imprisoned, but there was no happy ending , no true love' (232). Significantly the poems are interpreted by Joan's reviewers as an angry comment on married life (237), and Joan herself describes the collection as being 'about the male-female roles in our society' (227). They may be read as the transgressive eruption of semiotic desire into the ordered linguistic realm of the symbolic; but as long as they remain simply unconscious transgressions, a 'surprise within the rules', rather than a willed, intentional rewriting of the rules, their value is limited. Joan must (and later will) learn to perform a *conscious* rewriting of the prescriptive conventions of romance, in order to escape the destructive myth of victimized womanhood they encode. The fact that her 'subversive' poems are appropriated by her male publishers with the sole aim of making money from the collection, regardless of the quality of the writing ('"Don't you worry your pretty little head about good. We'll worry about good, that's our business, right?"' (226)) and that Joan is reduced to a seductive picture on the collection's cover suggests that this unconscious, passive mode of writing is not in itself sufficient to effect political change.[8]

These hidden indulgences and secrets are evidence of the larger, deeper secrets which Joan keeps from Arthur: her affair with the Royal Porcupine, for instance. 'This was the beginning of my double life', she writes soon after the affair commences, only to immediately qualify her assertion:

But hadn't my life always been double? There was always that shadowy twin, thin when I was fat, fat when I was thin, myself in silvery negative. . . . It was never-never land she wanted, that reckless twin. But not twin even, for I was more than double, I was triple, multiple, and now I could see that there was more than one life to come, there were many. (246)

By the time she met and married Arthur, she admits, 'I was two people at once, with two sets of identification papers, two bank accounts, two different groups of people who believed I existed' (213). Joan longs for Arthur's acknowledgement of her fiction-writing prowess, for his attention and admiration, but she realizes that this is impossible: 'In order for Arthur to appreciate me I'd have to reveal the identity of Louisa K., and I knew I couldn't do that. No matter what I did, Arthur was bound to despise me. I could never be what he wanted' (247). 'I wanted to be acknowledged', she writes, 'but I feared it. If I brought the separate parts of my life together . . . surely there would be an explosion' (217).

Other, more threatening duplicities pre-date the invention of her pseudonymic identity, Louisa K. Joan's life-story is a catalogue of role-playing escapist tactics: hiding, camouflage, disguise—all performed by her with the consummate skill engendered by lifelong practice. Discarded, hidden selves always threaten to surface and shatter her present patina of consistent, singular identity. If Joan

---

[8] For a discussion of Joan's automatic poetry writing as her means of accessing the subversive unconscious of her repressed female desire (Kristevan semiotic or Irigarayian *parler-femme* or Cixousian *écriture féminine*), see Christian Bök, 'Sibyls: Echoes of French Feminism in *The Diviners* and *Lady Oracle*', *Canadian Literature*, 135 (Winter 1992), 80–93. Unlike Bök, I read *Lady Oracle* as a parody, rather than an endorsement, of French feminism's idealization of unconscious subversion. Atwood stresses the need for women to consciously and actively engage in (masculine) language.

feared Arthur's discovery of her clandestine personae—Gothic novel-ist, lover of the Royal Porcupine—she is absolutely terrified that he will unearth her greatest secret: the truth about her 'fat' past. Joan, now beautiful and thin, was a fat, unattractive child and adolescent who ate copiously and dressed in violently flamboyant outfits in order to thwart the ideals of feminine beauty promoted by her mother, a 'made-up' paragon of social conformity. But by the time she met Arthur, Joan had traded her protective persona of fat fool for an equally defensive, if more socially acceptable, mask of slender femininity. In order to keep the truth of her past from Arthur, Joan made herself up; that is, she invented an utterly fallacious personal history, one more in keeping with the woman he perceived her to be, complete with details of a summer-camp seduction and a stint as a cheerleader. She completely omitted, in this rewriting, the true details of her past.

Her strategy was simple: 'I wanted to maintain his illusions for him intact, and it was easy to do, all it needed was a little restraint: I simply never told him anything important' (36). She lived in terror of his discovery of the truth, and in anguish at the self-betrayal the maintenance of his illusions required: 'I was terrified that sooner or later someone would find out about me, trace down my former self, unearth me' (251). They married as soon after his proposal as possible, 'before Arthur found out the truth'; Joan is 'terrified that [she'd] be exposed at the last minute as a fraud, liar and impostor' (199); she is desperately afraid that he will discover 'how deeply [she'd] deceived him' (200). Joan admits that 'Arthur loved [her] under false pretences' (345), but asks pathetically, 'If he'd known what I was really like would he still have loved me?' (36). She believes her 'hidden selves' to be 'unworthy' (268), and that she herself is 'hollow, a hoax, a delusion' (251). The past, unseen and unknown to Arthur, envelops her as surely as her discarded bulk once did:

When I looked at myself in the mirror, I didn't see what Arthur saw. The outline of my former body still surrounded me, like a mist, like a phantom moon, like the image of Dumbo the Flying Elephant super-imposed on my own. I wanted to forget the past, but it refused to forget me; it waited for sleep, then cornered me. (214)

The issue of fatness (repressed female desire) versus thinness (conformity with social expectations of femininity), the self-torturous repercussions of which are so painfully (if comically) portrayed in *Lady Oracle*, are a powerful visual expression of the dilemma which feminists ascribe to all women: repressed desire in conflict with social prescriptions.[9] Fatness symbolizes her repressed appetite, her submerged desires, a transgressive otherness strenuously denied, yet always present, which surround her 'like a mist'. Consciously disowned, prior, censored selves ascend, in moments of slippage, from the depths of Joan's unconscious, taunting her in a series of dreams and fantasies based on the imaginary life of a carnival Fat Lady she once saw as a child. Psychoanalytic analysis might seem an appropriate line to take in reading the novel: desire, repressed at the level of the semiotic with Joan's entry into socially conformist womanhood, finds expression in the irrationality of her 'dream-logic' and poetic writing, and constantly threatens to rupture the artifice of subjective wholeness that operates at the level of the symbolic order. Given the content of Joan's dreams, we might also find the novel (deliberately or fortuitously) amenable to reading in terms of Bakhtin's theory of the carnivalesque subversion/inversion of rational norms: the carnival Fat Lady, side-shows, and circus-tent settings of the dreams may evoke the 'gay parody of official reason' that Bakhtin associated with the transgressive energies of the carnival.

But psychoanalytic and carnivalesque readings remain inadequate. They are unable to account for the possibility of willed transgression

---

[9] For a reading of Margaret Atwood's fiction in these terms, see Maggie Humm, 'Going through the Green Channel', in *Border Traffic: Strategies of Contemporary Women Writers* (Manchester: Manchester University Press, 1991), 123–59. Humm writes: 'Femininity, then, has a vocabulary of repression, of stereotype and victimisation. Social representations of the female body do not coincide with a woman character's perception of her body and its possibilities. In fact the two are usually entirely at odds. It is this conflict which is a major feature of Atwood's novels' (128). She suggests that in Atwood's fictions, 'new accounts of the female body, and its potential cultural representations, amount to a feminist rewriting of culture' (124). While wholly endorsing Humm's interpretation of Atwood's fiction as a potentially revolutionary rewriting of cultural assumptions, I have difficulty accepting the rhetoric of victimization and repression which she evokes so continuously. This sits uncomfortably with her recognition of the power possessed by women to 'rewrite culture'. In constantly evoking the spectre of victimization, Humm only perpetuates the myth of passive reinscription which Atwood is so keen to dispel. The need for women to claim responsibility for their own (perhaps self-destructive) behaviour is central to Atwood's reformative vision. Joan must acknowledge and take responsibility for her *own* conformity to patriarchal norms of behaviour and appearance, for only in doing so will she be able to rewrite their prescriptions. See also Marilyn Patton, '*Lady Oracle*: The Politics of the Body', *ARIEL*, 22/4 (Oct. 1991), 29–48.

at the level of subjective consciousness or conscious interpretative choice at the level of the symbolic, the realm of intersubjectively shared meanings. The valorization of unconscious transgression, unmediated by conscious intention and untranslatable in terms of communal rationality, has little political efficacy. It may result in an advocacy of destructive rebellion *per se* as the only possible strategy for challenging restrictive social conventions, abandonment to the unsequestered expression of normless desire. Or it may offer subversion as merely 'a surprise within the rules', discovered rather than purposive: subversive subconscious energies, by definition, remain below the level of consciousness, unharnessable towards the achievement of deliberately conceived revisionary ends. We need to theorize the capacity of human subjects for reflexive evaluation of the norms that structure their intersubjective communities; we need to theorize their ability to move between a variety of interpretative and discursive sites, each offering different, even conflicting, settings for meaningful interpretation and narration. We need, in short, to theorize the possibility of conscious, willed transgression by communally situated human subjects; otherwise change can be understood only as the product of chance rather than intention. In preceding chapters I have argued that a measure of individual autonomy lies in the plural interpretative perspectives and discursive sites made available to us by our simultaneous situation in a variety of interpretative or discursive communities. Human agency, the capacity to interpret and create readable narratives of selfhood, inheres in a subject's placement in a plurality of communities, each providing a range of interpretative and discursive strategies that may interanimate and modify the others. *Lady Oracle* explores precisely this contestational, constitutive process of self-narration.

Instructive Parody

Lady Oracle is undeniably funny, although the instructive purpose of its humour is deadly serious. The humour in large part arises from a sophisticated parodic style not present in the painful introspective scrutiny evident in the two novels discussed in detail in the two previous chapters. Parody is an evaluative, self-consciously instructive stance which challenges various attitudes or assumptions through expository ridicule, it requires a certain capacity for distancing which enables one to stand apart from the situation or predicament (or self) being parodied.[10] It follows that self-parody is a potentially revisionary stance, one which, if possible, invalidates claims that we are merely passive victims embedded in the false 'reality' we inhabit, without the capacity to evaluate or change the prescriptive illusions it foists on us. If we are able to laugh *at* ourselves and our purported existential dilemma of ideological entrapment, then we are already some way out of it. The parodic humour of *Lady Oracle* is played off not against the 'patriarchy' (men are portrayed as equally victimized by the duality imposed by their adoption of social roles), but against the promoters of an exclusionist feminist literary theory which does nothing to eliminate, but only bemoans and in fact perpetuates, the destructive myths of social constitution and the disabling dualism of inside/outside. Such theory fears and retreats from the strategic battlefield of ideological discourse and intersubjective communication; *Lady Oracle* urges us to enter the fray and challenge the unacceptable prescriptions which are encoded in our language and literature.

In the final section of *Lady Oracle* Joan deliberately subverts stereotypical expectation by exploring the possibilities of conscious, revolutionary (self-)narrativization: she rewrites the prescriptive myth of (her own) womanhood in a manner that releases her from the bonds of a socially scripted narrative of mythical female perfection. The possibility and process of this revolutionary activity are exemplified in the meta-fictional portrayal of Joan's rewriting of her latest romance, *Stalked by Love*, which forswears conventional generic 'rules' and characterological stereotyping. In order to do so, Joan must reject the temptation of (impossible) escape, renounce the contrivance of flight, and relinquish the image of herself as a victim dependent on male 'rescue'.[11]

Joan's faked 'death' and subsequent flight to Italy were, she tells

---

[10] See Linda Hutcheon, *A Theory of Parody* (New York: Methuen, 1985).

[11] Wings are an important motif in the novel, suggesting flight as a means of escape. It is the winged costume that Joan most longed to wear in a childhood dance performance, although the longed-for role of butterfly was denied her because of her size. In subsequent years she continued to dream of, and enact, a variety of alternative flight strategies, culminating in her 'flight' to Italy. Allusions to the Daedalus–Icarus myth (in which the wings of artifice allow escape from an imprisoning labyrinth, but also bring about the death of Icarus through his hubristic flight) recur throughout the novel. For examples of Joan's flight fantasises which evidence her fear of enacting this fatal fall see pp. 102–3, 251, 274.

us, an attempt to reach the safety of an illusionary 'Other Side', a 'place where I would fit in at last, where I would be the *right shape*' (102; my emphasis). The other side she aspires to is a 'white paradise' of purity and fulfilment, a fantastic 'never-never land' that she reproduces in her own fictional heterocosms: 'I longed for the simplicity of that world where happiness was possible and wounds were only ritual ones. Why had I been closed out from that impossible white paradise where love was as final as death, and banished to this other place where everything changed and shifted?' (284). '[T]his other place' of fluidity and change, is, of course, the realm of conscious being and temporal alienation, the phenomenological flux of lived life. Conversely, 'that world', the other side she yearns to reach, is the petrified, inanimate condition of non-being, of unconsciousness, excommunication: literal or figurative death. 'What price safety', asks Joan, sitting alone on the balcony of her Italian flat soon after her escape from England, ostensibly dead to those she has 'left behind' (305). What is the cost of reaching that safe haven of fixity, of singular, 'essential' selfhood, of achieving an escape so absolute that one need never run away again? Her answer lies in a telling statement of dissatisfaction with the 'paradise' she has supposedly gained: 'The Other Side was no paradise, it was only a limbo. . . . the Other Side was boring. There was no one to talk to and nothing to do. [. . .] I was feeling marooned; the impulse to send out messages, in bottles or not, grew every day. *I am still alive.* . . . *Please rescue*' (309, emphasis original).

This is what Joan learns about the other side: attainment of it means death, or deathlike renunciation of recognizable (readable) selfhood, a limbo of eternal excommunication. This dreamed-of paradise is a penury of silence, a sentence to wordless, solitary confinement: 'there was no one to talk to.' In Italy she is 'a foreigner', alienated from the locals by her linguistic ignorance ('I didn't know the words' (312)), and her inability to understand their customs and codes of behaviour: 'The language was only one problem; there was also that other language, what is done and what isn't done' (17; see also 312). Here there is no one to recognize her, no one to appreciate the skilful accomplishment of her self-managed escape. Ironically, the success of her venture is conditional on maintaining the ignorance of her achievement in those she has left behind: 'freedom' in her new life depends on sustaining the illusion of her death. But Joan cannot bear being alone, unknown. She longs to be recognized, remembered;

she longs for an audience to applaud the cleverness of her artifice, this successful flight:

I was pleased with myself for having arranged it. And suddenly I wanted Arthur to know how clever I'd been. He always thought I was too disorganized to plot my way across the floor and out of the door, much less out of the country. . . . I would love him to know I'd done something complicated and dangerous without making a single mistake. I'd always wanted to do something he would admire. (27)

But her desired audience, 'everyone [she] had left on the other side' (8), is separated from her by their belief in her death.

Not surprisingly, having reached her imaginary haven of reclusion in Italy, Atwood's heroine still longs to escape, this time from the 'limbo' of her alienated paradise. Joan fluctuates between two wholly contrary dreams, both unsatisfactory because ultimately self-destructive. In the first she longs for rescue by a male figure (which entails conformity to the role of victimized female and thus repression of her rebellious impulses). She wants attention, she wants to be recognized, but is afraid of the inevitable loss of self-authorization in being recognized, subjected to the performative expectation of others. She sends an abortive rescue message to Arthur, her knight, and fantasizes about his sudden appearance, 'rescue-minded' (8), in this obscure village retreat. In the second she imagines attaining wholesale independence, absolute excommunication. In Italy she is not truly dead, not separated from interpreting others: she has merely traded one set of protocols of meaning (those of Arthur and the others she has left behind) for another (those of the Italian village). Integration into a new community—for example, that of the Italian village— means becoming the subject of its recognition, and entails the adoption of a whole new set of conventions; she must *learn* the new 'rules' linguistic and behavioural, of that community. Joan fantasizes about total emancipatory escape:

This time I really would disappear, without trace. No one at all would know where I was, not even Sam, not even Arthur. This time I would be free completely; no shreds of the past would cling to me, no clutching fingers. I could do anything I wanted. . . . I could merge into Italy, marry a vegetable man: we'd live in a little stone cottage, I'd have babies and fatten up, we'd eat steamy food and cover our bodies with oil, we'd laugh at death and live in the present. (333–4)

—only immediately to qualify its possibility: 'Why did every one of my fantasies turn into a trap?' (334). She is unable to imagine an existence that does not involve entrapment.

Joan's life so far has merely reinscribed a circular plot of flight and rescue from an endless series of perceived traps. Fleeing her Canadian parental home and the rituals of 'making up' enforced by her mother, Joan 'flew' to England, where, after falling from a bus, she was rescued by an archetypal chauvinist, Count Paul, whose lover she became. Disillusioned by Paul's failure to live up to her expectations of heroism and increasingly frightened by his possessiveness, Joan left him some months later, fleeing into the arms of another male rescuer, Arthur. But in this new relationship, nothing changes. Joan is still firmly ensconsed in a romantic life narrative in which self-value and identity are defined by the presence and demands of a heroic male partner. She has merely shifted the locus of external self-definition from one idealized male figure (Paul) to another (Arthur): 'the right man [Arthur] had come along, complete with a cause I could devote myself to. My life had significance' (171).

Her next major flight was to Italy, seemingly opting for excommunication, but she finds its condition of non-recognition unbearable. Once there, she dreams only of rescue, or of a 'magic transformation'. 'I was', she writes, 'caged on my balcony waiting to change. . . . I was waiting for something to happen, the next turn of events (a circle? a spiral?). All my life I'd been hooked on plots' (310). The plot she has been hooked on is one of futile circularity, lived out by Joan and self-destructively reinscribed in her Gothic fictions: a narrative of escape and recapture disguised as rescue, of flight and fatal fall. Joan has mistakenly imagined that the only escape from the patriarchal plot within which she believes herself to be entrapped lies in flight or exile. What is needed, however, is not an abandonment of plotting *per se*, but a revolutionary rewriting of received plot in manner that does not trade recognition for (unrecognizable) 'safety' or meaning for (meaningless) 'reality', yet which offers (partial) release from prescribed roles and conventions. It requires active, revolutionary self-(co-)authorization, not passive conformity to 'rules' constituted extra-personally or the defeatist refusal to engage with others at all.

Rejecting the Myths of Essentiality and Flight

In the final pages of Atwood's novel, Joan performs precisely this kind of redemptive rewriting. She manages to break with the cyclic non-progression of a conventional romance plot in *Stalked by Love*, and, as a consequence, is also able to discard the self-destructive plot of alternating flight and (male) rescue which has patterned her life to date. *Stalked by Love* is peopled by a cast of stereotypical characters. Charlotte, the stock heroine is an 'eternal virgin on the run' (131) who, at her mother's behest, is waiting for *'the right man'* (127); she is *'young and pretty'* (129) and thoroughly virtuous, having sworn an oath on her mother's deathbed to *'tell the truth, to be pure, circumspect and obedient'* (127; note the maternal source of constraining behavioural rules). She is lusted after by the Lord of Redmond Grange, who has employed her to mend the jewellery of his wife Felicia. Redmond, in appearance and demeanour, similarly fulfils the stock characteristics of a Gothic romance hero: he is (sexually) threatening, but a potential rescuer too. Tall and handsome, with *'strong arms'* and *'warm lips'* (333), his roving eye appraises Charlotte *'lustfully, ruthlessly'* (317). He has a tendency to dally with the serving maids, but Charlotte believes that *'if he were truly loved, unselfishly and purely . . . he would be a different man'* (193). Lady Felicia, who is Redmond's third wife, conforms to the stereotypical characterization of the 'evil wife' who must be killed off in order to make possible the 'happy ending' of Charlotte and Redmond's union. She is beautiful, spiteful, contemptuous, and vindictive; she has a *'scandalous reputation'* (129) which matches that of her husband for marital improbity, and is consumed by jealousy at Redmond's admiration for Charlotte.

On reappraising the manuscript of *Stalked by Love* soon after her arrival in Italy, Joan is initially pleased with it. The story is progressing well towards its expected conclusion. The heroine, Charlotte, is in peril: 'The house was after her, the master of the house as well, and possibly the mistress' (131). The conventional narrative ending seems to be clearly in sight. Charlotte has been taken through several narrow escapes: 'twice she'd been on the verge of rape, and she'd almost been murdered once' (316). All that remains is to write the expected ending: '[Joan] knew what had to happen. Felicia of course, would have to die; such was the fate of wives' (316). Charlotte and

Redmond, after some misunderstanding, would be blissfully united; Charlotte's virtue would be rewarded by 'the prize, the prizes in fact, for in addition to Redmond she would get the emeralds, the family silver, deeds of land stowed away in attics', and control over the running of the Grange (317).

This is what *should* happen, but as Joan's self-parodic tone in the above citations suggests, she finds herself struggling to write the expected story, overtly rebelling against the myth of feminine acquiescence it would sustain. She becomes increasingly sympathetic to the needs, desires, and monstrous jealousy of the soon-to-be ousted wife, Felicia. Joan breaks Gothic genre rules in order to detail Felicia's neglect by Redmond and her (meta-fictional) realization of the apparent necessity of her own demise: '*Perhaps she* [Felicia] *could foresee that life would have to be arranged for the convenience of Charlotte, after all, and that she herself would have to be disposed of. . . . She was afraid of death. All she wanted was happiness with the man she loved*' (319). Within the terms of conventional romance fiction, sympathy for Felicia is 'all wrong', as Joan realizes: it was 'out of the question, it was against the rules, it would foul up the plot completely' (319). Felicia *must* die because, as Joan explains, 'in my books all wives were eventually either mad or dead, or both' (319). But Charlotte's perfectly feminine 'intact virtue' and 'tidy ways' were beginning to pall; Joan longed for this paragon 'to fall into a mud puddle, have menstrual cramps, sweat, burp, fart' (319). The socially scripted role of feminist perfection which is epitomized in the figure of Charlotte, whose beautiful face and body model the heroinic 'shape' demanded by society, is stifling: 'Wearing Charlotte was like wearing a hair shirt, she made me itchy' (319).

Joan struggles to bring *Stalked by Love* to its expected conclusion. At first, in accordance with the expected plot, she 'kills' Felicia, writing her out of the fiction—or so it seems. But we soon learn that Felicia did not really die; she was only presumed dead after a drowning accident in which her body was never found. Like the 'dead' Joan who authors her, Felicia in fact lives on, unbeknown to her husband and his next wife in line, Charlotte. As Joan continues to write, the parallels between her own situation (her apparent death by drowning while remaining alive) and that of Felicia become increasingly evident. The setting and characters in Atwood's fiction (Joan in Italy) and those in Joan's fiction (Felicia and Charlotte at Redmond Grange) become increasingly hard to disentangle, as Joan vicariously enacts her own revolutionary rewriting of self through the agency of the rebellious character Felicia. Not only does Felicia look like Joan (she has the same long red hair, green eyes, and small white teeth), but she harbours the same secret beneath the disguise of her beauty: her perfect 'shape' was merely a socially acceptable mask. When Felicia reappears on the scene at Redmond Grange, after several months of absence during which Redmond and Charlotte busily make plans to marry, she is no longer thin and beautiful. Redmond is taking an evening stroll on the terrace when

> The shrubberies stirred and a figure stepped out from them, blocking his path. It was an enormously fat woman. . . . damp strands of red hair straggled down her bloated face like trickles of blood.
> 'Redmond, don't you know me?' the woman said in a throaty voice which, he recognised with horror, was Felicia's.
> 'Well,' he said with marked insincerity, 'I certainly am glad you didn't drown after all. But where have you been for these last two months?' (322)

This scene encapsulates all Joan's fears about a return from her self-imposed exile (to Canada, to Arthur, to the past) and her terror at the discovery of her duplicity: Redmond (as Arthur) reacts to Felicia's (as Joan's) unmasked appearance with 'repugnance' and 'disgust'. The confusing ontological migration of 'real' world characters (Joan and Arthur) into the fictional world of Joan's novel *Stalked by Love* becomes overt in the interpenetration of authorial and character-ological personae and ontologies.

> 'You don't want me,' [Felicia] said brokenly. She began to cry, her large body shaken by uncontrollable sobs. What could he do? 'You didn't want me to come back at all,' she wept. 'You're happier without me . . . and it was such an effort, Arthur, to get out of that water and come back all this way, just to be with you again. . . .'
> Redmond drew back, puzzled. 'Who is Arthur?' he asked.
> The woman began to fade, like mist, like invisible ink, like melting snow (323; Atwood's points of suspension)

From this point on, rather than being the means by which Joan passively reinscribes a conventional patriarchal plot, *Stalked by Love* becomes the arena for Joan's confrontation with the restrictive myths of idealized femininity. Furthermore, by writing herself (as Felicia) into this increasingly deviant text, Joan begins the revision of her own narrative of selfhood.

Before any final conclusion can be reached, however, Joan must relinquish one more self-deception: the belief in herself as the helpless victim of social demands of femininity, which are encoded, in her memory, in the figure of her mother. It is from her mother that Joan first learned the art of self-concealment, merely duplicating in her self-defensive mask of fatness, and later in her disguise of beauty and thinness, her mother's own defensive tactics of 'making up'. As a small child, Joan often watched, fascinated, as her mother 'put on her face' (66) in front of her triple-mirror vanity table.[12] She was particularly intrigued by her mother's mouth: 'Her lips were thin but she made a larger mouth with lipstick over and around them, like Bette Davies, which gave her a curious double mouth, the real one showing through the false one like a shadow' (68; see also 173 and 329). The image of the dual mouth is a recurrent motif throughout *Lady Oracle*, suggestive of the double standards and duplicity demanded by patriarchal society, in which conformity to (male) expectations of femininity often necessitates the masking—making over—of one's (women's) desires.[13] Women speak and act—make

---

[12] Atwood here draws attention to the repressed 'monster woman' famously theorized in Sandra Gilbert and Susan Gubar's *The Mad Woman in the Attic: The Woman Writer and the Nineteenth Century Literary Imagination* (New Haven: Yale University Press, 1979). Joan's mother's three-way mirror gave three images of the viewer: of the front and both sides of the head. In a persistent childhood dream Joan watched her mother make up in front of the mirror, suddenly realizing that 'instead of three reflections she [her mother] had three actual heads, which rose from her towelled shoulders on three separate necks' (66–7). In the dream there is a man outside the door, about to enter her mother's dressing-room. Joan experienced two versions of the dream: in the first she desperately feared the man's discovery of the truth that her 'mother was a monster' (67); in the second she wished him to enter the room and to discover the secret. The image of a 'triple-headed monster' continues to appear in Joan's fantasies and nightmares throughout the book, functioning as a symbol for the deception and monstrosity of making oneself up, an activity that involves repression of one's transgressive otherness, in accordance with social convention. Joan's purchase of a similar three-sided mirror while married to Arthur (219) suggests her conformity to social expectations of femininity, in appearance and behaviour. The motif of a man on the other side of the door, behind which some secret is kept, recurs throughout *Lady Oracle*, culminating in the figure of the newspaper reporter who threatens to enter Joan's Italian villa and expose the deception of her faked death.

[13] Atwood's concern is primarily with women's self-sublimation in the make-overs demanded by convention, particularly with the way in which this self-destructive pattern of behaviour is passed down from mother to daughter in the manner so clearly portrayed here. However, she is also aware of the way in which men are equally victims of (female) social expectation. Joan, e.g., continuously bemoans the fact that Arthur fails to fulfil her ideal of male heroism (8 and 197); he is, as she describes him, 'a man in a cage, like most men' (67).

themselves up—in ways that are often wholly contrary to their uncensored wants and needs. In this society, unattractive women are condemned to the apparent penury of a husbandless, childless existence. 'Don't you want to get married?' is the question repeatedly asked of the overweight teenage Joan (83; also 51).

In Italy, in the last of a series of daydreams and nightmarish fantasies, Joan imagines the appearance of her dead mother's ghost. Although Joan's mother has been physically absent from her daughter's life for some time (first because of the teenage Joan's deliberate separation from her by leaving home and later because of her death), she remains a potent psychological shaping presence throughout Joan's adult life, as evidenced by the frequent (imagined) appearance of her mother's 'astral body' (see 111, 173, 329). The final appearance of Joan's mother's ghost is of vital importance in *Lady Oracle*, for it marks the moment in which Joan first recognizes her need (and ability) to be responsible for her own narrative constructions. She is at last able to reject the inherited image of patriarchal femininity bequeathed by her mother, an image which Joan has adopted as her own. The ghost of her mother and its guilt-evoking prescriptive power (like the equally diaphanous figure of the ectoplasmic Fat Lady) is the product of Joan's own imaginings. It is no more than the imaginary embodiment of Joan's own guilt and fears with regard to her failure to conform to social expectations of femininity. In order to escape its admonishing presence and constitutive demands, Joan must disempower it by renouncing its (and hence her own learned) repressive injunctions. This she finally does. In the fantasy, the face of her mother's ghost is 'made up' as surely as it was in all Joan's memories of her: her lipsticked mouth is double, and she weeps black tears of mascara. It appears outside the window of Joan's Italian villa, on the other side of the glass, where Joan can see it but not touch it, and pleads with Joan to join it on the other side, the side of the dead. Joan resists the impulse to comply with this suicidal injunction: returning to the repressed 'maternal', the realm, of dyadic unity beyond or without consciousness, is suicidal, for it entails the relinquishment of one's consciousness (of oneself). And adopting her mother's stifling conformist mask in life is figurative death, another form of suicide. Joan realizes that the ghost of her mother is an image she can wilfully relinquish: 'She'd [Joan's mother] never really let go of me because I had never let her go. . . . She needed her freedom also; she had been my reflection too long' (329–30). This realization enables Joan to expunge the internalized (self-)image of ideal femininity which she has learned from her mother and maintained as her own, for she recognizes that it is she who writes the narrative of self-victimization, guilt, and repression previously attributed to her mother (and the society to whose expectations she conforms).

Having rejected the myth of femininity mistakenly thought to be imposed from without, Joan is now ready to take responsibility for rewriting the narrative within: to consciously revise her own narrative of selfhood, in contrast to the unconscious narrative subversions achieved earlier in her automatic writing. The power of creative subversion is given concrete expression as she completes her latest novel. She now writes two possible conclusions to her story, describing the entrance of both female protagonists into the forbidden maze at Redmond Grange: first Charlotte (the epitome of 'angelic' social conformity: pure, chaste, virginal), then Felicia (the 'madwoman' wife, evil and destructive).[14] The maze dominates the household at the Grange and the fiction *Stalked by Love*. It has been the site of extensive rumour amongst the cast of characters. Charlotte has been repeatedly warned of its danger by the Grange housekeeper, who tells her: '[s]ome say as how there's no center to the maze and that's how they get lost, they gets into it and they can't find their way out. Some say as how the first Lady Redmond and the second one are still in there, wandering around in circles' (186–7). Initially, Joan decides that Charlotte must enter the maze, and ponders the consequences of this action:

> Charlotte would have to go into the maze, there was no way out of it. . . . [But] did the maze mean certain death, or did it contain the answer to a riddle, an answer she must learn in order to live? More important: would she marry Redmond only if she stayed out of the maze, or only if she went in? Possibly she would be able to win his love only by risking her life and allowing him to rescue her. (331–2)

This version still manages to conform to romance genre requirements, providing a conventional 'happy ending' of rescue, union, and fulfilment. Once inside the maze, Charlotte is set upon by the murderous Felicia, only to be rescued by Redmond at the eleventh hour.

---

[14] In the terms of Gilbert and Gubar's analysis in *Madwoman in the Attic*, Felicia represents the repressed 'madwoman' condemned to silence/babble/death in a myth of feminine 'angelic' passivity embodied in the character of Charlotte.

But the myth in which virtuous heroinic femininity (Charlotte) is rewarded by male rescue, and anti-heroinic female transgression (Felicia) is punished by death, is no longer acceptable to Joan: 'that was the way it had always gone before, but somehow it no longer felt right' (333). The conventional happy ending must be rewritten. Joan writes a final version; this time Felicia goes into the maze. Unlike Charlotte, who wandered in circles without ever reaching the centre of the maze, Felicia soon finds herself in 'the central plot' where she is confronted by four women:

A stone bench ran along one side, and on it were seated four women. Two of them looked a lot like her, with red hair and green eyes and small white teeth. The third was middle aged, dressed in a strange garment that ended halfway up her calves, with a ratty piece of fur around her neck. The last was enormously fat. She was wearing a pair of pink tights and a short pink skirt covered with spangles. From her head sprouted two antennae, like a butterfly's, and a pair of obviously false wings were pinned to her back. . . .
'Who are you?' she asked.
'We are Lady Redmond,' said the middle-aged woman sadly. 'All of us,' the fat woman with the wings added.
'There must be some mistake,' Felicia protested. 'I myself am Lady Redmond.'
'Oh, yes, we know,' said the first woman. 'But every man has more than one wife. Sometimes all at once, sometimes one at a time, sometimes ones he doesn't even know about.' (341)

In tracing her own situational dilemma through the agency of her fictional characters, Joan has reached the central plot of her own subconscious meanderings. At the centre of the maze, Felicia confronts four figures that represent aspects of Joan: Joan the submissive wife of Arthur, Joan the lover of the Royal Porcupine and the mistress of Paul, Aunt Lou (the alternative maternal figure who does not endorse the strategy of making-up), and the Fat Lady (who is dressed in the butterfly costume—an image of flight and transformation—that Joan longed to wear as a child). Indoctrinated by a myth of the desirability of consistent singular selfhood, Joan has always run from the past and the recognition of her subjective plurality, in search of the impossible goal of essential, fixed personal identity. This has been her error to date; she has spent a lifetime 'looking, compulsively, for [her]self' (290).[15] But Atwood's novel is full of clues, often

[15] The error of a self-reflective, introspective search for essential selfhood (the Cartesian *cogito*) can be noted as early as the young Joan's Brownie days. Here she was taught to look into a mirror and say the 'magic word': 'Myself' (61).

uttered by the unaware Joan and directed to the ironically aware reader, about the error of seeking to escape one's plural selves and repressed desires. 'Pull yourself together' is a persistent refrain in the novel (see e.g. 13, 251, 328), '*I must be collected, I must collect myself*', Joan declares in a moment of blind panic at the end of the novel (339; emphasis original). Crucially, the centre of the conceptual maze is not the locus of a static, essential self; it offers the variety of difference rather than a fixed site of identity. Joan *is* the multiplicity of roles and personae she confronts here, '[s]ometimes all at once, sometimes one at a time'. She has many different selves; she exists in a variety of subject positions, each defined by their situation in a variety of determining communities, relationships, or contextual settings. Her sense of selfhood does not inhere in a fixed, essential self; it is the narrative of continuity which connects and interweaves the plurality of her disparate 'selves'.

Having come this far, one final myth needs revision: the pre-scripted plot of entrapment, escape, and rescue. Felicia is told by the women at the centre of the maze that the only way of escaping the maze is via a door which stands, enticingly, at its centre. The door appears to lead nowhere; it is framed, but otherwise unsupported, and it looks the same from both sides. Felicia turns the handle and the door swings open, revealing Redmond on the other side:

> *She was about to throw herself into his arms, weeping with relief, when she noticed an odd expression in his eyes. Then she knew. Redmond was the killer. He was a killer in disguise, he wanted to murder her as he had murdered his other wives. . . . He wanted to replace her with the other one, the next one, thin and flawless.* (342)

Felicia makes a momentous discovery: that 'as long as she stayed on her side of the door she would be safe' (342). In writing this, it appears that Joan has rejected the myth of escape to the other side, to an imaginary realm of stasis and wholeness. The interpretation of the ontological realms of writer and written, the words of *Lady Oracle* and *Stalked by Love*, continues as Redmond tries to lure Felicia through the door. Enacting a series of transformations, Redmond adopts the features of all the (duplicitous) men who have figured importantly in *Joan's* life: her father, Paul, the Royal Porcupine, and finally Arthur. In this last embodiment, Redmond-as-Arthur succeeds in tempting Felicia through the door with the words '*Let me rescue you. We will dance together forever, always*' (343). Resisting the seduction of this escapist lure, Felicia refuses Redmond, saying '*I know who you are*'. At this, '*the flesh fell away from his face, revealing the skull behind it*' (343). Male rescue, or escape to the other side, is finally exposed as deadly.

Having reached this point in her rewriting of the ending of *Stalked by Love*, Joan is interrupted by a knock on the door of her villa. She crouches behind the locked door, pondering whether or not to open the door to the man she knows is waiting outside. This scene is the culmination of behind-the-door images and references to the other side which permeate *Lady Oracle*: 'It struck me', writes Joan, 'that I'd spent too much of my time crouching behind closed doors, listening to the voices on the other side' (340). Thus cornered and waiting, she thinks: 'I still had options. I could pretend I wasn't there. I could wait and do nothing. I could disguise my voice and say that I was someone else. But if I turned the handle the door would unlock and swing outward, and I would have to face the man who stood waiting for me, for my life' (343). But Joan has learned with/through her character Felicia, and, rejecting the destructive, ultimately fatal nature of escape (she has, moreover, badly cut her feet, making flight impossible), she opens the door. It reveals not Arthur, as she expected, but an unknown man. The intruder is, it transpires, an investigative reporter who has tracked Joan down in her Italian hideaway following media speculation about whether her 'suicide' was in fact murder. He wants to write her (life-)story.

In opening the door, Joan rejects the 'options' of pretence, disguise, and the mask of otherness, which have proved so attractive to her in the past, and chooses instead to face, unmasked, the man who pursues her with (she imagines) murderous intent. Their confrontation is physical: Joan hits him over the head with a bottle, knocking him out and thereby (temporarily) silencing him and depriving him of his capacity to contradict Joan's version of events as she tells it to the police who arrive soon after (344). Importantly, when the reporter regains consciousness, Joan tells him her version of her story—the narrative of her life—which will form the basis of the story he will eventually write. In confronting him, rather than fleeing from him, she has literally taken into her hands her own power to contest his version of her. Rather than escape, she chooses to exercise her contestational voice in the activity of partial self-authorization; she has gained the power to speak/write (for) herself.

She now has the ability to controvert and challenge his and other readers' assumptions; she actively influences the story that others will know her by. Interpretative will-to-power, as I suggested in the chapter on Coetzee's *Foe*, is not (or need not be) the absolute power of an authoritative interpreter over a person subjected in the act of reading/writing. As potentially contestational speaking subjects, we are never simply passively written or read by an ontologically dominant author as are the characters in fiction. We exist within the same 'order' of language (to borrow a term from *Foe*) as those who attempt to comprehend us, and, from the variety of interpretative and discursive options available as a result of our plural placement in intersubjective communities, can actively influence and challenge others' interpretations of who we are, and the value-judgements others would make. Certainly, we can never wholly control the stories others write of us in their interpretative readings of who we are; but we can involve ourselves in the process of writing (our) meaning by engaging with our interpreters, communing and communicating with them, rather than escaping confrontation. Nor need we bind ourselves to some preconceived ideal of plotted causality or teleological resolution; we can celebrate the productivity of subjective open-endedness for the revisions and rewritings it makes possible. With Felicia, Joan has come to understand the need for the narrative integration of plural subject positions into her ongoing narrative of selfhood, a narrative that remains open to future change and adaptation: 'I don't have any definite plans', she writes, 'I don't think I'll ever be a very tidy person' (345).

In short, Joan has come to recognize the transgressive potential of willed deviance through the revisionary use of language and narrative. Eschewing escape, she chooses to challenge the potentially totalizing power of the journalist's interpretation of her, actively confronting him and asserting her own power of (partial) self-narrativization. This is very far from a utopian aesthetic that promotes excommunication from discursive authority. To utilize the spatial metaphors offered earlier, Joan chooses to situate herself in a transgressive marginal community (or rather communities, for the sites she occupies, the selves at the centre of the labyrinth, are plural), recognizing the revisionary capacity of such chosen positionality. She recognizes the need to challenge and controvert, *in* language, resisting the temptation of suicidal escape to an impossible other side, the penury/paradise of excommunication.

Agonistic Encounters

In Chapter 3 I considered a fundamental feminist claim about the victimization of women 'socialized' under the tyranny of patriarchal discourse. Adrienne Munich is exemplary: 'When women speak', she writes, 'they cannot help but enter male-dominated discourse; speaking women are silent women.'[16] I suggested that a theory of linguistic subjection and gender socialization, which posits the conformist 'making-up' by speaking women in accordance with patriarchal norms of femininity encoded in language, in fact overlooks the contestational power available to women if they choose to situate themselves as language-users in a variety of potentially contestational discursive sites within language. Bracketing the plurality of communities of language use and the transgressive interpretative tactics they make available to speaking subjects results in the kind of reductive dualism of inside/outside that underscores many poststructuralist accounts of subjectivity: either submission to the procedural dictates of language, to writtenness within the rule-bound structures of *langue*, or escape from language, release from the conventions that enable communication into the dissolute bliss of unrequited *différance*. In Adler's *Pitch Dark*, Kate's resigned acceptance of conformity and dismal hope for nothing more than 'a surprise within the rules' exemplifies this first stance; the renunciation of community for wilderness and language for silence by Atwood's protagonist in *Surfacing* exemplifies the second. All too readily, this may lead to an ostensibly revolutionary, but in fact defeatist, separatist feminist programme which advocates the abstention of women from prevailing modes of discourse for fear that speaking and writing in patriarchal language will only reinscribe its censorial ideology. Escape from communicative norms and rationality into the rarefied realm of an unmapped and unmappable female linguistic utopia is then endorsed.

In challenging the assumptions of such bleak theorizing, I have argued that if revolutionary changes in intersubjectively held (gender) values are to take place, what is needed is active confrontation with, not passive abstention from, those values and practices we find unacceptable. We need to theorize our ability to evaluate, retrospectively revise, and make choices between acceptable and unacceptable

---

[16] Adrienne Munich, 'Notorious Signs, Feminist Criticism and Literary Tradition', in Gayle Greene and Coppélia Kahn (eds.), *Making a Difference: Feminist Literary Criticism* (London and New York: Routledge, 1985), 239.

modes of discourse and the values they reinscribe, not advocate the abandonment of meaningful discursive practice altogether. Making such evaluations does not require objective placement outside language, which is clearly impossible if we are to remain conscious of ourselves as selves and be able to both act and communicate meaningfully. Simultaneously situated as speaking subjects in a variety of interpretative and discursive communities within language, we have at our disposal a variety of alternative possibilities for interpretation and meaningful communication. Becoming conscious of 'surprise' subversions and actively utilizing their challenging potential, we may reflexively (if retrospectively) evaluate the new possibilities they open to us as speaking subjects, and in doing so, modify, revise, and even replace existing communicative norms.

The idea that language use may be creative and constructive within certain structural restraints is one endorsed by a growing number of contemporary critics, and provides a much-needed counter to the unacceptable dualisms promoted by some poststructuralist theorists. In *Beyond Feminist Aesthetics*, for example, Rita Felski offers a feminist argument along these lines. She rejects both 'the notion of a self-determining ego' and also 'a theory of structural determination which defines subjectivity as an epiphenomenal product in the self-reproduction of social and discursive systems' in favour of 'a dynamic model of social reproduction and human communication'.[17] Utilizing the structuration theory developed by sociologist Anthony Giddens (see Chapter 5), she promotes a model 'which allows for a more dialectical understanding of the relationship between subjectivity and social structures'.[18] She continues, in a critique of theories of linguistic determinism:

The recognition that individuals are not 'spoken' by an abstract, pre-existing linguistic system, but that language is rather a social practice [or rather a plurality of social practices] which is contextually determined and open to varying degrees of modification and change makes possible a more differentiated understanding of discourse which is potentially more productive from the standpoint of feminist politics. The significance of particular communicative practices needs to be located in the

[17] Rita Felski, *Beyond Feminist Aesthetics: Feminist Literature and Social Change* (Cambridge, Mass.: Harvard University Press, 1989), 55.
[18] Ibid.

contexts of their use, in the functions they serve for particular social groups at specific historical conjunctures.[19]

This is not to suggest that we lose sight of the circumscribing power of unquestioned, blindly accepted discursive practices and social definitions. Feminist (and post-colonial) writers and theorists have done much to draw our attention to the prescriptive power of supposedly neutral definitions, descriptions, and communicative conventions. This warning note is clearly evident in *Lady Oracle*, which invites us to observe the way that social codes and inter-subjective expectations 'subject' subjects in the learned rituals of repression and making-up that are passed from mother to daughter and imposed on Joan by the various men in her life. But the novel is not content to lament rule-bound subjective writtenness or to endorse French feminist utopianism; it submits that, in language, strategies are at hand for subjective and social transformation through creative, rule-breaking narrativization. It warns against the twin dangers of essentialism and escape, urging instead active engagement with others in the communicative matrix that shapes our self-conceptions and the interpretations of others. In short, *Lady Oracle* offers a working model of what Allen Thiher describes as the 'rule-bound freedom' of literary and linguistic creativity, in which 'the writer can view his struggle with language less as a condemnation to defeat than as an agonistic encounter for which he can invent some of the rules'.[20] Actualization of revisionary possibility is never merely 'a surprise within the rules'. It is a creative power available to all who use language.

[19] Felski, *Beyond Feminist Aesthetics*, 65. Felski notes Giddens's reliance on Wittgenstein's theory of social communication, and uses both theorists to back her assertion that 'meaning is necessarily derived from use; language constitutes a form of social interaction which presupposes publicly shared intersubjective meanings'.

[20] Allen Thiher, *Words in Reflection: Modern Language Theory and Post-modern Fiction* (Chicago: University of Chicago Press, 1984), 156.

Bibliography of Works Cited

ADLER, RENATA, *Pitch Dark* (London: Hamish Hamilton, 1983).

ALTER, ROBERT, *Partial Magic: The Novel as a Self-Conscious Genre* (Berkeley and London: University of California Press, 1975).

ASHLEY, KATHLEEN; GILMORE, LEIGH; and PETERS, GERALD, *Autobiography and Postmodernism* (Amherst, Mass.: University of Massachusetts Press, 1994).

ATTRIDGE, DEREK, 'The Silence of the Canon: J. M. Coetzee's *Foe*, Cultural Narrative, and Political Oppression', in Karen Lawrence (ed.), *Decolonizing Tradition: New Views of Twentieth Century 'British' Literary Canon* (Urbana, Ill.: University of Illinois Press, 1992), 212–38.

ATWOOD, MARGARET, *Lady Oracle* (1977; London: Virago, 1982).

—— *Surfacing* (1979; London: Virago, 1984).

AVINERI, SHLOMO, and DE-SHALIT, AVNER (eds.), *Communitarianism and Individualism* (Oxford: Oxford University Press, 1992).

BAKHTIN, MIKHAIL M., *The Dialogic Imagination*, trans. Caryl Emerson and Michael Holquist. Ed. Michael Holquist (Austin, Tex.: University of Texas Press, 1981).

—— *Problems of Dostoevsky's Poetics* (1929), ed. and trans. Caryl Emerson (Manchester: Manchester University Press, 1984).

—— *Rabelais and his World*, trans. Helene Iwolsky (Bloomington, Ind.: Indiana University Press, 1984).

BALIBAR, ETIENNE, and MACHEEY, PIERRE, 'On Literature as an Ideological Form', in Robert Young (ed.), *Untying the Text: A Post-Structuralist Reader* (Boston, London, and Henley: Routledge and Kegan Paul, 1981).

BANVILLE, JOHN, *The Book of Evidence* (London: Secker and Warburg, 1989).

BARBER, BENJAMIN, *Strong Democracy* (Berkeley, University of California Press, 1984).

BARRETT, MICHÈLE, *Women's Oppression Today: Problems in Marxist Feminist Analysis* (London: Villiers Publications, 1980).

BARRETT, WILLIAM, *Death of the Soul: From Descartes to the Computer* (Oxford: Clarendon Press, 1987).

BARTH, JOHN, 'The Literature of Exhaustion', in Malcolm Bradbury (ed.), *The Novel Today: Contemporary Writers on Modern Fiction* (London: Fontana, 1977), 70–83.

—— 'The Literature of Replenishment', *Atlantic Monthly*, 245/1 (1980), 67–71.

BARTHES, ROLAND, *Image-Music-Text*, trans. and ed. Simon Heath (New York: Hill and Wang, 1977).
—— *The Pleasure of the Text*, trans. Richard Miller (London: Jonathan Cape, 1976).

BECKETT, SAMUEL, *Three Novels: Malloy, Malone Dies, and the Unnamable*, trans. Samuel Beckett (New York: Grove Press, 1955).

BEITCHMAN, PHILIP, *I am a Process with no Subject* (Gainesville, Fla.: University of Florida Press, 1988).

BENHABIB, SEYLA, *Critique, Norm and Utopia: Study of the Foundations of Critical Theory* (New York: Columbia University Press, 1986).

BENSTOCK, SHARI (ed.), *The Private Self: Theory and Practice of Women's Autobiographical Writings* (Chapel Hill, NC: University of North Carolina Press, 1988).

BENVENISTE, EMILE, *Problems in General Linguistics*, Vol. 1, trans. Mary E. Meek (Coral Gables, Fla.: University of Miami Press, 1971).

BERSANI, LEO, *Balzac to Beckett: Center and Circumference in French Fiction* (New York: Oxford University Press, 1970).
—— *The Freudian Body* (New York: Columbia University Press, 1986).
—— *A Future for Astyanax: Character and Desire in Literature* (London: Marion Boyars, 1978).

BLOOM, HAROLD, *The Anxiety of Influence* (New York and Oxford: Oxford University Press, 1973).

BÖK, CHRISTIAN, 'Sibyls: Echoes of French Feminism in *The Diviners* and *Lady Oracle*', *Canadian Literature*, 135 (Winter 1992), 80–93.

BONDI, LIZ, 'Locating Identity Politics', in Michael Keith and Steve Pile (eds.), *Place and the Politics of Identity* (London and New York: Routledge, 1993), 84–101.

BOOKER, M. KEITH, *Techniques of Subversion in Modern Literature: Transgression, Abjection, and the Carnivalesque* (Gainesville, Fla.: University of Florida Press, 1991).

BOOTH, WAYNE C., *The Company We Keep: An Ethics of Fiction* (Berkeley and London: University of California Press, 1988).

BORGES, JORGES LOUIS, 'A Note on (towards) Bernard Shaw', in D. A. Yates and J. E. Irby (eds.),*Labyrinthes* (New York: Penguin, 1970).

BOWIE, ANDREW, *Aesthetics and Subjectivity: From Kant to Nietzsche* (Manchester: Manchester University Press, 1990).

BOYNE, ROY, 'Power-Knowledge and Social Theory: The Systematic Misrepresentation of Contemporary French Social Theory in the Work of Anthony Giddens', in Christopher G. A. Bryant and David Jary (eds.), *Giddens' Theory of Structuration: A Critical Appreciation* (London and New York: Routledge, 1991), 52–73.

BROOKS, PETER, *Reading for the Plot: Design and Intention in Narrative* (1984; Cambridge, Mass., and London: Harvard University Press, 1992).

BRYANT, CHRISTOPHER G. A. AND JARY, DAVID (eds.), *Giddens' Theory of Structuration: A Critical Appreciation* (London and New York: Routledge, 1991).

BUTLER, CHRISTOPHER, *After the Wake: An Essay on the Contemporary Avant-Garde* (Oxford: Clarendon Press, 1980).

—— 'The Future of Theory: Saving the Reader', in Ralph Cohen (ed.), *The Future of Literary Theory* (New York and London: Routledge, 1989), 229–49.

BUTLER, JUDITH, 'The Body Politics of Julia Kristeva', *Hypatia: A Journal of Feminist Philosophy*, 3/3 (Winter 1989), 104–18.

CAHOONE, LAWRENCE E., *The Dilemma of Modernity: Philosophy, Culture, and Anti-Culture* (Albany, NY: State University of New York Press, 1988).

CALINESCU, MATEI and FOKEMMA, DOUWE (eds.), *Exploring Postmodernism* (Amsterdam and Philadelphia: John Benjamins, 1987).

CAMERON, DEBORAH, *Feminism and Linguistic Theory* (London: Macmillan, 1985).

CARAMELLO, CHARLES, *Silverless Mirrors: Book, Self and Postmodern American Fiction* (Tallahassee, Fla.: University Press of Florida, 1983).

CARROLL, DAVID, *Paraesthetics: Foucault, Lyotard, Derrida* (New York and London: Methuen, 1987).

—— *The Subject in Question: The Language of Theory and the Strategies of Fiction* (Chicago and London: University of Chicago Press, 1982).

CASCARDI, ANTHONY, *The Subject of Modernity* (Cambridge: Cambridge University Press, 1992).

CIXOUS, HÉLÈNE, 'Castration or Decapitation?', trans. Annette Kuhn, *Signs*, 7/1 (1981), 36–55.

CLADIS, MARK S., 'Wittgenstein, Rawls and Conservatism', *Philosophy and Social Criticism*, 20/1–2 (1994), 13–27.

COETZEE, J. M., *Foe* (1986; Harmondsworth: Penguin, 1988).

COHEN, ANTHONY PAUL, *The Symbolic Construction of Community* (London: Tavistock, 1985).

COLOMINA, B. (ed.), *Sexuality and Space* (New York: Princeton Architectural Press, 1992).

CONNOR, STEVEN, *Postmodernist Culture: An Introduction to Theories of the Contemporary* (Oxford: Basil Blackwell, 1989).

—— *Theory and Cultural Value* (Oxford: Basil Blackwell, 1992).

CORLETT, WILLIAM, *Community without Unity: A Politics of Derridean Extravagance* (Durham, NC, and London: Duke University Press, 1989).

CRITES, STEPHEN, 'Storytime: Recollecting the Past and Projecting the Future', in Theodore Sarbin (ed.), *Narrative Psychology: The Storied Nature of Human Conduct* (New York: Praeger, 1986).

CROSMAN, RICHARD, 'Do Readers Make Meaning?', in Susan Rubin

Suleiman and Inge Crosman (eds.), *The Reader in the Text: Essays on Audience and Reception* (Princeton: Princeton University Press, 1980), 149–64.

CULLER, JONATHAN, *On Deconstruction: Theory and Criticism after Structuralism* (London: Routledge and Kegan Paul, 1983).

DANTO, ARTHUR, *Narration and Knowledge* (New York: Columbia University Press, 1985).

DELAMOTTE, EUGENIA C., *Perils of the Night: A Feminist Study of Nineteenth-Century Gothic* (New York: Oxford University Press, 1990).

DELEUZE, GILLES, *Empiricism and Subjectivity: An Essay on Hume's Theory of Human Nature*, trans. and intr. Constantin V. Boundas (New York: Columbia University Press, 1991).

—— and GUATTARI, FELIX, *Anti-Oedipus: Capitalism and Schizophrenia*, trans. Robert Hurley, Mark Seem, and Helen Lane (New York: Viking, 1977).

DENNETT, DANIEL, *Elbow Room: The Varieties of Free Will Worth Wanting* (Oxford: Clarendon Press, 1984).

DERRIDA, JACQUES, *Dissemination*, trans. B. Johnson (London: Athlone Press, 1981).

—— *Glas*, trans. John P. Leavey, Jr., and Richard Rand (1974; Lincoln, Nebr.: University of Nebraska Press, 1986).

—— 'Limited Inc. abc . . .', trans. S. Weber,*Glyph*, 2 (1977), 162–251.

—— *Of Grammatology*, trans. Gayatri Chakravorty Spivak (1967; Baltimore: Johns Hopkins University Press, 1976).

—— *Positions*, trans. A. Bass (Chicago: University of Chicago Press, 1982).

—— 'Sending: On Representation', trans. Peter and Mary Ann Caws, *Social Research*, 49/2 (Summer 1982), 294–326.

—— 'Signature Event Context', *Glyph*, 1 (1977), 172–97.

—— *Speech and Phenomena: And Other Essays on Husserl's Theory of Signs*, trans. David B. Allison (Evanston, Ill.: Northwestern University Press, 1973).

—— 'Structure, Sign and Play in the Discourse of the Human Sciences', in Richard Macksey and Eugenio Donato (eds.), *The Structuralist Controversy: The Language of Criticism and the Science of Man* (Baltimore: Johns Hopkins University Press, 1972), 247–65.

—— *Writing and Difference*, trans. Alan Bass (1967; Chicago: University of Chicago Press, 1978).

DEWS, PETER, Editor's Introduction to *Jürgen Habermas: Autonomy and Solidarity: Interviews* (London: Verso, 1986).

—— *The Logics of Disintegration: Post-structuralist Thought and the Claims of Critical Theory* (London and New York: Verso, 1987).

DOCHERTY, THOMAS, *Reading (Absent) Character: Towards a Theory of Characterization in Fiction* (Oxford: Clarendon Press, 1983).

DONOGHUE, DENIS, 'Her Man Friday', *New York Times Book Review*, 22 Feb. 1987, p. 27.

DWORKIN, RONALD, 'Liberal Community', in Shlomo Avineri and Avner de-Shalit (eds.), *Communitarianism and Individualism* (Oxford: Oxford University Press, 1992), 205–24.

—— *A Matter of Principle* (Cambridge, Mass.: Harvard University Press, 1985).

EAGLETON, TERRY, *The Ideology of the Aesthetic* (Oxford: Basil Blackwell, 1990).

EAKIN, PAUL JOHN, *Fictions in Autobiography* (Princeton: Princeton University Press, 1985).

ELBAZ, ROBERT, *The Changing Nature of the Self: A Critical Study of the Autobiographical Discourse* (London: Croom Helm, 1988).

ENGSTRÖM, TIMOTHY H., 'The Postmodern Sublime?: Philosophical Rehabilitations and Pragmatic Evasions', *Boundary 2*, 20/2 (1993), 190–204.

FEDERMAN, RAYMOND, *Surfiction: Fiction Now and Tomorrow* (Chicago: Swallow Press, 1975).

—— *Take It or Leave It* (New York: Fiction Collective, 1976).

—— *The Twofold Vibration* (Bloomington, Ind.: Indiana University Press and Brighton: Harvester Press, 1982).

FELPERIN, HOWARD, *Beyond Deconstruction: The Uses and Abuses of Literary Theory* (Oxford: Clarendon Press, 1985).

FELSKI, RITA, *Beyond Feminist Aesthetics: Feminist Literature and Social Change* (Cambridge, Mass.: Harvard University Press, 1989).

FICHTE, JOHANN G., *The Vocation of Man* (La Salle, Ill.: Open Court, 1965).

FISH, STANLEY, *Doing What Comes Naturally: Change, Rhetoric, and the Practice of Theory in Literary and Legal Studies* (Oxford: Clarendon Press, 1989).

FLEENOR, JULIANN (ed.), *The Female Gothic* (London: Eden Press, 1983).

FLETCHER, JOHN, *The Novels of Samuel Beckett* (London: Chatto and Windus, 1972).

FOUCAULT, MICHEL, *The Foucault Reader*, ed. Paul Rainbow (New York: Pantheon, 1984).

—— *Madness and Civilisation: A History of Insanity*, trans. Richard Howard (New York: Vintage Books, 1965).

—— 'The Order of Discourse', in Robert Young (ed.), *Untying the Text: A Post-Structuralist Reader* (Boston, London, and Henley: Routledge and Kegan Paul, 1981), 48–78.

—— *The Order of Things: An Archaeology of the Human Sciences* (1966; New York: Vintage Books, 1973).

FRASER, NANCY, 'The Uses and Abuses of French Discourse Theories for Feminist Politics', *Boundary 2*, 17/2 (1990), 82–101.

FREEMAN, MARK, *Rewriting the Self: History, Memory, Narrative* (London and New York: Routledge, 1993).

FRIEDMAN, MARILYN, 'Feminism and Modern Friendship: Dislocating the Community', in Shlomo Avineri and Avner de-Shalit (eds.), *Communitarianism and Individualism* (Oxford: Oxford University Press, 1992), 101–19.

FULLBROOK, KATE, *Free Women: Ethics and Aesthetics in Twentieth Century Women's Fiction* (Hemel Hempstead: Harvester Press, 1990).

FUSS, DIANA, *Essentially Speaking: Feminism, Nature and Difference* (London: Routledge, 1989).

—— 'Inside/Out', in Diana Fuss (ed.), *Inside/Out: Lesbian Theories, Gay Theories* (New York: Routledge, 1991), 235–57.

GADAMER, HANS-GEORG, *Philosophical Hermeneutics*, trans. and ed. David E. Linge (Berkeley: University of California Press, 1976).

—— *Truth and Method* (New York: Seabury Press, 1975).

GALLOP, JANE, *The Daughter's Seduction: Feminism and Psychoanalysis* (Ithaca, NY: Cornell University Press, 1982).

GARDAM, JANE, 'The Only Story', *The* [London] *Sunday Times*, 7 Sept. 1986, p. 49.

GASCHÉ, RODOLPHE, *The Tain of the Mirror: Derrida and the Philosophy of Reflection* (Cambridge, Mass., and London: Harvard University Press, 1986).

GAUTHIER, XAVIÈRE, 'Is There Such a Thing as Women's Writing?', in Elaine Marks and Isabelle de Courtivron (eds.), (Brighton: Harvester Press, 1980), 161–4.

GIDDENS, ANTHONY, *The Consequences of Modernity* (Cambridge: Polity Press; Stanford Calif.: Stanford University Press, 1990).

—— *Modernity and Self-Identity: Self and Society in the Late Modern Age* (Cambridge: Polity Press, 1991).

—— *New Rules of Sociological Method: A Positive Critique of Interpretative Sociologies*, 2nd edn. (Cambridge: Polity Press, 1993).

—— *Social Theory and Modern Sociology* (Stanford, Calif.: Stanford University Press, 1987).

—— 'Structuration Theory: Past, Present and Future', in Christopher G. A. Bryant and David Jary (eds.), *Giddens' Theory of Structuration: A Critical Appreciation* (London and New York: Routledge, 1991), 201–21.

—— *Studies in Social and Political Theory* (London: Hutchinson; New York: Basic Books, 1977).

GILBERT, SANDRA, and GUBAR, SUSAN, *The Madwoman in the Attic: The Woman Writer and the Nineteenth Century Literary Imagination* (New Haven: Yale University Press, 1979).

GILMORE, LEIGH, *Autobiographics: A Feminist Theory of Women's Self-Representation* (Ithaca, NY: Cornell University Press, 1994).

GLOVER, JONATHAN, *I: The Philosophy and Psychology of Personal Identity* (Harmondsworth: Penguin, 1988).

GOODHEART, EUGENE, *The Cult of the Ego: The Self in Modern Literature* (Chicago and London: University of Chicago Press, 1968).

GOODMAN, NELSON, 'Twisted Tales; or, Story, Study, and Symphony', in W. J. T. Mitchell (ed.), *On Narrative* (Chicago and London: University of Chicago Press, 1981), 99–116.

GRAFF, GERALD, 'The Pseudo-Politics of Interpretation', in W. J. T. Mitchell (ed.), *The Politics of Interpretation* (Chicago and London: University of Chicago Press, 1982), 145–58.

GRANT, PATRICK, *Literature and Personal Values* (London and Basingstoke: Macmillan, 1992).

GUTMAN, AMY, 'Communitarian Critics of Liberalism', in Shlomo Avineri and Avner de-Shalit (eds.), *Communitarianism and Individualism* (Oxford: Oxford University Press, 1992), 120–36.

HABERMAS, JÜRGEN, 'The Dialectics of Rationalization', in Peter Dews (ed.), *Jürgen Habermas: Autonomy and Solidarity: Interviews* (London: Verso, 1986), 93–130.

—— 'Life-forms, Morality and the Task of the Philosopher', in Peter Dews (ed.), *Jürgen Habermas: Autonomy and Solidarity: Interviews* (London: Verso, 1986), 191–216.

—— *Moral Consciousness and Communicative Action*, trans. C. Lenhardt and S. Nicholson (Cambridge, Mass.: MIT Press, 1990).

—— *Philosophical Discourse of Modernity*, trans. Frederick Lawrence (Cambridge, Mass.: MIT Press, 1987).

—— *The Theory of Communicative Action*, Vol. I: *Reason and the Rationalization of Society*, trans. Thomas McCarthy (Boston: Beacon Books, 1984).

—— *Communication and the Evolution of Society*, trans. Thomas McCarthy (London: Heinemann, 1979).

HANSON, KAREN, *The Self Imagined: Philosophical Reflections of the Social Character of the Psyche* (New York and London: Routledge and Kegan Paul, 1986).

HARPHAM, GEOFFREY GALT, *Getting It Right: Language, Literature, and Ethics* (Chicago and London: University of Chicago Press, 1992).

HARTMAN, GEOFFREY, 'Literary Criticism and its Discontents', *Critical Inquiry*, 3 (Winter 1976), 203–20.

HARVEY, DAVID, *The Condition of Postmodernity* (Oxford: Basil Blackwell, 1989).

HASSAN, IHAB, *The Dismemberment of Orpheus: Toward a Postmodern Literature*, 2nd edn., (Madison: University of Wisconsin Press, 1982).

312   BIBLIOGRAPHY

HASSAN, IHAB, *The Literature of Silence: Henry Miller and Samuel Beckett* (New York: Knopf, 1967).
—— *Paracriticisms: Seven Speculations on the Times* (Urbana, Ill.: University of Illinois Press, 1975).
—— *The Right Promethean Fire* (Urbana, Ill., Chicago, and London: University of Illinois Press, 1980).
—— *Selves At Risk: Patterns of Quest in Contemporary American Letters* (Madison: University of Wisconsin Press, 1990).
HEBDIGE, DICK, Introduction to 'Subjects in Space', *New Formations*, 11 (1990), pp. vi–vii.
HEINRICH, DIETER, 'Fichte's Original Insight', trans. R. D. Lachterman, in *Contemporary German Philosophy* (University Park, Pa.: Pennsylvania State University Press, 1982), 15–52.
HELD, DAVID, *Introduction to Critical Theory* (Berkeley: University of California Press, 1980).
HENLEY, ROBIN, *Turning Life into Fiction* (Cincinnati: Story Press, 1994).
HIRSH, E. D. JR., 'The Politics of Theories of Interpretation', in W. J. T. Mitchell (ed.), *The Politics of Interpretation*, (Chicago and London: University of Chicago Press, 1982), 321–34.
HOGAN, PATRICK COLM, *The Politics of Interpretation* (New York and Oxford: Oxford University Press, 1990).
HONNETH, AXEL, 'An Aversion against the Universal: A Commentary on Lyotard's *Postmodern Condition*', *Theory, Culture and Society*, 2/3 (1985), 247–57.
HOOKS, BELL, *Yearning: Race, Gender, and Cultural Politics* (Boston: South End Press, 1990).
HUMM, MAGGIE, *Border Traffic: Strategies of Contemporary Women Writers* (Manchester: Manchester University Press, 1991).
HUTCHEON, LINDA, *A Theory of Parody* (New York: Methuen, 1985).
—— 'Colonialism and the Postmodern Condition: Complexities Abounding', *PMLA*, 110/1 (1995), 7–16.
—— *Narcissistic Narrative: The Metafictional Paradox* (Waterloo: Wilfrid Laurier University Press, 1980).
IRIGARAY, LUCE, *This Sex Which Is Not One*, trans. Catherine Porter (Ithaca, NY: Cornell University Press, 1985).
—— 'When Our Lips Speak Together', trans. Carolyn Burke, *Signs*, 6 (1980), 65–79.
JAMESON, FREDRIC, *Postmodernism, or, the Cultural Logic of Late Capitalism* (London: Verso, 1991).
JARDINE, ALICE, 'Pre-Texts for the Transatlantic Feminist', *Yale French Studies*, 62 (1981), 220–36.
JOHNSON, BARBARA, 'Writing', in Frank Lentricchia and Thomas McLaughlin (eds.), *Critical Terms for Literary Study* (Chicago and London: University of Chicago Press, 1990), 39–49.

Jolly, Rosemary, 'Rehearsals of Liberation: Contemporary Post-colonial Discourse and the New South Africa', *PMLA* 110/1 (1995), 17–29.

Jones, Ann Rosalind, 'Inscribing Femininity: French Theories of the Feminine', in Gayle Green and Coppélia Khan (eds.), *Making a Difference: Feminist Literary Criticism* (1985; London and New York: Routledge, 1988), 80–112.

—— 'Julia Kristeva on Femininity: The Limits of a Semiotic Politics', *Feminist Review*, 18 (1984), 56–73.

Jong, Erica, *Fear of Flying* (St Albans: Panther, 1973).

Kavanagh, James, 'Ideology', in Frank Lentricchia and Thomas McLaughlin (eds.), *Critical Terms for Literary Study* (Chicago and London: University of Chicago Press, 1990), 306–20.

Keith, Michael, and Pile, Steve (eds.), *Place and the Politics of Identify* (London and New York: Routledge, 1993).

Kennedy, Alan, *Reading Resistance Value: Deconstructive Practice and the Politics of Literary Criticism* (Basingstoke: Macmillan, 1990).

Kerby, Anthony Paul, *Narrative and the Self* (Bloomington and Indianapolis: Indiana University Press, 1991).

Kermode, Frank, 'Secrets and Narrative Sequence', in W. J. T. Mitchell (ed.), *On Narrative* (Chicago and London: University of Chicago Press, 1981), 79–97.

Kilminster, Richard, 'Structuration Theory as World View', in Christopher G. A. Bryant and David Jary (eds.), *Giddens's Theory of Structuration: A Critical Appreciation* (London and New York: Routledge, 1991), 74–115.

Klinkowitz, Jerome, *Literary Disruptions: The Making of a Post-Contemporary Fiction* (Urbana, Ill., Chicago, and London: University of Illinois Press, 1975).

Kristeva, Julia, *Desire in Language: A Semiotic Approach to Literature and Art*, trans. Thomas Gora, Alice Jardine, and Leon S. Roudiez, ed. Leon S. Roudiez (Oxford: Basil Blackwell, 1981).

—— *The Kristeva Reader*, ed. Toril Moi (Oxford: Basil Blackwell, 1986).

—— *The Revolution in Poetic Language*, trans. M. Waller (New York: Columbia University Press, 1984).

—— 'The System and the Speaking Subject', in Toril Moi (ed.), *The Kristeva Reader* (Oxford: Basil Blackwell, 1986), 24–33.

Kuhn, Thomas, *The Structure of Scientific Revolutions* (Chicago: University of Chicago Press, 1962).

Kuspit, Donald, 'The Contradictory Character of Postmodernism', in Hugh J. Silverman (ed.), *Postmodernism* (London and New York: Routledge, 1990), 53–68.

KYMLICKA, WILL, *Contemporary Political Philosophy: An Introduction* (Oxford: Clarendon Press, 1990).

—— *Liberalism, Community and Culture* (Oxford: Clarendon Press, 1989).

LACAN, JACQUES, *Écrits: A Selection*, trans. Alan Sheridan (New York: Norton, 1977).

—— *The Four Fundamental Concepts of Psycho-analysis* (London: Hogarth Press, 1977).

LAING, R. D., *The Politics of Experience* (New York: Random House, 1967).

LE CLAIR, TOM, and MCCAFFERY, LARRY, *Anything Can Happen: Interviews with Contemporary American Novelists* (Urbana, Ill.: University of Illinois Press, 1983).

LEFEBVRE, HENRI, *The Production of Space* (1974; Oxford: Basil Blackwell, 1991).

LEJEUNE, PHILLIPE, *On Autobiography* (Minneapolis: University of Minnesota Press, 1989).

LENTRICCHIA, FRANK, and MCLAUGHLIN, THOMAS (eds.), *Critical Terms for Literary Study* (Chicago and London: University of Chicago Press, 1990).

LEVINE, GEORGE (ed.), *Constructions of the Self* (New Brunswick, NJ: Rutgers University Press, 1992).

LINGIS, ALPHONSO, 'Some Questions about Lyotard's Postmodern Legitimation Narrative', *Philosophy and Social Criticism*, 20/1–2 (1994), 1–12.

LODGE, DAVID, *After Bakhtin: Essays on Fiction and Criticism* (London and New York: Routledge, 1990).

LYOTARD, JEAN-FRANÇOIS, *The Differend*, trans. Georges Van Den Abbeele (1983; Minneapolis: University of Minnesota Press, 1988).

—— *The Postmodern Condition: A Report on Knowledge*, trans. Geoff Bennington and Brian Massumi (1979; Manchester: Manchester University Press, 1984).

MACASKILL, BRIAN, and COLLERAN, JEANNE, 'Reading History, Writing Heresy: The Resistance of Representation and the Representation of Resistance in J. M. Coetzee's *Foe*', *Contemporary Literature*, 33/3 (Fall 1992), 432–57.

MACINTYRE, ALASDAIR, *After Virtue* (London: Duckworth, 1981).

—— *Whose Justice? Which Rationality?* (London: Duckworth, 1988).

MASSEY, DOREEN, 'Politics and Space/Time', in Michael Keith and Steve Pile (eds.), *Place and the Politics of Identity* (London and New York: Routledge, 1993), 141–61.

MCCABE, COLIN, *James Joyce and the Revolution of the Word* (London: Macmillan, 1979).

McCarthy, Thomas, *The Critical Theory of Jürgen Habermas* (Cambridge: Polity Press, 1984).
—— 'Kantian Constructivism and Reconstructivism: Rawls and Habermas in Dialogue', *Ethics*, 105 (Oct. 1994), 44–63.
McConnell, Frank D., *Four PostWar American Novelists: Bellow, Mailer, Barth and Pynchon* (Chicago: University of Chicago Press, 1977).
McHale, Brian, *Postmodernist Fiction* (London and New York: Routledge, 1987).
McNeil, Maureen, 'Dancing with Foucault: Feminism and Power-Knowledge', in Caroline Ramazanoğlu (ed.), *Up against Foucault: Explorations of Some Tensions between Foucault and Feminism* (London and New York: Routledge, 1993), 147–75.
Meaney, Gerardine, *(Un)like Subjects: Women, Theory, Fiction* (London and New York: Routledge, 1993).
Merod, Jim, *The Political Responsibility of the Critic* (Ithaca, NY: Cornell University Press, 1987).
Meyers, Diana Tietjens, *Subjection and Subjectivity: Psychoanalytic Feminism and Moral Philosophy* (New York and London: Routledge, 1994).
Michaels, Walter Benn, 'Is There a Politics of Interpretation', in W. J. T. Mitchell (ed.), *The Politics of Interpretation* (Chicago and London: University of Chicago Press, 1982), 335–46.
Millard, Elaine, 'French Feminisms', in Sara Mills, Lynne Pierce, Sue Spaull, and Elaine Millard (eds., *Feminist Readings/Feminists Reading* (Hemel Hempstead: Harvester Wheatsheaf, 1989), 153–86.
Miller, J. Hillis, *The Ethics of Reading: Kant, de Man, Eliot, Trollope, James and Benjamin* (New York: Columbia University Press, 1987).
—— 'Optic and Semiotic in *Middlemarch*', in Jerome Buckley (ed.), *The Worlds of Victorian Fiction* (Cambridge, Mass., and London: Harvard University Press, 1975), 125–45.
Mills, Sara; Pierce, Lynne; Spaull, Sue; and Millard, Elaine, *Feminist Readings/Feminists Reading* (Hemel Hempstead: Harvester Wheatsheaf, 1989).
Mink, Louis O., 'Narrative Form as Cognitive Instrument', in Robert H. Canary and Henry Kozicki (eds.), *The Writing of History* (Madison: University of Wisconsin Press, 1978), 129–49.
Mischel, Theodore (ed.), *The Self: Psychological and Philosophical Issues* (London: Basil Blackwell, 1977).
Mitchell, Juliet, *Woman's Estate* (Harmondsworth: Penguin, 1974).
Mitchell, W. J. T. (ed.), *On Narrative* (Chicago and London: University of Chicago Press, 1981).
—— *The Politics of Interpretation* (Chicago and London: University of Chicago Press, 1982).

MODELESKI, TANIA, *Feminism without Women: Culture and Criticism in a 'Postfeminist Age'* (London: Routledge, 1991).

MOI, TORIL, *Sexual/Textual Politics: Feminist Literary Theory* (1985; London and New York: Routledge, 1988).

MORGAN, PETER E., 'Foe's *Defoe* and *La Jeune Née*: Establishing a Metaphorical Referent for the Elided Female Voice', *Critique*, 35/2 (Winter 1994), 81–96.

MULHALL, STEPHEN, and SWIFT, ADAM, *Liberals and Communitarians* (Oxford and Cambridge, Mass.: Blackwell, 1992).

MUNICH, ADRIENNE, 'Notorious Signs, Feminist Criticism and Literary Tradition', in Gayle Greene and Coppélia Kahn (eds.), *Making a Difference: Feminist Literary Criticism* (London and New York: Routledge, 1985), 238–59.

NASH, CHRISTOPHER (ed. and intro.), *Narrative in Culture: The Uses of Storytelling in the Sciences, Philosophy and Literature* (London and New York: Routledge, 1990).

NEUHOUSER, FREDERICK, *Fichte's Theory of Subjectivity* (Cambridge: Cambridge University Press, 1990).

NOZICK, ROBERT, *Anarchy, State, Utopia* (Oxford: Basil Blackwell, 1984).

NUSSBAUM, MARTHA, *Love's Knowledge: Essays on Philosophy and Literature* (Oxford and New York: Oxford University Press, 1990).

OLNEY, JAMES (ed.), *Autobiography: Essays Theoretical and Critical* (Princeton: Princeton University Press, 1980).

OMMUNDSEN, WENCHE, *Metafictions? Reflexivity in Contemporary Texts* (Melbourne: Melbourne University Press, 1993).

PARFIT, DEREK, *Reasons and Persons* (Oxford: Clarendon Press, 1984).

PATTON, MARILYN, '*Lady Oracle*: The Politics of the Body', *ARIEL*, 22/4 (Oct. 1991), 29–48.

PAULSEN, A. B., '2', *Tri-Quarterly*, 26 (Winter 1973), n.p.

POST, ROBERT M., 'The Noise of Freedom: J. M. Coetzee's *Foe*', *Critique*, 30/3 (Spring 1989), 143–54.

RAWLS, JOHN, *A Theory of Justice* (Oxford: Oxford University Press, 1971).

—— 'The Domain of the Political and Overlapping Consensus', *New York University Law Review*, 64/2 (1989), 233–55.

—— 'Justice as Fairness: Political not Metaphysical', *Philosophy and Public Affairs*, 14/3 (1985), 223–51.

—— *Political Liberalism* (New York: Columbia University Press, 1993).

RAZ, JOSEPH, *The Morality of Freedom* (Oxford: Clarendon Press, 1986).

REVILL, GEORGE, 'Reading Rosehill: Community, Identity and Inner City Derby', in Michael Keith and Steve Pile (eds.), *Place and the Politics of Identity* (London and New York: Routledge, 1993), 117–40.

RICOEUR, PAUL, *The Conflict of Interpretations* (Evanston, Ill.: Northwestern University Press, 1974).

—— *Hermeneutics and the Human Sciences* (Cambridge: Cambridge University Press, 1981).

—— 'Narrative Time', in W. J. T. Michell (ed.), *On Narrative* (Chicago and London: University of Chicago Press, 1981), 165–86.

—— *Time and Narrative*, 3 vols. (Chicago: University of Chicago Press, 1984–8).

ROBINSON, LILLIAN S., 'Treason our Text: Feminist Challenges to the Literary Canon', *Tulsa Studies in Women's Literature*, 2/1 (Spring 1983), 83–98.

ROBINSON, SALLY, *Engendering the Subject: Gender and Self-Representation in Contemporary Women's Fiction* (Albany, NY: State University of New York Press, 1991).

RODERICK, RICK, *Habermas and the Foundations of Critical Theory* (Basingstoke: Macmillan, 1986).

RORTY, RICHARD, *Objectivity, Relativism and Truth* (New York: Cambridge University Press, 1991).

ROSENBLUM, NANCY, *Another Liberalism: Liberalism and the Reconstruction of Liberal Thought* (Cambridge, Mass., and London: Harvard University Press, 1987).

ROSENWALD, GEORGE C., and OCHBERG, RICHARD L. (eds.), *Storied Lives: The Cultural Politics of Self-Understanding* (New Haven and London: Yale University Press, 1992).

ROSOWSKI, SUSAN J., 'Margaret Atwood's *Lady Oracle*: Fantasy and the Modern Gothic Novel' in Judith McCombs (ed.), *Critical Essays on Margaret Atwood* (Boston: G. K. Hall, 1988, 197–207.

ROTH, JOEL, 'Excerpt: Typography that Makes the Reader Work', *Journal of Typographical Research*, 3 (Apr. 1969), 193–96.

ROTH, PHILIP, *The Facts: A Novelist's Autobiography* (1988; Harmondsworth: Penguin, 1989).

ROWE, JOHN CARLOS, 'To Live Outside the Law You Must Be Honest: The Authority of the Margin in Contemporary Theory', *Cultural Critique*, 2 (1985–6), 35–70.

SAGE, LORNA, *Women in the House of Fiction: Post-War Women Novelists* (Basingstoke and London: Macmillan, 1992).

SANDEL, MICHAEL, *Liberalism and the Limits of Justice* (Cambridge: Cambridge University Press, 1992).

—— 'Morality and the Liberal Ideal', *New Republic*, 7 May 1984, p. 17.

—— *Liberalism and its Critics* (1984; Oxford: Basil Blackwell, 1987).

SAPPORTA, MARC, *Composition No. 1* (Paris: Seuil, 1962).

SARBIN, THEODORE R., *Narrative Psychology: The Storied Nature of Human Conduct* (New York: Praeger, 1986).

SASS, LOUIS A., 'The Self and its Vicissitudes in the Psychoanalytic Avant-

Garde', in George Levine (ed.), *Constructions of the Self* (New Brunswick, NJ: Rutgers University Press, 1992), 17–58.

SCHEFFER, ISRAEL, *Science and Subjectivity* (Indianapolis: Bobbs-Merrill, 1967).

SCHOLES, ROBERT, *Fabulation and Metafiction* (Urbana, Ill.: University of Illinois Press, 1980).

—— *Protocols of Reading* (New Haven and London: Yale University Press, 1989).

—— *Textual Power: Literary Theory and the Teaching of English* (New Haven and London: Yale University Press, 1985).

SCHRAG, CALVIN O., *Communicative Praxis and the Space of Subjectivity* (Bloomington, Ind.: Indiana University Press, 1986).

SCHWARTZ, DANIEL, *The Case for a Humanistic Poetics* (Basingstoke and London: Macmillan, 1990).

—— 'The Ethics of Reading: The Case for Pluralistic and Transactional Reading', *Novel*, 21/2–3 (Winter/Spring 1988), 197–218.

SCOTT, CHARLES, 'Postmodern Language', in Hugh J. Silverman (ed.), *Postmodernism: Philosophy and the Arts* (London and New York: Routledge, 1990), 33–52.

SHIELDS, CAROL, *The Stone Diaries* (1993; London: Fourth Estate, 1994).

SHOTTER, JOHN, and GERGEN, KENNETH (eds.), *Texts of Identity* (London: Sage, 1989).

SHOWALTER, ELAINE, 'Feminist Criticism in the Wilderness', *Critical Inquiry*, 8/2 (Winter 1981), 179–205.

SIEBERS, TOBIN, *The Ethics of Criticism* (Ithaca, NY: Cornell University Press, 1988).

SILVERMAN, HUGH J. (ed.), *Postmodernism: Philosophy and the Arts* (London and New York: Routledge, 1990).

SMITH, BARBARA HERRNSTEIN, *Contingencies of Value: Alternative Perspectives for Critical Theory* (Cambridge, Mass., and London: Harvard University Press, 1988).

SMITH, NEIL, and KATZ, CINDI, 'Grounding Metaphor: Towards and Spatialized Politics', in Michael Keith and Steve Pile (eds.), *Place and the Politics of Identity* (London and New York: Routledge, 1993), 67–83.

SMITH, PAUL, *Discerning the Subject* (Minneapolis: University of Minnesota Press, 1988).

SMYTHE, E. J., *Postmodernism and Contemporary Fiction* (London: Batsford, 1991).

SOJA, EDWARD, *Postmodern Geographies: The Reassertion of Space in Critical Social Theory* (London: Verso, 1989).

—— and HOOPER, BARBARA, 'The Spaces that Difference Makes: Some Notes on the Geographical Margins in the New Cultural Politics', in Michael Keith and Steve Pile (eds.) *Place and the Politics of Identity* (London and New York: Routledge, 1993), 183–205.

SONTAG, SUSAN, 'The Aesthetics of Silence', in William J. Handy and Max Westbrook (eds.), *Twentieth Century Criticism: The Major Statements* (New York: Free Press, 1974), 453–73.

SPAIN, DAPHNE, *Gendered Spaces* (Chapel Hill, NC: University of North Carolina Press, 1992).

SPANOS, WILLIAM, *Martin Heidegger and the Question of Literature: Towards a Postmodern Literary Hermeneutics* (Bloomington, Ind.: Indiana University Press, 1979).

SPAULL, SUE, 'Margaret Atwood: *Surfacing*', in Sara Mills, Lynne Pierce, Sue Spaull, and Elaine Millard, *Feminist Readings/Feminists Reading* (Hemel Hempstead: Harvester Wheatsheaf, 1989), 109–16.

SPELMAN, ELIZABETH V., *Inessential Woman* (London: Women's Press, 1990).

SPIVAK, GAYATRI CHAKRAVORTY, 'Can the Subaltern Speak?', in Cary Nelson and Lawrence Grossberg (eds.), *Marxism and the Interpretation of Culture* (Basingstoke: Macmillan, 1988), 271–313.

—— 'The Politics of Interpretations', in W. J. T. Mitchell (ed.), *The Politics of Interpretation* (Chicago and London: University of Chicago Press, 1982), 347–66.

—— 'Theory in the Margin: Coetzee's *Foe* Reading Defoe's *Crusoe/Roxana*', *English in Africa*, 172 (1990), 1–23.

STEELE, MEILI, 'How Philosophy of Language Informs Ethics and Politics: Richard Rorty and Contemporary Theory', *Boundary 2*, 20/2 (1993), 140–72.

—— 'The Ontological Turn and its Ethical Consequences: Habermas and the Poststructuralists', *Praxis International*, 11/4 (1992), 428–46.

STONE, JENNIFER, 'The Horrors of Power: A Critique of Kristeva', in Francis Barker, Peter Hulme, Margaret Iversen, and Diana Loxley (eds.), *The Politics of Theory: Proceedings of the Essex Conference on the Sociology of Literature: July 1982* (Colchester: University of Essex, 1983), 38–48.

STURROCK, JOHN, *The Language of Autobiography: Studies in the First Person Singular* (Cambridge and New York: Cambridge University Press, 1993).

SUKENICK, RONALD, *In Form: Twelve Digressions on the Act of Fiction* (Carbondale, Ill.: Southern Illinois University Press, 1985).

SULLIVAN, WILLIAM M., *Reconstructing Public Philosophy* (Berkeley: University of California Press, 1982).

TAYLOR, CHARLES, *Hegel and Modern Society* (Cambridge: Cambridge University Press, 1979).

—— *Sources of the Self: The Making of the Modern Identity* (Cambridge, Mass.: Harvard University Press, 1989).

—— 'What is Human Agency?', in Theodore Mischel (ed.), *The Self:*

320 BIBLIOGRAPHY

Psychological and Philosophical Issues (Oxford, Basil Blackwell, 1977), 103–38.

TAYLOR, CHARLES, 'What's Wrong with Negative Freedom', in *Philosophical Papers*, vol. 2 (New York: Cambridge University Press, 1985), 211–29.

TAYLOR, MARK C., *ERRING: A Postmodern A/Theology* (Chicago: University of Chicago Press, 1984).

TEN KORTENAAR, NEIL, 'Beyond Authenticity and Creolization: Reading Achebe Writing Culture', *PMLA* 110/1 (1995), 30–42.

THIHER, ALLEN, *Words in Reflection: Modern Language Theory and Postmodern Fiction* (Chicago: University of Chicago Press, 1984).

VOLOSINOV, VALENTIN, *Marxism and the Philosophy of Language*, trans. L. Matejka and I. R. Titunk (New York and London: Seminar Press, 1973).

WALZER, MICHAEL, 'The Communitarian Critique of Liberalism', *Political Theory*, 18/1 (1990), 6–23.

—— *Spheres of Justice* (New York: Basic Books, 1983).

WATSON, STEPHEN, 'Colonialism and the Novels of J. M. Coetzee', *Research in African Literatures*, 17 (Fall 1986), 370–92.

WAUGH, PATRICIA, *Feminine Fictions: Revisiting the Postmodern* (London and New York: Routledge, 1989).

—— *Metafiction: The Theory and Practice of Self-Conscious Fiction* (London and New York: Methuen, 1984).

WEISMAN, LESLIE KANES, *Discrimination by Design: A Feminist Critique of the Man-made Environment* (Urbana, Ill., and Chicago: University of Illinois Press, 1992).

WELDON, FAY, *The Cloning of Joanna May* (London: Fontana, 1990).

WHITE, ALLON, 'Bakhtin, Sociolinguistics and Deconstruction', in Frank Gloversmith (ed.), *The Theory of Reading* (Brighton: Harvester Press and Totowa, NJ: Barnes and Noble Books, 1984), 123–46.

WHITE, HAYDEN, *Metahistory* (Baltimore: Johns Hopkins University Press, 1973).

—— *Tropics of Discourse* (Baltimore: Johns Hopkins University Press, 1978).

—— 'The Value of Narrativity in the Representation of Reality', *Critical Inquiry*, 7 (1980), 5–28.

WILDE, ALAN, *Horizons of Assent: Modernism, Postmodernism and the Ironic Imagination* (Baltimore: Johns Hopkins University Press, 1981).

WITTGENSTEIN, LUDWIG, *Philosophical Investigations*, trans. G. E. M. Anscombe (Oxford: Basil Blackwell, 1953).

WOLLHEIM, RICHARD, *The Thread of Life* (Cambridge, Mass.: Harvard University Press, 1984).

YAEGER, PATRICIA, *Honey-Mad Women: Emancipatory Strategies in Women's Writing* (New York: Columbia University Press, 1988).

YOUNG, ROBERT, *White Mythologies: Writing History and the West* (London: Routledge and Kegan Paul, 1990).

—— *Untying the Text: A Post-Structuralist Reader* (Boston, London, and Henley: Routledge and Kegan Paul, 1981).

ZAVARZADEH, MAS'UD, 'Critic as Conservator', *Poetics Today*, 3 (1982), 47–63.

Index

Lightning Source UK Ltd.
Milton Keynes UK
06 April 2011

170428UK00003B/5/A